The Southern Experience
in the American Revolution

The Southern Experience in the American Revolution

Edited by Jeffrey J. Crow
and Larry E. Tise

The University of North Carolina Press
Chapel Hill

Manufactured in the United States of America
Library of Congress Catalog Card Number 77-21519
Cloth, published 1978, ISBN 0-8078-1313-3
Paper, published 1979, ISBN 0-8078-4059-9
First printing, April 1978
Second printing, August 1979

Library of Congress Cataloging in Publication Data
Main entry under title:

The Southern experience in the American Revolution.

Based on lectures given at the University of North Carolina
at Chapel Hill, Duke University, and North Carolina State
University, in the fall of 1975, and sponsored by the North
Carolina Bicentennial Committee et al.
    1. Southern States—History—Revolution, 1775–1783—
Addresses, essays, lectures.   I. Crow, Jeffrey J.   II. Tise,
Larry E.   III. North Carolina Bicentennial Committee.
E230.5.S7S68   973.3'0975   77-21519
ISBN 0-8078-1313-3

*To the founders of the
revolutionary tradition in the South
and its past, present, and future heirs*

Contents

Introduction   ix

Part One   Social and Political Origins of the Revolution
            in the South

    1   Early Revolutionary Leaders in the South
         and the Problem of Southern Distinctiveness
         by Pauline Maier   3

    2   Rebelliousness: Personality Development
         and the American Revolution
         in the Southern Colonies
         by Robert M. Weir   25

    3   *"Virtus et Libertas"*: Political Culture,
         Social Change, and the Origins of the American
         Revolution in Virginia, 1763–1766
         by Jack P. Greene   55

    4   Class, Mobility, and Conflict in North Carolina
         on the Eve of the Revolution
         by Marvin L. Michael Kay and Lorin Lee Cary   109

Part Two   The War for American Independence:
            The "Southern Strategy" and Social Upheaval

    5   British Strategy for Pacifying the
         Southern Colonies, 1778–1781
         by John Shy   155

6   Carolina and Georgia Patriot
    and Loyalist Militia in Action, 1778–1783
    by Clyde R. Ferguson   174

Part Three   The Revolutionary Impact of War in the South:
             Ideals and Realities

7   "What an Alarming Crisis Is This":
    Southern Women and the American Revolution
    by Mary Beth Norton   203

8   British Caribbean and North American Slaves
    in an Era of War and Revolution, 1775–1807
    by Michael Mullin   235

9   "Taking Care of Business" in Revolutionary South
    Carolina: Republicanism and the Slave Society
    by Peter H. Wood   268

Contributors   295

Index   299

Introduction

Were the southern colonies in British North America already a distinctive cultural region at the onset of the American Revolution? Could the outlines of a later, if partially mythical, Defensive South, Benighted South, or Romantic South be discerned in the social and cultural experiences of southern colonists on the eve of the American Revolution? Did the experience of the American Revolution have a marked impact on the evolution of social and racial configurations of the Old South? Did the American Revolution—which, Bernard Bailyn has argued, released a "contagion of liberty"—reshape or redefine the roles of blacks and women in southern society?

These and other questions relating to the experience of the American Revolution and its influence on southern life were examined by nine historians during the course of a symposium entitled "The Experience of Revolution in North Carolina and the South" in the fall of 1975.[1] A jointly sponsored event initiated by the North Carolina Bicentennial Committee in association with the North Carolina Division of Archives and History, the Institute of Early American History and Culture of Williamsburg, Virginia, The University of North Carolina at Chapel Hill, Duke University, and North Carolina State University, the symposium took place on successive Thursdays on the campuses of the three participating universities. Each of the lectures has been revised and edited for inclusion in this volume.

A panel of historians from the participating institutions conceived the symposium in 1974 as an effort to generate a new assessment of the South's role in the Revolution, a period of southern history often ignored or neglected. Because

southerners of the 1960s and early 1970s had just experienced a
long decade of rearrangement in their basic social institutions—
particularly with regard to the rights and opportunities of black
Americans—and because historians were engaged in rewriting
large portions of southern history, the bicentennial of the American Revolution offered a propitious moment to take another look
at the South in a time of far-reaching political and social
upheaval. Moreover, historians, working primarily with sources
from other colonies, in recent years had begun to portray the
American Revolution as a liberating event of near millennial
proportions, which transformed or obliterated social and caste
distinctions in other locales.[2] Finally, except for one major
overview of the South in the American Revolution written in the
mid-1950s by John R. Alden, historians had largely overlooked
and disregarded the American Revolution as a significant event
in the growth of southern society. In the words of Charles G.
Sellers, Jr., "A modern reader could almost go through the whole
corpus of southern writings about the Revolution without
finding any evidence that a southern sectional consciousness
ever existed or that a sectional war ever took place."[3]

The paucity of major studies of the American Revolution
in the South either in early or more recent historiography is
suggestive of the manner in which southerners and southern
historians traditionally have dealt with the revolutionary era.[4]
While a southern statesman might promulgate the rights to life,
liberty, and the pursuit of happiness to justify or celebrate the
Revolution, the folks "down home" just as eagerly attempted to
maintain a caste society. While southerners have ever been
among the vanguard of flag-waving patriots, of those who
venerated the principles of the Revolution on the Fourth of July,
and of those who clamored longest and loudest to uphold the
nation's honor in seasons of foreign crisis, they nearly dealt the
nation a fatal blow by undertaking what they regarded as a
second American Revolution in the Civil War. The resulting
tensions between rhetoric and reality in the American South

have provided a rich, if violent, history, but also, all too often, have prevented southern historians from probing more deeply the nature of the Revolution in the South and its implications for southern society. In the two-hundred-year history of southern writings on the American Revolution, one will not find historians who seemed willing to measure the war in the same terms or with the same intensity with which they analyzed the Civil War.

The authors of these essays, then, have not had a body of southern writings, comparable to the detailed examinations of New England and the Middle Atlantic colonies, on which to build. Whether one wants to ask about the nature and goals of southern Whig leadership, sectional consciousness, or the outlines of class conflict in the southern colonies, one will find few studies with which to begin and fewer still that relate such concerns to the rising South.[5]

The four essays published here on the social and political origins of the Revolution in the South thus pose some fresh questions and in two cases employ new approaches to the revolutionary experience in the South. Pauline Maier addresses a fundamental question underpinning the symposium by asking whether southern revolutionary leaders were different from those of the Middle Atlantic and New England colonies. While she finds southern leaders diverse in their backgrounds, occupations, and interests, she discovers many similarities in values and ideology with northern Whigs. Maier argues that the southern Whig leaders examined in her essay, though members of the provincial elite, often found themselves on the peripheries of power because of factional or political disputes with an inner, ruling clique. Robert M. Weir, in a provocative departure from previous lines of inquiry, scrutinizes the southern colonial family in the eighteenth century and establishes links between family background, the southern elite, and the nature of the Revolution. Weir contends that the southern family was experiencing severe tensions during the latter part of the century that pitted child against parent. The Revolution, according to Weir, induced emotions that had been conditioned by childhood experiences, and so rebellion against parents easily became translated into rebellion against the mother country. Jack P. Greene takes a close look at the provincial elite in one colony, Virginia, where, Greene asserts, the members of the gentry long had taken pride in their British patriotism, moderation, and virtue. But in the mid-1760s these men were rocked by two challenges—parliamentary taxation and the Robinson and Chiswell scandals—that threatened to break their oligarchic control of provincial affairs by besmirching their corporate self-image. The gentry's response to these crises, concludes Greene, ensured its domination of the colony's politics for the next decade and the endorsement of its rule when the revolutionary crisis broke. While Greene argues against any sectional rift within the gentry or a "democratic" challenge from without by the lower and middling classes in Virginia, Marvin L. Michael Kay and Lorin Lee Cary paint quite a different portrait of North Carolina. Approaching "history from the bottom up," these authors focus on the North Carolina Regulation and discuss the most extensive and prolonged class attack by poorer farmers on a provincial elite in colonial America. Using quantifiable data, they analyze North Carolina society in terms of demography, economy, wealth distribution, and mobility patterns and find a tense class conflict culminating in the often misunderstood Battle of Alamance in 1771.

In recent years the military history of the Revolution has seen some new beginnings. Several studies have attempted to place military developments in the social and ideological context of colonial America.[6] The South's image of the revolutionary war, thanks in large part to antebellum southern memorialists, writers, and novelists, has sparkled with tales of glory and chivalry. In fact, the war in the South was a bloody and brutal civil war once the British had decided on their "southern strategy." The revolutionary character of the southern war is only now beginning to be explored,[7] and the two essays included here offer additional evidence of the social disorder, chaos, and dissension generated by the war. John Shy describes British plans for pacifying the American South and winning the war. The key to the strategy, Shy posits, was the "Americanization" of the war, that is, the employment of American loyalists in the war effort, thereby freeing British troops to move on to other areas. While not discounting the fact that estimates of loyalist sentiment in the South were exaggerated, Shy also attributes the failure of the British strategy to a loss of nerve, vacillation, and ambivalence in implementing the policy effectively. Clyde R. Ferguson shows why the "southern strategy" was foredoomed from an American standpoint. Both patriot and loyalist militia played a significant role during the southern war in suppressing political dissent and maintaining social stability. He insists that the patriot militia performed its functions better than the loyalist militia from as early as 1775–76. Often maligned by contemporaries—notably Nathanael Greene—and historians since, the Carolina and Georgia militias earn high marks from Ferguson.

While southerners and northerners alike have celebrated the vast implications of the Revolution for the rights of man, southern historians have generally overlooked the question of how the struggle itself related to the rights and social roles of nonwhite and nonmale segments of society.[8] Until a recent spate of publications on slavery and racism in the revolutionary period by such scholars as Benjamin Quarles, Winthrop D. Jordan, David Brion Davis, Duncan MacLeod, and Edmund S. Morgan (not to mention two contributors to this volume), the nature of black experiences and even the framework in which they occurred remained obscured. The experience of American women was even more vaguely understood.[9] The three essays in this volume on the impact of the war on women and blacks in southern society expand the boundaries of our present knowledge. Mary Beth Norton probes the trauma of war for southern women, black and white, rich and poor, loyalist and rebel. The devastating effects of the war, she contends, caused southerners to bend all efforts toward rebuilding colonial society and more firmly securing it on a foundation of slavery. The result was an unusually confining role for southern women at a time when a more independent concept of "republican" women was emerging in the North. In Norton's view, the seeds of the apotheosized antebellum lady were sown in the Revolution and its aftermath. Michael Mullin utilizes a comparative, hemispheric perspective to analyze two types of slave resistance in an era of revolutions. Examining African uprisings and Creole conspiracies as they erupted in the British Caribbean islands and North American colonies, Mullin attributes different black responses to the Western world's revolutions to varying rates of acculturation, African ethnicity, urbanization, and the nature of plantation management by blacks as well as whites. Peter H. Wood turns his attention more narrowly to the Negro experience in revolutionary South Carolina. Wood asserts that South Carolina blacks were "taking care of business" in several ways while white patriots were confronting the crown and Parliament. Wood sees subtle but revealing links between white demands for "liberty" and slave unrest.

The mere asking of questions about the social and political origins of the Revolution, its revolutionary character, or its impact on southern society, therefore, represents a new departure in southern historiography. By urging a group of distinguished revolutionary historians to explore these areas, the designers of the symposium were well aware that no new synthesis was likely to emerge. They, in fact, believed—as did the authors of the resultant essays—that the time had come to move beyond the limited parameters of southern historiography on the Revolution and to launch a discussion that long has been overdue. If historians and other students of southern history are to advance beyond the porous syntheses of the past, the carefully researched, though disparate essays in this collection should serve as a fillip to further scholarship.

We wish to thank the participating institutions that made the symposium possible and especially Thad W. Tate, Director of the Institute of Early American History and Culture; Don Higginbotham and William S. Powell of The University of North Carolina, Chapel Hill; Bernard Wishy and Rudolph Pate of North Carolina State University; and Sydney Nathans of Duke University. Our colleagues and friends at the Division of Archives and History have offered encouragement and support at each stage of the symposium and book, and to them we express our gratitude.

Raleigh, North Carolina   Jeffrey J. Crow
August 1976   Larry E. Tise

Notes

1. One of the nine historians invited to participate in the symposium, Marvin L. Michael Kay, read a paper that was written in cooperation with Lorin Lee Cary.
2. The most important study of this nature charting the impact of the Revolution on slavery, established religion, the rise of democracy, and the eroding of deferential social practices is Bernard Bailyn's *The Ideological Origins of the American Revolution* (Cambridge, Mass., 1967). A subsequent study with considerably greater social analysis is Gordon S. Wood's *The Creation of the American Republic, 1776–1787* (Chapel Hill, N.C., 1969).
3. John R. Alden, *The South in the Revolution, 1763–1789* (Baton Rouge, La., 1957). The best overview of the historiography of the revolutionary South, though somewhat dated, remains Charles G. Sellers, Jr., "The American Revolution: Southern Founders of a National Tradition," in Arthur S. Link and Rembert W. Patrick, eds., *Writing Southern History: Essays in Historiography in Honor of Fletcher M. Green* (Baton Rouge, La., 1965), pp. 38–66. Two excellent historiographical essays on the American Revolution, which include southern studies, are Esmond Wright, ed., *Causes and Consequences of the American Revolution* (Chicago, 1966), pp. 11–62; and Jack P. Greene, "Revolution, Confederation, and Constitution, 1763–1787," in William H. Cartwright and Richard L. Watson, Jr., eds., *The Reinterpretation of American History and Culture* (Washington, D.C., 1973).
4. Early national and antebellum historians recently have been the subject of a number of studies. See, for example, John Hope Franklin, "The North, the South, and the American Revolution," *Journal of American History* 62 (June 1975): 5–23; Lawrence H. Leder, ed., *Historians of Nature and Man's Nature: Early*

Nationalist Historians (New York, 1973); and Arthur H. Shaffer, *The Politics of History: Writing the History of the American Revolution* (Chicago, 1975).

5. Most studies of the revolutionary South have been at the state level, though the South occasionally is included in much broader analyses of the period. See, for instance, Jackson Turner Main, *The Social Structure of Revolutionary America* (Princeton, N.J., 1965), and *The Upper House in Revolutionary America, 1763–1778* (Madison, Wisc., 1967); and Elisha P. Douglass, *Rebels and Democrats: The Struggle for Equal Political Rights and Majority Rule during the American Revolution* (Chapel Hill, N.C., 1955). Jack P. Greene provides the fullest discussion of the southern colonies in *The Quest for Power: The Lower Houses of Assembly in the Southern Royal Colonies, 1689–1776* (Chapel Hill, N.C., 1963). Relevant state or regional studies include: Charles A. Barker, *The Background of the Revolution in Maryland* (New Haven, 1940); Philip A. Crowl, *Maryland during and after the Revolution* (Baltimore, 1943); Ronald Hoffman, *A Spirit of Dissension: Economics, Politics, and the Revolution in Maryland* (Baltimore, 1973); Hamilton J. Eckenrode, *The Revolution in Virginia* (New York, 1916); Robert E. Brown and B. Katherine Brown, *Virginia, 1705–1786: Democracy or Aristocracy?* (East Lansing, Mich., 1964); Charles S. Sydnor, *Gentlemen Freeholders: Political Practices in Washington's Virginia* (Chapel Hill, N.C., 1952); Thad W. Tate, "The Coming of the Revolution in Virginia: Britain's Challenge to Virginia's Ruling Class, 1763–1776," *William and Mary Quarterly*, 3d ser. 19 (July 1962): 323–43; Hugh T. Lefler and William S. Powell, *Colonial North Carolina: A History* (New York, 1973); Charles G. Sellers, Jr., "Making a Revolution: The North Carolina Whigs, 1765–1775," in J. Carlyle Sitterson, ed., *Studies in Southern History* (Chapel Hill, N.C., 1957); Kenneth Coleman, *The American Revolution in Georgia, 1763–1789* (Athens, Ga., 1958); William W. Abbot, *The Royal Governors of Georgia, 1754–1775* (Chapel Hill, N.C., 1959); and Carl Bridenbaugh, *Myths and Realities: Societies of the Colonial South* (New York, 1965).

6. The seeming obsession of southern historians with biographical and local studies or with battlefield strategies has largely precluded the emergence of studies examining socioeconomic aspects of the colonial militia, attitudes toward a standing army, or the social impact of the revolutionary war. One of the best of the political-military works is Hugh F. Rankin's *The North Carolina Continentals* (Chapel Hill, N.C., 1971). John Shy's *Toward Lexington: The Role of the British Army in the Coming of the American Revolution* (Princeton, N.J., 1965) opened the field for a different approach to the military history of the war as a whole. Don Higginbotham's *The War of American Independence: Military Attitudes, Policies, and Practice, 1763–1789* (New York, 1971) is perhaps the most important book on the subject.

7. See especially Paul H. Smith, *Loyalists and Redcoats: A Study in British Revolutionary Policy* (Chapel Hill, N.C., 1964); Franklin Wickwire and Mary Wickwire, *Cornwallis: The American Adventure* (Boston, 1970); and Ronald Hoffman, "The 'Disaffected' in the Revolutionary South," in Alfred F. Young, ed., *The American Revolution: Explorations in the History of American Radicalism* (DeKalb, Ill., 1976), pp. 273–316.

8. The impact of the southern war on Indians is not addressed in this book. A number of studies have been done on the subject but usually from a Euro-American perspective. See, for example, John R. Alden, *John Stuart and the Southern Colonial Frontier* (Ann Arbor, Mich., 1944); and James H. O'Donnell III, *Southern Indians in the American Revolution* (Knoxville, Tenn., 1973).

9. Benjamin Quarles, *The Negro in the American Revolution* (Chapel Hill, N.C., 1961); Winthrop D. Jordan, *White Over Black: American Attitudes toward the Negro, 1550–1812* (Chapel Hill, N.C., 1968); David Brion Davis, *The Problem of Slavery in the Age of Revolution, 1770–1823* (Ithaca, N.Y., 1975); Duncan J. MacLeod, *Slavery, Race and the American Revolution* (Cambridge, England, 1974); and Edmund S. Morgan, *American Slavery, American Freedom: The Ordeal of Colonial Virginia* (New York, 1975). On women, see Joan Hoff Wilson, "The Illusion of Change: Women and the American Revolution," in Young, ed., *American Revolution*, pp. 383–445.

Part One
Social and Political Origins
of the Revolution in the South

1

Early Revolutionary Leaders in the South and the Problem of Southern Distinctiveness

by Pauline Maier

The temptation to read mid-nineteenth-century assumptions back into the period before independence, to see the colonial South as a distinctive and separate section of North America, remains clear and present in any effort to examine the "experience of the Revolution in North Carolina and the South." As a result it is particularly important to define how the South was distinct during the revolutionary period, before differential population growths, the disappearance of slavery in the North, and divergent patterns of economic development made the division between those sections more marked and before a southern myth emerged to separate the world of "Cavaliers" from one of "Yankees."[1] This concern is as relevant to a study of the early champions of resistance to Britain as to that of other aspects of southern revolutionary history. Were southern revolutionary leaders different from those in the middle colonies and New England? If so, what was the nature of their differences? The answers are interesting not just for what they tell us about early revolutionary leadership in the South, but for their implications as to the place of the South in the nation both during the revolutionary era and in the century that bridged the War for Independence and the Civil War.

The revolutionaries who concern us here are not the "founding fathers" who won fame in designing and establishing the American republic during the last two decades of the eighteenth century, who have been called the "young men" of the Revolution.[2] They are a prior generation of Americans, born in the 1720s and 1730s, whose major contribution was in spearheading colonial resistance to Britain four decades later. The men emphasized here, preeminent leaders of the opposition to Britain in the Carolinas, Virginia, and Maryland, with one exception, led crowds against supporters of the Stamp Act. They characteristically favored the nonimportation associations that answered the Townshend duties of 1767 and opposed the importation of taxed East India Company tea. Above all, they joined and often led the extralegal organizations that institutionalized resistance to Britain. They were, in short, organizers, committeemen, congressmen—magistrates in what gradually became American revolutionary government. They constituted, as do all leadership groups, a minority and by definition an elite. But their power derived from the support of other colonists and reflected the appeal of their policies, their skill as popular politicians, and, to some extent, the continuing tendency of late colonial Americans to defer toward men of family or fortune for leadership.

In South Carolina, Christopher Gadsden (1724–1805) emerged during the Stamp Act crisis as a spokesman for Charleston's Sons of Liberty, an organization composed largely of local artisans. Later a leading advocate of nonimportation, he was identified as one of the "Tribunes" of the people by Lieutenant Governor William Bull, and remained "the chief figure at every meeting under the 'Liberty Tree' " through the 1760s and 1770s until the final break with Britain. Not all his service was "without doors": he served nearly thirty years in the South Carolina assembly, beginning in 1757. He was a conspicuous member of the Stamp Act Congress of 1765, participated in the South Carolina Provincial Congress, and was one of his state's first four delegates to the Continental Congress, which he left in January

1776 to assume command as senior colonel of South Carolina's military forces.[3]

North Carolina's resistance movement centered in the Cape Fear region, and its preeminent leader was Cornelius Harnett (1723–1781), who served as spokesman for an uprising at Brunswick in February 1766 that demanded the release of ships seized by British customsmen for lack of stamped papers. He was also a "ringleader" of those daring North Carolinians who in July 1775 set fire to British-held Fort Johnston. His main contributions to the colonial cause were made as chairman of the Cape Fear Sons of Liberty and of the region's nonimportation association of 1770, as presiding officer of both the Wilmington and the New Hanover County committees of safety, as a delegate to the provincial and later the Continental Congress, and as chairman of the North Carolina Provincial Council as well as of its successor, the provincial Council of Safety. These last offices made him "in all but name the first chief executive of the newborn State."[4]

Aside from a clique of Sons of Liberty in Norfolk, Virginia's resistance movement centered in the Northern Neck, where initiative often was taken by Richard Henry Lee (1732–1794). Fully as much as other resistance leaders, Lee proved willing to act "out of doors," as when he arranged a demonstration against stampman George Mercer at Westmoreland Courthouse on 24 September 1765, or when he organized the Westmoreland Association of February 1766 that forced a local merchant, Archibald Ritchie, to renounce any intention of clearing vessels on stamped paper. Lee served in the Virginia House of Burgesses and in the provincial revolutionary conventions. Unlike Patrick Henry, whom Thomas Jefferson described as lazy in reading and committee work, at best a "silent and almost unmeddling" congressman, Lee proved to be one of the busiest members of the Continental Congress, just as he had been the "work-horse of the Assembly" in Virginia. Within a four-month period, for example, he served on eighteen different congressional committees. Finally, like Harnett, who consistently complained of the fatigue and financial losses incurred by service at Congress, Lee "panted for retirement from the most distressing pressure of business" he had ever conceived of, much less experienced.[5]

In Maryland no one leader emerged above all others throughout the decade before independence. Some individuals who gained prominence in the Stamp Act resistance retained importance into the mid-1770s: the Annapolis lawyers William Paca and Samuel Chase, for example, or William Lux, who helped transform Baltimore's "mechanical company," a civic organization that included both merchants and tradesmen, into the Baltimore Sons of Liberty. Chase organized local mechanics and small tradesmen not just against the Stamp Act, but against the corrupt city government of Annapolis, thereby winning the mayor's and aldermen's denunciation as a "busy restless Incendiary—a Ringleader of Mobs—a foul mouth'd and inflaming Son of Discord and Passion—a common Disturber of the public Tranquility." When a cohesive revolutionary movement formed in Maryland, it centered instead around Charles Carroll of Carrollton (1737–1832), whose prominence dated from his "First Citizen" letters, published in the *Maryland Gazette* during 1773. Although his correspondence reveals that Carroll was a strong opponent of the Stamp Act, he had far greater reservations on the use of direct popular force than did Lee, Gadsden, or even his own colleague Chase. Disqualified from office during the colonial period because of his Catholicism, Carroll first appeared in a political body during 1774 when he attended the Maryland Convention, but he became in rapid succession a member of the provincial Committee of Correspondence and Committee of Safety and of the Annapolis Committee of Correspondence. He, too, served in the Continental Congress and signed the Declaration of Independence.[6]

Contemporaries regularly compared southern leaders to their counterparts in the North. Josiah Quincy, Jr., the Massachusetts patriot, once described Harnett as the "Samuel Adams of North Carolina (except in point of fortune)." After hearing Christopher Gadsden speak at the Continental Congress, Silas Deane of Connecticut concluded that Gadsden had if anything outdone Deane's neighbors at their own game. "Mr. Gadsden leaves all New England Sons of Liberty far behind" in the extremity of his devotion to the cause, he wrote.[7] The constituencies of southern leaders also were much like those of their counterparts further north. Harnett's following was somewhat unusual in that it included the principal gentlemen and freeholders of the Cape Fear region, and Lee's Westmoreland Association was signed by members of several leading families of Virginia's Northern Neck. But the tradesmen and shopkeepers who followed Chase in Annapolis, Lux in Baltimore, and Gadsden in Charleston were much like the men who lent their strength to the Sons of Liberty in Boston and New York. Nor were the southerners' techniques characteristically more "genteel" than those of northerners. Stamp supporter Archibald Ritchie was so harassed in Virginia that one of his opponents feared Ritchie would commit suicide and so deprive patriots "of the Satisfaction of seeing the Wretch who so insolently defied his Country, mortified." Nine years later the young James Madison considered Virginians significantly more "spirited" than some northerners. "A fellow was lately tarred & feathered for treating [one] of our county committees with disre[s]pect," he wrote his friend William Bradford, while "in NY. they insult the whole Colony and Continent with impunity!"[8] Finally, southerners won the wrath of the British in equal measure with their northern peers. Just as John Hancock and Samuel Adams were excepted from General Thomas Gage's Proclamation of Amnesty at Boston in 1774, Cornelius Harnett and his colleague Robert Howe were excluded from Sir Henry Clinton's proclamation of May 1776 that offered pardon to all North Carolinians who would lay down arms and submit to British law. Two years earlier, Harnett and three other North Carolina patriots were identified by Governor Josiah Martin "as persons who have marked themselves out . . . by their unremitted labours to promote sedition and rebellion here from the beginnings of the discontents in America to this time" and who "stand foremost among the patrons of revolt and anarchy"[9]—words used with only minor variations by loyalists and British officials throughout the colonies to describe Harnett's fellows in the American cause.

The marked differences between individual southerners within this "first generation" of revolutionary leaders makes more exact comparisons with their northern counterparts unnecessary. If the existence of a typical southern leader is suspect at best, that of a leadership distinctive to the South is still more unlikely. Even in temperament southern leaders were notably diverse. The group included the ardent Gadsden, whose pungent language Josiah Quincy, Jr., described as "plain, blunt, hot, and incorrect, though very sensible" (Gadsden once suggested that the British considered the Americans a parcel of very tame asses), but also Harnett, a man of dedication and reserve, as sparing of words for contemporaries, it seems, as for posterity. It encompassed Chase, "big, fun-loving, uncouth, unthinking . . . and quick to anger" along with Carroll, aloof and possessed of a remarkable self-discipline forged through years of dealing with his outspoken father. And it included Lee, Spartan in prose and body, perhaps as complex a man as any in the revolutionary movement. Educational backgrounds also were dissimilar. Some were schooled or otherwise prepared for their occupations in America, others in Europe. Harnett, Lux, and Chase apparently did not study abroad. Gadsden was schooled in England for a few years before being apprenticed at age sixteen to a merchant in Philadelphia; Lee attended Wakefield Academy in Yorkshire until age nineteen. Carroll had perhaps the most extensive formal education of any American, attending Jesuit schools in Flanders, Paris, and Bourges before reading law in London, a task that required separation from his family in Maryland from the ages of eleven to twenty-seven.[10]

The level of wealth among these revolutionary leaders ranged widely, although most were either in, or near enough to aspire to, the upper orders of colonial society. Their different occupations dramatize the economic diversity of the late colonial South. Southern revolutionary leadership included men on the make like Chase, the son of a debt-ridden Episcopalian minister, himself a lawyer who specialized in defending debtors. Gadsden, a merchant, was better born than Chase but also was upward mobile: he wrote during the Stamp Act crisis that he had "not a large but . . . a clear Estate," and later built one of the largest wharves in prosperous Charleston. William Lux, by contrast, was a dry goods merchant who expanded a business inherited from his father by acquiring vessels, establishing branch stores, and opening a rope walk. Cornelius Harnett inherited a fortune once estimated at £7,000 from his father, a self-made Irish immigrant whose profits were won, it seems, largely through land speculation. But the elder Harnett had been "one of the leaders in the industrial development of the Cape Fear section," operating an inn, ferry, and sawmills. His son was similarly involved in diverse economic activities, including a partnership in a local distillery.[11]

That early southern revolutionary leaders often were involved in commercial activities suggests that if there was a typical southern revolutionary leader, he was not, as the stereotype goes, a gentleman planter. Major planters were, of course, often deeply involved in commerce, selling not only the products of their own lands but those of their neighbors and importing products for the use of planters with smaller holdings. But Lee and Carroll, both members of the planter class, were so deeply involved in activities beyond the plantation as to make any simple categorization of them as planters extremely problematic. Carroll, the sole heir to one of the largest fortunes in America (in 1764 his father listed assets worth nearly £89,000 sterling), was given a ten-thousand-acre estate when he completed his education and returned to Maryland. He served, however, less as a planter than as the manager of several Carroll plantations, as an entrepreneur engaged in marketing Carroll products, putting out loans, carrying on land speculations, and, above all, presiding over the family's substantial interest in the Baltimore Iron Works. Richard Henry Lee was a landlord whose livelihood came from rents paid for the use of his land and slaves. He himself was in fact a tenant. His home in Westmoreland County, "Chantilly," stood on land leased from his eldest brother, Philip Ludwell Lee. Although Lee was committed to the interests of planters by tradition and by family, he was also concerned with the state of the Atlantic trade since he managed the estate of his younger brother, William, a merchant based in London.[12]

There were few if any equivalents elsewhere in the resistance movement of Carroll's fortune or Lee's family. But social position did not free Carroll or Lee from the anxieties over rank characteristic of the upward mobile. Lee's fears were particularly acute. Though born into one of the first families of Virginia, he was chronically short of funds. Not for him the largess of a Gadsden, who could claim in old age that he had never accepted compensation for public service except during his years in the Continental Congress. Lee's critics claimed that he squeezed every farthing, maneuvering wherever possible to maximize his compensation for attending the House of Burgesses. To relieve his financial want, Lee sought office under the crown and even applied for the Virginia stamp distributorship in 1764. But financial problems stemming from his possession of a small estate and a large family continued to haunt him and to shape the future of his progeny. His two eldest sons could not hope to become gentlemen planters. Mainly because he found English schooling cheaper than its colonial alternatives, Lee sent his sons to England for their education, with instructions that their expenses be carefully restricted and that they prepare for careers in the church and in trade.[13] Nor was Carroll, a man of far greater assets, free of the specter of downward mobility. "All

the descendants of the House of Butler established in this
Province soon after the settlement are extinct or so miserably
reduced by poverty as to be unknown," he wrote a correspondent in 1771: "In a commercial nation"—a significant description
of his world—"the glory of illustrious progenitors will not screen
their needy posterity from obscurity and want."[14]

These leaders were of boisterous temperament, but also
reserved and disciplined; educated in England, trained in
America; raised in debt, raised in affluence; concerned with
upward mobility, concerned with downward mobility; lawyer,
merchant, landlord, planter, early industrialist. The variety represented by southern revolutionary leaders, not their common
characteristics, demands emphasis. If their differences make it
difficult to define a typical southern revolutionary, much less to
distinguish that hypothetical creature from his counterparts
further north, they also reinforce a conclusion Crane Brinton
drew from a much larger, cross-national study of revolutions and
revolutionaries. "It takes almost as many kinds of men and
women to make a revolution as to make a world," Brinton
decided. Revolutionaries are on the whole "quite ordinary men
and women," superior to their less active fellows only in administrative ability, property holding (for revolutionaries generally have been persons of substance), and, finally, "energy and
willingness to experiment."[15]

But why should these particular persons have been willing to experiment, to transform the established system? None
became a revolutionary from some overt or covert plan for the
reconstitution of society or government, but their commitment to
the status quo was weak enough that they were willing if not to
court at least to risk change. Indeed, change might offer a
prospect of improvement. The standing order certainly promised
little future to Richard Henry Lee. His effort to win through
political preferment an income sufficient to maintain the social
rank he had won by birth came to nothing and exacerbated his
disillusionment. Little favor could be expected from the British

ministers, Arthur Lee wrote him in 1770, since it was "openly the Plan" in England "to bestow for the future all places in America, on those who prove themselves the more active instruments of oppression."[16] Carroll, too, had his differences with the standing order, above all in its treatment of Roman Catholics. Since they were excluded from both holding office and voting, the Catholics' property was as vulnerable to forces beyond their control as that of the colonists in general would have been if Parliament had been left free to tax them. During the Seven Years' War the Maryland assembly had imposed a double tax on Catholics, which prompted Carroll's father to consider selling his Maryland properties and begin anew in a French colony. Catholic emancipation in Maryland remained unlikely while that colony was linked to a mother country whose laws had prevented Carroll, as a young law student, from entering the English bar unless he bought an exception, which he had refused to do.[17] Only in the course of the Revolution were Catholics absorbed into the public life of Maryland—a half century earlier, as it turned out, than their coreligionists were emancipated in Britain.

    None of these revolutionary leaders was among the "inner circles" of power in his colony, even though all but Carroll had been active in local government and had served in their provincial assemblies even before the Anglo-American conflict. Instead they characteristically were involved in major political crises as opponents of those favored with influence and power. Gadsden had so alienated the royal governor by his role in South Carolina's Grant-Middleton feud that the governor tried to unseat him from the assembly in 1762. Later Gadsden supported assembly prerogatives in the Wilkes fund controversy, which led to a total breakdown of royal government on the eve of Revolution. Harnett's involvement in North Carolina's court law controversy, Carroll's in Maryland's proclamation fee crisis, even Lee's opposition to John Robinson, speaker of the House of Burgesses and Virginia's treasurer, put these men in positions within their respective provinces during the mid-1760s much like that of Gadsden in South Carolina. All were, to some extent, outsiders, opponents, as they saw it, of an inner clique of powerful men, whether crown appointees or, as in Virginia, a set of influential James River planters whom the Lees considered haughty "aristocrats," unlike themselves and the mass of Virginians.[18]

From these circumstances in part arose the language of the Revolution, which imbued the American cause in the South, as in the North, with great moral meaning. Like revolutionary leaders elsewhere, and with great fervor and urgency, southern revolutionary leaders defended the cause of the public against that of the few and urged austerity, self-sacrifice, and industriousness upon the partisans of freedom. Patriotism for Harnett consisted of "disinterested public behaviour"; those who opposed the public cause, whether in the colonies or, as Gadsden put it, on "the other side of the great herring pond," were selfish men who lacked "virtue enough to resist the allurement of present gain." The revolutionary movement demanded that the *"private partial interest* of a few INDIVIDUALS . . . not . . . be put in competition with the *lasting welfare* of ALL America," Gadsden said; the moral message of the Revolution was flung in the face of what Richard Henry Lee called the "universal selfishness" of his age.[19] Even private pleasures—horse racing, billiards, dancing—had to be sacrificed on the "altar of freedom," according to Harnett's New Hanover Committee of Safety. Gadsden won a reputation for extremism by his emphatic profession of these ideals. He would rather see his "own family reduced to the utmost Extremity and half cut to pieces," he claimed, than submit to Britain's "damned Machinations."[20]

Even their advocates seem to have found these values to some extent alien to the South. New England seemed far more as a homeland of revolutionary values, a place where the virtues of self-sacrifice and industriousness were most fully realized. Gadsden deplored his South Carolina countrymen's suspicions of that section and wished they might "imitate instead of abusing" New England, which, he hoped, would provide "an Assylum that honest Men might resort to in the time of their last Distress." Lee considered retiring to New England, whose people he characterized as "wise, attentive, sober, dilligent & frugal." By contrast, he wrote John Adams, the "hasty, unpersevering, aristocratic genius of the south suits not my disposition, and is inconsistent with my ideas of what must constitute social happiness and security."[21]

How, then, did the creed of sacrifice, austerity, and industriousness appear in the South? Not, it seems, through Calvinistic tradition. A majority of southerners might have belonged to Calvinist denominations, but the revolutionary leaders considered here were Anglican or Catholic. Nor did southern revolutionaries have the same sense of connection with seventeenth-century revolutionary Calvinism as did, for example, their admired friend Samuel Adams, who saw himself as upholding the traditions and habits of his Puritan ancestors. Lee's forebears took the side of the crown in the tumults of the seventeenth century; his grandfather believed in the divine right of kings and considered James II the lawful king of England even after the Glorious Revolution of 1688. Lee himself once suggested that Oliver Cromwell was a usurper.[22] Carroll's grandfather had fled the oppression of Cromwell in Ireland only to be displaced again by Puritan militants in Maryland during the Glorious Revolution. Clearly, the grandson could have little nostalgia for England's revolutionary tradition.

The writings of seventeenth- and eighteenth-century English "Commonwealthmen" or "Real Whigs" provided to some extent a source of "revolutionary principles," and southern leaders were familiar with the writings of men like John Locke and Algernon Sidney. The leaders' affiliation with legislative opposition "parties" within their colonies no doubt increased the appeal of English revolutionary ideology. In the eighteenth century the justifications of resistance, revolution, and what modern observers easily identify as "politics" were closely related; in each case the opposition group took the stance of disinterested defenders of the public good confronting a "faction" of self-serving men in power.[23]

But the southern leaders' espousals of civic virtue were not only public but intensely personal, suggesting that their professions had roots beyond the political sphere. Carroll, for example, was obsessed from youth with the virtues of frugality and industry. "I would not accept my Father's estate upon condition of consuming the annual profits, in gaudy equipages, empty pomp & show and in company more empty than these," he wrote. (Nor would his father have offered it to him on those terms. The elder Carroll was, if anything, more addicted to an ethic of frugality and industry than his son.) For Carroll and for Lee, as for other revolutionary partisans North and South, the "mistaken policy of England" had one redeeming quality: it might force Americans to a greater achievement of self-sacrifice and industry. Here Carroll found a special role for the wealthy: "In this hour of necessity and oppression," he wrote, "it is the duty of every man of fortune . . . to set an example of frugality & industry to ye common people."[24]

This peculiar ethic of the American Revolution took root among southern leaders because it expressed needs and fears that were to some extent distinctive to a southern elite. Frugality and industry were valued, first, because they fostered self-sufficiency, or, as the South would have it, independence—a point of honor, even obsession, to all southern gentlemen, real or aspiring. Personal independence implied freedom from debt or financial anxiety, living within one's means, avoiding excessive luxury. It was endangered by uncontrolled costs, whether in the form of British taxes or, to men like Lee, in the excessive prices charged by local Scottish merchants. Lee, who was, in his words, easily "warmed up" at the prospect of parliamentary taxation, also tried to organize a "patriotic store" to supply the "industrious planter . . . with every frugal necessity at a price at least 50 per cent cheaper than he has for many years been able to purchase them" and thus help free him from the blight of debt.[25] But not even a "large & independent Fortune" could assure independence, as the elder Charles Carroll recognized, for dependence had many forms. Public office might entail obligations that corroded independence. In this way the younger Carroll consoled himself for being barred from office. "Who so happy as an independent Man," he asked, "and who more independent than a private gentleman?" Even Socrates had "declined all offices of state from a persuasion that a man cou'd not long be great & virtuous." For this elusive independence the elder Carroll demanded that his son "Struggle & Labour"— words evocative of Puritan oratory—to learn English law. It would be a shame, he wrote, for a gentleman "to be dependent on ev'ry dirty Petty fogger whose Interest it may be to lead him by such a dependence into endless difficulties," and "commendable . . . for a Gent[leman] of an Independent fortune not only to stand in [no] need of Mercenary Advisors but to be able to advise & assist his friends, Relations & Neighbors."[26]

Self-sacrifice and work were also understood as an obligation to posterity. "Can fine furniture Cloaths &c be put in Competition with a provision for Children," the elder Carroll asked. "Pride & Vanity are not to be indulged at their Expence"; be content, he urged his son and daughter-in-law in 1770, with "what is neat Clean & Necessary." The younger Carroll once suggested that a lack of work discipline also accounted for downward mobility among gentry families in Maryland where the well-being of estates required close and unremitting attention.[27] This fixation with providing for posterity was not confined to Maryland; it may have been as widespread as the interest of southern elites in western land purchases. Some such ventures were speculative, geared to quick profit. But in Virginia, at least, investors more often sought a reserve of fertile soil. Rented out to tenants who improved the land, which they held on leases that often spanned three lives, these tracts were meant to assure future generations of landed status once primitive cultivation methods robbed fertility from ancestral lands nearer the coast. No similar means of protecting or entrenching wealth was available to colonial Bostonians, according to G. B. Warden; but then, the New Englanders had other traditions that called on men to make current sacrifices for the good of the young and unborn. When Samuel Adams talked of passing on to posterity the heritage of New England, he referred to institutional and moral legacies, whereas in the South injunctions to discipline and frugality in the name of freedom, which was essentially a state of moral independence, had very personal economic meaning as well. In both places, however, the plea for revolutionary partisanship was made above all in the name of posterity. "No people ever yet procured their liberty so as to be benefitted themselves," Charles Carroll wrote. "To do it for posterity to reap the advantage is what has ever been aimed at."[28]

Finally, frugality and industriousness were honored because in fostering independence and freedom they averted what Richard Henry Lee called the greatest human evil, slavery. Within English political thought slavery was a technical term for an ultimate state of dependence and unfreedom. In this sense it was a standard word in revolutionary rhetoric throughout the colonies, but it had particular emotional meaning in the South because of the prevalence there of black chattel slavery. Southerners knew firsthand the degradation of slavery and very explicitly linked the fate they sought to avoid for themselves with that of their own black slaves. "We are as real Slaves as those we are permitted to command, and differ only in degree," Gadsden wrote in 1769, "for what is a slave, but one that is at the will of his master, and has no property of his own, but on the most precarious tenure." And the future had still worse in store: "If we have but eyes that see, and ears that hear, we can not but discover that the deepest scheme of Systematical Slavery is preparing for Us, to which the acts now complained of seem only to be mere preludes." Who could hesitate, he wrote five years later, "to avert by every means in our Power the abject Slavery intended for us and our posterity."[29]

Lee was particularly obsessed with the danger of slavery. By trying to take American property without the Americans' consent, he wrote in 1764, Britain menaced the colonists with a slavery far worse than that endured by their own black slaves, for the colonists would become slaves "of five hundred masters instead of one." If the Stamp Act were to go into effect, he wrote some years later, Virginians' wives and children would be made slaves, their estates taken from them without their consent and by violence. Thus their "nipping in the bud this wicked design" was extremely important. This was not symbolic language. Lee's fears were real and literal. In 1777 he wrote Patrick Henry that only the East India Company's refusal had prevented the British ministry from "sending American prisoners to the East Indies for slaves," but, foiled there, ministers were "on the verge" of sending to Africa all colonial prisoners then in England. The threat of slavery encompassed other southern fears as well, for it suggested a final failure of their dreams for personal independence and their hopes for posterity. "Every scheme that cunning can form, or power execute" was being used, Lee claimed, to reduce to slavery all Americans, both of the present and of future generations.[30]

Was there perhaps a cosmic justice in the fate these southerners feared for the slaveholding South? Gadsden saw in the Anglo-American conflict the "general perceptible workings of Providence" whereby crime was punished by its like, such that "slavery begets slavery." A decade later Virginia's George Mason expressed a similar conviction that slaveholding brought the "judgment of heaven on a Country," that "providence punishes national sins, by national calamities."[31] Mason also claimed that slavery made every master a "petty Tyrant," inured to despotism and cruelty, to "all the finer feelings of the Soul," a view shared by several of his countrymen and argued with particular eloquence by Thomas Jefferson. Slavery, moreover,

discouraged artisans and manufacturers: both Mason and
Richard Henry Lee blamed slavery for inhibiting the emigration
to Virginia of industrious white men, thus perpetuating the
state's dependence on its lazy, incompetent blacks and retarding
both the settlement and the economic development of Virginia.
These views were endorsed by the freeholders of several Virginia
counties in 1774. Gadsden witnessed the negative effects of
slavery on white industriousness and virtue in still more graphic
terms. In Charleston, he noted, slaves who worked as artisans
took jobs from the "prudent sober poor [white] man," reducing
him to idleness and poverty.[32]

Lee and Gadsden, then, like many other southerners, saw
a deep enmity between slavery and freedom, not a paradoxical
affinity, as Edmund Morgan recently argued. They shared no
sense that the poorest southerners had to be kept in slavery lest
their dependency, idleness, and dissipation be left free to
undermine American liberty, as Morgan suggests. Even in slavery, their arguments indicate, the South's impoverished black
Americans posed a threat to white freedom. If the South was to
realize fully the ethic of a Revolution fought not just for political
independence but for the personal habits essential to freedom, it
would have to be freed of the slave trade—a trade that many
Virginians, including Lee, actively opposed, and that New
Hanover County, North Carolina, condemned explicitly as
dangerous to both the "virtue and the welfare of this country."
With time, moreover, the South would have to be freed of all
slavery, for all southerners, black and white. But since dependency, laziness, and improvidence often seemed to white observers an integral part of the Africans' nature, black emancipation
was tightly linked with colonization—with robbing the slaves of
their American and their southern identity even as they were
freed of their chains.[33]

In personal characteristics and concerns, in values and
ideology, then, southern leaders were much like their northern
counterparts. To be sure, the bases of shared beliefs were

different in the South: the southern leaders considered here were
moved by an intense desire for personal independence or
freedom that was in their society a mark of honor; by a concern
for posterity that reflected at once the possibility and the
difficulty of passing on to children the gains of earlier generations; and, finally, by an abhorrence of slavery. But these
concerns were distinctive to the South in degree only and served
ultimately to buttress a network of beliefs that welded North and
South ever more tightly in the battle against Britain. The most
significant geographical division of the revolutionary era was
not, it would seem, between North and South. Contemporary
scholarship suggests that it was instead between east and west
or, more exactly, between the cosmopolitan coastal regions
(Carroll's "commercial nation") and the more isolated hinter-
land.[34]

But what of the future? Political, demographic, and economic change soon defined more substantial distinctions between North and South. As a result the revolutionary tradition
may also have met a different fate in each section. In the North a
literal belief in the right of revolution declined in the late
eighteenth and early nineteenth centuries, just as it had declined
in England after her seventeenth-century revolutions. Even old
revolutionaries like Samuel Adams condemned mobs and extralegal committees and congresses as threats to the new republic.
By the 1860s supporters of the northern cause had come to sound
much like the loyalists of nine decades earlier, demanding order
and subordination to authority, damning southern "anarchy."
Those northerners who most resembled their revolutionary
ancestors, defending men's essential right to decide how they
would be governed and by whom, and to overthrow a government they no longer supported, were often condemned as
Copperheads.[35]

The history of the South during the early decades of the
new nation must have been far different from that of the North.
There the revolutionary tradition survived, much as it had

continued in eighteenth-century America. But as southerners increasingly felt themselves an embattled minority, they did more than perpetuate an Anglo-American tradition of resistance and revolution. They threw off the Calvinistic values of the Carrolls and Lees for a new image of southern elites as "cavaliers" and transformed their own Anglo-American revolutionary tradition so as to justify an attempt at independence not in the name of frugality and industry, but of grace and leisure, not for a society at odds with slavery, but for one that would perpetuate it, not for a united America, but for a separate southern Confederacy.

Notes

1. William R. Taylor, *Cavalier and Yankee: The Old South and American National Character* (New York, 1961). John R. Alden discussed the emergence of a separate southern identity during the late eighteenth century in *The First South* (Baton Rouge, La., 1961).

2. Stanley Elkins and Eric McKitrick, "The Founding Fathers: Young Men of the Revolution," *Political Science Quarterly* 76 (1961): 181–216, esp. pp. 202–6.

3. Richard Walsh, ed., *The Writings of Christopher Gadsden* (Columbia, S.C., 1966), esp. p. xxi; Walsh, *Charleston's Sons of Liberty* (Columbia, S.C., 1959); Walsh, "Christopher Gadsden: Radical or Conservative Revolutionary?" *South Carolina Historical Magazine* 113 (1962): 195–203; and Robert L. Meriwether, "Christopher Gadsden," in *Dictionary of American Biography* (New York, 1931), 7: 82–83.

4. R. D. W. Connor, *Cornelius Harnett: An Essay in North Carolina History* (Raleigh, N.C., 1909), quotation p. 89.

5. Oliver Perry Chitwood, *Richard Henry Lee: Statesman of the Revolution* (Morgantown, W. Va., 1967), and John Carter Matthews, "Richard Henry Lee and the American Revolution" (Ph.D. diss., University of Virginia, 1939), esp. pp. 61, 120–22, 191. Jefferson to William Wirt, 12 April 1812, in Paul L. Ford, ed., *The Writings of Thomas Jefferson*, 10 vols. (New York, 1898), 9: 343; Lee to John Page, Philadelphia, 26 May 1771, in James Curtis Ballagh, ed., *The Letters of Richard Henry Lee*, 2 vols. (1911, 1914; reprint ed., New York, 1970), 1: 295–96. See also Harnett to his wife, York, Pa., 28 Dec. 1777, in Walter Clark, ed., *The State Records of North Carolina*, 16 vols. (Winston and Goldsboro, N.C., 1895–1907), 11: 825–27.

6. Ronald Hoffman, *A Spirit of Dissension: Economics, Politics and the Revolution in Maryland* (Baltimore, 1973), esp. pp. 38–40, 44, 48–50, 113–17; Francis F. Beirne, "Sam Chase, 'Disturber,'" in *Maryland Historical Magazine* 107 (1962): 78–89, quotation p. 78; and Neil Strawser, "Samuel Chase and the

Annapolis Paper War," ibid., pp. 177–94. Peter S. Onuf, ed., *Maryland and the Empire, 1773: The Antilon-First Citizen Letters* (Baltimore, 1974), esp. pp. 81, 87–88; Thomas O'Brien Hanley, *Charles Carroll of Carrollton: The Making of a Revolutionary Gentleman* (Washington, D.C. 1970), p. 232, and Hanley, ed., "The Charles Carroll Papers," microfilm edition (Scholar Resources, Inc.; Wilmington, Del., 1971), roll 1, introduction.

7. Connor, *Harnett*, p. 79 (Quincy); Walsh, ed., *Writings of Gadsden*, p. xxi (Deane).

8. Richard Parker to R. H. Lee, 23 Feb. 1766, in Paul P. Hoffman, ed., "Lee Family Papers, 1742–1795," University of Virginia microfilm (Charlottesville, Va., 1966), roll 1; Madison to William Bradford, [early March 1775], in William T. Hutchinson and William M. E. Rachal, eds., *The Papers of James Madison* (Chicago, 1962), 1: 141.

9. Connor, *Harnett*, pp. 158–59, 100–101.

10. Walsh, ed., *Writings of Gadsden*, p. xix (Quincy); Gadsden letter, 20 Feb. 1766, in Robert Weir, ed., "Two Letters by Christopher Gadsden, February 1766," in *South Carolina Historical Magazine* 125 (1974): 175; Strawser, "Chase," p. 179. General biographical information here and henceforth is mainly from Walsh, "Gadsden"; Connor, *Harnett*; Chitwood, *Lee*; and Hanley, *Carroll*.

11. Hoffman, *Spirit of Dissension*, pp. 48–49 (Chase), and pp. 39–40 (Lux). Gadsden to James Pearson, Charleston, 12 Feb. 1766, in Weir, ed., "Two Letters," p. 173. For a more precise description of Gadsden's occupation as a "Country Factor" who assembled colonial products on his wharf and sold them for the best price possible—unlike the factors of British mercantile houses, who tried to buy cheap in America and sell high in Europe—see George C. Rogers, "The Charleston Tea Party: The Significance of December 3, 1773," *South Carolina Historical Magazine* 125 (1974): 156. Gadsden was apparently also an importer: we know, for example, that he imported slaves on at least two occasions. See W. Robert Higgins, "Charleston Merchants and Factors in the External Negro Trade, 1735–1775," ibid. 115 (1964): 212; Connor, *Harnett*, p. 18.

12. Charles Carroll of Annapolis to Charles Carroll of Carrollton, 9 Jan. 1764, listing assets, in *Maryland Historical Magazine* 12 (1917): 27; Hanley, *Carroll*, pp. 174–75. Hoffman argues that Carroll was more a merchant than a planter (*Spirit of Dissension*, pp. 117–18). Chitwood, *Lee*, passim.

13. Gadsden, as "A Steady Federalist," 30 Jan. 1797, in Walsh, ed., *Writings of Gadsden*, pp. 279–80; accusation of Lee by John Mercer in *Virginia Gazette* (Purdie and Dixon), 25 Sept. 1766. Chitwood, *Lee*, esp. pp. 16–17, 36–37, 228–29; and R. H. Lee to William Lee, Chantilly, 12 July 1772, in Ballagh, ed., *Letters of Lee*, pp. 70–73.

14. Carroll to the Countess of Auzoüer, 20 Sept. 1771, in "A Lost Copy-Book of Charles Carroll of Carrollton," *Maryland Historical Magazine* 32 (1937): 203–4.

15. Crane Brinton, *The Anatomy of Revolution* (New York, 1952), pp. 131–33.

16. Arthur Lee to R. H. Lee, 20 Oct. 1770, in Hoffman, ed., "Lee Family Papers," roll 2.

17. Hanley, *Carroll*, esp. p. 209.

18. This attitude is clear in the Lee family papers. See, for example, Thomas Ludwell Lee to Richard Henry Lee, 1 June 1776, in Hoffman, ed., "Lee Family Papers," roll 2, where he wrote of a "certain set of Aristocrats, for we have such monsters here." Also Matthews, "Lee," passim. For a general summary of southern legislative politics in this period, see Jack P. Greene, *The Quest for Power: The Lower Houses of Assembly in the Southern Royal Colonies, 1689–1776* (Chapel Hill, N.C., 1963).

19. Harnett to South Carolina Sons of Liberty, 1770, in Connor, *Harnett*, pp. 57–58; Gadsden to William Samuel Johnson, Charleston, 16 April 1766, in Walsh, ed., *Writings of Gadsden*, pp. 73–74; and Gadsden in *South Carolina Gazette*, 22 June 1769. Lee letter, 31 May 1764, in Ballagh, ed., *Letters of Lee*, 1: 5, 7.

20. Committee of Safety in Connor, *Harnett*, p. 90; Gadsden to Samuel Adams, Charleston, 5 June 1774, in Walsh, ed., *Writings of Gadsden*, p. 95.

21. Gadsden to Samuel Adams, Charleston, 4 April 1779, in Walsh, ed., *Writings of Gadsden*, p. 163; Lee to Arthur Lee, 11 Feb. 1779, and to John Adams, 8 Oct. 1779, in Ballagh, ed., *Writings of Lee*, 2: 33, 155. On the place of these themes in the American Revolution see Bernard Bailyn, *Ideological Origins of the American Revolution* (Cambridge, Mass., 1967); Edmund S. Morgan, "The Puritan Ethic and the American Revolution," *William and Mary Quarterly*, 3d ser. 24 (1967): 3–43; and C. Vann Woodward, "The Southern Ethic in a Puritan World," ibid. 25 (1968): 343–70.

22. To Arthur Lee, Chantilly, 20 Dec. 1766, in Ballagh, ed., *Letters of Lee*, 1: 21–22. For a succinct summary of the Lee family's politics from the mid-seventeenth to the mid-eighteenth centuries, see Paul P. Hoffman, ed., *Guide to the Microfilm Edition of the Lee Family Papers, 1742–1795* (Charlottesville, Va., 1966), pp. 11–15.

23. Edmund S. Morgan, *American Slavery, American Freedom: The Ordeal of Colonial Virginia* (New York, 1975), pp. 369–75; Bernard Bailyn, *The Origins of American Politics* (New York, 1967).

24. Carroll to his father, 4 Feb. 1758, and to William Graves, 15 Sept. 1765, in Hanley, "Carroll Papers," microfilm roll 1. See also Lee letter of 31 May 1764, in Ballagh, ed., *Letters of Lee*, 1: 7.

25. *Virginia Gazette* (Rind), 31 Jan. 1771. Arthur Lee also referred to a freedom from economic obligation when, in 1770, he wrote that he wished he could help Richard Henry Lee achieve a "state of independence" (Letter of 20 Oct. 1770 in Hoffman, ed., "Lee Family Papers," roll 1).

26. Charles Carroll of Annapolis to William Graves, 23 Dec. 1768, *Maryland Historical Magazine* 12 (1917): 179; Charles Carroll of Carrollton to Graves, 15 Sept. 1768, and to his father, 14 June 1763, in Hanley, ed., "Carroll Papers," roll 1; Charles Carroll of Annapolis to his son, 26 June 1759, ibid.

27. Charles Carroll of Annapolis to his son, 30 Nov. 1770, *Maryland Historical Magazine* 13 (1918): 71; Hanley, *Carroll*, p. 152; and Charles Carroll of Carrollton to William Graves, 15 Sept. 1765, Hanley, ed., "Carroll Papers," roll 1.

28. See Willard F. Bliss, "The Rise of Tenancy in Virginia," *Virginia*

Magazine of History and Biography 108 (1958): esp. 427–28, 430; and G. B. Warden, "Inequality and Instability in Eighteenth-Century Boston," *Journal of Interdisciplinary History* 6 (April 1976): 585–620. Carroll quoted in Hoffman, *Spirit of Dissension*, p. 250.

29. Lee to James Monroe, 5 Jan. 1784, Ballagh, ed., *Letters of Lee*, 2: 287. Gadsden as "Pro Grege et Rege," 10 June 1769, and to Samuel Adams, 5 June 1774, in Walsh, ed., *Writings of Gadsden*, pp. 77–78, 95.

30. Lee letter, 31 May 1764; Lee to Henry, Philadelphia, 15 April 1777, and to Samuel Adams, 4 Feb. 1773, in Ballagh, ed., *Writings of Lee*, 1: 6, 275, 82, and as "A Virginia Planter," draft, 1766, misdated 1776 in Hoffman, ed., "Lee Family Papers," roll 2.

31. Gadsden to William Samuel Johnson, 16 April 1766, in Walsh, ed., *Writings of Gadsden*, p. 72; Mason, at the Constitutional Convention, quoted in Andrew C. McLaughlin, *The Confederation and the Constitution* (New York, 1967), p. 176.

32. Mason in McLaughlin, *Confederation*, p. 176, and in Richard K. MacMaster, "Arthur Lee's 'Address on Slavery': An Aspect of Virginia's Struggle to End the Slave Trade, 1765–1774," *Virginia Magazine of History and Biography* 130 (1972): 145–46, 151–52n. This article includes an excellent brief introduction to Virginia's debate over slavery. See p. 152 for county resolutions of 1774. Jefferson in Morgan, *American Slavery*, p. 375; Lee quoted in Chitwood, *Lee*, p. 18; Gadsden to William Henry Drayton, Charleston, 1 June 1778, in Walsh, ed., *Writings of Gadsden*, pp. 126–27.

33. Morgan, *American Slavery*, esp. pp. 384–85. See also McMaster, "Arthur Lee's 'Address on Slavery,'" p. 145, for Lee's discussion of African inferiority, and p. 153, for a contrary suggestion that slavery induced the slaves' vices.

34. For a discussion of this theme in recent historical writing see Pauline Maier, "Why Revolution? Why Democracy?" *Journal of Interdisciplinary History* 6 (April 1976): 711–32.

35. Pauline Maier, "Coming to Terms with Samuel Adams," *American Historical Review* 131 (1976): 27. George Fredrickson, *The Inner Civil War: Northern Intellectuals and the Crisis of Union* (New York, 1965).

2

Rebelliousness: Personality Development and the American Revolution in the Southern Colonies

by Robert M. Weir

About three miles south of the Ashley River shortly after one o'clock on the afternoon of 23 December 1765, four young men on horseback barred the road to Charleston, South Carolina. Seizing the reins of the horses drawing several vehicles belonging to the family of Robert Williams, they dragged his stepson from the buggy in which he had been riding with his fourteen-year-old sister. While the others held the rest of the party at gunpoint, one of the men leaped into the vehicle, whipped up the horses, and sped off down the road with the girl. Sometime after the pair were out of sight, the highwaymen released the rest of the party. Not far down the road, Williams came upon the vehicle wrecked in a ditch, some of the girl's clothing strewn about in the bushes, and the couple nowhere in sight.[1]

Though we may have our suspicions, we, like Mrs. Williams, want to know exactly what was happening. She posed the question while confronting a cocked pistol; we raise it as a topic of scholarly discussion more than two hundred years later. Whereas she understandably was interested in quick and detailed answers, we can defer them while we seek to put the matter in a wider perspective. In the process, because we know that two of the most active highwaymen later became revolutionary leaders, we, in effect, shall be assessing an observation made by a loyalist, Jonathan Boucher, who sought partly to explain the Revolution by noting that the "chief Abettors of Violence . . . are young men of Good Parts, but spoil'd by a strange, imperfect, desultory kind of Education." Children, he previously had remarked, were "no longer so respectful and dutiful as they ought to be, and as they used to be."[2] Accordingly this essay will attempt to explore some possible relationships between family life, especially in the plantation colonies, and the nature of the American Revolution.

Admittedly, the limited state of our present knowledge makes the enterprise somewhat speculative, but there are reasons for believing that the attempt might be worthwhile. First, though the southern family of the late colonial period has yet to be subjected to widespread and intensive scrutiny, social and demographic historians have learned a good deal during the last few years about the situation farther north.[3] Second, though contemporary "studies of family relationships have not yet progressed to the point that . . . well-documented conclusions can be drawn . . . in regard to politically relevant dimensions," as one scholar noted, they tend to indicate that "early learning is an important factor in the developmental psychology of political attitudes." Attempts to correlate specific political beliefs held by parents and children have produced disappointingly negative results, but a number of recent investigations suggest that the "study of the direct transmission of more basic personality orientations might be a fruitful area for future research." Thus, despite considerable criticism since its publication nearly thirty years ago, the central assumption underlying the now classic study of *The Authoritarian Personality* still appears to be viable.[4] And thus, though Boucher failed to coin neologisms like the "rebellious personality," modern scholarship suggests that he may have been at least partially correct, not only in perceiving the existence of such a phenomenon, but also in accounting for it.

Several recent scholars have attempted to postulate direct
or indirect relationships between changes in the colonial family
and the coming of the American Revolution. Most of these
hypotheses relate to the concept of "modernization." Although
its definitions and manifestations appear to be equally innumerable, one of the most important features of the process seems to
be a change in the traditional patterns of authority. In North
America between the seventeenth and the nineteenth centuries
the trend was clearly away from authoritarianism: deference
waned; voluntary associations proliferated; and even in the
family, children seem to have acquired greater independence
at earlier ages. Intimately involved with all of these developments—both as cause and result—was the emergence of
a new personality type, the psychologically autonomous individual.[5] To explain the rapid emergence of this new man,
especially in the colonies outside of New England, Jack Greene
has developed a sophisticated version of the Turner thesis in
which he argues that the economic opportunities and necessities
of the New World placed a premium upon adaptive behavior.
Flexibility, in turn, required personal autonomy. But having
acquired the requisite personality (presumably over several successive generations) Americans found themselves confronted
with British restraints threatening to their "autonomy as
individuals"—an autonomy that had become essential to their
self-esteem as well as to their success in colonial society. Thus
they responded angrily and rebelliously.[6]

Intrinsically plausible, the argument is also tactically
adroit, for it does not depend upon a particular model of the
colonial family. Whether the family was authoritarian or permis-
sive, patriarchal or contractual, Greene implies by his scant
attention to the matter, was less important than the character of
the father figure a son sought to emulate. All other factors being
equal, autonomous fathers, he appears to assume, tended to
produce even more autonomous sons, and empirical evidence
seems to validate this assumption. One investigator found

recently that among contemporary families "with the effects of all of the other variables held constant, the strongest single predictor of our respondents' level of personal control was their parents['] level of personal control."[7] Thus one of the strong points of Greene's interpretation is its ability to cope with widely differing patterns of authority in American families. Indeed, the chief weakness of his point of view may be merely that he has yet to claim enough for it.

Be that as it may, any attempt to link the Revolution more closely to prior changes in the colonial family must confront the nature of these changes directly. Thus, Philip Greven, whose suppositions were based upon a very detailed knowledge of the situation in Andover, Massachusetts, suggested that by the mid-eighteenth century earlier independence for sons meant that "their attitudes toward parent-son relations had changed significantly from those of their fathers' and their grandfathers' generations. For Andover's fourth generation, Thomas Paine's call for independence . . . from the mother-country and from the father-king might have been just what Paine claimed it to be—common sense."[8] More recently, Edwin Burrows and Michael Wallace have elaborated this hypothesis in a subtle and suggestive essay. During most of the colonial period, they argue, "Americans accepted British control and authority because the objective disparity between British power and colonial power created in them a deep personal sense of comparative weakness and inferiority." Colonial dependence and weakness in turn produced affection and imitation of British standards by individual Americans who were "inclined to be acquiescent toward authority and authority figures," in part because of the "structure of both colonial society and the colonial family." But demographic and economic growth of the colonies, along with their increasing military prowess, "transformed the collective image of the colonies from one of weakness and inferiority to one of strength and capability." Furthermore, "the decline of patriarchalism in both colonial society and the colonial family . . .

tended to produce less authoritarian and more autonomous personality types," for whom the "arbitrary exercise of imperial authority was likely to be extremely objectionable." Thus British restrictions of the 1760s and 1770s "shattered the personal trust and affection that Americans had had for the English and their King. A widespread feeling of betrayal aroused still more anger against Britain, and may also have released previously repressed resentments at dependency."[9]

Undoubtedly, as Bruce Mazlish has put it, Burrows and Wallace basically "have the picture right,"[10] although a few areas may still be a bit out of focus. For example, their contention that the growth of the colonies, in the perception of many Americans, bespoke a "concomitant transformation in the personal identity of significant masses of people" is not entirely convincing. Admittedly, recent studies of the psychology of nationalism appear to substantiate the current existence of such a phenomenon.[11] But what holds true after the advent of modern nationalism may be more doubtful before it. In fact, to assume the existence of such a link between personal and collective capability is to complicate the problem of explaining the Revolution in those southern colonies whose inhabitants remained acutely conscious of their economic weakness or military impotence. Nor can this objection be answered entirely by assuming that men from such areas identified themselves with America collectively instead of with their local communities. After all, even Patrick Henry's famous statement that he was "not a Virginian, but an American" was uttered during the course of a debate in which he advocated greater voting strength in the Continental Congress for Virginia.[12]

The other major difficulty with Burrows and Wallace's hypothesis arises from their assumption that changes in the family were as rapid and as great elsewhere in America as in Andover, Massachusetts. Not only does that assumption exceed present knowledge, it is also implausible. Even in regard to New England we might argue—as we could ten years ago—whether the role of the family was expanding or contracting during much of the colonial period. Elsewhere, to paraphrase Edward Saveth, our ignorance remains to this day "almost unmitigated." Perhaps the safest course would be to take a cue from the work of Robert Wells and other demographic historians who have been impressed by the "tremendous complexity and diversity" among families in the New World.[13] That patterns of authority varied as widely as the composition of households appears possible, if not probable. Furthermore, even if one accepts the dubious proposition that the decline of patriarchalism was universal, the rate in most places was almost certainly very gradual. In poetry, the "one-hoss shay" may collapse all at once; in history, such processes are apt to be agonizingly slow. One would expect, therefore, to find an extended period of transition, fraught with ambiguity and tension, during which children attempted to assert earlier independence while parents struggled to maintain their authority.

Much evidence indicates that this is precisely what happened in much of the Western world. John Locke, whose *Some Thoughts Concerning Education* made him the Dr. Spock of the eighteenth century, illustrates the nature of the transition. Recognizing that "the time must come" when children "will be past the rod and correction," he noted that the influence of a parent must then be based upon "love and friendship." But until that time, he also believed, "children . . . should look upon their parents as their lords, their absolute governors; and, as such, stand in awe of them."[14] When and where to draw the line between the two conditions was then as now the subject of contention. During the eighteenth century child-rearing manuals began advocating that parents instill independence in their children. Yet as late as the first half of the next century, travelers' accounts reported considerable stress and strain in American families over the subject. And in New England during the late eighteenth century, magazines catering to a middle-class audience (which was doubtless relatively quick to adopt newer trends) expressed values that recently have led a number of sociologists to conclude that "the colonial family was undoubtedly a family in transition, perhaps in some areas in a *more marked transition* than is commonly recognized."[15]

Nowhere is the nature of that transition more clearly revealed than in the changing pattern of parental control over marriage. As Daniel Scott Smith has observed, up until the early eighteenth century "there existed a stable, parental-run marriage system, in the nineteenth century a stable participant-run system." Intervening was "a period of change and crisis." More recently, Smith and Michael Hindus have further illuminated characteristics of that crisis by their analysis of premarital conception rates. Using a broad sample of American marriages between 1640 and 1971, they discovered the existence of a cyclical trend that reached an all-time high in the last half of the eighteenth century, when approximately one-third of all brides appear to have been pregnant at marriage. Noting that the similarity of economic status between bride and groom indicates that in all probability these courtships remained at least partially constrained by traditional norms, they interpret the high level of premarital conceptions as evidence of conflict within the family. As one contemporary observer put it, these couples "would do the same again, because otherwise they could not obtain their parent's [sic] consent to marry." In short, these were shotgun weddings in which the weapon was turned on the older rather than the younger generation. Their frequency, Smith and Hindus persuasively contend, reveals not the "contractual, Lockean and republican nature of the family," but tensions generated by power relationships being challenged.[16]

Though Smith and Hindus draw only a small part of their evidence from the southern colonies, there are reasons to suspect that such tensions may have been especially characteristic there. On the one hand, as Greene and others have pointed out, personal independence was almost a fetish among the local elites, and the development of personal autonomy appears to have proceeded apace.[17] On the other hand, however, scholars have noted that the antebellum South retained many features of a traditional society—including a high degree of patriarchalism.[18] Thus it appears that geographic dispersal, institutional weaknesses, the exigencies of plantation life, and a number of other factors accentuated contradictory thrusts. The patriarch demanded obedience and subordination; the youth who modeled himself upon the father sought independence and personal control over his own life. For members of the upper classes at least, slavery probably exacerbated conflict. "Boy," that traditional but now dying southern term for a black man, illustrates why: black slaves and white children shared a similar state of dependency. Quite naturally, therefore, as the diary of Philip Fithian, a tutor in Virginia, clearly shows, planters' children used the slaves as a touchstone by which to determine the appropriateness of their own treatment. Thus attempts to distinguish themselves from those who were in a similarly dependent situation doubtless resulted in exaggerated displays of independence. Moreover, parents like Maurice Moore of North Carolina clearly sought to make the same distinction and therefore occasionally may have treated some of these displays with unwonted indulgence.[19] This possibility suggests two explanations for widely varying reports of very lax as well as very strict discipline in southern households. Undoubtedly, the diversity among families was great, but inconsistencies within single households may have been almost as widespread and frequent.[20] And inconsistent discipline has ever been a notorious cause of friction between parent and child.

In addition, two other features especially characteristic of life in the southern colonies probably further increased the prevailing level of conflict. One was the tendency of southern planters to send their children to England for schooling; the result, undoubtedly, was often a generation gap like that between John Drayton of South Carolina who, according to his grandson, "was a man of indifferent education [and] . . .

confined mind" and his son William Henry, whose prose style betrays a clever, polished, and somewhat snobbish prig.[21] The other characteristic feature of the area appears to have been an unusually high rate of early mortality among parents. The South Carolina lowcountry was undoubtedly exactly what it was reputed to be—a most unhealthy place. Even among Virginians an astonishing number of future revolutionary leaders—including Washington, Jefferson, George Mason, Edmund Pendleton, and Peyton Randolph—lost fathers at an early age.[22] Thus in all probability a disproportionately high percentage of youths grew up under forms of tutelage that could be perceived as less legitimate than that of their natural parents. That fact, of course, by no means signifies that they all experienced difficulty with surrogate father figures. Undoubtedly, many were like Edward Rutledge who was reputed to have been known for his "filial affection and obedience," though he grew up under the care of his older brother John. Nevertheless, the parental death rate almost certainly increased the potential for conflict during childhood and youth, for even in the eighteenth century the stepchild relationship was a byword for contention.[23] Thus conditions widespread in the southern colonies make it reasonable to suppose that many revolutionary leaders matured in homes where the boundaries of the permissible occasionally were vague, the situation ambivalent, and relationships with authority figures not infrequently strained.

Much scattered evidence appears to support these suppositions. Boucher, as we have seen, believed children to be increasingly disobedient. If one prefers Whig to Tory testimony, he can turn to Landon Carter whose mature son Robert Wormley, "Wild Bob," delighted in vexing him—or at least so the old man thought. Schoolmasters' reports from Virginia and North Carolina both before and after the Revolution contain frequent accounts of difficulty in managing rebellious youths. Among prominent individuals, John Drayton appears to have had an especially hard time with his sons. "Very wild and

ungovernable" was the report on one of the younger, Glen, who
was studying in Britain, while his older brothers prompted their
father to write: "I am so unhappy and made so miserable in two
of my Sons . . . [who take] no Council from me nor yet pay no
obedience." They in turn apparently considered him a "Tyrant."[24] Only a great deal of further research will permit us to
evaluate these examples with much certainty, but such friction
may have been common, though perhaps the Draytons' was
unusually intense. If this was indeed the case, during childhood
and adolescence members of the local elites in the southern
colonies acquired a large and explosive emotional baggage.

This probability suggests that Smith and Hindus may
have been especially perceptive when they observed that the
"very ambiguity of the relationship between parents and children heightened the salience of the familial analogy for the
parallel struggle that was developing between the colonies and
the mother country." Ambiguity and conflict in each case obviously facilitated the conscious perception of the one as an
analogue of the other. So, too, did the traditional propensity—
despite Locke's work—to conflate patriarchal and royal authority.[25] But significant as such conscious perceptions were, the
subconscious transfer of emotions from the one context to the
other was doubtless even more important. For as Benjamin
Rush—who was both a pioneer psychiatrist and a revolutionary
leader—noted, emotional reactions "may be induced by causes
that are forgotten; or by the presence of objects which revive the
sensation of distress with which at one time it was associated,
but without reviving the cause of it in the memory."[26] Accordingly, the figures of speech employed by revolutionary leaders
help to account for the intensity of their reaction to British
measures. The "epithets of parent and child have been so long
applied to Great Britain and her colonies," George Mason
fumed, "that . . . we rarely see anything from your side of the
water free from the authoritative style of a master to a schoolboys
. . . Is not this a little ridiculous?" Equally revealing is the ten-

dency of Americans to refer to Britain not only as an " 'illiberal stepdame' " but also as a " 'vile imposter—an old abandoned prostitute.' " The old prostitute is perhaps more significant than the stepdame, for the latter could be—and no doubt was in part—used in a conscious attempt to sanction resistance by stigmatizing British authority as illegitimate. But cursing Britain as an old imposter went beyond conscious utility. Rather, it recapitulated a pattern of behavior frequently observed among adolescents who attempt to assuage guilt over their increasing estrangement from their parents by imagining that these ugly old people are not really their parents but imposters.[27]

Why, one should ask at this point, is it worth knowing that the Revolution called forth and drew upon emotions that had been conditioned by the childhood experiences of revolutionaries? Was it not primarily a political revolution, understandable in conventional political terms, without the necessity of recourse to what at first glance appear to be only marginally relevant considerations? Certainly, at least on one level, the Revolution is largely comprehensible in purely political terms. But some aspects remain puzzling from most conventional perspectives. As Pauline Maier observed in reviewing Robert Calhoon's fine book about the loyalists, "after 500 pages, the reader may well conclude that the Loyalists were not much different from other Americans." Thus many of them remain enigmas; and thus Burrows and Wallace have postulated the existence of a "distinctive Loyalist 'personality' " that remained "psychologically dependent on England. The prospect of living without a system of external supports and restraints filled them with anxiety."[28] Doubtless, this is an accurate characterization of some loyalists, but it scarcely fits others. Among the others, some—but not all—may perhaps be more readily understood from the perspective outlined here. William Bull II and Alexander Garden may be good examples. Bull was lieutenant governor of South Carolina; Garden was the most distinguished contemporary physician in Charleston. There appears to be little evidence—other than their loyalism—for considering either a dependent personality; to each, the influence of an oath—for one, the royal oath of office, for the other, the Hippocratic—may have been decisive. Each, however, especially disliked and avoided contention. Bull was "so very obliging that he never obliged," according to one very contentious Whig, Christopher Gadsden. Garden refused to serve in the revolutionary army, even as a doctor, because he wished to remain "a peaceable Person to follow his Profession."[29] In short, loyalism or vacillation may have been associated with a personality type that was less dependent than fearful of contention. Although there is insufficient evidence to be certain about Bull and Garden, some youths may have found conflict with their parents so threatening that they could not bear to go through a similar experience again—which is not to say that they were dependent personalities.

The phenomenon of lingering allegiance may also be easier to understand when the Revolution is approached as a drama that evoked childhood emotions. Richard Henry Lee voiced a commonly accepted axiom when he remarked that "nothing can be more certain than that allegiance & protection are reciprocal duties." Thus allegiance made little intellectual sense after August 1775 when Americans were proclaimed to be in rebellion and thereby formally denied the protection of the crown. Indeed, it can be argued, allegiance to a king always makes the most sense when seen as the culturally sanctioned projection of attitudes and emotions that first have been developed and conditioned in the family setting. Accordingly, several scholars have come close to suggesting that in abandoning the nurturing and protective role, British authorities unleashed upon George III all of the repressed hostilities of Americans toward their own fathers. The flood of hostility was in some ways remarkable, and perhaps no other perspective will account fully for the popularity of the assault upon the king in Thomas Paine's *Common Sense*.[30] Less commonly observed is that "anger at an unnatural 'parental' betrayal" did not, as has been claimed, sweep "away once and for all that affection for England." That affection remained resilient in the lower South, even among such leading revolutionary figures as John Rutledge, Henry Laurens, and Rawlins Lowndes, who retained strong vestiges of their former loyalty—at least until the British occupation of 1780 and 1782.[31] In fact, the evocation of this undertone of lingering affection is part of what gives the Declaration of Independence its somber dignity. Doubtless one of the main reasons the document still can move men who have had no experience with rebellion on a national scale is because they have had such experience on a personal level; it is also equally probable that the Declaration and the movement it epitomized took the form they did partly because revolutionary leaders were sons before they became revolutionaries, and their emotions were equally ambivalent in both cases.

All of which is to say that there was a significant irrational component to the American Revolution. Without an understanding of this element the movement may be inexplicable, at least in Georgia and South Carolina. In the populous colonies to the north resistance may have appeared to have a reasonable chance of success. Thus William Lee could report from London that "the ministers attend much to the motions in Virginia, for they think *you will fight.*" But in the two southernmost of the thirteen colonies Whigs and loyalists alike were acutely aware not only of their prosperity under imperial control but also of their extreme vulnerability without the concomitant British protection. With slaves in their midst and Indians on their borders, sparsely scattered South Carolinians and Georgians believed they needed outside assistance against even relatively weak foes. From any rational point of view, challenging Britain was virtually tantamount to suicide. Knowing this, British observers like Richard Oswald, a slave merchant with close ties to the area, assumed that southerners were only bluffing, that they would never dare to revolt. In short, British authorities expected them to act rationally, and the expectation proved wrong. There were, of course, many reasons why men were willing to run the awesome risks that rebellion entailed, but one of the most important was emotion. For if, as Edmund Morgan has remarked, self-interest can strengthen one's commitment to principles,[32] it also can undermine the commitment. And in this case something had to supplement self-interest. Without anger, it is therefore doubtful that there would have been a Revolution in this area. And without the tensions that appear to have characterized families in the southern colonies, whether there would have been enough anger is a question about which one can only speculate.

Ultimately, of course, that question can never be answered with certainty. Yet the hypothesis that prompts it can be tested in various ways. Among these, one of the more interesting may be to extend its application. If conflict and tension at home during youth accentuated emotions that fueled the Revolution, it should be possible to establish plausible links between this putative family background and the goals of revolutionary leaders. In Jefferson's case, Fawn Brodie and Erik Erikson recently have sought to make precisely such connections. As the latter notes, Jefferson, who had struggled to discharge the responsibilities of an eldest son while still lacking full control of his own property, was as "a lawgiver . . . forever preoccupied with matters of the generations." High on the list of all the tyrannies over the mind of man that he opposed were those, like entail, that might be called the tyranny of the older generation. No doubt the effect of his own experience contributed to his belief that constitutions should terminate every two decades.[33] The idea, to be sure, represented an attempt to combine the safeguards of a written constitution with the flexibility of British practice. But that the life span of constitutions was to be identical to the minority of each new generation is most suggestive.

If Jefferson's career appears to provide grounds for suspecting that the ends as well as the means of the Revolution can be correlated to its leaders' earlier struggles for personal independence, the relationship also raises a more important and complex question. Why were the results in each case—of youthful rebellion and of colonial revolt—so creative and successful? The scope of the question and of the present paper obviously preclude anything but a most tentative answer. But I can suggest, once again, that the revolutionary crisis and its outcome recapitulated the earlier adolescent crisis—that the successful resolution of the one prepared the way for the successful outcome of the other. In one form or another, this argument has been applied to other revolutionary situations by other scholars. In particular, Erikson has suggested that Luther and Gandhi resolved their own identity crises in ways that uniquely fitted them for the role of charismatic leaders in their respective societies. And Bruce Mazlish, who rejects the notion that American revolutionary leadership was predominantly charismatic, has modified Erikson's interpretation to fit Washington.[34] Thus—to reverse an old biological metaphor—there is little that is new in the general belief that phylogeny recapitulates ontogeny, or that the developing revolutionary situation recalls the previous psychological evolution of the individuals involved. What may be novel in the American situation, however, is the scale of the phenomenon. The relative absence of charismatic leaders suggests that they were superfluous—or, perhaps, ubiquitous. Having sought and achieved personal autonomy during youth, most American leaders doubtless felt little need to subordinate themselves to a charismatic figure, for they were he.

If so, a closer look at the conditions that promoted the successful quest for personal autonomy in America may be worthwhile. If our suspicions about the situation in the southern colonies are correct, that quest appears to have been both unusually successful and unusually contentious. How to account for the apparently unlikely conjunction of these two characteristics therefore becomes the question. One explanation may be that the harmonious family is a vestige of the Garden of Eden, perhaps equally mythical. Increasingly, students of the family

are beginning to suspect that not harmony but a considerable
degree of conflict may have been the rule. In addition, they are
beginning to discover that such conflict may be far less damaging
than they used to believe. As some notably candid researchers,
who followed a group of men and women from birth to adult-
hood only to find that many of their early predictions proved to
be wrong, observed, " 'we had not appreciated the maturing
utility of many painful . . . experiences which in time, if lived
through, brought sharpened awareness, more complex integra-
tions, better skills in problem solving, clarified goals, and increasing stability.' "[35] Less immediately apparent, however, is
what enabled Americans to overcome the guilt necessarily entailed by rebellion against a previously accepted authority figure.

In particular, if there was an intimate connection between
family life in the southern colonies and the nature of the
American Revolution, the mechanisms by which individuals
justified rebellion in each case must have been closely related.
The explanation offered by Greene, who observed that British
authorities forfeited their mantle of authority by violating what
colonials perceived as the moral order, covers the political but
not the familial rebellion. The interpretation advanced by Lewis
Feuer subsumes both kinds of revolts, but even he would not
argue for its particular relevance to the American Revolution. In
other cases, however, he notes that rebels frequently have
sought to cope with their guilt feelings by seeking " 'back to the
people' identification." A "would-be parricide," the rebel "can
conquer his guilt only with the demonstration that he is selfless
and by winning the comforting maternal love of the oppressed."
Among American revolutionaries, Thomas Burke of North Carolina is one of the very few who might fit this model. Having
quarreled with his Irish uncle who raised him, Burke came to
America where he soon became identified with the revolutionary
movement. "My zeal," he later wrote, "was a passion for the
liberty of mankind. I could not stand aloof from the struggle."[36]
Even allowing for words written in retrospect under the

influence of Enlightenment rhetoric, Burke sounds atypical enough to make one suspect that the psychological mechanisms by which he assuaged guilt were not the same as those of most of his fellow southerners. The question therefore remains: how did young men nerve themselves to revolt against their fathers, how did American revolutionaries sanction their rebelliousness? In the final analysis, we must return to the notion that maturation of the individual, in the one case, and colonial growth, in the other, appeared to render illegitimate authority that hitherto had been perceived as legitimate.

Why? Because in colonial society the son sought to emulate the father, to behave as he would have under similar circumstances. That is, sons internalized parental standards and values. A most illuminating symbolic representation of the process occurs in the nether world of myth and Freudian fantasy where men killed and ate the tribal patriarch. Such cannibalism presumably conferred his extraordinary power upon his successors who sought to ingest its magical sources with the father. Amid the restraints of civilization and the conscious mind, the model takes the place of the flesh, while values substitute for magic. In each case, parricide is carried on in the name of the father, and the system of beliefs that sanctioned his authority legitimizes the revolt of the sons. Thus it is not really surprising to find that in the American Revolution men who called themselves Sons of Liberty resisted a king whose crown and lineage had symbolized British freedom. Nor is it even surprising to find, as Winthrop Jordan has done, that Americans figuratively and in some ways quite literally consumed the crown. Indeed, it seems entirely natural that they did so in the firm belief that their forefathers would have been proud of them.[37]

Ultimately, therefore, to understand both the American Revolution and the men who led it, we must know what qualities parents esteemed in their sons. One was independence, but independence was generally considered to be a manly virtue; obedience a boyish one. Indeed, independence in manhood depended upon obedience in childhood, for only the discipline of the one made possible the freedom of the other. As Locke noted, "Every man must some time or other be trusted to himself, and his own conduct; and he that is a good, a virtuous, and able man, must be made so within." The man who had not learned regular habits and self-control in childhood was a threat as well as a "burthen to Society and himself," as Eliza Lucas Pinckney observed. Industry was most prized for its utility in maintaining a well-regulated life. "The greatest conquest is a Victory over your own irregular passions," she reminded her brother in urging him to "lay down betimes a plan" for his "conduct in life." Some forty years later, Jefferson revealed that he shared the same belief when he wrote to his daughter that work was the way to avoid hysteria.[38] So, too, did a less prominent revolutionary leader from South Carolina, Thomas Ferguson, who directed the executors of his will to be especially careful in keeping his sons busy until they were twenty-one, "so as to give a true Relish for Industry, being well convinced that the Habit of Idleness is productive of the most fatal Consequences to Youth." However anachronistic it would be to apply Michael Walzer's recent insight to these men and women, they frequently acted as if they understood that only the discipline of the Puritan saints made possible the liberalism of Locke.[39]

In the socialization of their children, as in virtually every area of life from architecture to zoology, they exhibited a rage for order and regularity. Nothing could be farther from the truth in most cases, one suspects, than Henry Adams's comment that the "life of boyhood in Virginia was not well fitted for teaching self-control or mental discipline."[40] In fact, the frequency of injunctions like those quoted above, as well as the surprising depth of commitment to what Edmund Morgan has termed the Puritan Ethic on the part of wealthy Anglicans in the southern colonies, suggests that local circumstances may have given these virtues special and continued relevance. Relatively weak institutional support made self-discipline socially and psychologically more important. So, too, undoubtedly, did the presence of slaves. Certainly, if Fithian's impression was accurate, planters like Robert Carter of Nomini Hall strove to make their plantations, like their minds, islands of good order and regularity in a potentially chaotic world.[41] Furthermore, the flux and tension within the family itself may have heightened the commitment of many among both fathers and sons to stability and order.

At any rate, personal order and regularity clearly were among the most pervasive, earliest, and persistently inculcated of all cultural imperatives, and the inculcation depended at least in part upon the threatened deprivation of love. As Richard Henry Lee wrote to his sons, Thomas and Ludwell, "whilst you continue to behave as well as you have done, my tenderest affection shall always be placed on you," and the same sentiment was expressed by many other parents—including Jefferson and Henry Laurens.[42] However cruel the technique may appear to be, and whatever its hidden costs, it seems to have been effective. Certainly the revolutionary generation contained some of the most rigorously self-disciplined individuals one would want to meet—like Jefferson—whose lives were, insofar as the contingencies of life and the vagaries of the human heart permit, models of good order and regularity.[43] If ever men were schooled to be masters of their own lives, these were they.

Just as surely, however, if ever men were reared to resist external authority, these also were they. For to threaten the withdrawal of love for the failure to live up to certain standards was to say, in the plainest possible manner, that some values were greater than love—greater even than the nurturing love of a parent upon which, to a young child, life itself seemed to depend. Implicit here was the notion that some values were great enough to sanction resistance against even the most legitimate of authorities. And among these imperatives one of the most important was self-control—the imposition of order and regularity upon one's own life. A trivial incident from John Rutledge's childhood therefore becomes illuminating. The first recorded episode of his rebelliousness, at age eleven, involved a refusal to study "literature and the arts" because, he claimed to believe, such pursuits were corrupting and conducive to idleness. Naturally, as an individual developed greater control of himself, external controls became increasingly irksome, superfluous, and—most important—potentially disruptive of the internally imposed patterns of order. The process of maturation therefore dictated that self-control ultimately meant both control of self and independence from the control of others. Of necessity, the two were inseparable. Thus the revolutionary generation was being taught that the dependent and disordered life was not worth living. This form of tutelage was not apt to produce boys or men who, because of fear or guilt, would be incapable of challenging authority. Rather, it was a form of schooling that tended to make self-evident Mason's observation that there was "a passion natural to the mind of man, especially a free man, which renders him impatient of restraint." Finally, however, it was a form of education that produced men who justified their impatience by their restraint. Not all were moderate revolutionaries, though most were, but they were men for whom order was the ultimate sanction of rebelliousness and revolution.[44]

Herein may lie some of the most important links between the family background of the southern elite and the nature of the Revolution. Youthful experience taught that rebellion need not lead to chaos, that in fact it might be a prerequisite for order, and that the risk was worth taking. Thus Americans could resist, on a piecemeal basis, imperial restraints that threatened to limit de facto colonial autonomy; thus, too, when less drastic measures proved ineffective, they could pledge their lives, their fortunes, and their sacred honor in defense of independence. Significantly, they increasingly justified their rebelliousness in the name of order. According to Henry Laurens, British measures threatened to produce "dire confusion," while William Henry Drayton believed that Britain had created a situation "pregnant with horrible uproar and wild confusion." Over and over again, these charges were repeated until Jefferson immortalized them in the Declaration of Independence.[45] For the gist of the indictment against George III was not merely that he failed to protect colonial liberty—or even that he had actively infringed it—but that in doing both he had created disorder and confusion. In the final analysis the perception of this fact may have been a large part of what helped to make the Declaration acceptable to many Americans. It is therefore not surprising that, as many scholars have observed, the culmination and most characteristic expression of the American Revolution was to be found in the constitutions it produced.[46] Because "domestic Tranquillity" and the "Blessings of Liberty" seemed to be one and inseparable at some of the deepest levels of consciousness, as well as of political prudence, these constitutions became the ultimate sanction of rebellion.

Thus we have some fascinating paradoxes: violence undertaken in the name of order, and a revolution that drew energy and direction from the irrational and yet remained among the most rational of revolutions on record—one that was, despite its substratum of emotion, "infused," as one commentator has observed, "by *mind* to a degree never approximated since and perhaps never approximated before."[47]

To quote this apt description is to put the present interpretation in perspective. My attempt here has not been to reject more conventional interpretations, nor even to supplant some of the more unconventional ones, but to supplement them. Briefly and starkly stated, the thesis of this essay has been that family life and child-rearing practices in the southern colonies contributed to a particular kind of rebelliousness that revealed itself on the grand as well as lesser scales. Hitherto we have sought to demonstrate this proposition by an abstract discussion of developments in the larger sphere. But if the point of view is valid, it should be equally useful in helping us to understand concrete events at the domestic level. Let us therefore return to the earthy plane upon which we began to see if the present perspective helps to make the sequel of our opening drama more understandable—indeed, perhaps almost predictable.

Williams and his stepson, you will recall, had found the vehicle wrecked in a ditch, clothes strewn about, and the young couple, William Ward Crosthwaite and Sarah Hartley, gone. Obviously acquainted with the highwaymen and apparently suspecting collusion on Sarah's part, the two men sought to convince all the ministers in the area not to marry the pair, though it was lamentably clear that Crosthwaite had had Sarah "a Considerable time in the woods by himself." But the efforts of the two men proved to be in vain, for within hours of the kidnapping the couple, who lacked a marriage license, took their vows before the rector of the local parish. To justify his participation the minister posed the crucial question: "Suppose Mr. Crosthwaite shou'd debauch or has debauched your Sister?" To which her brother could only reply that he "would rather have her an honest Woman than a Whore."[48]

This was one of those times, it seems, when even the literal shotgun could be effectively turned against the restraints imposed by familial authority and when one might engage with impunity in flagrant acts of rebelliousness. In response to Mrs. Williams's demand to know what was going on, one of the highwaymen, Barnard Elliott, replied, "God damn you[,] Madam[,] Crosthwaite is my friend[.] I dont care if it should cost me £10,000 & all the money'd Men in the Province will approve our Conduct & stand by us." He was correct. Though arrested and indicted for a felony, the kidnappers had no difficulty in finding sureties for their bonds, nor in being quickly pardoned after the girl testified that she had gone willingly. Indeed, the minister claimed that Crosthwaite had acted like "a Man of Courage & an officer."[49] Regularization of the couple's relationship by marriage and the ensuing community approval suggest that the episode was a peculiarly eighteenth-century act of American rebelliousness—a minirevolution in which the end was not liberation from restraints but the "foundation of freedom."[50] Thus it is not surprising to find that at the time of her kidnapping, Sarah Hartley "was legally intitled unto a Considerable Substance in Lands and Goods." Nor is it anticlimactic to learn that her second marriage, after Crosthwaite's premature death, was to a widower merchant. Finally, it appears somehow fitting that one of the gunmen, Benjamin Huger, died while fighting the British in 1779; while another, Barnard Elliott, became the orator who read the Declaration of Independence at the ceremonies in Charleston celebrating its adoption.[51]

Notes

1. Examination and Deposition of Robert Williams, 14 Jan. 1766, South Carolina Council Journal No. 32, pp. 688–92, and Pardon of W. Ward Crosthwaite, Barnard Elliott, Benjamin Huger, and John Miles, 3 April 1766, Miscellaneous Records, MM, p. 361, both at South Carolina Department of Archives and History, Columbia, S.C.

2. Quoted in Edwin G. Burrows and Michael Wallace, "The American Revolution: The Ideology and Psychology of National Liberation," *Perspectives in American History* 6 (1972): 266.

3. For citations to much of this literature, which clearly reveal its geographic imbalance, see Robert V. Wells, "Family History and Demographic Transition," *Journal of Social History* 8 (Fall 1975): 1–19; and Rudy R. Seward, "The Colonial Family in America: Toward a Socio-Historical Restoration of its Structure," *Journal of Marriage and the Family* 35 (Feb. 1973): 58–70.

4. Richard G. Niemi, "Political Socialization," in Jeanne N. Knutson, ed., *Handbook of Political Psychology* (San Francisco, 1973), pp. 129, 136; Nevitt Sanford, "Authoritarian Personality in Contemporary Perspective," ibid., pp. 139–70; R. W. Connell, "Political Socialization in the American Family," *Public Opinion Quarterly* 36 (Fall 1972): 330; Stanley A. Renshon, *Psychological Needs and Political Behavior: A Theory of Personality and Political Efficacy* (New York, 1974), p. 240; T. W. Adorno et al., *The Authoritarian Personality* (New York, 1950). The first two quotations are from Niemi; the third from Renshon.

5. Richard D. Brown, "Modernization and the Modern Personality in Early America, 1600–1865: A Sketch of a Synthesis," *Journal of Interdisciplinary History* 2 (1971–72): 201–28, esp. pp. 215–20; Neil J. Smelser, "The Modernization of Social Relations," in Myron Weiner, ed., *Modernization: The Dynamics of Growth* (New York, 1966), pp. 110–21.

6. Jack P. Greene, "Autonomy and Stability: New England and the British Colonial Experience in Early Modern America," *Journal of Social History* 7 (Winter 1974): 171–94; Jack P. Greene, "An Uneasy Connection: An Analysis of the

Preconditions of the American Revolution," in Stephen G. Kurtz and James H. Hutson, eds., *Essays on the American Revolution* (Chapel Hill, N.C., 1973), pp. 59–61.

7. Renshon, *Psychological Needs and Political Behavior*, p. 150.

8. Philip J. Greven, Jr., *Four Generations: Population, Land, and Family in Colonial Andover, Massachusetts* (Ithaca, N.Y., 1970), p. 281.

9. Burrows and Wallace, "The American Revolution," pp. 167–306. Quotations are from pp. 274, 281, 284, 287–88, and 289.

10. Bruce Mazlish, "Leadership in the American Revolution: The Psychological Dimension," in *Leadership in the American Revolution* (Washington, D.C., 1974), p. 122.

11. Burrows and Wallace, "The American Revolution," p. 273, n. 13.

12. Hugh T. Lefler and William S. Powell, *Colonial North Carolina: A History* (New York, 1973), pp. 172, 174; John Shy, "A New Look at Colonial Militia," *William and Mary Quarterly*, 3d ser. 20 (April 1963): 181; Noble Wymberly Jones, Archibald Bulloch, and John Houstoun to President of Continental Congress, 6 April 1775, in William T. Northen, ed., *Men of Mark in Georgia*, 6 vols. (Atlanta, 1907–12), 1:214; Merrill Jensen, *The Articles of Confederation* (Madison, Wisc., 1963), p. 58.

13. David J. Rothman, "A Note on the Study of the Colonial Family," *William and Mary Quarterly*, 3d ser. 23 (Oct. 1966): 627–34; Bernard Bailyn, *Education in the Forming of American Society: Needs and Opportunities for Study* (Chapel Hill, N.C., 1960, and New York, 1972), pp. 21–29; Edward N. Saveth, "The Problem of American Family History," *American Quarterly* 21 (Summer 1969): 314; Robert V. Wells, "Household Size and Composition in the British Colonies in America, 1675–1775," *Journal of Interdisciplinary History* 4 (Spring 1974): 570; Arlene Skolnick, "The Family Revisited: Themes in Recent Social Science Research," *Journal of Interdisciplinary History* 5 (Spring 1975): 712–14, 718.

14. The advice of child-rearing manuals doubtless was not always followed, but some parents tried to teach their children "according to Mr. Lock's [sic] method (which I have carefully studied)" (Eliza Lucas Pinckney to Mrs. Bartlett, 20 May 1745, in Harriott Horry Ravenel, *Eliza Pinckney* [New York, 1896; reprint ed., Spartanburg, S.C., 1967], p. 113); John Locke, "Some Thoughts Concerning Education," in Robert H. Bremner, ed., *Children and Youth in America: A Documentary History*, 3 vols. (Cambridge, Mass., 1970), vol. 1, *1600–1865*, p. 133.

15. Abigail J. Stewart , David G. Winter, and A. David Jones, "Coding Categories for the Study of Child-Rearing from Historical Sources," *Journal of Interdisciplinary History* 5 (Spring 1975): 701; Frank J. Furstenberg, Jr., "Industrialization and the American Family," *American Sociological Review* 31 (June 1966): 326–37; the quotation is from Herman R. Lantz, Raymond Schmitt, Margaret Britton, and Eloise C. Snyder, "Pre-Industrial Patterns in the Colonial Family in America: A Content Analysis of Colonial Magazines," *American Sociological Review* 33 (June 1968): 425.

16. Daniel Scott Smith, "Parental Power and Marriage Patterns: An Analysis of Historical Trends in Hingham, Massachusetts," *Journal of Marriage and*

the Family 35 (Aug. 1973): 426; Daniel Scott Smith and Michael S. Hindus, "Premarital Pregnancy in America, 1640–1971: An Overview and Interpretation," *Journal of Interdisciplinary History* 5 (Spring 1975): 538, 556, 557.

17. Greene, "An Uneasy Connection," pp. 59–60; Landon Carter, *The Diary of Colonel Landon Carter of Sabine Hall, 1752–1778*, ed. Jack P. Greene, 2 vols. (Charlottesville, Va., 1965), 1:19–20; Robert M. Weir, "The South Carolinian as Extremist," *South Atlantic Quarterly* 74 (Winter 1975): 91–92; Greene, "Autonomy and Stability," pp. 189–93.

18. Eugene D. Genovese, *The World the Slaveholders Made: Two Essays in Interpretation* (New York, 1971), pp. 121–22; Brown, "Modernization and the Modern Personality," p. 212; Paul Connor, "Patriarchy: Old World and New," *American Quarterly* 17 (Spring 1965): 48–62. See also Arthur W. Calhoun, *A Social History of the American Family from Colonial Times to the Present*, 3 vols. (Cleveland, Ohio, 1917–19), 2:69, 334, 337.

19. Entry of 5 April 1774, Philip Vickers Fithian, *Journal and Letters of Philip Vickers Fithian, 1773–1774: A Plantation Tutor of the Old Dominion*, ed. Hunter Dickinson Farish (Charlottesville, Va., 1957), p. 92; Philippe Ariès, *Centuries of Childhood: A Social History of Family Life* (New York, 1962), p. 26; Maurice Moore, "The Justice of Taxing the American Colonies, in Great-Britain, Considered," in William K. Boyd, ed., *Some Eighteenth Century Tracts Concerning North America* (Raleigh, N.C., 1927), p. 174.

20. On the one hand, there were parents like Gabriel Manigault who was, as Maurice Crouse has noted, "a stern father, with a short temper and little tolerance for the follies of youth," and the description might apply equally well to other South Carolinians like Henry Laurens and his own father, John. The Carters of Nomini Hall, Fithian originally believed, also attempted to keep their children "in perfect subjection." On the other hand, Fithian later discovered, obedience was not always the rule, and travelers like Nicholas Cresswell, the Marquis de Chastellux, and Francisco de Miranda often remarked about undisciplined children. It should be noted, however, that observers frequently revealed biases and assumptions that may have caused them to underestimate the degree of parental control in American families. Maurice A. Crouse, "The Manigault Family of South Carolina, 1688–1783" (Ph.D. diss., Northwestern University, 1964), p. 120; David D. Wallace, *The Life of Henry Laurens* (New York, 1915), p. 470; Fithian to Rev. Enoch Green, 1 Dec. 1773, and entries of 11 Feb. and 6 June 1774, Fithian, *Journal and Letters*, pp. 26, 64, 116; entry of 19 July 1777, *The Journal of Nicholas Cresswell, 1774–1777*, ed. Samuel Thornely (New York, 1924), p. 270; entry of 31 Dec. 1780, Marquis de Chastellux, *Travels in North America in the Years 1780, 1781 and 1782*, ed. Howard C. Rice, Jr., 2 vols. (Chapel Hill, N.C., 1963), 1:221; entry of Aug. 1783, John S. Ezell, ed., and Judson P. Wood, trans., *The New Democracy in America: Travels of Francisco de Miranda in the United States, 1783–1784* (Norman Okla., 1963), pp. 23–24; Calhoun, *Social History*, 2:64. For evidence suggesting that inconsistencies in discipline sometimes may have resulted from conflicting lines of authority within the family, see Edward M. Riley, ed., *The Journal of John Harrower, An Indentured Servant in the Colony of Virginia, 1773–1776* (Williamsburg, Va., 1963), p. 103; and John Davis, *Travels of*

Four Years and a Half in the United States of America During 1798 . . . *1802*, ed. A. J. Morrison (New York, 1909), p. 97.

For further discussions of ambiguity, ambivalence, and variety in parent-child relationships, see Edmund S. Morgan, *Virginians at Home: Family Life in the Eighteenth Century* (Charlottesville, Va., 1952), p. 8; and John Walzer, "A Period of Ambivalence: Eighteenth-Century American Childhood," in Lloyd de Mause, ed., *The History of Childhood* (New York, 1974), pp. 351, 362–63.

21. Carl Bridenbaugh, *Myths and Realities: Societies of the Colonial South* (New York, 1963), pp. 35, 101; John Drayton, *The Carolinian Florist of Governor John Drayton of South Carolina, 1766–1822*, ed. Margaret B. Meriwether (Columbia, S.C., 1943), p. xxv; William Henry Drayton, ed., *The Letters of Freeman, Etc.* (London, 1771).

22. Bridenbaugh, *Myths and Realities*, p. 69. Without attempting to be exhaustive, one might add to this list: Benjamin Harrison and George Wythe (Virginia); John Penn (North Carolina); Christopher Gadsden, Ralph Izard, Rawlins Lowndes, Andrew Pickens, Edward, Hugh, and John Rutledge, Thomas Sumter (South Carolina); Lachlan McIntosh and George Walton (Georgia). Relatively early loss of a mother would add many more, including Henry Laurens and his son John, Thomas Lynch, Jr. (South Carolina); Abraham Baldwin, Jonathan Bryan, and the Habersham brothers, John and Joseph (Georgia). Unfortunately, most research on the effects of a parent's death upon a child has tended to neglect the historical context and is therefore of limited value for present purposes, but see Elizabeth Herzog and Cecelia E. Sudia, "Fatherless Homes: A Review of Research," *Children* 15 (Sept.–Oct. 1968): 177–82; and Carmi Schooler, "Childhood Family Structure and Adult Characteristics," *Sociometry* 35 (June 1972): 255–69.

23. Quoted in Dorothy C. Smith, "The Revolutionary Service of Edward Rutledge" (M.A. thesis, University of South Carolina, 1947), p. 2. For the spectrum of relationships between mothers and stepchildren, see Julia Cherry Spruill, *Women's Life and Work in the Southern Colonies* (Chapel Hill, N.C., 1938), pp. 62–63.

24. Carter, *Diary*, 1:52–54; Walker Maury to Theodorick Bland, 14 Sept. 1786, in Jane Carson, *James Innes and His Brothers of the F. H. C.* (Charlottesville, Va., 1965), p. 50; entry of 6 June 1774, Fithian, *Journal and Letters*, p. 116; James Reed on the School at New Bern, 15 Feb. 1772, in Edgar W. Knight, ed., *A Documentary History of Education in the South before 1860*, 5 vols. (Chapel Hill, N.C., 1949–53), 1:95; John Drayton to James Glen, 24 Dec. 1769, and 14 March 1770, James Glen Papers, 1738–77, South Caroliniana Library, Columbia, S.C.; Drayton *Carolinian Florist*, p. xxv.

25. Smith and Hindus, "Premarital Pregnancy in America," p. 557; Gordon J. Schochet, "The Family and the Origins of the State in Locke's Political Philosophy," in John W. Yolton, ed., *John Locke, Problems and Perspectives: A Collection of New Essays* (Cambridge, England, 1969), pp. 81–98; Winthrop D. Jordan, "Familial Politics: Thomas Paine and the Killing of the King, 1776," *Journal of American History* 60 (Sept. 1973):299–301.

26. Quoted in Erik H. Erikson, *Dimensions of a New Identity: The 1973 Jefferson Lectures in the Humanities* (New York, 1974), p. 101. For a more technical discussion of some varieties of this phenomenon, see Fred Weinstein and Gerald M. Platt, *The Wish to Be Free: Society, Psyche, and Value Change* (Berkeley and Los Angeles, 1969), p. 148.

27. George Mason to the Committee of London Merchants, 6 June 1766, in Edmund S. Morgan, ed., *Prologue to Revolution: Sources and Documents on the Stamp Act Crisis, 1764–1766* (Chapel Hill, N.C., 1959), pp. 158–59; David Ramsay, *History of the American Revolution*, and *New York Journal*, 25 May 1775, both quoted in Burrows and Wallace, "The American Revolution," pp. 192, 202; Lea Barinbaum, "Identity Crisis in Adolescence: The Problem of an Adopted Girl," *Adolescence* 9 (Winter 1974): 547.

28. Jack P. Greene, "The Social Origins of the American Revolution: An Evaluation and an Interpretation," *Political Science Quarterly* 88 (March 1973): 20; *New York Times Book Review*, 3 Feb. 1974, p. 33; Burrows and Wallace, "The American Revolution," pp. 295–99.

29. For Bull see Allen Johnson et al., eds., *Dictionary of American Biography* 20 vols. (New York, 1928–36), 2:252–53; for Garden see Edmund B. Berkeley and Dorothy Smith Berkeley, *Dr. Alexander Garden of Charles Town* (Chapel Hill, N.C., 1969), p. 269 and passim. Richard Walsh, ed., *The Writings of Christopher Gadsden, 1746–1805* (Columbia, S.C., 1966), p. 71.

30. Richard Henry Lee to Patrick Henry, 8 Sept. 1777, in James C. Ballagh, ed., *The Letters of Richard Henry Lee*, 2 vols. (New York, 1911–14), 1:320–21; Merrill Jensen, ed., *English Historical Documents*, vol. 9, *American Colonial Documents to 1776* (New York, 1969), pp. 850–51. Jordan hints at such an interpretation, especially in regard to Thomas Paine. Greene and Burrows and Wallace approach the matter somewhat more warily. See Jordan, "Familial Politics," pp. 296, 301–4; Greene, "An Uneasy Connection," pp. 63–64, 79–80; Burrows and Wallace, "The American Revolution," pp. 270, 304.

31. The quotation is from Burrows and Wallace, "The American Revolution," p. 291; Wallace, *Life of Henry Laurens*, pp. 377–78; Rawlins Lowndes to James Simpson, 20 May 1780, Clinton Papers, William L. Clements Library, University of Michigan, Ann Arbor, Mich.; Edward McCrady, *The History of South Carolina in the Revolution, 1780–1783* (New York, 1902), p. 587; Edward McCrady, *The History of South Carolina in the Revolution, 1775–1780* (New York, 1901), p. 238. See also Fred R. MacFadden, Jr., "Popular Arts and the Revolt Against Patriarchalism in Colonial America," *Journal of Popular Culture* 8 (Fall 1974): 286–94.

32. William Lee to Rodham Kenner, 15 May 1775, Worthington C. Ford, ed., *Letters of William Lee, 1766–1783*, 3 vols. (New York, 1968), 1:157; M. Eugene Sirmans, *Colonial South Carolina: A Political History, 1663–1763* (Chapel Hill, N.C., 1966), pp. 334–42; McCrady, *History of South Carolina, 1775–1780*, p. 314; William W. Abbot, *The Royal Governors of Georgia, 1754–1775* (Chapel Hill, N.C., 1959), p. 159; Richard Oswald to Lord Dartmouth, 21 Feb. 1775, Dartmouth Papers, pp. 3, 13, Staffordshire County Record Office, Stafford, England; Edmund S. Morgan, *The Birth of the Republic* (Chicago, 1956), pp. 52–53.

33. Fawn M. Brodie, *Thomas Jefferson, An Intimate History* (New York, 1974), pp. 38–39, 53–54, 244, 326; Erikson, *Dimensions of a New Identity*, p. 72; Merrill D. Peterson, *Thomas Jefferson and the New Nation: A Biography* (New York, 1970), pp. 113–17.

34. Erik H. Erikson, *Young Man Luther: A Study in Psychoanalysis and History* (New York, 1962), pp. 15, 22, 206; Erik H. Erikson, *Gandhi's Truth: On the Origins of Militant Nonviolence* (New York, 1969), p. 407; Mazlish, "Leadership in the American Revolution," pp. 116, 117, 127–31. For the view that Washington was a charismatic leader, see Seymour M. Lipset, *The First New Nation: The United States in Historical and Comparative Perspective* (New York, 1963), pp. 16–23; and Marcus Cunliffe, *George Washington: Man and Monument* (London, 1959), pp. 158, 163.

35. Skolnick, "The Family Revisited," pp. 710, 714–15, 718.

36. Greene, "An Uneasy Connection," pp. 77–78; Lewis S. Feuer, *The Conflict of Generations: The Character and Significance of Student Movements* (New York, 1969), pp. 529–30; Elisha P. Douglass, "Thomas Burke, Disillusioned Democrat," *North Carolina Historical Review* 26 (April 1949): 151, quotation p. 153.

37. Jordan, "Familial Politics," pp. 294–308; Advertisement for History of Carolina from 1663–1721, *South Carolina Gazette and Country Journal* (Charleston), 18 Feb. 1766; Letter of 25 April 1770, *South Carolina Gazette* (Charleston), 17 May 1770; Brodie, *Thomas Jefferson*, p. 39.

38. Locke, "Some Thoughts Concerning Education," p. 133; Eliza Pinckney to [Daniel Horry, Jr.], 16 April 1782, Elise Pinckney, ed., "Letters of Eliza Lucas Pinckney, 1768–1782," *South Carolina Historical Magazine* 76 (July 1975): 167; Eliza Lucas Pinckney to George Lucas, Jr., 1745, in Ravenel, *Eliza Pinckney*, pp. 64–65; Bernard Bailyn, "Boyd's Jefferson: Notes for a Sketch," *New England Quarterly* 33 (Sept. 1960): 390.

39. Will of Thomas Ferguson, proved 20 May 1786, Charleston County Wills, vol. 22 (1786–93), p. 18, Works Progress Administration Transcripts, South Carolina Archives. Ferguson was a member of the First and Second Provincial Congresses, 1775–76; the General Assembly, 1776–78; the Legislative Council, 1776; the House of Representatives, 1778–80; and the Privy Council, 1776–82. Michael Walzer, *The Revolution of the Saints: A Study in the Origins of Radical Politics* (New York, 1968), pp. 302–3.

40. Although Winthrop Jordan termed it a "penchant for order," it may have been more what eighteenth-century men would have called a "ruling passion" (Jordan, *White Over Black: American Attitudes toward the Negro, 1550–1812* [Chapel Hill, N.C., 1968], p. 482). Henry Adams, *John Randolph* (Boston, 1898), p. 6. The interest shown by early biographers in Patrick Henry's boyhood "indolence" suggests that they may have realized such a background would have been unusual among his contemporaries as well as surprising for a man of his later accomplishments. See, for example, Moses Coit Tyler, *Patrick Henry* (Boston, 1898), p. 5. That this picture is distorted even in Henry's case is suggested by Richard R. Beeman, *Patrick Henry: A Biography* (New York, 1974), p. 4.

41. Edmund S. Morgan, "The Puritan Ethic and the American Revolu-

tion," *William and Mary Quarterly*, 3d ser. 24 (Jan. 1967): 1–43, esp. p. 7; entry of 15 Dec. 1773, Fithian, *Journal and Letters*, pp. 31–32. See also Abraham Baldwin's comments on education quoted in Northen, ed., *Men of Mark in Georgia*, 1:8–9.

42. Richard Henry Lee to sons Thomas and Ludwell, 10 May 1777, in Ballagh, ed., *Letters of Lee*, 1:288; Brodie, *Thomas Jefferson*, p. 51; Wallace, *Life of Henry Laurens*, p. 470.

43. Wallace, *Life of Henry Laurens*, p. 46, and passim; Eliza Lucas Pinckney, *The Letterbook of Eliza Lucas Pinckney, 1739–1762*, ed. Elise Pinckney and Marvin Zahniser (Chapel Hill, N.C., 1972), pp. 34–35; Brodie, *Thomas Jefferson*, pp. 21–22. Although Brodie termed Jefferson the most "orderly" and "most controlled" of our "great presidents," Jordan observed that even then she probably underrated the "power of the eighteenth-century cultural atmosphere. This is to say, that in any other age" a man of Jefferson's emotions "would have devoted himself to quarreling, wenching, boozing, and generally messing up his historical reputation." Obviously, the cultural atmosphere was British as well as American and the young Englishman who later became a leader of the Revolution in North Carolina, James Iredell, had been in the colonies less than two years when on 22 August 1770 he began a journal by observing, "As I spend too much time in an unprofitable, idle manner, I have thoughts of an Expedient, which may perhaps correct my Conduct a little. I am determined to set down the history of every day. . . , so that by this method, I shall review the Conduct of my time." Perhaps, however, it is significant that this resolution came to him in Edenton, North Carolina! See Jordan's review of Brodie's *Thomas Jefferson* in *William and Mary Quarterly*, 3d ser. 32 (July 1975): 510–11; Don Higginbotham, ed., *The Papers of James Iredell*, 2 vols. (Raleigh, N.C., 1976), 1:23, 171.

44. Richard Barry, *Mr. Rutledge of South Carolina* (New York, 1942), p. 12. Although Barry's work is neither documented nor very reliable, this episode is plausible. Mason to Committee of London Merchants, 6 June 1766, in Morgan, ed., *Prologue to Revolution*, p. 162. Cf. Greene, "Autonomy and Stability," p. 192. For a suggestive discussion of the ways in which this impulse could lead to attempts to impose order on others, see Charles G. Sellers, Jr., "Making a Revolution: The North Carolina Whigs, 1765–1775," in J. Carlyle Sitterson, ed., *Studies in Southern History* (Chapel Hill, N.C., 1957), pp. 23–46.

45. Henry Laurens to John Laurens, 8 Feb. 1774, in "Letters From Hon. Henry Laurens to His Son John, 1773–1776," *South Carolina Historical and Genealogical Magazine* 3 (July 1902): 140; [William Henry Drayton], "A Letter from 'Freeman' of South Carolina to the Deputies of North America, Assembled in the High Court of Congress at Philadelphia," 10 Aug. 1774, in Robert W. Gibbes, ed., *Documentary History of the American Revolution*, 3 vols. (New York, 1853–57; reprint ed., Spartanburg, S.C., 1972), vol. 1, *1764–1776*, p. 27; Thomas Jefferson, "A Summary View of the Rights of British Americans," conveniently available in Merrill D. Peterson, ed., *The Portable Thomas Jefferson* (New York, 1975), pp. 10, 14–16; "Declaration of the Causes and Necessity for Taking Up Arms," 6 July 1775, in Jensen, ed., *American Colonial Documents to 1776*, pp. 846–47; South Carolina "Association," adopted 3 June 1775, in William E. Hemphill and Wylma

A. Wates, eds., *Extracts from the Journals of the Provincial Congresses of South Carolina, 1775–1776* (Columbia, S.C., 1960), p. 36.

46. Hannah Arendt, *On Revolution* (New York, 1965), pp. 139–41; R. R. Palmer, *The Age of the Democratic Revolution: A Political History of Europe and America, 1760–1800* (Princeton, N.J., 1959), pp. 214–35.

47. Irving Kristol, "The Most Successful Revolution," *American Heritage* 25 (April 1974): 37.

48. Examination and Deposition of Robert Williams, and Information and Deposition of Thomas Hartley, 14 Jan. 1766, S.C. Council Journal No. 32, pp. 692, 697, South Carolina Archives.

49. Williams's Deposition, Petition of Robert Williams and Thomas Hartley, and Hartley's Deposition, 14 Jan. 1766, ibid., pp. 690, 686–87, 698; Pardon of W. Ward Crosthwaite, Barnard Elliott, Benjamin Huger, and John Miles, 3 April 1766, Miscellaneous Records, MM, pp. 361–62, South Carolina Archives. For Crosthwaite, see "Officers of the South Carolina Regiment in the Cherokee War, 1760–1761," *South Carolina Historical and Genealogical Magazine* 3 (Oct. 1902): 205.

50. The distinction between revolution and mere rebellion is Hannah Arendt's. If the point is valid in this context, one might expect to find that among the middle and upper classes, at least, illegitimacy remained low even though the rate of premarital conceptions skyrocketed during the late eighteenth century. Although isolating the operative values might prove to be a monumental task, statistically parallel trends in illegitimacy and premarital pregnancy probably mask significant variations in the behavior of different classes. This paper has focused upon values and behavior doubtless characterizing individuals of relatively high socioeconomic status. Arendt, *On Revolution*, p. 140; Smith and Hindus, "Premarital Pregnancy in America," p. 539; Edward Shorter, "Illegitimacy, Sexual Revolution, and Social Change in Modern Europe," in Theodore K. Rabb and Robert I. Rotberg, eds., *The Family in History: Interdisciplinary Essays* (New York, 1971), pp. 67–70.

51. Williams's Deposition, 14 Jan. 1766, S.C. Council Journal No. 32, p. 692, South Carolina Archives. For Crosthwaite's death, see *South Carolina Gazette*, 2 Nov. 1769. For Sarah's second marriage, see Robert G. Stewart, *Henry Benbridge, American Portrait Painter* (Washington, D.C., 1971), p. 40; and "Records Kept by Colonel Isaac Hayne," *South Carolina Historical and Genealogical Magazine* 10 (Jan. 1909): 167. McCrady, *History of South Carolina, 1775–1780*, pp. 179, 358.

3

"Virtus et Libertas": Political Culture, Social Change, and the Origins of the American Revolution in Virginia, 1763–1766

by Jack P. Greene

Oh Britain how thou suffered thy renowned Arms to be degraded, by employing them in the cause of Tyranny and Oppression, when Virtue and Liberty was the Sheild and Spear which made them formidable![1]

I

On 6 May 1776, the elected delegates of the people of Virginia met in convention in Williamsburg to determine the political future of their "Country." Over the next two months they took a series of momentous decisions. On 15 May they committed Virginia to independence by voting to instruct the colony's delegates to Congress to propose independence for all of the thirteen colonies then in arms against Great Britain. On 12 June they approved the Virginia Declaration of Rights, the prototype for all later American bills of rights. On 29 June they adopted a constitution for the independent Commonwealth of Virginia and elected a governor and privy council. On 5 July, the last day of the convention, they settled on the design for "a great Seal" for the new commonwealth.[2] Adopted as the capstone of the new political edifice and as the final step in a sustained and intense process of corporate self-redefinition, the design of this seal could scarcely have been more revealing of the contemporary meaning of the Revolution in Virginia.

The seal was to have two sides. On the first was "Virtus, *the genius of the Commonwealth*, dressed like an Amazon, resting on a spear with one hand, and holding a sword in the other, and treading on *tyranny*, represented by a man prostrate, a crown fallen from his head, a broken chair in his left hand, and a scourge in his right." Over the head of Virtus was "the word 'Virginia' . . . and underneath, the words 'Sic semper tyrannis.'" On the reverse side was a group: in the center was "Libertas, with her wand and pileus; on one side of her, Ceres, with the cornucopia in one hand and an ear of wheat in the other; on the other side Aeternitas . . . with the globe and phoenix." Beneath the group were the words " 'Deus nobis hoc otia fecit.' "[3]

This juxtaposition of virtue and liberty was not novel;[4] indeed, it was a cliché of eighteenth-century Anglo-American political thought. The two qualities, or conditions, were thought to be inextricably intertwined: to separate them was to unravel the whole political fabric. A people's virtue was a certain measure of the extent of its liberty: liberty without virtue was licentiousness. The composition of the reverse side of the seal was less conventional, albeit the symbolism was as appropriate for the other twelve colonies as for Virginia. It emphasized the dependence of civil liberty, as represented by Libertas, upon the bountifulness of the American environment, as depicted by Ceres, the goddess of agriculture, and the hope, as illustrated by Aeternitas, the goddess of permanence, both for the "timeless sovereignty of the new commonwealth" and for the perpetuation of the civil liberty and bountifulness on which it was based.[5] The Latin motto, meaning "God endowed us with these retreats," was simply an invocation of another familiar eighteenth-century cultural theme: the association of virtue and liberty with retirement in a country setting, a theme that was especially appropriate to Virginia, perhaps the most rural of all of the colonies.[6]

But it was the obverse of the seal that was freighted with the most profound emotional content. If almost every segment of the emerging American political community emphasized the intimate connection between virtue and liberty and if Boston could claim a special affinity for the "generous Principles of *Liberty*," which, as one earlier Bostonian had asserted, had "always distinguish'd this METROPOLIS,"[7] only Virginia claimed virtue "as the genius of the Commonwealth." Nor was this a new claim, a utopian vision evoked by the exhilarating contemplation of the possibilities of revolution. Rather, it represented a dramatic restatement of a self-conception—an elusive aspiration—that stretched back at least two generations and had been sharpened vividly over the previous fifteen years by the counterexample of Britain, whose behavior seemed to make patently clear that it had followed the tragic example of Rome and, as Edmund Pendleton remarked, abandoned "virtue and Liberty. . . the Sheild and the Spear" that had made it "Formidable" for "Tyranny and Oppression." But this self-conception also had been seriously shaken over the previous twenty-five years by a series of ominous social and political developments within Virginia that seemed to portend moral and social decline of the most disturbing variety.[8] The claim of virtue as the special characteristic of Virginia was thus an expression—in the midst of revolution—both of a continuing commitment to a political and social ideal that long had animated the leaders of the Virginia polity and of deep-seated fears, grounded in experience, about the present and future moral state of the commonwealth. The design of the seal thus suggests that revolution and independence were ways of overcoming two powerful threats to Virginia's corporate self-image as it had taken shape over the previous half century. One threat was external and was represented by the tyrannical acts of the imperial government; the other was internal and was manifest in the frightening decline of virtue in Virginia. Vividly evident in the heavy symbolism of the new seal of the commonwealth, the intense anxieties arising from these two challenges—the interlocking fears of the loss of both liberty and virtue—as well as the determined commitment to preserve both underlay and to a considerable extent determined the behavior of Virginia's political leaders during the dozen years immediately preceding the Declaration of Independence. The nature and origins of Virginia's corporate self-image and the emerging dialectic between the self-image and these two formidable challenges during the crucial years 1764–66, at the very beginning of the prerevolutionary crises, are the subjects that will be explored in this essay.

II

By 1760 a large native oligarchy had dominated the political life of Virginia at both the local and provincial levels for over a century. Until near the end of the second decade of the eighteenth century, public affairs had been riven with strife and discord, the stability that had obtained under Governor Sir William Berkeley between the Restoration in 1660 and Bacon's Rebellion in 1676 being only the exception that proved the rule. The seemingly endless struggles for ascendancy in an extremely fluid social and economic environment that had characterized political life from the founding of the colony in 1607 to the Restoration was followed in the wake of Bacon's Rebellion by a series of recurrent conflicts over the crown's efforts to gain more control over the economic and political life of the colony. For the next forty years, these conflicts both split the gentry—a combination of leading tobacco magnates, overseas merchants, and professional men and the colony's political elite—into warring factions and led to the expulsion or removal of one royal governor after another. Not until 1718, when, following the failure of a vigorous and sustained attempt to undermine the extraordinary power of the Virginia Council, Lieutenant Governor Alexander Spotswood (1710–22) reached an accommodation with local leaders, was this pattern finally broken.[9]

By casting themselves in the role of "patriot" governors

and carefully cultivating the gentry as well as the new Walpolean emphasis upon harmony and cooperation among all branches of government, Spotswood's immediate successors, Hugh Drysdale (1722–26) and, especially, Sir William Gooch (1727–49), joined with the leading local politicians to fashion a new political stability that remained essentially intact for the rest of the colonial period. Political factions disappeared, and, unlike their counterparts in many other colonies, Virginia legislators routinely supported the administration and increasingly took special pride in the colony's intense British patriotism and loyalty to the crown. With the exception of Robert Dinwiddie during the first years of his tenure in the early 1750s, subsequent governors, including Francis Fauquier (1758–67) and Norborne Berkeley, Baron de Botetourt (1767–70), obtained similar results by following the successful example of Gooch.[10]

From 1720 through the early 1760s, Virginia politics was a classic model of what Samuel P. Huntington has described as a situation of "traditional stability." In the absence of large or important urban centers, with overall economic prosperity, and without serious social divisions, the countryside was dominant, and the rural elite governed unchallenged by endogenous opposition. The tenantry and yeomanry assumed a largely passive or only marginally active role in politics, and the numerically weak intermediate class of merchants and lawyers allied itself with the dominant elite. Virginia, as Sir John Randolph, speaker of the House of Burgesses, informed that body in August 1734, had attained a degree of public "Happiness, which seems almost peculiar to our selves, of being under none of the Perturbations which we see every where else arising from the different Views and Designs of Factions and Parties."[11]

The central figures in this political nirvana during the early 1760s were Francis Fauquier, the lieutenant governor, and John Robinson, since 1738 speaker of the House of Burgesses and treasurer of the colony. The council included several "very respectable [and politically influential] characters," including its

aging president, John Blair, Sr.; William Nelson, perhaps the
colony's largest resident merchant; Thomas Nelson, William's
brother and a prominent lawyer; and Richard Corbin, receiver
general and scion of an old gentry family. But none of these men
approached Fauquier and Robinson in political power and popularity. Fauquier, the urbane and cosmopolitan Englishman, and
Robinson, the amiable "native, educated wholly in Virginia,"
were the same age—in 1763, fifty-nine years old—and very
much alike in political personality: judicious, conciliatory, pragmatic, and benevolent. At the time of his appointment in 1758,
Fauquier had been advised by Lord Anson, who knew the
"people you are going to preside over well," that Virginians were
a "good Natured people whom you may lead but whom you
cannot drive." Fauquier found this advice extraordinarily conge-
nial. Although he had been charged by his political superiors in
London to obtain Robinson's resignation from one of his two
powerful offices and to secure the permanent separation of the
offices of speaker and treasurer, Fauquier instead proceeded, to
the great displeasure of London officials, to form an intimate
alliance with Robinson. By this action he securely established his
reputation among Virginians as a "kind and benevolent patriot
Governor" who could be counted on to defend the colony's
established constitution and fundamental interests against all
external enemies, whether imperial officials or British mercantile
interests, and who helped to ensure the perpetuation of the
colony's traditional internal political stability. Robinson was
equally devoted to the politics of moderation and compromise.
He took his seat in the House of Burgesses in 1727, the first year
of Gooch's gubernatorial tenure, and subsequently received his
political tutelage from Gooch and Sir John Randolph, his predecessor as speaker and, next to Gooch, the principal architect of
Virginia's remarkable political stability. During his long tenure in
office, Robinson had acquired such extraordinary political popularity that by the early 1760s he could be described by Fauquier as
the "darling of the Country."[12]

Robinson's enormous popularity—and power—derived in part from the "weight and influence" of the "Speaker's . . . Chair" among "those, who" were "candidates for his countenance and favour" and in part, it was discovered after his death in 1766, from the liberal disposition of public funds entrusted to him as treasurer. But his power and popularity were much too general to be explained entirely in these terms. Far more important were his "sound political knowledge," his public reputation as a man of "great integrity, assiduity, and ability in business," and his personification of the politics of prudence and restraint so much admired by the gentry. Contemporaries found his "acquaintance with parliamentary forms" and the grace with which he filled the speaker's chair remarkable. "When he presided," wrote Edmund Randolph,

the decorum of the house outshone that of the British House of Commons, even with Onslow at their head. When he propounded a question, his comprehension and perspicuity brought it equally to the most humble and the most polished understanding. To committees he nominated the members best qualified. He stated to the house the contents of every bill and showed himself to be a perfect master of the subject. When he pronounced the rules of order, he convinced the reluctant. When on the floor of a committee of the whole house, he opened the debate, he submitted resolutions and enforced them with simplicity and might. In the limited sphere of colonial politics, he was a column.

No less important as an ingredient of Robinson's political power was an extraordinary warmth of personality, "a benevolence which created friends and a sincerity which never lost one," qualities that won for him wide applause and admiration as "a jewel of a man" whose "opinions must [always] be regarded."[13] Around Robinson in the house revolved an impressive array of political talent that was broadly representative of the ruling gentry and genuinely and, in most cases, effectively responsive to the needs of the larger society. Among the leading members were several men who were closely attached to Robinson, including Attorney General Peyton Randolph, who would

succeed him as speaker in 1766; his special protégé Edmund
Pendleton, a lawyer of great probity and stature; and Benjamin
Harrison and Archibald Cary, two James River planters from
prominent gentry families. But Robinson never tried to use his
associates as the nucleus of a political machine or to prefer them
to the exclusion of other "qualified" members. He distributed
committee assignments widely, and not only among such relatively independent, if usually supportive, men as Richard Bland,
Benjamin Waller, George Wythe, Robert Carter Nicholas, and
Dudley Digges—all, like Randolph and Pendleton, members of
that "constellation of eminent lawyers and scholars" who practiced before the General Court. He also utilized the talents of
those who most often opposed his policies and were potential
political rivals, including the two brothers, Charles Carter of
Cleve, the last person to contest Robinson for the speakership in
1742, and Landon Carter, the petulant squire of Sabine Hall,
and, in very recent years, Richard Henry Lee, the brilliant,
ambitious, and hot-tempered young planter from Westmoreland
County. Until his death in 1764, Charles Carter of Cleve was,
next to Robinson, the most powerful and prominent man in the
house, while Robinson repeatedly assigned Lee to major committee posts even though Lee had launched his career in the
burgesses in 1758 with a vigorous attack upon the speaker.[14]

Several historians have discussed mid-eighteenth-century
Virginia politics in terms of a split between a James River faction
under the leadership of Robinson and his associates and a
Northern Neck interest revolving around the Carters, Lees,
Masons, and other prominent families from the Rappahannock
and Potomac river valleys. During the 1740s, competition over
western lands by rival speculating groups roughly corresponded
to such a division, and the fact that Northern Neck representatives such as the Carters and Lee were among Robinson's
most consistent critics lends some plausibility to such a categorization. But if such a factional split existed, it does not seem to
have been very serious or to have had any major impact upon the

politics of the house. Both the house and the council frequently divided over such fundamental issues as the extent of Virginia's contribution to the Seven Years' War and any of the myriad questions involved with the several paper money emissions made during that war. But these divisions, as St. George Tucker, still another prominent member of the Virginia bar who emigrated from Bermuda to Virginia in 1772, later testified, were the results not "of *party spirit*" but "only" of such "differences of opinion . . . as different men, coming from different parts of our extensive Country might well be expected to entertain." Prior to the mid-1760s, at least, no issue arose of sufficient force to create deep or lasting political divisions.[15]

To have organized themselves into parties would in any case have constituted a serious and disturbing violation of a clear and proud corporate self-image that Virginians had carefully nurtured over the previous half century. "The pride of Virginia," later wrote Edmund Randolph, who had grown into manhood during the years when that self-image was assuming concrete and durable shape,

had so long been a topic of discourse in the other colonies that it had almost grown into a proverb. Being the earliest among the British settlements in North America, having been soon withdrawn from the humiliation of proprietary dependence to the dignity of a government immediately under the crown, advancing rapidly into wealth from her extensive territory and the luxuriant production of her staple commodities, the sons of the most opulent families trained by education and habits acquired in England and hence perhaps arrogating some superiority over the provinces not so distinguished, she was charged with manifesting a cons[c]iousness that she had more nearly approached to the British model . . . of excellence, and what was claimed as an attribute of character in a government readily diffused itself among the individuals who were members of it.[16]

Among the attributes of character thus assigned by Virginians to their political system, six were primary. The first was *unanimity*, the successful transcendence, celebrated by Sir John Randolph in a quotation given earlier, of "private Broils" and

"Party-Rancour." A second was *moderation*. Virginia, said Edmund Randolph, had "received from the parent country an original stamina, perhaps I might add something phlegmatic in her temper, which inclined her to regulated liberty by saving her from those ebullitions which teem with violence and insubordination." Virginians took special pride in the "spirit of mildness" that both pervaded social relations among whites and animated the colony's uniformly "cool and deliberate" political counsels. A third was hardheaded *pragmatism*. It was the "happiness of Virginia character," according to Edmund Randolph, "hardly ever to push to extremity any theory which by practical relations may not be accommodated." Believing, as Edmund Pendleton later remarked, that "perfection in any institute devised by *man*, was as vain as the search for a philosopher's stone," Virginians were willing when—"as in all . . . Political cases"—they could not "get the very best" to "take the best we can get."[17] Moderation and practicality were closely related to *virtue*, still a fourth—and, for contemporary Virginians, the central defining attribute of Virginia's political character. Virginians, said the German traveler, Johann David Schoepf conceived of themselves as having "an inborn higher morality" that had infused itself into the political system. Because it was composed of fallible men, that system occasionally might make mistakes. But its leaders prided themselves upon always trying to work for the corporate welfare of the whole community rather than the particular interests of any of its parts and upon keeping the polity almost totally free from the corruption that had tainted—and eventually destroyed—so many other political systems. "The possession of soil," said one observer, "naturally turns the attention to its cultivation, and generally speaking, men who," like Virginians, "are occupied by labor in the country are more exempt from the vices prevailing in towns." But the virtue of a political system also depended upon a fifth attribute of political character and an extremely important component of Virginia's corporate self-image: the vaunted *independence* of its leaders. A "high sense of personal independence," said Edmund Randolph, "was universal" among white Virginians. Nourished by the "system of slavery, however so baneful to virtue," a "quick and acute sense" of personal liberty, a disdain for every "abridgement of personal independence" was, thought Randolph, the "ornament" of the "real Virginia planter." A sixth and final attribute of the character of the Virginia political system was its *loyalty*. "Every political sentiment, every fashion in Virginia," Randolph said, "appeared to be imperfect unless it bore a resemblance to some precedent in England." Virginians liked to think that this "almost idolatrous deference to the mother country" was reciprocated by "a particular regard and predilection for Virginia." Obviously, a polity thus characterized by its unanimity, moderation, pragmatic realism, virtue, independence, and loyalty was, said Randolph proudly, "in a political view inferior to [that of] no other colony."[18]

This image had been both sharpened and reinforced—if also somewhat shaken—by events during the early 1750s and 1760s. Between 1752 and 1764, various actions by the metropolitan government and its servants had called into question the confident assumption that Britain "had a particular regard and predilection" for Virginia and had eaten away at the foundations of the colony's celebrated British patriotism. Having found, said one anonymous bard, probably the respected Stafford County lawyer John Mercer,

> . . . this loyal land in peace
> nor striving nor contending
> than how to prove its loves increase
> tow'rds one of George's sending,

Lieutenant Governor Robert Dinwiddie, through his unilateral imposition in 1752 of a fee of a pistole for signing and sealing all land patents, had raised the specter of arbitrary royal power in the colony for the first time in nearly thirty-five years. The pistole fee controversy was only the first in a trio of political contests through which "Virginians hitherto distinguished for their loyalty" found themselves "shamefully traduced, were Oppressed,

Insulted, & treated like rebells, by the very persons from whom
they" had been so "long taught to expect Succour."[19] The other
two disputes erupted in 1759 and commanded the intermittent
attention of the Virginia political community for the next five
years. They revolved around the British merchants' opposition to
the colony's wartime paper money emissions and the Virginia
clergy's attack upon the Two-penny Acts, measures that enabled
people to pay public obligations, including the salary of the
established clergy, in money instead of tobacco in two years of
extremely short crops.[20]

As in the case of the pistole fee controversy, in both of
these disputes metropolitan officials had supported a person or a
group that the vast majority of Virginia political leaders believed
was trying to extend its power or gain private advantage at the
expense of the general welfare of the whole colony. In the classic
manner of British colonial administration, crown officials never
had sided wholly with the colony's opponents in any of the three
controversies. But the cumulative effect of their behavior was to
persuade Virginia's political leaders that Virginia's political institutions, specifically the elected House of Burgesses, were the
only agencies that could be trusted to act in the best interests of
the colony and to make them—for the first time in almost fifty
years—especially sensitive to a dangerous defect in the Virginia
political system: the vague constitutional arrangements that
obtained under the empire made the Virginia polity particularly
vulnerable to the awesome might of the parent state. To remedy
this defect, Virginia's political leaders vigorously sought to
secure precise constitutional limitations upon royal power that
would provide the colony with permanent protection against any
ill-considered or corrupt exertion of imperial authority. The
anxiety arising from their inability to achieve such limitations,
which haunted Virginians through the early 1760s and fed a
mounting suspicion of the intentions of the metropolitan government, had however been tempered by two other developments: first, the intensification of British patriotism as a
result of the justifiable pride Virginians took in their impressive

contribution to the great British victory in the Seven Years' War and of the conciliatory behavior of Dinwiddie's successor, Francis Fauquier; and, second, the perpetuation of the belief, fostered by the few concessions extended to the colony by metropolitan officials in each of the controversies, in the essential justice of the mother country and its basic goodwill toward Virginia. Moreover, the behavior of the colony's political leaders throughout these disputes could only reinforce the colony's corporate self-image. They had behaved, said Edmund Randolph, with a "loyalty debased by no servile compliance and . . . a patriotic watchfulness never degenerating into the mere petulance of complaint" and had displayed "an elevation of character" that would render Virginians "incapable of being seduced by the artifices" of any set of men, however corrupt or designing, who might gain control of the metropolitan government. Besides, if the British government was in fact as just and benignly disposed toward Virginia as Virginians wanted to believe, "to know when to complain and how to complain with dignity" was all that was necessary to avoid any evils that might descend upon the colony as a result of a deleterious exertion of its power.[21]

More disturbing by far to the Virginia political community and potentially far more damaging to the colony's corporate self-image were the abundant signs of rampant internal moral decay that had become increasingly manifest in the years after 1740. Slavery, some observers noted, had had a vicious effect "upon the Morals & Manners of our People," undermining a respect for labor and feeding lamentable "Habits of Pride, and Cruelty in . . . Owners."[22] Even more serious—and much more widely condemned—was a perceptible falling away from the old values of industry, thrift, and sobriety and an exorbitant increase in luxury, gambling, and drunkenness. More and more after 1745, travelers and native Virginians alike remarked on the "extravagance, ostentation, and . . . disregard for economy" in the colony, especially and, most menacingly, among the wealthy. Fauquier expressed great alarm in 1762 at the planters' rising indebtedness to British merchants which he attributed to the planters' unwillingness to "quit any one Article of Luxury." In a sermon celebrating the peace of 1763, the Reverend James Horrocks of the College of William and Mary warned the colony in moderate Anglican tones against too "great a Tendency amongst us to Extravagance and Luxury" and admonished his readers to eschew the "insignificant Pride of Dress, the empty Ambition of Gaudy Furniture, or a splendid Equipage . . . which must undoubtedly serve more for Ostentation and Parade, than any real Use or valuable Purpose." Equally sinister in its meaning, an uncontrollable "spirit of gaming" had broken "forth . . . in ways destructive of morals and estates." This "prevailing Passion and Taste for Gaming . . . Racing, Cards, Dice and all other such Diversions," "wretched practice[s]" that, said one critic, "fifty years ago [were] . . . scarcely . . . known," had devastating effects upon the character of Virginians at all levels of society, especially the young, and thus carried a potentially "fatal Tendency" for Virginia society. Said one erstwhile poet:

> Honor it stabs; religion it disgraces,
> It hurts our trade, and honesty defaces.
> But, what is worse, it so much guilt does bring,
> That many times distraction thence does spring.

Many thought that Virginia was already too far "infatuated & Abandoned" to feel any guilt. "The Vice and Wickedness of a Nation," Reverend William Stith, also of the college, told the colony's political leaders in a sermon before the House of Burgesses in 1752, "are the certain Forerunners and Cause of its Disgrace and Destruction." Clergymen of every religious stamp agreed that all indications suggested that the destruction of Virginia was imminent and could be averted only by an uncompromising and permanent return to the solid virtues of earlier generations.[23]

If this widespread moral declension obviously had touched some of the colony's first families, and if it constituted an omnipresent and menacing threat to several aspects of the colony's corporate self-image, especially its belief in its own moderation, prudence, virtue, and independence, there were still in the early 1760s no ostensible signs that it had touched— much less damaged—the colony's political system. The system was dominated by men who had been performing capably in positions of power and responsibility for at least a generation. Thirteen of the most powerful members of the House of Burgesses between 1750 and 1764 were still active and alive in the mid-1760s and had a combined total of over two hundred years of legislative service. The median number of years of service was fifteen, ranging from thirty-six for Speaker Robinson to five for Richard Henry Lee, and the median age was forty-two, with Robinson, at fifty-nine, being the oldest, and Lee, at thirty-one, the youngest. Men reached such positions of top leadership, moreover, not from the "vanity of pedigree" but from the "positive force of character." "Fortune, birth, and station" might be sufficient to get a man elected to the house but not to gain for him a place of leadership and the confidence of his colleagues that such a position represented. Such places were reserved for men of "Ability and Distinction." And not just Robinson, but the whole group, enjoyed wide public esteem. These men, said Charles Hansford, a blacksmith turned poet, in 1752, were "stars of the first magnitude" who "in their several stations" combined

> The great support and ornament to be
> Of Britain's first and ancient colony.[24]

Satisfaction with the colony's political system was not, of course, universal. There were occasional complaints about the growth of corruption in elections, of ambition and demagoguery among politicians, and of the number of men standing for elections "who have neither natural or acquired parts to recommend them."[25] Far more important, perhaps, an increasing number of people began to worry about the excessive power lodged in the hands of John Robinson in his joint capacity as speaker and treasurer. "How unhappy must a Country be," Landon Carter confided to his diary in March 1752 after witnessing Robinson's extraordinary influence upon the members of the House of Burgesses, "should such a man be byased with vitious Principles." "The gentleman who has filled that chair for several Assemblies, I hope is a good man and very worthy of his promotion," Alexander White wrote to Richard Henry Lee in 1758, "but still he is but a man, and so much power lodged in one man's hands, seems to me to be inconsistent with the freedom and independency of an English Legislature." One writer, perhaps Landon Carter, circulated a piece in manuscript entitled "*Lady Virginia*, to prove the . . . Speaker's great influence, and arbitrary conduct, in the House of Burgesses," a piece, Richard Bland later declared, "that stood very high in the opinion of most men . . . [and] must have made [a] deep impression on those to whom he communicated" it "to the Speaker's disadvantage." There were even widespread "suspicions . . . among the people" that Robinson was converting public funds to private uses, and Arthur Lee charged in a private letter from Britain in November 1763 that Robinson was "a Man, more mercenary & abandoned, but far less able, than Sr. Robert Walpole." But Robinson met these rumors by placing his most vocal critic, Richard Henry Lee, on a committee to investigate the state of the treasury, and the failure of this committee to turn up any irregularities only confirmed people in their "high opinion of" Robinson's "good conduct and" in their belief in his honesty in "complying with the laws relating to the management of the Treasury."[26] From all appearances in the early 1760s, Sir John Randolph's 1734 remark that the Virginia political system as "yet [had] no Footsteps of Corruption" within it still applied.[27] But the general moral declension in Virginia nevertheless had created residual fears among many of the colony's political leaders for the continuing virtue of the political system.

III

Beginning in the spring of 1764 and continuing over the next thirty months, a series of developments revealed just how justified had been the anxieties of the early 1760s, anxieties arising from the conjoint fears of external oppression from the imperial government and internal corruption within the Virginia political system. In quick succession, Virginia's political leaders had to face a grave external challenge and a severe internal shock. The external challenge was posed by the Stamp Act and the threat of taxation by the British Parliament; the internal shock derived from two separate sources: first, the disclosure at the death of Speaker John Robinson in May 1766 that he had loaned over £100,000 from public funds to members of the gentry and, second, the special treatment accorded a member of the gentry, Robinson's son-in-law Colonel John Chiswell, by other gentrymen on the General Court when he was accused of murdering a social inferior in a tavern in a fit of anger. The Stamp Act made it abundantly clear, as Richard Bland, Landon Carter, and others had been warning over the previous five years, that the colony had no certain protection against the overpowering might of the imperial government, while the Robinson and Chiswell affairs constituted a powerful blow to the colony's traditional corporate self-image. Both demonstrated the inadequacy of constitutional safeguards within the colony and raised serious doubts about the health of the Virginia body politic and, more especially, about the extent of the devotion of its gentry leaders to its hallowed political beliefs. The immediate result of this simultaneous display of the evils of unbounded power from both without and within was a political, moral, and psychological crisis that might have destroyed a less stable and adaptable political system. Out of this crisis, however, emerged a new reformist impulse in Virginia politics that called for a purification of the political system and the uncompromising reaffirmation of the gentry's commitment to the old political values. Only by bringing political reality into harmony with the colony's traditional corporate self-image, the proponents of the new impulse insisted, would the colony be able to combat either the challenge from Britain or the internal moral laxity that, temporarily they hoped, had seized the Virginia polity.

News that the House of Commons had resolved on 10 March 1764 that it was proper to levy stamp duties on the colonies reached Virginia within six weeks and appeared in the *Virginia Gazette* on 27 April.[28] The immediate reaction was widespread alarm, and the response of Richard Henry Lee was a preview of the collective sentiments the colony's leaders expressed over the next two years. A "very clever Man" of great spirit and driving ambition, Lee was the younger son of Thomas Lee of Stratford, who had been president of the council and in 1749–50 acting governor of the colony. The son early had chosen politics as the best means to gratify a boundless passion for fame and in 1758 at age twenty-six had entered the House of Burgesses as representative from his native county of Westmoreland. By 1764, after six years of service in the house, he had made his reputation as a brilliant, polished, and impassioned orator—"one of the first Speakers in the House of Burgesses"—and "an ornament to his Country."[29] Reacting with characteristic warmth to the news of the Commons' resolutions, Lee expressed his alarm in a letter to a friend in Britain in May 1764. The " 'free possession of property, the right to be governed by laws made by our representatives, and the illegality of taxation without consent,' " he declared, were "such essential principles of the British constitution, that it is a matter of wonder how men, who have imbibed them in their mother's milk, whose very atmosphere is charged with them, should be of opinion that the people of America were to be taxed without consulting their representatives." It was hard to believe that Britons could treat the colonists, "by whose distress and enterprise they saw their country so much enlarged in territory, and increased in wealth, as aliens to their society, and meriting to be enslaved by their superiour power." But Lee thought he had an explanation. In combination with many other "late determinations of the great" in Britain, the Commons' vote seemed to him "to prove a resolution, to oppress North America with the iron hand of power, unrestrained by any sentiment, drawn from reason, the liberty of mankind, or the genius of their own government" to keep the colonists "low, in order to secure our dependence." Although Lee did not counsel open resistance, he did express the hope that the scheme would be subversive of the ends it was intended to effect. "Poverty and oppression, among those whose minds are filled with ideas of British liberty," he warned, "may introduce a virtuous industry, with a train of generous and manly sentiments, which, when in future they become supported by numbers, may produce a fatal resentment of parental care being converted into tyrannical usurpation."[30]

Lee's letter indicated both how devoted Virginia's leaders were to the preservation of their constitutional rights as Englishmen and what a highly charged emotional issue parliamentary taxation might be, at least among less temperate Virginia politicians; equally important, it put forth two important ideas about the meaning of Parliament's behavior and its possible effects upon Virginia society. The first was the—in my view, essentially correct—perception that parliamentary taxation was part of a design formed by the "great" in Britain not to establish an internal tyranny in Britain by beginning gradually with the distant colonies, as a few nervous American observers would later charge, but to secure colonial dependence by keeping the colonies "low." The second, an idea that would be amplified and become increasingly attractive to Virginians in response to developments over the next decade, was the notion that British oppression might be the means for recovering the lost—or at least the declining—virtue of the colony. By depriving Virginians of the means to gratify their increasing passion for luxury and pleasure, such a severe economic blow as that to be expected from the Stamp Act might force them to return to the old values, produce that moral regeneration being called for by Anglican and dissenting clergy alike, and endow the old dominion with renewed vigor.

The official response was somewhat more measured but no less emphatic. On 15 June 1764 the Committee of Correspondence—a joint committee composed of four councillors and most of the leading members of the House of Burgesses and charged with corresponding with Edward Montague, a London barrister who represented Virginia in London—met to consider Montague's 10 March letter informing the committee of Parliament's resolutions on the proposed stamp duties. The committee immediately and emphatically declared its opposition to the duties and ordered George Wythe and Robert Carter Nicholas, two of the colony's most respected lawyers and prominent leaders in the House of Burgesses, to draft a reply. Raising all of the obvious objections to the duties, Wythe and Nicholas, as moderate in their politics as Lee was warm, attacked them as being both economically unwise and unjust. Such duties, they complained, would be "an additional heavy burthen . . . upon a People already laden with Debts, contracted chiefly," they reminded the agent, "in Defence of the Common Cause" during the Seven Years' War. They found the proposal the "more extraordinary" in view of the part taken by the colony during the war when "with the greatest Cheerfulness" it had "always . . . submitted to & comply'd with every Requisition . . . made . . . with the least Colour of Reason or Pretence of Necessity." But the main focus of their objections was constitutional. Going right to the heart of the constitutional problem that had plagued Virginia's relations with the imperial government over the previous twelve years, they expressed the "wish that our just Liberties & Privileges as free born British Subjects were once properly defin'd." What those liberties and privileges might be, they did not spell out in detail, and they carefully disavowed any intention of trying to put a "restraint upon the controlling Power of Parliament." But they did assert that the "most vital Principle of the British Constitution" was the exemption of the subject from laws made "without either their personal Consent, or the Consent by their representatives" and suggested that for Parliament to "fix a Tax upon such Part of our Trade & concerns as are merely internal, appears . . . to be . . . a long & hasty Stride . . . of the first importance."

Before the committee met to approve this letter of 28 July, it had received a subsequent letter from Montague informing it of the ministry's determination "to carry their Intentions of taxing the Colonies at pleasure into Execution." Now that the threat of parliamentary taxation seemed more certain, the committee felt compelled to make its constitutional claims both more explicit and more emphatic. In a postscript to the Wythe and Nicholas letter, it applied the traditional distinction between power and right to the case. That Parliament had the power to do what it pleased, that it was mighty enough even to give the king power to tax the "people of England by Proclamation," it did not deny. "But no man surely dare be such an Enemy to his Country," it argued, "as to say they have a Right to do this." "We conceive," the committee declared, "that no Man or Body of Men however invested with power, have a right to do anything that is contrary to Reason & Justice, or that can tend to the Destruction of the Constitution."[31]

Exactly what was reasonable and just in this situation and what constitutional rules applied were worked out over the next few weeks by the colony's most respected political writer, Richard Bland. Like Wythe and Nicholas, Bland was an outstanding lawyer who was noted for his political moderation. In 1764 he was fifty-four years old, had been a representative for Prince George County for twenty-two years, and was widely respected for his scholarship, especially his knowledge of political theory and Virginia history: "staunch & tough as whitleather," one observer later remarked, with "something of ye look of musty old Parchme'ts w'ch he handleth & studieth much."[32] Although he was a member of the Committee of Correspondence, Bland had not been at either of the meetings at which it had considered the proposed stamp duties. That he approved of the committee's proceedings, however, was made clear in *The Colonel Dismounted*, his last salvo against the clergy in the polemic over the Two-penny Acts. To counter the clergy's claim that royal instructions were binding upon the Virginia legislature, Bland argued in the pamphlet that Virginians, like all Englishmen, were subject only to laws made with their own consent, that only the House of Burgesses could give the consent of Virginians, and that instructions could not have the force of law because the house had not approved them. Upon learning of the proposed stamp duties, Bland simply extended his argument to include acts of Parliament as well as royal instructions. Because Virginians had no voice in the decisions of Parliament, it could not, he insisted, "impose laws upon" them "merely relative to" their "INTERNAL Government" without depriving them of the "most valuable Part" of their "Birthright as *Englishmen*, of being governed by Laws made with" their "own Consent." Bland was careful to point out that the "Term INTERNAL Government" excluded "from the Legislature of the Colony all Power derogatory to their Dependence upon the Mother Country." He declared, in fact, that Virginians could never withdraw their "Dependence without destroying the Constitution" and that in "every instance" of "EXTERNAL Government" they were and "must be, subject to the Authority of the *British* Parliament." But, he argued, just as "all Power . . . is excluded from the Colony of withdrawing its Dependence from the Mother Kingdom, so is all Power over the Colony excluded from the Mother Kingdom but such as respects its EXTERNAL Government." By thus assigning to the House of Burgesses exclusive jurisdiction over Virginia's internal affairs and limiting Parliament's authority over the colony to matters of "EXTERNAL Government," Bland sought to define the constitutional relationship between Virginia and Great Britain in a way that would protect Virginia from the overwhelming power of Parliament—as well as the crown—without lessening the colony's dependence upon the parent state. Characteristically, Bland had attempted to find a reasonable and moderate solution, but he left no doubt about where the logic of his argument led. "Parliament, as the stronger Power," he observed, could certainly "force any Laws it shall think fit upon us." But the question, he added with a firm and gentle warning, was "not what it can do, but what Constitutional Right it has to do so. And if it has not any constitutional Right, then any Tax, respecting our INTERNAL Polity, which may hereafter be imposed upon us by Act of Parliament, is arbitrary, as depriving us of our Rights, and may be opposed."[33]

Bland's pamphlet was published on 27 October 1764, just three days before the House of Burgesses convened for the first time since news of the proposed stamp duties had reached the colony.[34] On 7 November, Peyton Randolph in behalf of the Committee of Correspondence placed the various communications with the agent before the house. Denunciation of the duties in the house seems to have been universal, and Speaker Robinson appointed a committee to draw up formal protests to the king, Lords, and Commons. Composed of eight of the most distinguished members and broadly representative of the spectrum of political tempers in the house, including such moderates as Randolph, who acted as chairman, Wythe, Edmund Pendleton, Benjamin Harrison, Archibald Cary, and such firebrands as Landon Carter, Richard Henry Lee, both of whom seem to have taken the lead in opposing the duties, and John Fleming, a Cumberland County lawyer, the committee submitted on 30 November an address to the king, a memorial to the Lords, and a remonstrance to the Commons. After making a number of amendments, both the house and the council unanimously adopted all three documents on 18 December.[35]

These documents, by which the Virginia assembly joined the New York assembly as the first American legislatures to protest the constitutionality of the proposed stamp duties, were a model of moderation—but moderation expressed "with decent Firmness." To authorities in London, Fauquier described them as merely "praying that Virginians be permitted to tax themselves." In fact, they went considerably beyond that. Citing the colony's "ready Compliance with Royal Requisitions during the late War" as evidence of its "firm and inviolable Attachment to your sacred Person and Government," the address to the king implored him

"to protect your People of this Colony in the Enjoyment of their
ancient and inestimable Right of being governed by such Laws
respecting their internal Polity and Taxation as are derived from
their own Consent, with the Approbation of their Sovereign or
his Substitute"—an official endorsement of Bland's claim that
the Virginia legislature had exclusive jurisdiction over all of the
internal affairs of Virginia, including matters of legislation as well
as taxation. The address thus committed the legislature of the
colony to a claim of constitutional jurisdiction that went way
beyond that advanced by the assembly of any other colony
during the Stamp Act crisis. Like the statements of the Stamp
Act Congress, these documents claimed no more than exclusive
jurisdiction over matters of taxation.

The memorial to the Lords and the remonstrance to the
Commons pointed out the adverse economic consequences such
duties might have upon a colony already overburdened with a
large war debt and threatened by a renewal of Indian hostilities
on its frontiers at a time of "Scarcity of circulating Cash," "little
Value of their Staple at the *British* Markets" to which it was
confined, and the "late Restrictions upon the Trade of the
Colonies"—a reference to other aspects of the Grenville program. Stamp duties would render the "Circumstances of the
People extremely distressful." But the memorial and remonstrance also firmly denied that Parliament had any right to exercise
"a Power never before constitutionally assumed" of taxing the
colonists "without the Consent of Representatives chosen by
themselves" and asked "by what Distinction" Virginians could
"be deprived of that sacred Birthright and most valuable Inheri-
tance by their Fellow Subjects" in a "Parliament, wherein they
are not, and indeed cannot, constitutionally be represented." For
Parliament to exercise such a power would be to "establish this
melancholy Truth, that the Inhabitants of the Colonies are Slaves
of *Britons*, from whom they are descended, and from whom they
might expect every Indulgence that the Obligations of Interest
and Affection can entitle them to." But the evil consequences to

be expected from parliamentary taxation were not limited to the colonies. By reducing the colonists to such "extreme poverty" that they would be compelled to manufacture most of the items they customarily bought from Britain, parliamentary taxation would prove destructive of that "happy Intercourse of reciprocal Benefits" that had so much advanced "the Prosperity of both" the colonies and Britain. Nor would it be wise, said the remonstrance to the Commons, for "*British* Patriots" ever to "consent to the Exercise of anticonstitutional Power, which even in this remote Corner may be dangerous in its Example to the interiour Parts of the *British* Empire." To prevent all such measures for the future and to achieve constitutional security, the lack of which Virginians had lamented over the previous five years, the memorial asked the assistance of the Lords in the Virginians' endeavors "to establish their Constitution upon its proper Foundation"—a "Necessity" required by the "Duty" the memorialists "owed to themselves and their Posterity."[36]

If these documents put the Virginia legislature unequivocally on record in behalf of the principles that no society should be subject to power beyond its control, that Parliament was beyond the control of Virginia society, and that, therefore, Parliament could have no legitimate claim to jurisdiction over the internal concerns of Virginia, they did so in the traditional Virginia mode: "in a respectful Manner" and amid great—and doubtless sincere—protestations that its conduct had been animated by "Principles . . . of the purest Loyalty and Affection as they always endeavoured by their Conduct to demonstrate that they consider their Connexions with *Great Britain*, the Seat of Liberty, as their greatest Happiness." Not so the next official Virginia statement on the stamp duties. By the time the assembly met again on 24 May for the primary purpose of trying to resolve a financial crisis arising out of the treasury's inability to redeem paper money whose currency ended on 1 March, unofficial news had reached the colony of Parliament's passage of the Stamp Act on 17 February. For whatever reason—ostensibly because the

colony had received neither an official answer to its earlier
protests nor official news of passage of the Stamp Act, but
probably because the established leaders, in the absence of both
Landon Carter and Richard Henry Lee, the "warmest" patriots
among them, were genuinely ambivalent about what course to
adopt—house leaders failed to take any notice of the matter. This
failure opened the way for several "young hot and giddy
members," as Fauquier described them, "whose habits and
expectations had no relation to men in power," to seize the
initiative. The group included three young lawyers: John Fleming, George Johnston of Fairfax County, and Patrick Henry.
Henry, who was barely twenty-nine years old and had just been
returned at a by-election as a new member for Louisa County,
had the primary role in the drama that unfolded in the chambers
of the house on 29 May. Son of an Anglican vestryman and
militia colonel, Henry was an "improving" young lawyer with a
brilliant vernacular speaking style and a boundless ambition for
fame and popular applause. Having already achieved some
renown for his work in the county courts, specifically his bold
defense of his clients in the Parson's Cause, Henry was now
anxious both to shine in the colony's highest political counsels
and to obtain recognition from the colony's political establishment.[37]

Henry achieved these objectives and more by his actions
on 29 May. After the main business of the session had been
aborted and many of the members had left for home, he
succeeded, with the help of Johnston and against the opposition
of the established leaders, in pushing through five resolutions
roundly and unequivocally condemning the Stamp Act as illegal
and destructive of "British as well as American Freedom."
Asserting that Virginians possessed all of the rights of Englishmen and that those rights had been guaranteed to them by
two royal charters, the resolutions argued that of all of those
rights no taxation without representation was the "distinguish-
ing Characteristic of British Freedom," that Virginians had "un-

interruptedly enjoyed the Right of being thus governed by their own Assembly in the Article of their Taxes and internal Police," and that their assembly had the *"only and sole exclusive* Right and Power to lay Taxes upon" them. The last resolution declaring the assembly's exclusive right of taxation passed by one vote and was rescinded the next day after Henry, perhaps anticipating Fauquier's dissolution of the house in response to the resolves, had left for home. But the resolves, including a sixth and a seventh that Henry apparently had not introduced, had already been transmitted, by whom is not certain, to the other colonies, where they were widely reprinted, applauded, and copied. Indeed, by providing the rallying call for strong resistance to the Stamp Act and serving as a model for similar resolutions from most of the other colonies, they placed Virginia at the forefront of the continental protests against the Stamp Act.[38]

The absence of substantive differences between the Henry resolutions and the protests adopted by the unanimous vote of both house and council the previous December has made it difficult for historians to understand why the established leadership opposed them and strongly suggests that it was not the content but the tone, source, and circumstances of the passage of the resolutions that elicited establishment opposition. For such immoderate resolutions, introduced by surprise and passed precipitously, diverged sharply from the customary Virginia mode of firm but considered, sober, and judicious protest combined with profuse expressions of loyalty and affection and therefore constituted an obvious deviation from the political system's corporate self-image. Equally important, perhaps, the introduction of such resolutions by a man with a public reputation for emotional oratory and their hasty passage on the basis of a highly emotional appeal without the establishment's considered approval carried ominous portents for the future of Virginia politics. For Henry's resolutions and the circumstances of their passage raised the specter of emotionalism and unreason. Were they a harbinger of a totally new—and frightening—political mode that would replace the politics of self-control and disinterest with the politics of passion and ambition, a new style of politics in which the electorate would be more widely involved in the political process, the distinctions between rulers and ruled would become hopelessly blurred, and men of mean intentions would, in the manner of Henry, manipulate the people for their own self-interests by appealing to their emotions rather than to their reason? This was not to say that Henry was such a man, but only that his success could be interpreted as a potential challenge to the elevated politics of moderation, restraint, and enlightened upper-class leadership to which Virginians of all categories long had been committed.[39]

Henry's resolutions turned out to be only a temporary lapse from the traditional moderation of Virginia politics. Fauquier did not again call a meeting of the General Assembly until the fall of 1766 after he had received official word of the repeal of the Stamp Act because he feared that it could not be controlled, as in the past, by "cool reasonable men." In the meantime, the several public meetings that subsequently assumed responsibility for preventing enforcement of the Stamp Act were not taken over by men from the middle and lower orders, but, as in most of the other colonies, were dominated by the gentry. "This Concourse of People, I should call a Mob," Fauquier wrote of the group who forced Stamp Distributor George Mercer's resignation in Williamsburg in late October 1765, "did I not know that it was chiefly composed of Gentlemen of Property in the Colony—some of them at the Head of their respective Counties, and the Merchants of the Country whether English, Scotch, or Virginians, for few absented themselves." Similarly, the 115 signers of the Westmoreland Association, the nucleus of the group of 400 men who marched the following 28 February to Hobbs' Hole in neighboring Essex County to force Archibald Ritchie, a Scottish merchant who had publicly threatened to use stamps, to sign the association, included virtually every prominent resident of Westmoreland and surrounding counties. Finally, the movement to defy the Stamp Act and to conduct judicial and commercial business without stamped paper was led by the county magistrates upon the advice of the colony's leading lawyers who, concerned to "convince the people that there is not a total end of laws," ruled that the act was invalid "for want of . . . constitutional authority . . . in the Parliament to pass it."[40]

Indeed, the gentry emerged from the Stamp Act crisis with its position as strong as ever. At new elections to replace the House of Burgesses dissolved by Fauquier following passage of Henry's resolutions, the turnover of members was less than one-third, which was about normal for a house that had been sitting for several years. All of the old leaders who were still alive were returned, and none of the known opponents of the Henry resolutions lost his seat.[41] The traditional leadership was in fact united with the vast majority of the public in opposition to a common enemy and around a clearly articulated intellectual position vis-à-vis Parliament's constitutional authority in the colony. In the months following Henry's resolves, Virginians, in private letters, newspaper essays, and pamphlets, revealed a remarkable consensus in both the tone and the content of their opposition to the Stamp Act. Although they continued to complain about the economic distress that would result from the enforcement of the act, especially in view of the large—and largely unpaid—public debt accumulated by Virginia during the war, it was really, said a "Gentleman in Virginia" to his Bristol correspondent, the "matter of right that Tingles in every vein of Americans," for "If the p[arliamen]t have a right to tax Americans, to speak in their favor, it thence must follow, that Americans have no benefit of the British constitution, or the great charter, which says, 'No man's life, liberty, or property, shall be taken from him, or harm'd, but by known and established laws, made by his own consent, or the consent of his representatives chosen by himself!' " They continued to insist that parliamentary taxation was a constitutional innovation, an "extension of arbi-

trary unconstitutional power"; to deny—in elaborate treatises by
Richard Bland and Landon Carter—that Parliament had any
jurisdiction over the internal government of the colony; and to
demand that the constitutions of the colonies be defined in such
a way as to safeguard American liberty and thereby ensure that
"men who derive their original from Britons" would not "become slaves." "I know of no civilized people, in like situation
with the Americans, at this time," wrote one Virginian: "All have
some constitution, but I really cannot find a name for ours. We
seem to be entirely at the mercy of the m[inistr]y for the time
being, and are considered only as a machine to be made useful to
Britain, without the least regard how we may be affected
ourselves." Clearly, the Stamp Act was "arbitrary" and unconstitutional and was a part, as John Mercer put it, of those
"Chains forging for us" across the Atlantic. Less obvious was
why the ministry and Parliament would deal such a "fatal blow
to American liberty." What was to account for the sudden
transformation of "the mother country . . . into an arbitrary,
cruel, and oppressive stepdame"? No one in Virginia, at this
early date, seems to have attributed that transformation to a
conspiracy of power "to reduce," as Landon Carter later said,
"the subjects of Great Britain" to "slavery . . . though beginning
only by degrees with those in America." Many explained it as the
result of simple malice—the roots of which were never
explained—on the part of George Grenville and his followers.
But the most rational—and widespread—explanation was the
one offered by Richard Henry Lee when the Stamp Act was first
suggested. By keeping the colonies low through taxation and
other restrictive measures, the British hoped to keep them
dependent and, as Landon Carter surmised, thereby increase the
profits annually derived from the colonies.[42]

Whatever the explanation, Virginia's active and undeviat-
ing determination "to convince the world that we are as firm and
unanimous in the cause of Liberty, as so noble and exalted a
principle demands" was enormously reinforcive of the colony's

corporate self-image. However enervated by luxury and pleasure, the colony's political system still had vigor—and virtue—
enough to dare "to despise power, when that power was
opposed to Liberty." Its leaders had not yet become so "unmanly
[and] . . . ignominious, [as] to yield to such impositions, which
confirms on us the condition of slavery," but had shown by their
rejection of "passive obedience" and their pursuit of active
opposition that in the manner of free, independent, and virtuous
men—true Virginians—they despised "sycophants, and all
kinds of servility." Indeed, said George Washington, the Stamp
Act had opened the "Eyes of our People" to the fact that "many
Luxuries which we lavish our substance to Great Britain for, can
well be dispensed with whilst the necessaries of Life are (mostly)
to be had within ourselves." This recognition, he predicted,
would inevitably "introduce frugality, and be a necessary stimu-
lation to Industry" and a means of reviving the declining virtue
of Virginia. Indeed, in but short retrospect, even Henry's resolutions, though they deviated from the colony's customary political
moderation, seemed to have been a fitting exertion of Virginia's
firmness against a flagrant exertion of arbitrary power. Many
moderates did continue to condemn those resolutions, chiefly for
their redundancy and emotionalism. But the favorable reception
they received in the other colonies clearly placed Virginia in the
vanguard of opposition to the Stamp Act and thereby nourished
Virginian pride in taking the lead in the essential concerns of the
American colonies, a position the colony would assiduously seek
to maintain throughout the next twenty-five years. It was
gratifying, said the Norfolk Sons of Liberty in March 1766, to be
"a part of that colony, who first, in General Assembly, openly
expressed their detestation" to the Stamp Act.[43]

So pleased were Virginians with their manly and virtuous
opposition to a flagrant attempt to "rivet the shackles of slavery
and oppression on ourselves, and millions yet unborn" that they
openly chided the British upon the impurities of their political
system and contrasted it with the more virtuous system of

Virginia. "The unequal representation of the people of England has long been called the *rotten* part of the constitution," said one writer, and, said Richard Bland, was certainly "a great Defect in the present part of the Constitution, which has departed so much from its original Purity." "It would," Bland suggested condescendingly, "be a Work worthy of the best patriotick Spirits in the Nation to effectuate an Alteration in this putrid Part of the Constitution; and by restoring it to its pristine Perfection, prevent any 'Order of Rank of the Subjects from imposing upon or binding the rest without their Consent.' But," he added, "I fear, the Gangrene has taken too deep Hold to be eradicated in these Days of Venality." And in an open letter to the British press, George Mason reminded "our fellow-Subjects in Great Britain . . . that We are still the same People with them, in every Respect; only not yet debauched by Wealth, Luxury, Venality & Corruption."[44]

IV

Within a matter of weeks after the Stamp Act had been repealed and almost contemporaneously with these pious lectures, the death of Speaker Robinson on 10 May 1766 revealed the existence of the deepest and most extensive example of government corruption in any of the British colonies in America up to that time—and in the proud colony that claimed virtue as the special attribute of its political system. Immediately after his death there was no hint of scandal. The newspapers praised Robinson as a "worthy Member of Society," the "greatest of human kind," and the "best of men" who had been always "animated with every Social Virtue." But the old rumors of the diversion of public funds soon resurfaced, and Fauquier's appointment of Robert Carter Nicholas, a respected lawyer with impressive family connections and a reputation for impeccable honesty, as interim treasurer until the burgesses met to make a permanent election led to the discovery of great irregularities, the extent of which was not immediately clear and the exact nature not made public until the 1950s! By late June, Nicholas had speculated in the newspapers that the total deficiency might approach £100,000.[45] Within a month after Robinson's death, a second—and equally appalling—scandal broke upon the public. Colonel John Chiswell, burgess from Williamsburg and a prominent and well-connected member of the gentry (John Robinson was his father-in-law, and he had been married to a Randolph), during a tavern brawl in Cumberland County on 3 June 1766, ran his sword through and killed Robert Routledge, a local merchant who, in the heat of argument and deep in his cups, had thrown some wine in Chiswell's face. Chiswell was immediately committed to the county jail, from which the local examining court ordered him to public prison to be tried for murder without bail. But three judges of the General Court and members of the governor's council—including the council president, John Blair, Sr., William Byrd III, and Presly Thornton, all of whom were closely attached to Chiswell through family or friendship—took him out of the custody of local officials and gave him bail—without looking at the record of the examining court that had confined him or hearing a single witness. This flagrant display of favoritism elicited an enormous outcry of public disapproval.[46]

This outcry and an intense public discussion of the implications of both it and the Robinson scandal were facilitated by the newly opened press in Williamsburg. Virginia had no newspapers until 1736 and only one from then until May 1766. The refusal of its publisher, Joseph Royle, who was also public printer to the colony, to publish several essays against the Stamp Act had forced several writers, including John Mercer and Landon Carter, to send their essays to newspapers in neighboring colonies and had provided dramatic evidence of the "undue influence the press, in Virginia, has long laboured under" by being too "complaisant" to the royal administration. To remedy this situation, "some of the hot Burgesses invited a printer from Maryland" to set up a rival and "uninfluenced" newspaper. Published by William Rind, the new paper first appeared on 16

May on the very eve of the Chiswell murder case and the first
revelations of the Robinson scandal. Over the next several
months, the fierce competition between Rind and Alexander
Purdie and John Dixon, who, Royle having died in December
1765, together had resumed publication of the old *Gazette* the
previous March with promises that their newspaper would "be
as free as any Gentleman can wish or desire," stimulated a
wide-ranging canvas of the meaning of both the Chiswell and
Robinson cases, a debate that for the first time in nearly forty
years created a fundamental rift of opinion among the ruling
gentry. The upholders of Robinson, now headed by Peyton
Randolph and firmly defending the old Robinson system of
personal government, a system, they pointed out, that had provided the colony with a long period of uninterrupted stability
and public peace, emphasized the necessity of tempering the
constitution and the letter of the law with "lenient applications
and the good offices of men of virtue." An opposing group,
consisting of many previously independent leaders including
Nicholas, Richard Bland, Richard Henry Lee, Severn Eyre, and
Robert Bolling, demanded disinterested, impartial, and *impersonal government* and an uncompromising return to and rigorous
implementation of the traditional values of the Virginia political
system.[47]

The latter group considered the special treatment accorded Chiswell by the judges of the General Court especially
ominous. Public discussion of the case was spearheaded by
Robert Bolling and James Milner. Bolling was a member of an
old, if no longer quite so prominent, gentry family. He had
studied law in Britain and Virginia, but had become a planter in
Buckingham County. A member of the burgesses, he was also, in
the judgment of a modern scholar, "probably the most prolific
poet of Pre-Revolutionary America." Milner was a young lawyer
who practiced in the county courts in the western piedmont. A
new man on the Virginia political scene, Milner had credentials
that, had he not later moved to North Carolina, would have

enabled him to enter the ranks of the politically influential. As Bolling put it, the behavior of the judges in the Chiswell case posed the questions whether the judges' action was legal and, if it was not, whether it did not have "a tendency to overturn the laws and constitution of the country, by their exercising an extrajudicial power and controuling the course of law in a case of the highest consequence to the safety of the subject." Bolling's principal contention was that the action was not legal and that it was "in fact a [mere] rescue" of a powerful man by his powerful friends, "a most flagrant injury, both to Prince and people" that reserved to the judges of the General Court "nothing less than a power of licensing homicides." John Blair offered a weak public defense of the judges' behavior. Because the murder was not premeditated but the result of "a most unhappy drunken affair," he declared, leniency was justifiable. But Bolling mockingly replied that the judges clearly had violated the letter of the law and that if the judges could so behave then "your fellow subjects in Virginia live only at discretion of your sublime Board; a Board," he added, "which having an unreasonable power by law already, should at least be prevented from usurping one, subversive both of law and reason." Blair had indicated that making a public defense had required him to waive "the dignity of our [the judges'] stations." To Bolling, the very suggestion that the dignity of office should exempt any group from public accountability was outrageous. "I begin to think myself an inhabitant of some other country than Virginia," he wrote: "Is there a *dignity* in this land which exempts any person whatever from a duty to satisfy, if possible, a people which conceives itself injured? Methinks I hear a general negative from every part of Virginia."[48]

But it was not Bolling but Milner writing under the pseudonym Dikephilos—a lover of justice—who first spelled out the full—and sobering—implications of the judges' misbehavior. That behavior gave rise to the suspicions that the "influence of Mr. Chiswell's friends" would "prevent the truth from being published," that "justice" would be "perverted, and law trampled on." But for "an atrocious murderer" to be thus "screened from justice," to be "cleared, by means of great friends," said Milner, was not only "an act of wonderful partiality" but an "opprobrius stain . . . on our colony" that justifiably had enraged Routledge's family and friends and deeply alarmed "Patriots, . . . foreigners, [and] the middle and lower ranks of men, who are acquainted with the particulars." "They said," according to Milner, "that one of the worthiest of men had been not only murdered, but defamed; and that the murderer was treated with indulgence and partiality inconsistent with our constitution, and destructive of our security and privileges." "People in general," wrote Milner, said that "every true American justly detested the late intolerable Stamp Act" and laudably expressed willingness to risk their lives and fortunes to prevent so dreadful an attack on American liberty and property: "But now they apprehend that this partiality may be attended with still more dreadful consequences than ever that detestable Act of power could have been, because this must affect our lives, while that could only affect our estates." Milner agreed with one of the anonymous defenders of the judges who had objected to the public outcry against the judges on the grounds that "men in power should be treated with great deference." But this deference, said Milner, "should be consistent with British freedom, and not like slaves to a [Turkish] Bashaw. If British subjects know the power of men in high stations, and if men in high stations will exceed their due bounds, has not the meanest subject a right to mention his apprehension and grievance?" No man deserved British privileges, Milner declared, "who would not protect them." Obviously, added Bolling, the country had to be preserved "from a stretch of jurisdiction, which, if allowed, may probably, one day or other, form its greatest infelicity." "To pass over, without attention," such an obvious violation of the constitution, he declared, "would be a proof of great deficiency in public virtue, insomuch as to leave us but a melancholy prospect of futurity." Virginians had to make sure that "some Virginians" could not "massacre other Virginians (or sojourners among them) with impunity." Bolling summarized the issue acidly and succinctly in verse:

> The Laws, in Vulgar Hands unkind,
> The worthy Gentleman confined;
> But in the Hands of Gentlemen
> Politer, they released again.
> But then began a strange Fracas:
> Some swore it was, some 'twas not, Law.
> 'Twas not for common Men, 'twas plain;
> But was it not for Gentlemen?

Did Virginia, that ancient repository of virtue, have a double standard in the law, one for the rich and powerful and another for the rest of society?[49]

Public debate over the Chiswell case came to an abrupt end on 15 October when Chiswell was found dead on the eve of his murder trial; his death was attributed to "Anxiety of Mind." But suspicions ran so deep that many believed that Chiswell's death had been fabricated to permit him to escape punishment, and a mob insisted upon opening the casket to verify the identity of the corpse before it was interred.[50]

The charge of murder was not the only source of Chiswell's "Anxiety of Mind," for he had been one of the principal beneficiaries of Robinson's largess with the public funds, and the public debate over the Chiswell case paralleled a vigorous discussion of the significance of Robinson's default at the treasury and how such behavior might be prevented in the future. Outrage at this notorious "shock to the constitution" was balanced by a widespread reluctance to condemn the man responsible for it, and the general consensus seems to have been, as William Nelson put it, that a "good . . . man . . . in private Life" had been "prevail'd upon by a set of men he was connected with, & who pretended to be his Friends" to engage in conduct that stained "a character otherwise so amiable." "The Truth is," said Nelson, Robinson "had a Benevolence for all Mankind & so great a Desire to please everybody & make them happy, that he never could resist an application to him for money which he hoped to be able to replace before he should be called upon for it. This humane Disposition of his they took Advantage of. Therefore on them lay the Balance: his was the Error, or rather let me say the Weakness of carrying even his Virtues to too great an Excess." Even the most vociferous critics of Robinson's actions conceded that the old speaker had always intended "to charge himself with every shilling, which came into his hands, or for which he ought to have been accountable." Some defenders even contended that Robinson's actions were "a publick good." Given the prevailing shortage of specie and Parliament's prohibition of further emissions of paper money by the Currency Act of 1764, Robinson's loaning out paper money instead of retiring it, they said, was a patriotic action that "immediately relieved many worthy families from ruin and indigence." What was good for indigent "worthy families" was good for Virginia![51]

    But the drift of opinion seems to have run strongly in the opposite direction. "Private virtues, amiable as they are," said Nicholas in turning Bernard Mandeville's famous aphorism on its head, easily could "become publick vices, and prove the means of destroying a whole country." Although he praised Robinson's "humane disposition" and "many brilliant virtues," Landon Carter expressed the predominant view when he declared that "charity . . . is certainly condemnable when extended out of any office of trust." Many others took an even less charitable view of Robinson's charity. "To metamorphose a notorious breach of the publick confidence into charity and munificence," sputtered Robert Bolling, was to subvert "all ideas of virtue and morality." Far from being praised for his private generosity with public funds, he had to be condemned, said an anonymous and uncompromising critic writing under the pseudonym Elizabeth Barebones, for what he was: "a misapplier of the publick revenues, a destroyer of his country's credit, [and] . . . a subverter of its liberty." Robinson had not acted in behalf of the public welfare, as many of his defenders had seemed to imply: he had only contributed to hasten Virginia's ruin by helping some of the colony's "untowardly degenerate brats, who would not be ruled, nor satisfied with a wholesome allowance; but by intemperance, and a rich diet, quite unsuitable to [either] their constitutions" or their resources, enmeshed themselves ever further in "an impoverished luxury." Consider, warned Elizabeth Barebones,

what convulsions were produced in old Rome by the ambitious compassion of proud and luxurious debtors for their dear selves. Is it not the judicious *Sallust* who puts these words into the mouth of *Cato*? . . . *And shall any one talk to me in this case of mildness and mercy? We have long since indeed lost the right names of things from amongst us. The giving what belongs to other people is called generosity, and the courage to venture upon wickedness is named fortitude, by which it is that the state has been brought upon the very brink of destruction*. Is it not the mild and good natured *Addison* who, after he had caused Decius to assert that the *virtues of humanity are Caesar's*, makes Cato reply, with a proper vehemence and resentment, *Curse his virtues, they have undone his country. Such popular humanity is treason!*

Robinson's behavior, wrote Richard Hartswell, revealed "vices of a very deep die," and the gentry, whose role it was to provide a laudable example for the rest of society, could not possibly afford "to connive at vices that ought to be punished" or in any way "give . . . a sanction to any thing that may be injurious to their country." Once it was revealed, said "A Planter," quoting Alexander Pope, that

> . . . beneath the Patriot's Cloak
> From the crack'd Bag the dropping Guinea spoke,
> And gingling down the Back Stairs told the Crew,
> "Old Cato is as great a Rogue as you,"

and became clear to the public that the gentry was willing to tolerate the corruption of which Robinson was guilty, social disaster could be the only result. Inferiors would rush to imitate their superiors, and the last vestiges of the vaunted virtue of Virginia would be swept away in a tide of social corruption.

Clearly, the stakes were too high for Virginians to be content with merely "shinning over our ulcers." Far more drastic remedies were required: "probing to the bottom, . . . laying *bare the bone*, and scraping it . . . to obtain a real and unequivocal cure." "Neither the interest of any individual, while alive, nor his posthumous fame, when dead," could be suffered to prevent "an impartial attention to the true interests of the colony" at such a critical juncture in its history. Obviously, Robinson had been tempted into his excesses because of his extraordinary power that shielded him from immediate discovery. Robinson, charged Nicholas, "knew he had a power superiour to the whole Legislature; and that he could dispense with . . . laws made to regulate his own steps." But no man could be permitted to put himself above the law. "With what face," asked Hartswell, "can any one deny the absolute necessity of executing the laws with the utmost vigour upon *all* who" chose to live under them? "No rule ought ever to be more regarded, than the law of equality" before the law, declared Nicholas, "this being equity and justice itself."[52]

As in the Chiswell case, this demand for powerful remedies to cleanse the colony of political corruption came largely from within the gentry itself, as the proponents of impersonal government and a return to the traditional political values of the colony spearheaded a movement to separate the offices of speaker and treasurer as the only means to prevent similar abuses in the future. Nicholas, who hoped for appointment as treasurer on a permanent basis, as well as Richard Bland and Richard Henry Lee, who were both candidates for the speakership, led a spirited campaign against the supporters of Peyton Randolph, who hoped to succeed Robinson as both speaker and treasurer. Randolph received support from many who were probably indebted to the Robinson estate, who hoped that he would take a more lenient view of his predecessor and feared that Nicholas might insist upon rapid repayment so as to "distress many familys" as well as from close connections like

Benjamin Grymes and his brother John Randolph, who professed themselves to be, in principle, "enemies to [all] innovations in Government, which" tended—as a general rule—"to destroy liberty." He also was favored by independent men who, like Landon Carter, predicted that separation might produce an even "greater evil" by presenting the crown with an opportunity to do what it had been endeavoring to do for nearly a decade: wrest the power to appoint the treasurer "out of controul of the House of Burgesses." "I see," said Carter, "a power somewhere too apt to be abused, and fond of extending the right to lucrative employments." Should the crown succeed in such a venture, Carter declared, "Then farewell Dear Liberty."[53]

But the traditional values of the gentry made the arguments in favor of separation far more powerful. "Whenever . . . the publick happiness can be promoted by abrogating a *constitutional custom*," said Bland, "it is the duty of the national Council to banish such a custom from the constitution, which by its continuance might prevent that happiness, and the establishment of the perfection of the state upon the firmest foundation." Old customs, said Nicholas, "if found inconvenient . . . surely ought to be abolished." That the union of the two offices had indeed proved inconvenient seemed obvious to the proponents of separation. Under Robinson, the union demonstrably had given so "much weight and influence to the Chair" as to permit the "weight of dignity" to "intrude itself into the place of reason and just argument and bear everything before it," thereby destroying that "just . . . equilibrium" that "in every state . . . is necessary for the publick weal." Such a union had the unfortunate effect of setting in motion "a kind of action and reaction, that the one [office] might become almost unbounded in its influence and the other placed almost out of the reach of publick controul." "Where two such offices are enjoyed by one person," said the freeholders of James City County, "it must convey a great degree of power and superiority, which may lay a foundation for such undue influence as is inconsistent with the liberty of a free people." Clearly, the legislature had to consider "how far the power of any single man in authority ought to be limited" and take proper steps to eliminate "too exhorbitant [a concentration] of power" in the hands of any man and all possibility of his obtaining an "undue influence." Moreover, opposition to separation in the face of such an extravagant misuse of power as that of which Robinson had been guilty only lent credence to "a strong suspicion that there was *and is* an influence or something very much like it, still [even after Robinson's death] prevailing." Should "a man destitute of any real Goodness of Heart, and Benevolence of Disposition" ever succeed both to the chair, "the greatest Post of Honour conferr'd on him in the Power of the Country to give," *and* the treasury, "what dreadful Things may we not fear from him?" asked "A Planter" in the *Gazette*: "Is it not in his Power (if not to breed Convulsions in the State) at least to dispose [as had Robinson] of our Property by his own Will, and build his Greatness on his Country's Ruin?" "Will ye then, O ye Guardians of the People, any longer suffer Things to remain in a Channel that so evidently does and must tend to produce great Hardships and Inconveniences on Ourselves and Posterity?" queried "A Planter," who called upon the voters "not to suffer" their representatives to depart from their "respective Counties without positive Instructions, not only to separate those two Offices, but to fix that of Treasurer in such a Manner" that public monies no longer could be misapplied. This and other similar appeals to the public had their effect: on one of the few occasions in colonial Virginia politics up to that time meetings of constituents publicly instructed their representatives to work for a separation.[54]

When the House of Burgesses convened in November 1766 for the first time since it had been dissolved for passage of the Henry resolutions in the late spring of 1766, the reform impulse was running very strong. The reform group carried a motion to separate the offices of speaker and treasurer "by a great majority," and the house chose Robert Carter Nicholas as treasurer, put him under severe penalties for any mismanagement at the treasury, authorized him to conduct a thorough investigation of the scandal, and insisted upon immediate repayment from the forced sale of Robinson's estate. Yet the burgesses did not reject the old Robinson system in its entirety. Perhaps in part because it was not clear that all of the borrowers from Robinson had known they were dipping into public funds and in part because Robinson's records were sufficiently confused as to prevent immediate verification of the names of debtors and the amounts owed, the burgesses did not insist upon a full public revelation of the details of the scandal. Despite the diligent efforts of Edmund Pendleton as trustee for Robinson's estate, the difficulty of verifying details and of collecting many of the debts prevented full repayment to the treasury for several decades. For speaker the house selected Peyton Randolph, Robinson's chief protégé. In temperament and political style, the new speaker could scarcely have been more similar to Robinson, though Randolph was widely respected for his honesty and untainted by the scandal. To compensate Randolph, who had to give up the attorney generalship to accept the speakership, for the loss of income resulting from the separation of the treasury from the speakership, the house, against the strong wishes of one segment of the reform group that argued against giving the speaker a salary that not only would "burthen the people" but might "hereafter . . . tempt men of corrupt minds, or mercenary principles, to solicit the honour for the sake of the profit," voted, for the first time ever, an annual salary to the speaker. In the manner of Robinson, Randolph quickly moved to mollify discontent by diffusing political power within the burgesses. He increased the size and thereby broadened the base of membership on the powerful standing committees in the house and distributed assignments upon major committees much more widely than Robinson had done. Although a relatively few talented and influential men continued to dominate the work of the burgesses, this diffusion of committee assign-

ments slightly increased the number of burgesses who thenceforth played a visible role in the proceedings of the house.[55]

Because of their temporal relationship to the Stamp Act
crisis and their simultaneous revelations, the Robinson scandal
and the Chiswell case hit the Virginia political community much
harder than either might have done in isolation. Only a few
weeks before these two developments broke, political writers
had drawn a sharp contrast between the corruption of the British
polity and the virtue of the Virginian. But these two developments, one coming immediately on top of the other,
strongly suggested both that the Virginia gentry was guilty of the
same inner corruption and was suffering from the same decay of
public virtue as so recently had been charged against Britain's
governing classes and that Virginia's liberty was at least as much
endangered from the unrestrained lust for gain and social
privilege among its own gentry as from the wanton exertion of
imperial power by greedy and designing politicians in Britain.
The many questions raised by these developments constituted a
profound and disturbing challenge to the colony's flattering
corporate self-image. Had, as these developments both implied,
Virginia already and "so early quit the paths of wisdom" and
virtue and degenerated into a base aristocratic oligarchy in which
mere "family and fortune" raised men to such a "superiority"
above the rest of society that they could, without fear of
retribution, place themselves entirely beyond the law? Had the
government of the colony fallen into the hands of "men, who
had more influence than merit, and men who have patronized
villains (or have been duped by them) and defended what they
ought to have detected," men "whose vices, extravagances, and
follies" were of that very species that always had been "inconsistent with the prosperity of any society" and had "formerly
brought ruin and desolation upon the most powerful states and
kingdoms"? Had the celebrated public virtue of the gentry so far
declined as to prevent them from making any distinction between their own private interests and the public welfare?[56]

The rising fear throughout the summer and fall of 1766 was that the answer to all of these questions was yes, but the fear finally was allayed by the vigorous and self-critical reaction of the gentry itself. This reaction made it abundantly clear that the gentry would not condone unconstitutional and corrupt actions by any of its members—not even the powerful and popular John Robinson—much less, as one earlier historian has suggested, "present a solid, silent phalanx to the rest of society whether" or not the cause was "just or unjust, good or bad, right or wrong." Far from uniting in a cover-up, some members of the gentry inaugurated and dominated the public protest against the favoritism extended to Chiswell and the successful campaign to get to the bottom of the Robinson scandal and to prevent similar occurrences in the future by detaching the treasury from the speakership. And when William Byrd III, one of the judges who had granted Chiswell bail, and John Wayles, a lawyer friend of Chiswell's who had given evidence in Chiswell's behalf at the hearing, sued Robert Bolling and all three of the colony's printers for libel, a grand jury in Williamsburg including such well-known gentry figures as Mann Page, John Page, and Lewis Burwell, Sr., threw out the actions on the grounds that they were "NOT TRUE BILLS" and, for doing so, were celebrated publicly as "GOOD MEN AND TRUE, FRIENDS TO LIBERTY." Moreover, the full and open discussion of both matters by the gentry and others in the press, as one writer remarked, "had the salutary Effect of correcting the haughty Spirits of some of our great Men, who, from their Fortunes, Connections, and Stations, had conceived very high Ideas of Self-Importance,—but who are now convinced, that *a Bashaw opposed against a Man, is but a Man*." Even more important, perhaps, the very conception of *"great men"* had been restored to its ancient Virginia meaning: *great* men were identifiable not through their "outward grandeur" but through their vigorous and honest "service to the publick."[57]

By all these actions in behalf of reform, as well as by the obvious moral outrage that underlay them, the gentry, or at least

those many "worthy patriots" among them, put itself firmly on
record as opposed to the "confederacy of the great in place,
family connections, and that more to be dreaded foe to public
virtue, warm and private friendship" and left no doubt that it
was not yet ready to "seal [the] . . . ruin" of the colony either by
continuing to unite "in one person the only two great places in
the power of her assembly to bestow" or by countenancing
special treatment under the law for wealthy and well-connected
inhabitants. Thenceforth, *personal* government was to be replaced by *impersonal* government. Merit and virtue, not wealth
and family, would be the central criteria for political leadership.
Behavior and practice once again would be brought into harmony with the colony's cherished corporate self-image. Old
ideas would be revitalized. The malignant humors that gradually
had taken hold of the body politics during Robinson's thirty-year
domination of public life would be exorcised. Public virtue once
again would become the central defining quality of the Virginia
political system.[58]

V

The reformist impulse generated within the ranks of the gentry
by the events of 1764–66 continued to have a strong—and
ramifying—influence in Virginia politics for at least another
generation. In combination, those events had intensified the
movement for constitutional security, first generated during the
late 1750s by the growing recognition of the inadequacy of
existing constitutional safeguards for the colony's rights and
liberties against the extraordinary might of the imperial state,
and stimulated a searching examination of the entire structure of
constitutional arrangements within Virginia. The excessive concentration of power in the council, each of whose members
united the "discordant and heterogeneous dignities of Privy
Consellor, Judge of the General Court, and Member of the
intermediate body of the Legislature"; the total absence of that
"one very essential security, namely the Right of" the voters to

choose a new House of Burgesses to meet "in a certain time after being dissolved, as in Britain"; and the crown's excessive influence through its appointment of both the governor and council which together constituted "⅔ of the Legislature & all the judicial power"—these were all identified in 1764–66 as serious "imperfection[s] in the constitution" that put the liberty and property of Virginians "on a very precarious footing."[59] Even the ancient and rarely criticized economic restrictions imposed on the colony's trade by the navigation system, restrictions that, however quietly, had "ever been regarded here as oppressive in many Respects," received modest criticism.[60] Perhaps the most important result of this new critical posture, however, was the increasing sensitivity of Virginia's leaders to any indications of corruption *within* their political system, as they subsequently watched the conduct of each other and the operation of their own polity with the same jealous avidity that they accorded distasteful measures of the imperial government. From this new critical posture, the Virginia gentry was in a position both to continue to "claim the Honour of" taking "the Lead" in the opposition to Britain over the next decade and to assert—with some measure of credibility once again—that, as one writer put it in 1769, "the prevailing principle of *our* government is *virtue*," albeit the continuing proliferation of luxury, gaming, and other forms of vice among large segments—and within every stratum—of Virginia society contributed to feed the powerful currents of anxiety about the moral health of the society that were so vividly manifest in the symbolism of the new state seal in 1776.[61]

Despite the vigor of the gentry's response to the Stamp Act, developments within Virginia—the Robinson scandal and the special treatment accorded Chiswell—had called into question the legitimacy of the gentry's claim both to public virtue and to political leadership and generated a strong movement—within the gentry—toward self-reform, a movement that received its strength less from desire of the gentry to perpetuate its political power as a corporate group than from the devotion of individual members of the gentry to the traditional ideals and the ancient corporate self-image of the Virginia political system. Through self-reform, through the powerful reassertion of an active commitment to the preservation—and exemplification—of the hallowed values of the Virginia polity, the reformist group among the gentry managed in 1766 to reestablish, more firmly than ever perhaps, the viability of the gentry's long-standing claim to political dominance. The success of the reform effort and the rededication of the gentry to *virtus et libertas* represented by that effort may, moreover, have been the primary reason why the Revolution in Virginia constituted not a rejection but an endorsement of government by the gentry, of a set of political arrangements under which, as Edmund Pendleton later put it, "those of more information on political subjects" instructed the "classes who have not otherwise an opportunity of acquiring that knowledge . . . in their *rights* and *duties* as freemen, and taught [them] to respect them."[62] In the midst of a revolutionary upheaval, a political gentry regenerated by events a decade earlier managed to infuse the traditional Virginia political modes and the old ideals into a new state government, to carry out still further reforms in the political and social system without altering in any fundamental way the existing structure of politics, and to retain the confidence of the politically relevant segments of Virginia society.

Notes

1. Edmund Pendleton to Richard Henry Lee, 20 April 1776, David J. Mays, ed., *The Letters and Papers of Edmund Pendleton*, 2 vols. (Charlottesville, Va., 1967), 1:164. Emphasis added.

2. The best modern study of the work of the Virginia convention of May–June 1776 is Keith B. Berwick, "Moderation in Crisis: The Trials of Leadership in Revolutionary Virginia" (Ph.D. diss., University of Chicago, 1959).

3. The great seal is described virtually verbatim from the original resolution by Edmund Randolph, *History of Virginia*, ed. Arthur H. Shaffer (Charlottesville, Va., 1970), p. 276.

4. See the important discussions in Gordon S. Wood, *The Creation of the American Republic 1776–1787* (Chapel Hill, N.C., 1969), pp. 65–70; Gerald Stourzh, *Alexander Hamilton and the Idea of Republican Government* (Stanford, Calif., 1970), pp. 63–75; and J. G. A. Pocock, *The Machiavellian Moment: Florentine Political Thought and the Atlantic Republican Tradition* (Princeton, N.J., 1975), pp. 406–552.

5. The meaning of the seal is analyzed in W. Edwin Hemphill, "The Symbolism of Our Seal," *Virginia Cavalcade* 2 (1952): 27–33.

6. See especially Maynard Mack, *The Garden and the City* (Toronto, 1969), and Maren-sofie Røstvig, *The Happy Man*, 2 vols. (Oslo, 1958–62).

7. *The Invitation* (Boston, 1755), p. 3.

8. The background to these developments is discussed in Jack P. Greene, "Society, Ideology, and Politics: An Analysis of the Political Culture of Mid-Eighteenth Century Virginia," in Richard M. Jellison, ed., *Society, Freedom, and Conscience: The American Revolution . . .* (New York, 1976), pp. 14–76.

9. See, especially, Bernard Bailyn, "Politics and Social Structure in Virginia," in James Morton Smith, ed., *Seventeenth-Century America: Essays in Colonial History* (Chapel Hill, N.C., 1959), pp. 90–115; John C. Rainbolt, "The Alteration in the Relationship between Leadership and Constituents in Virginia, 1660–1720," *William and Mary Quarterly*, 3d ser. 27 (1970): 411–34; and Jack P. Greene, "The Opposition to Lieutenant Governor Alexander Spotswood, 1718," *Virginia Magazine of History and Biography* 80 (1962): 35–42.

10. The social and political conditions that underlay this new political stability are discussed in Greene, "Society, Ideology, and Politics," and, more broadly, in Greene, "The Growth of Political Stability: An Interpretation of Political Development in the Anglo-American Colonies, 1660–1760," in John Parker and Carol Urness, eds., *The American Revolution . . .* (Minneapolis, 1975), pp. 26–52.

11. Samuel P. Huntington, *Political Order in Changing Societies* (New Haven, 1968), p. 76; Randolph's Speech, 24 Aug. 1734, in Henry R. McIlwaine and John P. Kennedy, eds., *Journals of the House of Burgesses of Virginia*, 13 vols. (Richmond, Va., 1906–15), 1727–40, pp. 175–76 (hereafter cited as *Burgesses Journals*).

12. Randolph, *History of Virginia*, p. 173; Fauquier to Earl of Egremont, 19 May 1763, PRO 30/47/14, Bundle 1, Egremont Papers, Public Record Office, London; Jack P. Greene, "The Attempt to Separate the Offices of Speaker and Treasurer in Virginia, 1758–1766," *Virginia Magazine of History and Biography* 71 (1963): 11–18; Fauquier to Board of Trade, 12 May 1761, CO5/1330, ff. 129–35, Public Record Office; James Maury to John Camm, 12 Dec. 1763, *Burgesses Journals, 1761–65*, pp. li–liii; James Horrocks, *Upon the Peace* (Williamsburg, Va., 1763), pp. iii–iv; St. George Tucker to William Wirt, 25 Sept. 1815, *William and Mary College Quarterly*, 1st ser. 22 (1914): 253.

13. Randolph, *History of Virginia*, pp. 173–74; Robert Carter Nicholas to the Printer, *Virginia Gazette* (Purdie and Dixon), 27 June 1766; entry of 9 Oct. 1776, Landon Carter, *Diary of Colonel Landon Carter of Sabine Hall, 1752–1778*, ed. Jack P. Greene, 2 vols. (Charlottesville, Va., 1965), 2:738.

14. Jack P. Greene, "Foundations of Political Power in the Virginia House of Burgesses, 1720–1776," *William and Mary Quarterly*, 3d ser. 16 (1959): 485–506; Randolph, *History of Virginia*, pp. 174, 179.

15. Tucker to Wirt, 25 Sept. 1815, *William and Mary College Quarterly*, 1st ser. 22 (1914): 253. Historians who have treated Virginia politics in terms of a north-south split include David Alan Williams, "Political Alignments in Colonial Virginia" (Ph.D. diss., Northwestern University, 1959); Joseph Albert Ernst, "The Robinson Scandal Redivivus: Money, Debts, and Politics in Revolutionary Virginia," *Virginia Magazine of History and Biography* 77 (1969): 146–73; and J. A. Leo Lemay, "Robert Bolling and the Bailment of Colonel Chiswell," *Early American Literature* 6 (1971): 99–142.

16. Randolph, *History of Virginia*, p. 177.

17. Ibid., pp. 157–58, 247–48; John Markland, *Typographia: An Ode to Printing* (Williamsburg, Va., 1730), pp. 9–10; David Mossum, Jr., "Ode," *Virginia Gazette*, 26 Nov. 1736; Pendleton, "Address to the Va. Ratifying Convention," 12 June 1788, in Mays, ed., *Pendleton Papers*, 2: 528.

18. Johann David Schoepf, *Travels in the Confederation* [1783–1784], trans. and ed. Alfred J. Morrison, 2 vols. (Philadelphia, 1911), 1:91–95; Randolph, *History of Virginia*, pp. 161, 176, 178, 193, 197, 257; Marquis de Chastellux, *Travels in North America in the Years 1780, 1781, and 1782*, ed. Howard C. Rice, Jr., 2 vols. (Chapel Hill, N.C., 1963), pp. 428–30.

19. [Mercer], "Dinwiddianae," in Richard Beale Davis, ed., *The Colonial Virginia Satirist: Mid-Eighteenth-Century Commentaries on Politics, Religion, and Society* (Philadelphia, 1967), pp. 21, 27. On the pistole fee controversy, see Jack P. Greene, ed., "The Case of the Pistole Fee," *Virginia Magazine of History and Biography* 66 (1958): 406–22. The points covered in this and the following three paragraphs are developed more fully in Greene, "Society, Ideology, and Politics."

20. These disputes are treated in detail by Thad W. Tate, "The Coming of the Revolution in Virginia: Britain's Challenge to Virginia's Ruling Class, 1763–1776," *William and Mary Quarterly*, 3d ser. 19 (1962): 324–35; Rhys Isaac, "Religion and Authority: Problems of the Anglican Establishment in Virginia in the Era of the Great Awakening and the Parsons' Cause," ibid. 30 (1973): 3–36; and Joseph Albert Ernst, "Genesis of the Currency Act of 1764: Virginia Paper Money and the Protection of British Investments," ibid. 22 (1965): 34–59.

21. Randolph, *History of Virginia*, pp. 160–61, 163, 248. See Greene, "Society, Ideology, and Politics," for a fuller discussion of these points.

22. George Mason, "Scheme for Replevying Goods . . .," [23 Dec. 1765], in Robert A. Rutland, ed., *The Papers of George Mason*, 3 vols. (Chapel Hill, N.C., 1970), 1:61–62. See also the citations in note 65 of Greene, "Society, Ideology, and Politics."

23. See Andrew Burnaby, *Burnaby's Travels through North America*, ed. Rufus Rockwell Wilson (New York, 1904), p. 55; Fauquier to Board of Trade, 3 Nov. 1762, CO5/1330, ff. 339–40, Public Record Office; Horrocks, *Upon the Peace*, pp. 9–10, 14; "My Country's Worth," [1752], in James A. Servies and Carl R.

Dolmetsch, eds., *The Poems of Charles Hansford* (Chapel Hill, N.C., 1961), pp. 62–64; William Stith, *The Sinfulness and Pernicious Nature of Gaming* (Williamsburg, Va., 1752), pp. 11–12; Randolph, *History of Virginia*, p. 61.

24. Randolph, *History of Virginia*, pp. 177–78; Greene, "Foundations of Political Power," pp. 485–506; "My Country's Worth," *Poems of Charles Hansford*, p. 58.

25. Alexander White to R. H. Lee, [1758], "Selections and Excerpts from the Lee Papers," *Southern Literary Messenger* 286 (1858): 118; Landon Carter, *The Rector Detected* (Williamsburg, Va., 1764), p. 8. See also Gordon S. Wood, "Rhetoric and Reality in the American Revolution," *William and Mary Quarterly*, 3d ser. 22 (1965): 27–28.

26. Entry of 13 March 1752, Carter, *Diary*, 1:85, and generally, 1:65–124; White to Lee, [1758], and Richard Bland to R. H. Lee, 22 May 1766, "Lee Papers," pp. 116–17; "The Freeholder" [Richard Bland] to Printer, *Virginia Gazette* (Purdie and Dixon), 17 Oct. 1766; Arthur Lee to Philip Ludwell Lee, 5 Nov. 1763, Arthur Lee Papers (Ms. Am 811 F), I, f.2, Houghton Library, Harvard University, Cambridge, Mass.; Robert Carter Nicholas to Printer, *Virginia Gazette* (Purdie and Dixon), 1 Sept. 1766. On Lee's challenge to Robinson, see Ernst, "Robinson Scandal Redivivus," pp. 149–50.

27. Randolph's Speech, 24 Aug. 1734, *Burgesses Journals, 1727–40*, pp. 175–76.

28. According to John Mercer in a letter of 12 Sept. 1766 to the *Virginia Gazette* (Purdie and Dixon), 26 Sept. 1766. Because the issue for 27 April 1764 is no longer extant, there is no way to verify Mercer's statement. But there is no reason to doubt it, although no announcement appeared in the *Maryland Gazette* (Annapolis) until 24 May 1764.

29. Harry Piper to Dixon and Littledale, 29 May 1773, Henry Piper Letter Book, 1767–76, Alderman Library, University of Virginia, Charlottesville, Va.

30. R. H. Lee to ——, 31 May 1764, in James C. Ballagh, ed., *The Letters of Richard Henry Lee*, 2 vols. (New York, 1911–14), 1:5–7.

31. Committee of Correspondence to Edward Montague, 28 July 1764, "Proceedings of the Virginia Committee of Correspondence," *Virginia Magazine of History and Biography* 12 (1905): 5–14.

32. Roger Atkinson to Samuel Pleasants, 1 Oct. 1774, in A. J. Morrison, ed., "Letters of Roger Atkinson, 1769–1776," ibid. 15 (1908): 356.

33. Richard Bland, *The Colonel Dismounted* (Williamsburg, Va., 1764), esp. pp. 21–23.

34. Virginia Gazette Daybook, 1764–66, 24, 27 Oct. 1764, pp. 108, 110, Alderman Library.

35. *Burgesses Journals, 1761–65*, 7 Nov.–18 Dec. 1764, esp. pp. 240, 254, 257, 279, 293, 299, 300, 301, 302–4. For the roles played by Carter and Lee see entries for 14, 25 July 1776, 23–24 Feb. 1777, Carter, *Diary*, 2:1057, 1063, 1082–84; Jack P. Greene, *Landon Carter: An Inquiry into the Personal Values and Social Imperatives of the Eighteenth-Century Virginia Gentry* (Charlottesville, Va., 1967), pp. 85–86; and R. H. Lee to William Rind, *Virginia Gazette* (Rind), 25 July 1766.

36. Fauquier to Board of Trade, 24 Dec. 1765, CO5/1331, pp. 1–2, Public Record Office; Address, Memorial, and Remonstrance, 18 Dec. 1764, *Burgesses Journals, 1761–65*, pp. 302–4.

37. Memorial and Remonstrance, 18 Dec. 1764, *Burgesses Journals, 1761–65*, pp. 302–4; Fauquier to Board of Trade, 25 June 1765, CO5/1331, Public Record Office; Randolph, *History of Virginia*, p. 167; Robert Douthat Meade, *Patrick Henry*, 2 vols. (Philadelphia, 1957–69), 1:169–82. On the Parson's Cause, see Glenn C. Smith, "The Parson's Cause, 1755–1765," *Tyler's Quarterly Historical and Genealogical Magazine* 21 (1940): 140–71, 291–306; Richard R. Beeman, *Patrick Henry: A Biography* (New York, 1974), pp. 11–43; and Tate, "Coming of the Revolution in Virginia," pp. 323–43. The interpretation of Henry's motivations is my own. The continued opposition but ambivalence of the establishment leaders is suggested by Edmund Pendleton to James Madison, Sr., 17 April 1765, in Mays, ed., *Pendleton Papers*, 1:20.

38. Henry's resolutions are conveniently reprinted in William J. Van Schreeven, comp., and Robert L. Scribner, ed., *Revolutionary Virginia: The Road to Independence* (Charlottesville, Va., 1973), 1: 17–18. The circumstances surrounding their passage is discussed by Ernst, "Robinson Scandal Redivivus," pp. 152–57. Their transmission to and reception in other colonies is discussed in Edmund S. Morgan and Helen M. Morgan, *The Stamp Act Crisis: Prologue to Revolution* (Chapel Hill, N.C., 1953), pp. 88–98.

39. An alternative explanation for the division over the Henry resolutions interpreting it in terms of a "democratic," "outside," or sectional challenge to an entrenched, aristocratic, and eastern elite runs through most of the literature on the subject from Randolph, *History of Virginia*, pp. 167–68, to Ernst, "Robinson Scandal Redivivus," pp. 152–57. Closer to my own view is Tate, "Coming of the Revolution in Virginia," pp. 323–43.

40. Fauquier to Board of Trade, 25 June 1765, CO5/1331, Public Record Office; and 3 Nov. 1765, in *Burgesses Journals, 1761–65*, pp. lxviii–lxxi; Resolutions of the Westmoreland Association, 27 Feb. 1766, and Declaration of Magistrates of Northampton Co., 11 Feb. 1766, in Van Schreeven, comp., and Scribner, ed., *Revolutionary Virginia*, pp. 20–26; *Maryland Gazette* (Annapolis), 17 Oct. 1765; Edmund Pendleton to James Madison, Sr., 11 Dec. 1765, 15 Feb. 1766, in Mays, ed., *Pendleton Papers*, 1:20, 23; *Virginia Gazette* (Rind), 16 May 1766. On the Ritchie affair, see John C. Matthews, "Two Men on a Tax: Richard Henry Lee, Archibald Ritchie, and the Stamp Act," in Darrett B. Rutman, ed., *The Old Dominion: Essays for Thomas Perkins Abernethy* (Charlottesville, Va., 1964), pp. 100–108.

41. See *Burgesses Journals, 1761–65* pp. 5–9.

42. Letters from A Gentleman in Virginia, 5 June [Sept.] 1765, in Walter E. Minchinton, ed., "The Stamp Act Crisis: Bristol and Virginia," *Virginia Magazine of History and Biography* 73 (1965):147–51; Anglo-Americanus (John Mercer) to Printer, *New York Gazette, or, The Weekly Post-Boy* (New York), 4 July 1765; Richard Henry Lee to ——, 4 July 1765, and to Arthur Lee, 4 July 1765, in Ballagh, ed., *Letters of Lee*, 1:9–10; Jack P. Greene, ed., "'Not to be *Governed* or Taxed, But By . . . Our Representatives': Four Essays in Opposition to the Stamp Act by

Landon Carter," *Virginia Magazine of History and Biography* 76 (1968): 259–300, esp. p. 294; Greene, *Landon Carter*, p. 53.

43. R. H. Lee to Landon Carter, 22 June 1765, in Ballagh, ed., *Letters of Lee*, 1:8; Northamptoniensis to Printer, 24 March 1766, in *Virginia Gazette* (Purdie), 4 April 1766; Algernon Sydney to Printer, 16 May 1766, ibid., 30 May 1766; George Washington to Francis Dandridge, 20 Sept. 1765, in John C. Fitzpatrick, ed., *The Writings of George Washington*, 39 vols. (Washington, D.C., 1931–44), 2: 425–26; Resolutions of Norfolk Sons of Liberty, 31 March 1766, in Van Schreeven, comp., and Scribner, ed., *Revolutionary Virginia*, p. 46.

44. Resolutions of Norfolk Sons of Liberty, 31 March 1766, in Van Schreeven, comp., and Scribner, ed., *Revolutionary Virginia*, p. 46; Richard Bland, *An Inquiry into the Rights of the British Colonies* (Williamsburg, Va., 1766), as reprinted in ibid., pp. 33–34; Gentleman in Va. to ——, [Sept.] 1765, in Minchinton, ed., "Stamp Act Crisis," p. 149; George Mason to Committee of Merchants in London, 6 June 1766, in Rutland, ed., *Mason Papers*, 1: 68.

45. Obituary, *Virginia Gazette* (Rind), 16 May 1766; Nicholas to Printer, ibid. (Purdie), 27 June 1766. The best published treatments are Ernst, "Robinson Scandal Redivivus," pp. 146–73, and David J. Mays, *Edmund Pendleton*, 2 vols. (Cambridge, Mass., 1952), 1:174–208, 358–85.

46. Carl Bridenbaugh, "Violence and Virtue in Virginia, 1766: or, the Importance of the Trivial," *Proceedings of the Massachusetts Historical Society* 76 (1964): 3–29, and Lemay, "Robert Bolling," pp. 99–142, are the best published accounts.

47. See Bridenbaugh, "Violence and Virtue in Virginia," pp. 14–16; Jack P. Greene, *The Quest for Power: The Lower Houses of Assembly in the Southern Royal Colonies, 1689–1776* (Chapel Hill, N.C., 1963), pp. 288–90; Greene, ed., " 'Not to be *Governed* or Taxed,' " pp. 268–69; *New York Gazette*, 4 July 1765; and Lemay, "Robert Bolling," pp. 102, 119–20; Nicholas to Printer, *Virginia Gazette* (Purdie and Dixon), 5 Sept. 1766.

48. Bolling's letters, all published anonymously, are printed in *Virginia Gazette* (Purdie), 20 June, 11, 25 July 1766. Blair's defense is in ibid., 4 July 1766.

49. Dikephilos [James Milner] to Printer, ibid., 18 July, 29 Aug. 1766; [Bolling] to Printer, ibid., 11 July 1766; Marcus Fabius and Marcus Curtius [Bolling] to Metriotes, ibid., 12 Sept. 1766; Bolling, "The Gentleman, 1766," as quoted by Lemay, "Robert Bolling," pp. 100–101.

50. *Maryland Gazette* (Annapolis), 30 Oct. 1766.

51. Nicholas to Printer, *Virginia Gazette* (Purdie), 27 June 1766; ibid., (Purdie and Dixon), 5 Sept. 1766; Philautos [Peter Warren?] to Printer, ibid. (Purdie), 25 July 1766; William Nelson to Edward and Samuel Athawes, 13 Nov. 1766, Nelson Letter Book, p. 19, Virginia State Library, Richmond.

52. Nicholas to Printer, *Virginia Gazette* (Purdie), 5 Sept. 1766; Honest Buckskin [Carter] to Printer, ibid., 1 Aug. 1766; Marcus Fabius and Marcus Curtius [Bolling] to Metriotes, ibid., 12 Sept. 1766; Elizabeth Barebones to Printer, ibid., 27 Nov., 11 Dec. 1766; Richard Hartswell to Printer, ibid., 19 Sept. 1766; A Planter to Printer, ibid. (Rind), 8 Aug. 1766; Anonymous to Editor, ibid. (Purdie and Dixon), 4 July 1766.

53. Richard Bland to Printer, 20 June 1766, *Virginia Gazette* (Purdie), 11 July 1766; Nicholas to Printer, ibid., 27 June 1766; ibid. (Purdie and Dixon), 5 Sept. 1766; Honest Buckskin [Carter] to Printer, ibid., 1 Aug. 1766; Benjamin Grymes to Printer, ibid., 15 Sept. 1766; Philautos [Peter Warren?] to Printer, ibid., 25 July 1766; Nicholas to William Preston, 21 May 1766, Preston Papers 2QQ97, Wisconsin Historical Society, Madison; Bland to R. H. Lee, 22 May 1766, and Nicholas to Lee, 23 May 1766, in "Lee Papers," pp. 116–17; John Wayles to John T. Ware, 20 Aug. 1766, American Loyalist Claims, PRO T. 79/30, Public Record Office. See also Greene, "Attempt to Separate the Offices of Speaker and Treasurer."

54. Nicholas to Printer, *Virginia Gazette* (Purdie and Dixon), 27 June 1766; ibid., 5 Sept. 1766; A Planter to Printer, ibid. (Rind), 8 Aug. 1766; The Freeholder [Richard Bland] to Honest Buckskin [Carter], ibid. (Purdie and Dixon), 17 Oct. 1766; Address of Freeholders of James City County to Lewis Burwell, ibid., 30 Oct. 1766; see also Philautos to Printer, ibid., 15 Aug. 1766; Principal Inhabitants of Accomack Co. to Thomas Parramore and Southy Simpson, 1 Oct. 1766, ibid., 17 Oct. 1766; Anonymous to Printer, 11 Nov. 1766, ibid. (Rind), 27 Nov. 1766.

55. Inhabitants of Accomack Co. to Parramore and Simpson, 1 Oct. 1766, ibid. (Purdie and Dixon), 17 Oct. 1766; ibid., 27 Nov. 1766; *Maryland Gazette*, 27 Nov. 1766; Greene, "Foundations of Political Power," p. 486; and *Quest for Power*, p. 248; Mays, ed., *Pendleton Papers*, 1:174–208, 358–85.

56. Speech of R. H. Lee, 1766, in "Lee Papers," p. 121; Anonymous to Printer, *Virginia Gazette* (Purdie and Dixon), 27 Feb. 1766; Dikephilos [Milner] to Printer, Sept. 1766, ibid., 6 Nov. 1766; [R. R.] John Camm to Printer, ibid.; [Thomas Burke], "A Prophecy from the East," ibid. (Rind), 15 Aug. 1766.

57. *Maryland Gazette*, 30 Oct. 1766; Bridenbaugh, "Violence and Virtue in Virginia," pp. 27–28; Lemay, "Robert Bolling," pp. 115, 120; Richard Hartswell to Printer, *Virginia Gazette* (Purdie and Dixon), 19 Sept. 1766.

58. Richard Hartswell to Printer, *Virginia Gazette* (Purdie and Dixon), 19 Sept. 1766; David Boyd to R. H. Lee, 17 Nov. 1766, in "Lee Papers," p. 118.

59. See Greene, *Quest for Power*, pp. 386–87; R. H. Lee to Arthur Lee, 20 Dec. 1766, in Ballagh, ed., *Letters of Lee*, 1:19–21; Lee, "State of the Constitution in Virginia," n.d., Lee-Ludwell Papers, Virginia Historical Society, Richmond; Marcus Fabius and Marcus Curtius [Bolling] to Metriotes, *Virginia Gazette* (Purdie and Dixon), 12 Sept. 1766; Letter of Phileleutheros, 10 April 1769, Va. Misc. MSS, Library of Congress, Washington, D.C.; George Mason, "Comments on the Va. Charters," 1773, in Rutland, ed., *Mason Papers*, 1:174–75.

60. A Virginian to Printer, *Virginia Gazette* (Rind), 11 Dec. 1766.

61. Benjamin Franklin's Marginalia in Israel Mauduit, *A Short View . . .* (London, 1769), in Leonard W. Labaree et al., eds., *The Papers of Benjamin Franklin*, 18 vols. to date (New Haven, 1959–), 16:296–97; Brutus to Printer, *Virginia Gazette* (Rind), 1 June 1769, as printed in Jack P. Greene, ed., *Colonies to Nation: A Documentary History of the American Revolution, 1763–1789* (New York, 1975), pp. 156–57.

62. Pendleton to Citizens of Caroline, Nov. 1768, in Mays, ed., *Pendleton Papers*, 2:650.

4

Class, Mobility, and Conflict in North Carolina on the Eve of the Revolution

by Marvin L. Michael Kay and Lorin Lee Cary

Historians who stress the liberal and consentaneous qualities of the late colonial and revolutionary era have appreciated neither the meaning of class and mobility in the colonies nor the importance of the conservative ideology that helped to define colonial Anglo-America.[1] Even the concept of "deference," although widely used to comprehend the age, has not really been understood. During this period deference was a particular expression of the objective class and power arrangements in society and of the pervasive and demanding notion that "the people" must accept these arrangements and defer to their "betters." Deference, then, was the ideological cement that helped to solidify the "natural" and supposedly benevolent union of wealth, power, and prestige in a ruling class. Ignoring the subtleties of these and other conservative factors has enabled historians to belittle radical challenges to the status quo. For by defining the prerevolutionary colonies in liberal, capitalistic, democratic, and consentaneous terms, and by stressing the calming effects of social mobility, they have erroneously constructed colonials who were not class conscious and who thus were incapable of becoming involved in class conflicts. Such conflicts as occurred, therefore, have been comprehended largely as sectional rather than as class struggles.[2]

Ironically, this last quality of their work links the "consensus historians" with an earlier school of American historians, the followers of Frederick Jackson Turner, who stressed sectional variation and conflict to understand the American past. Most students of North Carolina's colonial-revolutionary past have used this sectional interpretation. Normally less explicit and dogmatic in rejecting the explanatory power of class than the consensus historians, they nevertheless have, if ambiguously, underplayed its importance in their emphasis upon the contrast between North Carolina's eastern and western counties.

Selecting data to justify their interpretation and using inadequate quantitative techniques, they have exaggerated the demographic differences between eastern and western North Carolina, overstated the homogeneity of property holdings within the western counties, and virtually ignored variations within regions throughout the province. Consequently, these historians have been incapable of describing accurately the objective class characteristics of North Carolina.[3]

This essay will argue that *throughout* North Carolina an inequitable distribution of wealth and limited application of political democracy produced a wealthy and prestigious upper class that controlled political offices on the county and provincial levels. Second, it will contend that such economic mobility as existed did not deter North Carolinians, of all classes, from comprehending their social, economic, and political conditions in class terms. Finally, it will argue that the organizers of the most serious challenge to the rule of colonial authorities in eighteenth-century America prior to 1775, the Regulators in North Carolina, were, as children of their age, necessarily class conscious. They were, nevertheless, in the vanguard of those who radically challenged the prevailing conservative class ethos by rejecting the alleged benevolence of upper-class rule. In so doing they translated a class consciousness that stressed deference into one that stressed class conflict and the need for democratic reforms that would give farmers control over government and their own destinies. As all do in class struggles, the Regulators claimed that such class rule equaled the common weal.

To demonstrate these assertions, we will analyze primarily quantifiable data to discuss North Carolina during the 1760s and 1770s in terms of its economy and demography, its wealth distribution, its mobility patterns, its political power makeup, and the class differences between the Regulators and their opponents. We will then analyze the Regulation in North Carolina essentially along class lines.

Economy and Demography
An analysis of white and black populations (not taxables) in North Carolina around 1767 demonstrates that contrasting the coastal and piedmont areas alone overlooks important variations within the east and within the west as well as similar trends in the two regions.[4] The economy and demography of the Lower Cape Fear region in the southeast (New Hanover and Brunswick counties), for example, were unlike those in the rest of the colony with the limited exception of the Upper Cape Fear (Bladen County). Adequate transportation facilities and capital accumulation in the Lower Cape Fear resulted in a large slave population concentrated in the hands of a relatively large number of wealthy landowners who primarily produced naval stores and lumber for export. Sixty-two percent of the population in the region was black, representing 12 percent of the province's black population. The region's white population, however, comprised only 2 percent of the colony's white population (see Table 1).

Elsewhere, the highest concentration of blacks was in the tobacco, lumber, and commodities-producing Albemarle Sound region (the seven northeastern coastal counties). Here blacks comprised 35 percent of the population. This area had relatively few large slaveholdings, a condition true throughout North Carolina except in the Lower and Upper Cape Fear regions. Thus, the range (the difference between the number of slaves

Table 1. Regional Slave Ownership and Distribution Patterns in North Carolina, Circa 1767

Region and Sample Counties for each Region and Year	Percent of Households with Slaves; x̄ Slaves per Household; x̄ Slaves in Slaveowning Households	Total Households (percent)			Slaveholding Households (percent)			Slave Distribution per Household (percent)			Range
		5 or More Slaves[1]	10 or More Slaves[2]	20 or More Slaves[3]	5 or More Slaves	10 or More Slaves	20 or More Slaves	5 or More Slaves	10 or More Slaves	20 or More Slaves	
Albemarle Sound counties: Bertie, 1768; Pasquotank, 1769	37.8% 2.461 6.502	16.5	7.8	1.4	43.7	20.8	3.8	77.1	54.1	21.1	87
Neuse-Pamlico Coastal region: Beaufort, 1764; Onslow, 1771	36.7% 2.304 6.286	15.1	7.5	1.6	41.0	20.4	4.1	74.7	54.0	22.1	91
Lower Cape Fear region: Brunswick, 1769; New Hanover, 1767	49.9% 9.575 19.184	31.3	24.7	11.8	62.7	49.4	23.6	94.6	90.2	72.9	242
Upper Cape Fear region (Inner-Outer Plain region): Bladen, 1763	35.1% 3.232 9.202	16.4	9.0	3.6	46.7	25.5	10.2	83.8	69.1	47.5	93

Central Inner Plain counties: Pitt, 1764	27.0%	1.499	5.549	11.1	2.9	0.6	41.1	14.9	2.1	72.0	41.1	9.7	27
Northern Inner Plain-Piedmont region: Granville, 1769	36.3%	2.421	6.672	16.5	8.7	1.5	45.5	24.0	4.1	77.9	56.6	18.2	51
Western counties: Anson County, 1763	11.4%	0.474	4.161	1.8	0.7	0.0	16.1	6.5	0.0	51.5	25.0	0.0	17

Notes and Sources: During the Regulator period, Randolph and Caldwell counties were part of Orange County, and Montgomery County was part of Anson County. We converted the slave taxable totals found in the following sources to slave population estimates by using a multiplier of 1.89. State Archives: County Records, Bertie County, Taxables, 1765–71; Secretary of State, Tax Lists, 1720–1839; Legislative Papers, Tax Lists, 1771–74. The differences between mean slaveholdings in the counties in Tables 1 and 7 are explained by refinements that were appropriate for Table 7 but not for Table 1.

[1]Three or more slave taxables.
[2]Five or more slave taxables.
[3]Eleven or more slave taxables.

owned by the largest slaveowner and zero) of slaveownership in the Albemarle was eighty-seven, and the percentage of slaves living in the households with twenty or more slaves was 21.1 percent; comparable figures for the Lower Cape Fear were 242 and 72.9 percent, and for the Upper Cape Fear 93 and 47.5 percent.

The slaveholding patterns of the Cape Fear region contrast most strongly with those of the western counties of Orange, Rowan, Anson, Mecklenburg, and Tryon. This is piedmont country, generally five hundred to one thousand feet above sea level, rising gradually westward; swift-flowing rivers, unsuitable for navigation, necessitated dependence upon overland wagon routes for inland transportation.[5] Western counties grew rapidly from their political organization in the 1750s through the Regulator period. The taxable population grew from about 2,000 in 1754 to approximately 10,500 in 1767. During these years the black population grew even more rapidly, from about 50 to 730 in Orange County, for example.[6] Towns also developed during this period. In Orange, Childsburg was established in 1759 (it became Hillsboro in 1766), and Salisbury was formed in Rowan about 1755. By 1760 the towns were commercially viable. Stores preceded towns, but multiplied as towns developed.[7]

Equally as important as the late settlement of this region and its rapid population growth, therefore, was early establishment of stores to handle the marketing, supply, and credit needs of the backcountry. Along with commerce came a political and a juridical development that resulted in a rapid movement of lawyers into the area.

Despite this development, in the sample western county of Anson in 1763 slaveholdings averaged less than .5 among all households. Only 11.4 percent of all households owned slaves, and those households held an average of slightly more than four slaves. By comparison, in the Lower Cape Fear, slaveholdings averaged 9.6, 50 percent of the households owned slaves, and the average number of slaves among slaveholding households was nineteen (see Table 1).

Wealth Distribution
To determine wealth distribution in North Carolina during the
years 1762–72 we analyzed the estate records of two sample
counties: Orange County, in the west, and Bertie County, in the
east[8] (see Tables 2A and 2B). In Orange County the lower 30
percent of the free population owned 6 percent, the middle 30
percent owned 15 percent, the upper 30 percent owned 36
percent, and the wealthiest 10 percent owned 43 percent of the
wealth (see Table 2A). This distribution reflected the early, if
incomplete, development of commercial farming in the region.

Table 2A. Distribution of Wealth in Orange County, 1762–1772, as Measured
by Inventories[1]

Percentile	N	Total Inventories	x̄	Percent of Total Wealth
Lower 30%	36.3	£1,297	£35:14	6
Middle 30%	36.3	£3,352	£92:7	15
Top 30%	36.3	£7,826	£215:12	36
Top 10%	12.1	£9,388	£775:18	43
Totals	121.	£21,865	£180:14	100
Top 1%	1.21	£2,407	£1,989:5	9

Table 2B. Distribution of Wealth in Bertie County, 1762–1772, as Measured
by Inventories[2]

Percentile	N	Total Inventories	x̄	Percent of Total Wealth
Lower 30%	17.1	£426	£24:18	1.7
Middle 30%	17.1	£1,967	£115:0	7.9
Top 30%	17.1	£7,837	£458:6	31.6
Top 10%	5.7	£14,592	£2,560:0	58.8
Totals	57.	£24,822	£435:9	100
Top 1%	.57	£3,112	£5,459:13	12.5

[1]See State Archives: Orange County Estates, 1758–85 (this is a bound volume of estate
records).
[2]State Archives: Secretary of State's Records, North Carolina Wills, 1763–89, vols. 10, 15;
County Records, Bertie County, Estates Papers.

Although wealth distribution in the western counties was inequitable when compared with many colonial farming communities, it was not as inequitable as in the more economically mature eastern counties of North Carolina. This is illustrated by comparing the distribution in Orange County (Table 2A) with that in Bertie County (Table 2B) where the free poor were poorer, the rich were richer, and the distribution of wealth was more inequitable. The mean inventoried wealth (personalty including slaves) of the lower 30 percent of the population per household head was £35:14 in Orange County, compared with £24:18 in Bertie, while that of the top 10 percent and 1 percent were £775:18 and £1989:5 for Orange County and £2560 and £5459:13 for Bertie. And in Bertie County the lower 30 percent of the free population owned 1.7 percent, the middle 30 percent owned 7.9 percent, the upper 30 percent owned 31.6 percent, while the wealthiest 10 percent owned 58.8 percent of the wealth.

Mobility Patterns

Here, in an econometric analysis of mobility, we present and test a quantitative model of economic mobility among taxable households. This was done by using extant tax lists for the period 1748–72 to gauge the economic status of a household as defined by the number of slaves (aged twelve years and over) that it owned. Mobility is measured by changes in the *relative* number of slaves owned.

This analysis has two principal steps. The first simply measures the extent of mobility for selected counties and periods in colonial North Carolina. This was done by correlating, for each household that could be identified in two successive periods, the number of slaves shown on the tax lists in the two periods. The second step consists of a set of multiple-regression equations designed to provide a statistical explanation of the observed variation, among counties and periods, in the degree of economic mobility. Both steps are based on the previously described

data for six counties, covering various periods falling within the 1748–69 interval, providing a total of nine unduplicated data sets.
The results of the first phase of the analysis are shown in Table 3. The more closely the correlation coefficient approaches +1.0, the smaller the measured economic mobility in the sample population: a perfect correlation would mean that the relative status of a household, as gauged by its slaveholding at one point in time, would provide a totally accurate prediction of its relative status at a subsequent point in time, which is another way of describing a situation of zero mobility. Conversely, an r value of zero would reflect a situation of total fluidity, the theoretical maximum of mobility, in which relative status is completely unrelated between two points in time. As expected, the actual

Table 3. Correlation Analysis of Mobility[1]

			Households in Sample	Correlation Coefficients		
Rank (by r)	County	Period		r	Lower Limit[2]	Upper Limit[2]
1	New Hanover	1755–62	115	.91	.88	.93
2	New Hanover-Brunswick	1762–67 (69)	145	.89	.86	.92
3	Bertie	1751–63	133	.80	.74	.85
4	Beaufort-Pitt	1755–64	172	.66	.58	.73
5	Pasquotank	1748–54	89	.53	.39	.65
6	Bertie	1763–68	223	.50	.41	.55
7	Pasquotank	1754–69	95	.47	.32	.59
8	Granville	1755–69	101	.38	.20	.49
9	Cumberland	1755–67	74	.23	.04	.44

[1]The following records were used to develop Tables 3–6. State Archives: Colonial Court Records, Taxes and Accounts, 1679–54; County Records, Bertie County Taxables, 1755–64, 1765–71; Treasurer's and Comptroller's Papers—County Settlements with the State; Secretary of State Tax Lists, 1720–1839.
[2]Refers to upper and lower limits of r at the 10 percent level of probability.

measurements yielded by the present study fall between these
hypothetical extreme values.

In Table 3, the data sets—counties and time periods—are
ranked in (descending) order of the correlation coefficient, from
the least to the greatest in social mobility. In addition, confidence
intervals at the 10 percent level of probability are shown for each
observed value of r, which may be used to adjust the comparisons of the data sets for the probable influence of statistical error.
The table shows that mobility varied significantly among counties (but not, in the main, over time periods). If the confidence
intervals are used as an approximate means of identifying
categories, the highest degree of immobility seems to occur in the
New Hanover-Brunswick area (in both time periods) and Bertie
County (to a lesser extent and only in the earlier comparison).
The remaining counties and time periods comprise a virtually
continuous set, but with a considerable and highly significant
range between the relative immobility in Beaufort-Pitt and the
high mobility in Cumberland.

Unfortunately, it was not possible to construct adequate
data sets for a true western county. Given supportive findings,
however, we presume that western mobility patterns were much
like those in neighboring Cumberland, a county with similar
slaveholding characteristics.

Having found substantial mobility differentials, the next
step is to attempt a statistical explanation of these differentials,
to identify the underlying determinants, and to measure their
separate effects. For this purpose, multiple-regression methods
are used, in which the dependent variable is the correlation
coefficient for each of the nine data sets. The regression equations, their rationale, and the results of their application to the
empirical data all are described in a technical footnote to Table 5.
The main conclusions based on this analysis are summarized
immediately below.

The regression analysis reveals that mobility differentials
among counties and time periods may be explained with re-

Table 4. Means and Standard Deviations of
          Regression Variables

Variable[1]	Mean	Standard Deviation
I	.60	.23
$T_1 - T_0$	9.56	3.78
N_0/U_0	.28	.10
S_0	1.74	2.02
S_1/S_0	1.78	.70
σ_0/S_0	2.23	.38
U_1/U_0	1.44	.59

[1]Variables defined in Technical Note to Table 5.

ference to three statistically significant determining factors.
Taken together, these three factors explain, in the statistical
sense, four-fifths of the observed variance in mobility. The
factors are shown to operate in the initially hypothesized
directions and are approximately equal in the magnitude of their
separate effects. The three identified determinants are as follows:

a. *The greater the average number of slaves owned per household
at the start of each time period, the smaller the amount of mobility*. A
high average level of ownership may be taken to represent a
socioeconomic structure in which the barriers to upward changes
in status have become more formidable.

b. *The more unequal the distribution of slaveholding at the start
of the periods studied, the smaller the degree of mobility observed in the
subsequent period*. Inequality appears, therefore, to have a self-
perpetuating tendency, intensifying the difficulties of movement
up the economic scale and, perhaps, acting to buttress the
positions of those already at the upper levels.

c. *The higher the rates of population growth (as gauged by rates
of change in the total number of taxable households), the more mobility
shown*. It is reasonable to expect population growth, insofar as it
reflects net immigration, to be conducive to greater economic
mobility.

Table 5. Regression Results (Dependent Variable is I)[1]

	Equation 1[2]	Equation 2
Constant	−.135	−.124
T_1-T_0	.002[3] (.16) [.04]	
N_0/U_0	−.850[3] (−1.05) [−.35]	
S_0	.138 (4.85) [1.19]	.117 (5.64) [1.01]
S_1/S_0	−.107[3] (−1.83) [−.32]	
σ_0/S_0	.636 (4.06) [1.02]	.494 (2.96) [.79]
U_1/U_0	−.360 (−3.60) [−.91]	−.405 (−4.11) [−1.02]
$\bar{R}^2$	.88	.82
(F)	(10.60)	(13.42)

Note: $\bar{R}^2$ adjusted to two degrees of freedom in equation 1 and to five degrees of freedom in equation 2.

[1]Variables defined in Technical Note below.
[2]Regression coefficients shown in first row, t-ratios in second row (in parentheses) and beta weights in third row [in brackets].
[3]Denotes a coefficient not significant at the 10 percent level of probability (based on a two-tailed t-test).

Technical Note: Multiple Regression Anaylsis
The initial estimating equation is shown below:

$$I = a_0 + a_1(T_1 - T_0) + a_2 N_0/U_0 + a_3 S_0 + a_4 S_1/S_0 + a_5 \sigma_0/S_0 + a_6 U_1/U_0 + \mu$$

where, for each county and period,

I = correlation coefficient for household slaveholding in successive periods.

$T_1 - T_0$ = time difference, in years, between beginning and end of period.

N_0/U_0 = number of households in mobility sample at beginning of period divided by number of households in universe.

S_0 = mean slaveholding per sample household at beginning of period.

S_1/S_0 = mean slaveholding per sample household at end of period, divided by corresponding mean at beginning of period.

σ_0/S_0 = coefficient of variation at beginning of period, that is, standard deviation of slaveholding per household divided by sample mean.

U_1/U_0 = number of households in universe at end of period, divided by number at start of period.

μ = statistical error term.

$a_1, a_4, a_6 < 0$
$a_3, a_5 > 0$

Briefly stated, the underlying rationale of the foregoing equation is, first, that immobility (directly measured by I), will be greater wherever the initial level of slaveholding is high and the holdings are relatively unequal (that is, the coefficient of variation is large), both indicative of barriers to changes in status; and, second, that immobility will be smaller wherever the time period covered by the data is relatively long, where a relatively large increase occurs in the average household's ownership of slaves, and where growth in the total number of households is comparatively rapid, suggesting fluidity in the social structure. The N_0/U_0 term is included to test for the effect of sample size; its sign is not hypothesized, a priori. Means and standard deviations of all regression variables are shown in Table 4.

The regression results appear in Table 5. It is evident, from equation 1, that the length of the time period, the relative size of the sample, and the change in average slaveholding per household all lack statistical significance (although the last variable is somewhat marginal in this respect). However, mean slaveholding per household in the base period, the coefficient of variation, and the relative change in the universe population of households emerge as highly significant determinants and operate in the directions initially hypothesized.

In equation 2, the insignificant variables have been omitted, without materially affecting the coefficients of the retained variables, all of which are significant at the 5 percent level, with five degrees of freedom. (The effect of increasing the degrees of freedom raises the significance level of $\bar{R}^2$ from 10 percent in the first equation to 1 percent in the second.) The beta weights shown in the third row of entries for each variable provide a simple means of gauging the relative importance of each of the separate determinants of mobility. Assuming that causation operates as hypothesized, they indicate that an increase of one standard deviation in each variable has the following separate effects on the amount of measured immobility: S_0 and σ_0/S_0 cause increases of 1.10 and .79 standard deviations, respectively, and U_1/U_0 results in a decrease of 1.02 standard deviations. Thus, it may be concluded from the present analysis that a high average level of slaveholding and inequality in the distribution of slaves acted as major, positive forces on economic immobility (in the times and places studied) and that these forces were partially offset by population growth.

Thus, the western counties, where the Regulation occurred, almost certainly experienced high economic mobility
rates during the 1760s and 1770s. If they followed Cumberland's
pattern, this mobility essentially involved a large number of
slight fluctuations (upward or downward) in wealth. As seen in
Table 6, with a sample of seventy-four household heads for each
year, 1755 and 1767, in Cumberland County, the status of
thirty-nine remained the same (as measured by slaveholdings),
while the status of thirty-five changed—twenty-seven upward
and eight downward. Of the thirty-five whose status changed,
seventeen household heads acquired one or two slave taxables
and seven lost one or two slave taxables (one to three or four

Table 6. Frequency Distribution of Cumberland County's Changes in Slave
Ownership, 1755–1763, as Stated in Slave Taxables[1]

Change in Number of Slave Taxables Owned	Upward	Downward	Total
0	—	—	39
1	12	4	16
2	5	3	8
3	2	1	3
4	5	0	5
5	0	0	0
6	1	0	1
7	2	0	2

[1]Column one indicates the extent of the change in the number of taxables owned per
household within the time period, 1755–63. Column two indicates the number of
households that experienced gains in slaveholding. Thus, column one conjoined with
column two tells us, for instance, that twelve households had one more slave taxable in
1763 than in 1755. Column three indicates the number of households that experienced
losses in slaveholding. Column four indicates the total mobility in each category. Thus,
thirty-nine households had the same number of slaves in 1763 as in 1755, sixteen
households experienced a gain or loss of one slave taxable during this period, and so on.

It is of further interest to note that of the thirty-nine households that had zero mobility
during these years, thirty-six owned no slaves, two owned one slave taxable, and one owned
two slave taxables. The largest slaveholders owned seven slave taxables in 1755 (one) and
seven in 1767 (two). Seven slave taxables on the average signified the ownership of about
thirteen slaves.

slaves). The rest, eleven family heads, fluctuated between gaining and losing three to seven slave taxables (five to thirteen slaves), with only three having gains or losses of five or more slave taxables.

In the counties farther west where the Regulation occurred, there were probably even greater property fluctuations among the masses than in Cumberland County, but the size of individual changes undoubtedly was smaller. Thus, while small economic gains or losses were frequent, dramatic gains or losses were not. Or, stated differently, while economic mobility was great in the west, class mobility rarely occurred. The evidence of lack of mobility *among classes* in no way contradicts the earlier finding of relatively large mobility which pertains essentially to *intraclass* movement. This being the case, it is most unlikely that mobility patterns could have significantly lessened the deep feelings of class consciousness that were part of the ethos of the period and the consciousness of the mass of the people.

Political Power Arrangements
In Tables 7A–D through 9A–D, we measured the relationship between three different forms of wealth and officeholding for seven counties in three regions: the western counties of Anson, Orange, and Rowan (where the Regulation was centered), the northeastern (Albemarle) counties of Bertie and Pasquotank, and the southeastern (Lower Cape Fear) counties of New Hanover and Brunswick.

Using slaveholdings as recorded in tax lists as one gauge, we can see in Table 7A–D that the officers in all sections were the leading slaveholders. If we include all officers in the analysis, the statistical picture resembles that of the leading 10 percent of the slaveholding heads of households of each county. Thus, for example, in Anson County the mean slaveholding among household heads in 1763 was 0.61; the average holding among the top 10 percent of the slaveholders was 4.62 and among the officers 3.64. In Pasquotank County in 1769 the mean slavehold-

Table 7A. Wealth of Anson County Officers Compared with County Totals and Those of Top 10 Percent of County Household Heads as Measured by Slaveholdings in 1763[1]

Group or County	N	Total Number of Slaves	$\bar{x}$
Anson County	291	177	0.61
Top 10% of county household heads	29	134	4.62
Anson County Officers	11	40	3.64

Table 7B. Wealth of Bertie County Officers Compared with County Totals and Those of Top 10 Percent of County Household Heads as Measured by Slaveholdings in 1768[2]

Group or County	N	Total Number of Slaves	$\bar{x}$
Bertie County	595	1,898	3.19
Top 10% of county household heads	59.5	1,125	18.9
Bertie County officers	36	587	16.31
Leading Bertie County officers[3]	11	304	27.64

Table 7C. Wealth of Pasquotank County Officers Compared with County Totals and Those of Top 10 Percent of County Household Heads as Measured by Slaveholdings in 1769[4]

Group or County	N	Total Number of Slaves	$\bar{x}$
Pasquotank County	769	1,453	1.89
Top 10% of county household heads	76.9	877	11.4
Pasquotank County officers	36	370	10.28
Leading Pasquotank County officers	14	108	18

Table 7D. Wealth of Cape Fear Counties' (New Hanover and Brunswick) Officers
Compared with Region's Totals and Those of Top 10 Percent of Region's
Household Heads as Measured by Slaveholdings in 1767–1769[5]

Group or County	N	Total Number of Slaves	$\bar{x}$
Cape Fear	527	5,038	9.56
Top 10% of county household heads	52.7	3,455	65.56
Cape Fear officers	64	3,343	52.23
Leading Cape Fear officers	19	1,332	70.11

[1]Officers' names for Anson County during the Regulator period were obtained from State Archives: Anson County, Minute Docket County Court, July 1771–July 1777; Minutes, County Court of Pleas and Quarter Sessions, 1771–77; Governor's Office, Lists of Taxables, Militia, and Magistrates, 1754–70, Undated; Governor's Office, Council Papers, 1761–79; Military Collection, Troop Returns (1747–1859), Militia and Continental Returns, 1770–78. In addition see Clark, ed., *State Records*, 22:381–82; Saunders, ed., *Colonial Records*, 4:889, 951; 6:799. For 1763 slaveholdings see State Archives, Secretary of State Tax Lists, 1720–1839.

[2]Officers' names for Bertie County during the Regulator period were obtained from State Archives: Governor's Office, Lists of Taxables, Militia, and Magistrates, 1754–70; County Court Minutes, Bertie, 1758–69, 1767–72; Council Papers, 1761–79; also see Saunders, ed., *Colonial Records*, 6:80, 636. For 1768 slaveholdings see State Archives, County Records, Bertie County, Taxables, 1765–71.

[3]Officers included all traceable assemblymen, militia officers (captain through colonel), clerks, registers, sheriffs, and justices of the peace. Leading officers were defined as the above except justices of the peace and militia captains.

[4]Officers' names for Pasquotank County during the Regulator period were obtained from State Achives: Governor's Office, Lists of Taxables, Militia, and Magistrates, 1754–70; Pasquotank County Court Minutes, 1737–85; Council Papers, 1761–79. Also see Saunders, ed., *Colonial Records*, 5:163, 320, 975–86; 6:122; Clark, ed., *State Records*, 22:306–99, 815, 831, 855–63. For 1769 slaveholdings see State Archives, Secretary of State, Tax Lists, 1720–1839.

[5]Officers' names for Cape Fear counties during the Regulator period were obtained from State Archives: Governor's Office, Lists of Taxables, Militia, and Magistrates, 1754–70; County Court Minutes, New Hanover, 1738–98; Council Papers, 1761–79. Also see Saunders, ed., *Colonial Records*, 5:822, 975–86, 991; 6:58–60, 209–15, 237, 335, 1008, 1070; 7:526–29, 698, 702; 9:298; Clark, ed., *State Records*, 22:306–500, passim. For 1767–69 slaveholdings see State Archives, Secretary of State, Tax Lists, 1720–1839.

Table 8A. Wealth of Orange County Officers Compared with County Totals and Those of Top 10 Percent of County Household Heads as Measured by Inventoried Wealth during the Years 1762–1772[1]

Group or County	N	Total Inventoried Wealth	$\bar{x}$
Orange County	121	£21,865	£ 180:14
Top 10% in county	12.1	£ 9,388	£ 775:18
County officers	2	£ 2,218	£1,109:5

Table 8B. Wealth of Bertie County Officers Compared with County Totals and Those of Top 10 Percent of County Household Heads as Measured by Inventoried Wealth during the Years 1762–1772[2]

Group or County	N	Total Inventoried Wealth	$\bar{x}$
Bertie County	57	£24,822	£435:10
Top 10% in county	5.7	£14,592	£2,560
County officers	4	£11,416	£2,854

[1]Officers' names for Orange County during the Regulator period were obtained from State Archives: Orange County Court Minutes, 1752–66; Governor's Office, Lists of Taxables, Militia, and Magistrates, 1754–70, Undated; Governor's Office, Council Papers, 1761–79; Hillsboro District Minute Docket, 1768–88, Part I. In addition see Saunders, ed., *Colonial Records*, 5:320, 365, 835; 6:340, 573, 798, 1016; 7:91, 821, 827, 832, 833, 863–64, 888; 8:574-600, 659–77. Leading Orange County officers included only assemblymen, sheriffs, clerks, registers, and militia colonels, lieutenant colonels, majors, and adjutants. All other citations of officers in this table included the above leading officers plus justices of the peace and militia captains. For inventories see State Archives, Orange County Estates, 1758–85 (this is a bound volume of estate records).
[2]See n. 1, Table 2B and n.2, Table 7B.

ing among household heads was 1.89; the average holding among the top 10 percent of the slaveholders was 11.4 and among officers 10.28. If we exclude justices of the peace and militia captains from the officers' list, the remaining leading officers in each county were men whose holdings averaged substantially higher than the mean holding for the top 10 percent of slaveholders. In Pasquotank, for instance, such officers' mean holding was 18.

Use of inventoried wealth for the years 1762–72 as the gauge reveals a similar story in Orange and Bertie counties. In Table 8A–B, we can see that Orange County's mean wealth in personalty was £180:14; the wealthiest 10 percent averaged £775:18, and officers averaged £1109:5. Comparable figures for Bertie County were £435:10 (average for the county), £2560 (average for the wealthiest 10 percent), and £2854 (average for the county's officers). The fact that officer affluence is even greater when inventoried wealth is measured than when only slaveholdings are considered probably indicates the importance of nonagricultural wealth among the officers.

To measure the total wealth (personalty and realty) of the officeholders, we used tax lists compiled eight to eleven years after the period in question. The historian working with quantitative data often does not have the luxury of choice: the 1779 to 1782 tax lists are the best complete records available to evaluate the total wealth of the western county officials. Use of records from a later period exaggerates the wealth of the officials. For our purposes, however, the resulting bias is not important, and the findings complement those just discussed. In Montgomery County (formed from Anson County) the wealth of the officers averaged slightly higher than the wealthiest 10 percent of the county (Table 9A), while in counties formed largely from Orange County, the officers' wealth averaged about twice that of the wealthiest 10 percent of the population (Table 9B). Similarly, in Rowan and Brunswick officers' wealth averaged about twice that of the wealthiest 10 percent of the population (Table 9C–D).

Class Differences between the Regulators and Their Opponents
Statistical evidence also supports the Regulators' class descriptions of themselves and their antagonists. To demonstrate this, we traced on available tax lists the names of all known Regulators and anti-Regulators. Thus, using slaveownership in 1763 as the gauge of wealth, Table 10 shows that in Anson County a slightly smaller percentage of the Regulators owned slaves than was the

Table 9A. Wealth of Anson County Officers Compared with County Totals and
Those of Top 10 Percent of Taxables as Measured by Slaveholdings
and Total Assessments in Montgomery County in 1782[1]

Group or County	N	Total Number of Slaves and $\bar{x}$	Total Assessed Wealth and $\bar{x}$
Montgomery County	455	474; $\bar{x}$ = 1.04	£62,254; $\bar{x}$ = £136:16
Top 10% of Montgomery County taxables	45.5	377.8; $\bar{x}$ = 8.3	£32,328; $\bar{x}$ = £712
Anson County officers	5	33; $\bar{x}$ = 6.6	£ 2,980; $\bar{x}$ = £745

Table 9B. Wealth of Orange County Officers Compared with County Totals and
Those of Top 10 Percent of Taxables as Measured by Total Assessments
in Orange County (1779), Randolph County (1779), and Caswell
County, (1780)[2]

Group or County	N	Total Assesed Wealth	$\bar{x}$
Orange, Randolph, & Caswell Counties	2,607	£4,038,856	£ 1,549:5
Top 10% of counties' taxables	261	£2,038,451	£ 7,810:3
Orange County officers	27	£ 336,952	£13,395:13
Leading Orange County officers	7	£ 109,352	£15,621:14

Table 9C. Wealth of Rowan County Officers Compared with County Totals and
Those of Top 10 Percent of Taxables as Measured by Total Assessments
in Rowan County in 1778[3]

Group or County	N	Total Assessed Wealth	$\bar{x}$
Rowan County	2,254	£1,271,200	£ 564:20
Top 10% of county's taxables	225.4	£ 645,388	£2,863:6
Rowan County officers	25	£ 124,291	£4,971:13

Table 9D. Wealth of Brunswick County Offiicers Compared with County Totals
         and Those of Top 10 Percent of Taxables as Measured by Total
         Assessments in Brunswick County in 1782[4]

Group or County	N	Total Assessed Wealth	$\bar{x}$
Brunswick County	145	£78,939:16	£ 544:8
Top 10% of county's taxables	14.5	£60,542:10	£4,175:7
Brunswick County officers	3	£25,595	£8,531:13

[1]See n. 1, Table 8A. For assessed wealth in 1782 see Legislative Papers, Tax Lists.
[2]See n. 1, Table 8A. For 1779 and 1780 wealth totals see State Archives: Legislative Papers, Tax Lists; Secretary of State, Tax Lists, 1720–1839.
[3]Officers' names for Rowan County during the Regulator period were obtained from State Archives: Governor's Office, Lists of Taxables, Militia, and Magistrates, 1754–70; Governor's Office, Committee of Claims Reports, 1760–64; Council Papers, 1761–79; Rowan County Court Minutes, 1753–72. For assessed wealth in 1778 see State Archives, County Records, Rowan County, Tax Lists, 1758–1819.
[4]See n. 4, Table 7D. For assessed wealth of Brunswick County officers see State Archives, Legislative Papers, Tax Lists.

case in the county at large and that the mean number of slaves held by the Regulators was also slightly less than that of the county. On the other hand, somewhat over 69 percent of Regulator antagonists owned slaves, in comparison with about 17 percent of the county's householders, and the mean number of slaves they held was six times larger than the average in the county.

The findings are similar when we investigate the total wealth of the Regulators and their opponents (Table 11). Tax lists compiled eight to eleven years after the Regulation are the best and earliest data available to compare the total wealth of Regulators and known anti-Regulators. Such data very likely exaggerate the wealth of both groups, with the greatest exaggeration among the Regulators. Thus, use of these later tax lists results in a conservative bias (an overestimate) in measuring Regulator

Table 10.   Slaveholdings of Regulators Compared with Those of Anti-Regulators and the Entire County's Population Anson County, 1763[1]

Group or County	Total Number of Slaves Owned Within Group or County	N and Number of Households in Group or County That Owned Slaves	Percent of Households in Group or County That Owned Slaves	$\bar{x}$ Slaveholding in County or Group	Group's Percentage of County's Population	Group's Percentage of County's Slaves	Proportion between Slaveholdings and Population
Anson County	177	291 49	16.84	0.61	100	100	1
Regulators in Anson County[2]	36	62 9	14.52	0.58	21.31	20.34	0.95
Anti-Regulators in Anson County[3]	49	13 9	69.23	3.77	4.47	27.68	6.19

[1]State Archives: Secretary of State, Tax Lists, 1720–1839.
[2]Three hundred and twenty Regulators were uncovered for Anson County and traced in the 1763 Anson County tax list. To obtain these names, we used all available Regulator petitions, advertisements, court records, pamphlets, letters, and statements along with comments of other contemporaries. Identical techniques were used to uncover Regulator names for other counties.
[3]Forty-two anti-Regulators were uncovered for Anson County and traced in the 1763 Anson County tax list. Documents similar to those used to identify the Regulators, but also including official correspondence among officers, were used to obtain the names of the anti-Regulators for Anson County as well as the other counties.

wealth. The tendency to exaggerate the wealth of both groups was caused additionally by the records used to compile the lists of Regulators and their opponents. This once again resulted in an acceptable conservative bias in measuring Regulator wealth. On the other hand, poorer westerners who opposed the Regulators have not been traced. We know they were there; the number of western militiamen who mustered against the Regulators in 1768 and 1771 is proof even though the vast majority of the poorer folk in Anson, Orange, and Rowan counties supported or joined the Regulators. A consequence of not identifying the poorer anti-Regulators is that our analyses demonstrate only the affluence of the most outspoken and influential anti-Regulators. Nevertheless, almost all wealthy westerners have been identified as being opposed to the Regulators, although many of them could not be traced on the available tax lists. Thus, the emphasis on the wealth of the opponents of the Regulators is not seriously questioned by the limits of our data. The data in Table 11 from both counties suggest that the Regulators were poorer than average while their antagonists were relatively affluent. This is strikingly illustrated in Orange County where the traceable anti-Regulators comprised most of the wealthiest 1 percent of the population.

Other evidence supports the Regulators' understanding of the class differences between themselves and their adversaries. A partial check of land records, for example, helps to establish that Regulators were landowners, squatters, tenants, or dependents of various kinds.[9] Very few were affluent. On the other hand, of the twelve merchants (eight of whom also held important offices) operating in Orange County whose affiliations can be traced, all were antagonists of the Regulators. Similarly, of the twelve persons who have been identified as Orange County sheriffs, clerks, registers, coroners, and Hillsboro commissioners during the period, none became Regulators. Of the twelve attorneys who practiced law in Orange County whose affiliations can be traced, all opposed the Regulation. Of the

Table 11. Total Wealth of Regulators in Select Western Counties Compared with Anti-Regulators and Population of County

Group or County; Years of Survey	N	Assessed Wealth (£) for Groups or Counties			Group's Percentage of County Totals		Proportion between Wealth and Population
		Total	Mean	Range	Population	Assessed Wealth (£)	
Orange (1779), Randolph (1779), & Caldwell (1780) counties combined	2,607	4,038,856	1,549:4	21–70,431	100	100	1
Regulators in these counties	146	180,105	1,233:12	100–17,038	5.60	4.45	0.79
Anti-Regulators in these counties	47	460,733	9,802:16	100–70,431	1.80	11.41	6.34
Montgomery County (1782)	455	62,254	136:16	1–1,975	100	100	1
Regulators in Montgomery County	35	2,715	77:12	4–280	7.69	4.36	0.57
Anti-Regulators in Montgomery County	7	2,759	394:2	17–1,187	1.54	4.44	2.89

Notes and Sources: Four hundred and forty-five Regulators were uncovered for Orange County, 19 for Rowan County, and 67 who resided in one of the three counties, for a total of 851. An additional 72 names that were not used were gathered from Granville County and Halifax County petitions concerning problems similar to those that bothered the Regulators. The 851 names were checked off against each of four tax lists. One hundred and twenty-nine anti-Regulators were in Orange County, 61 in Rowan County, and 42 in Anson County, for a total of 232. They were treated in the same manner as were the Regulator names. For a published list of 883 Regulator names that Kay corrected in developing his own list, see Elmer D. Johnson, "The War of the Regulation," pp. 155–73. State Archives: Legislative Papers, Tax Lists; Secretary of State, Tax Lists, 1720–1839.

twenty-three militia officers serving between 1768 and 1771, none became Regulators, and of fifty-nine justices of the peace who served between 1766 and 1771 only three became Regulators. In Rowan County, sixty-two officers and ten lawyers were traced; only one, a justice of the peace, was a known Regulator.[10] Anson County, however, had a somewhat higher Regulator representation among militia officers (one captain and five junior officers out of thirty). This tendency was also true among Anson's civil officers: five out of twenty-six justices of the peace and one out of nine county court officers were Regulators. Almost all the known anti-Regulators, on the other hand, were officers either during or close to the Regulator period.

The exceptions to these generalizations should not be ignored. Some Regulators were affluent. Leaders or spokesmen, whether they ever formally joined the movement or not, such as Herman Husband of Orange County, Charles Robinson of Anson County, and Christopher Nation of Rowan County, were relatively well-to-do farmers. But the leaders of rebellions and revolutions frequently have been more affluent than the rank and file. And the presence of a handful of such men does not indicate that an important section of the western elite joined the western rebels; the elite of the west showed a remarkable unity in the face of the threat to their interests.

The quantitative evidence is suggestive concerning the allegiances of whites at the other end of the social structure—dependents, that is, propertyless sons of farmers, indentured servants, or apprentices. An analysis of the Anson County tax list of 1763 gives us conservative estimates concerning the number of Regulators and anti-Regulators who were dependents: they comprised 22.5 percent of the Regulators, while none has been found among the anti-Regulators. The number of dependents who were apprentices and servants is unclear. Certainly, they were no more than one-third of the total. More traditional sources buttress the view that servants were of minor importance among the Regulators; the Regulators never expressed servant grievances. Last, neither quantitative nor traditional evidence has revealed the participation of blacks, slave or free, in the uprising.

The Regulator movement, therefore, took place in counties in which the distribution of wealth was inequitable enough to enable a wealthy upper class to establish control over both elected and appointed offices. As we shall see, the class descriptions of the Regulators, their opponents, and the officials of the western counties outlined here correspond closely with how the Regulators viewed themselves and their enemies.

The North Carolina Regulation was an organized movement of white farmers that swept the three western counties of Orange, Anson, and Rowan from 1766 until 1771. By the last year, it was supported by six to seven thousand men out of a total white taxable population of about eight thousand.[11] As might be expected in a popular movement that lasted five years, the Regulation also attracted sympathetic but less organized backing in seven surrounding counties.[12] During this time span participants grew in awareness and broadened their program while adopting a variety of methods of protest: they used political pressure applied directly upon local officials, law suits, civil disobedience, limited acts of violence, petitions to the governor, council, and assembly, election campaigns, and finally a military confrontation at the Battle of the Alamance on 16 May 1771, in which a Regulator "army" was defeated in a two-hour battle by an army of loyal militia led by the royal governor.[13]

The Regulator movement was not, as it is usually described, a sectional struggle between western farmers and the aristocratic easterners who controlled provincial government. Rather, the Regulators were class-conscious white farmers in the west who attempted to democratize local government in their respective counties and to replace their wealthy and corrupt elected officials with farmer representatives who would serve the interests of the farmers and hence of the people. In time, they assailed the governor, and obliquely the eastern elite, but this was simply an acknowledgment that many problems were provincial in origin and, therefore, demanded provincial rather than local solutions. Thus the dissenting farmers eventually fought against their wealthy and powerful exploiters wherever they lived, east and west, but they never regarded the conflict as sectional in nature.

The class consciousness of the Regulators reflected both the existing maldistribution of wealth and power and the prevailing ideology of an age that openly asserted the necessity and benevolence of upper-class rule and demanded that "the people" defer to rule by their "betters."[14] The apostasy of the Regulators was to proscribe upper-class rule as malevolent and then to replace class deference with class conflict.

The Regulators were able to reject deferential behavioral patterns and attitudes in part because in the more recently settled western counties, where wealth was growing rapidly, the ruling class was neither as long established nor as wealthy as its counterpart in the east. Wealth was inequitably distributed in all sections of the province, but the range was narrowest in the west, and the area had the province's largest concentration of small-to-middling nonslaveholding farmers. When they felt themselves exploited, therefore, they had both the numbers and relative lack of inhibitions to protest vigorously.

The ethos of the age together with the bitter class antagonisms and refusal of Regulators to defer to the ruling class led them to describe themselves and their adversaries in class terms. They saw themselves as "farmers," as "planters" (a term with none of the later connotations associated with large plantation owners), as "poor Industrious peasants," as "poor people," as "oppressed" or "helpless" people or families, as "the wretched poor," and as productive, hard-working "labourers."[15]

Although they did not reject the accumulation of land, slaves, and liquid wealth, and normally owned, rented, or squatted on the land they worked, the Regulators saw no

inconsistency in calling themselves "labourers" and "poor peasants." As laborers they characterized themselves and their class
as the producers in society and all others as either economic
dependents or parasites. Use of the term "peasants" and the
emphasis upon "family" suggest both the Regulators' sense of
community, of which the family was an integral part, and the
permanence of their economic condition. Community and family, joined with deference, were important elements of the
conservative ideology of the period. In rejecting deference,
however, the Regulators were free to use their belief that they
comprised a community of laboring peasant families to develop a
radical attack upon the ruling class. And, during this transitional
period in Anglo-American history, when liberal capitalistic values were gaining acceptance, the Regulators' petty capitalistic-
acquisitive thrust, though in tension with the peasant values,
acted as a catalyst to deepen class tensions and further to
encourage their demands for democracy.

As a corollary of their view of themselves, Regulators saw
their western opponents (and by extension antagonists throughout the province) as expropriators of the fruits of "the people's"
labor—"rich and powerful," "designing" "Monsters in iniquity"
who (practicing "every Fraud, and . . . threats and menaces")
were parasitically "dependent in their Fortunes, with great
Expectations from others." Such men could be wealthy farmers
or in other occupations. More often, Regulators saw that most of
the wealth accumulated by the affluent in the western counties
stemmed from multiple economic pursuits: store owning, the
practice of law, land speculation, milling, tavernkeeping, and
moneylending, all in addition to or instead of farming. Consequently, although the Regulators attacked the rich in general,
they assailed in particular those they considered nonproductive,
especially merchants and lawyers. The Regulators, however,
never understood their enemies solely in economic terms. They
believed that the wealthy also controlled the political and legal
systems and used this control to aggrandize themselves further

at the expense of the poor farmers. Thus, much of the Regulators' attack was concentrated upon the affluent county officers.

Rhetoric often colors reality. But Regulator insistence on the interrelation of wealth and political power, as we have seen, coincided with reality. In North Carolina the royal governor and council appointed the affluent to local militia and civil posts. These men, in turn, ensured their continued appointment in part by their control over the executive, administrative, legislative, judicial, police, and military functions of each county. These same officials invariably were elected to the vestry and assembly as a consequence of the dexterous use of their wealth and appointive power, including effective control over the nominating and electoral processes and the peoples' habitual attitudes of deference. Elected officials, the Regulators argued, were those "whose highest Study is the Promotion of their wealth" and who consequently would allow "the Interest of the Public, when it comes in Competition with their private Advantages . . . to sink."[16]

Officials pursued public policies that added to private fortunes in many ways: by the awarding of public contracts to favorites; by locating and building bridges, harbors, ferries, and towns to satisfy the rich and powerful; by issuing licenses for mills to favorites; by ensuring that the public offices the wealthy controlled were remunerative; by granting compensation to masters for executed slaves; and by awarding exorbitant commissions to a favored few to handle the mechanics of currency emissions.[17]

Affluent officeholders also exploited more directly their poorer and weaker constituents. They collected unlawful taxes and fees and corruptly handled public monies. Such actions not only stole money from the people, but also further increased the tax levels that had remained high after the French and Indian War to pay off war debts and to finance growing peacetime public expenditures. The ruling provincial elite also early instituted a regressive tax system that consisted primarily of poll taxes, duties, fees, and work levies—all of which inequitably and harshly burdened the poor. The scarcity of currency, though not a deliberate policy of the elite, made even greater the burden of taxation on the poor, especially those in the west who were farthest from the centers of commerce.[18]

In addition, creditors, merchants, lawyers, and public officers brought an increasing number of court suits against indebted farmers while lawyers and officers charged exorbitant or extortionate court fees.[19] All of these groups cooperated in distraining excessive amounts of property from moneyless farmers and corruptly selling the property at public auctions below its value to members of the "in" group—with nothing returned to the victims. The wealthy and powerful were able to maintain these conditions both by passing and by manipulating the application of biased laws.[20] For example, small claims procedures would have been expensive even if court officers had acted honestly and with moderation, but statutes concerning fees were sufficiently vague to invite misconstruction and misconduct by officers and lawyers.[21]

These matters formed the substance of Regulator protest. Clearly, the Regulators' grievances were rooted in class, not sectional, differences and exploitation. This is why they did not challenge the disproportionately small number of western representatives in the assembly. In 1769, when the Regulators urged dividing western counties to create additional counties, their goal was not to gain parity in representation, but to decrease the size of counties in order to provide western farmers with readier access to public facilities.[22]

From the beginning, the Regulators proposed and fought for reforms calculated to replace upper-class control over the polity and economy with control by smaller farmers. The precursor of the Regulators in Orange County, the Sandy Creek Association, organized in the summer of 1766, proposed that constituents gain direct access to and control over county officers and elected representatives by giving instructions in regularly scheduled meetings. This proposal had far-reaching democratic ramifications, for if successful it would have challenged both upper-class notions of virtual representation and control over local and provincial government.

The Sandy Creek Association borrowed from the North Carolina Sons of Liberty's arguments against the Stamp Act. Adapting the Whig arguments to democratic ones, the association called for direct control by the people over local government to prevent, ironically, "Officers under" the Sons of Liberty from carrying on "unjust oppression in our own Province." All men were corruptible unless directly accountable to their constituencies.[23]

Throughout the Regulator movement, which formally began early in 1768 after the demise of the Sandy Creek Association, direct control was the basic means by which the Regulators hoped to replace corrupt upper-class rule with rule by the farmers. They also attempted to elect farmer representatives who not only would pass needed remedial legislation, but also would enable the Regulators to control better the appointed local officials. In the elections of 1769 and again in 1770, the Regulators in Orange, Rowan, and Anson counties collaborated in an effort to elect farmer legislators. They appealed primarily to class. One campaign document asserted that

a majority of our assembly is composed of Lawyers, Clerks, and others in Connection with them, while by our own Voice we have excluded the Planter.—Is it not evident their own private Interest is, designed in the whole Train of our Laws?—We have not the least Reason to expect the Good of the Farmer, and consequently of the Community, will be consulted, by those who hang on Favors, or depend on the Intricacies of the Laws.—What can be expected from those who have ever discovered a Want of good Principles, and whose highest Study is the Promotion of their wealth; and with whom the Interest of the Public, when it comes in Competition with their private Advantages, is suffered to sink?— nothing less than the Ruin of the Publick.[24]

The same appeal then called upon citizens "for once [to] assert your Liberty and maintain your Rights" and to resist all strategems (including plying them with liquor) by incumbents who, if elected again, would "draw from you the last Farthing."[25]

In the 1770 campaign that followed the dissolution of the 1769 assembly, Husband in his *Impartial Relation* urged the farmers to elect either farmers or those who would support farmers' needs. Especially to be shunned were the "clerk[s], lawyer[s], or Scotch merchant[s], or any sect who are connected with certain companies, callings and combinations, whose interests jar with the interest of the public good.—And when they come to solicit you with invitations to entertainments, etc., shun them as you would a pestilence.—Send a man who is the choice of the country, and not one who sets up himself, and is the choice of a party; whose interest clashes with the good of the publick."[26]

The Regulators' opponents were no less class-conscious. In supporting Edmund Fanning for the assembly, they stressed that his "considerable" property ostensibly ensured that the "interest of the public must be his interest." Those who questioned Fanning's "attachment to the welfare and interest of his constituents" were both "assassin[s] who . . . stab in the dark" and "persons courting the voice of popularity." This was a classic appeal to the masses to defer to their "betters" who, in turn, would act benevolently to promote the interests of all their constituents.[27]

One result of the October 1769 assembly elections was an abnormally high turnover: of the eighty-four men elected, thirty-eight had not served previously and displaced incumbents. This was a turnover of 45.24 percent as compared with the turnover in November 1766 of 26.61 percent. Very likely there was some relationship between the unusual turnover in 1769 and the Regulation, but exactly what must be explained.[28]

The invariable explanation that two Regulator spokesmen

(Herman Husband of Orange County and Christopher Nation of Rowan County) and some sympathizers were elected in 1769, but that there were some reversals in the 1770 election is inadequate. A more precise and meaningful statement can be made by analyzing changes in the class composition of the assembly by tracing fluctuations in the election of the two overlapping groups the Regulators abhorred most: economic (merchants, lawyers, placemen, and physicians) and political (clerks, registers, sheriffs, and coroners).

Such an analysis supports the hypothesis that the only significant change in the class character of assemblymen occurred where the Regulators were most active politically. In the 1776 election the Regulator counties (Orange, Rowan, and Anson plus neighboring Granville) returned four freshman assemblymen. Three of them were merchants, lawyers, or placemen, and three also held major county offices in addition to the office of justice of the peace. A dramatic change occurred in the 1769 elections. Only one of eight newly elected assemblymen was of the commercial elite, and only two held important county offices. Six of the eight incumbents who were defeated were of the commercial elite and five were important county officeholders. Some reversals occurred in the 1770 elections: one of the four freshmen was of the commercial elite, and two of the four were important officeholders.[29]

After their limited successes in the 1769 elections, the Regulators concentrated on sending petitions to their spokesmen in the assembly. Calling themselves "poor Inhabitants," "poor Petitioners," "poor Industrious peasant[s]," and "honest industrious familys," they proposed legislative remedies to old and new grievances. Anson County Regulators asked that the chief justice receive a salary instead of fees; Orange and Rowan Regulators jointly petitioned that all clerks be paid in the same way. Both groups urged an end to the collection of unlawful fees, but the Orange-Rowan petition also called upon the legislature to dismiss all clerks, to prohibit clerks and lawyers from serving in the assembly, and to freeze the fees of lawyers.[30]

To cut court costs further, Orange and Rowan advocated a small claims court with a single magistrate who would handle cases involving £6 or less with six-man juries if either litigant so requested. Anson suggested that all debts between 40s. and £10 be tried without lawyers by a six-man jury impaneled by a single magistrate whose judgment could not be appealed. In the context of such proposals the Regulators first formally proposed that large counties be divided because of the expense of traveling to court.

Orange and Rowan demanded that sheriffs be replaced as tax collectors, called for reforms in the clearing of accounts, and urged that the corrupt handling of public monies and the "mystery" of the sinking fund be investigated. Both petitions mentioned the currency shortage, and Anson County demanded that no further taxes be levied until a sufficient money supply was emitted and that currency be backed by land and not be "call'd in by a Tax." To enable westerners to pay their taxes in "the produce of the country," Anson proposed constructing inspection warehouses in the west. The Orange and Rowan Regulators requested a more inclusive law to make inspectors' notes for "imperishable commodities" legal tender for all payments throughout the province.

The petitions went beyond elaborating upon prior grievances. The Regulators perceived the inequitable nature of the tax system and argued that the poor in the province were disproportionately taxed. Since western farmers were "generally in mean circumstances," the Anson Regulators argued that they were particularly oppressed and urged that each person "pay in proportion to the profits arising from his Estate."

Orange and Rowan counties proposed the same reform, but for somewhat different reasons: "And may it please you to consider of and pass an Act to Tax everyone in proportion to his Estates; however equitable the law as it now stands, may appear to the inhabitants of the Maritime parts of the province, where estates consist chiefly in slaves; yet to us in the frontier, where very few are possessed of slaves, tho' their estates are in proportion (in many instances) as of one Thousand to one, for all to pay equal, is with submission, very grievious and oppressive."[31] While many historians read this as a protest against a tax system that favored the east, the Regulators actually were saying just the reverse. They admitted the possibility that easterners paid their share of taxes because a large portion of their wealth —their slaves—was taxed. But the petition protested that westerners who were rich in property other than slaves paid no more taxes than their poorer western neighbors. The petitioners attacked the poll tax and called for an equitable levy on all forms of wealth (although in so doing they underestimated or ignored the wealth of easterners in property other than slaves and the degree to which easterners were being subsidized by the province).[32]

Anson Regulators also, for the first time, raised the land-related grievances of pre-Regulator dissidents. They complained of court suits over delinquent quitrents, charging that the corrupt administration by the governor and council resulted in favorites engrossing the best lands. To relieve the squatters' fears, Anson proposed that the assembly pass a preemption law guaranteeing squatters with improved lands in the Granville District first choice in purchasing their farms when the land office reopened.[33]

The petitions not only asked for reforms to redress particular grievances but also outlined proposals to achieve more democratic elections, more open legislative procedures, and representatives who would serve the needs of the farming community. Orange and Rowan demanded that lawyers and clerks be prohibited from the house because, "intent on making their own fortunes [they] are blind to, & solely Regardless of their Country's Interest are ever planning such schemes or projecting such Laws, as may best Effect their wicked purposes, witness the Summons and Petition Act calculated purely to enrich themselves, and Creatures at the expense of the poor Industrious peasant."[34] Anson asked that the *viva voce* method of voting that was subject to pressures and abuses be replaced by voting by "Ticket and Ballot." Orange and Rowan called for recording the votes in the legislative journal with copies to be sent to each justice of the peace so that constituents might "have an Opportunity to Distinguish our friends, from our foes among you, and to act accordingly at any future choice."[35]

During the 1770 election campaign, Herman Husband raised still another significant new issue, arguing that people spent, on the average, fully one-twelfth of the year at militia musters or working on roads. Work levies were a highly inequitable method of taxation because the time the poor and wealthy had to work on the roads was not proportionately divided and because the poor could least afford and were most adversely affected by the loss of labor time. No specific reforms were recommended to alleviate these problems other than to suggest that the militia question might be made more tolerable if the officers were selected by the people.[36]

Husband also appealed for the abolition of a tax-supported church establishment, probably as much for fiscal as for religious reasons.[37] The only previous religious reform proposed by the Regulators was that members of all sects be allowed to marry "according to their respective Mode . . . after due publication or License," as urged in both 1769 petitions.[38]

While the Regulators united the vast majority of the inhabitants of Anson, Orange, and Rowan counties behind their demands for reforms to redress specific grievances and to ensure farmer control over the government, the elite, east and west, including the governor, were equally united in opposition. The Regulators constituted too great a challenge to the economic and political wealth and power of the provincial elite for incipient Whigs and Tories alike not to clasp hands with the governor to put down the rebellious farmers.[39]

In 1771, nevertheless, not all members of the provincial establishment supported Governor William Tryon's military solution. The Albemarle region refused to contribute either troops or money. Their leaders may have agreed with Samuel Johnston, wealthy Whig leader and author of the Riot Act, that severe application of the act would quell the uprisings without a military expedition. Other elite leaders berated the assembly and governor for passing ill-advised reform laws and for not suppressing the Regulators quickly enough. Whatever differences existed among the elite, all agreed they must end the uprising and punish its leaders, and those proposing military action to do this were in a position to achieve success.[40]

In conclusion, historians who argue that class consciousness and class conflict were denied in the colonies by the equitable distribution of wealth and social mobility, as compared with England, are merely prescribing shibboleths to replace hard analysis. The Regulation in North Carolina took place in counties where over 40 percent of the wealth was controlled by the upper 10 percent of society, where economic mobility was great but class mobility was slight, where class consciousness was a normal, preferred condition, and where class exploitation was great. The Regulation took place when and where it did because of past disturbances in the area, the exaggeration of certain traditional grievances resulting from commercial growth, a ruling class that was new and not firmly entrenched in a recently settled and fast-growing west, the end of the French threat, and sensitivities heightened by increasing revolutionary tensions. The movement grew among a numerous class of poor farmers who saw nothing wrong in either using the term "peasants" or in asserting that they were farmers and laborers. Their class consciousness was a sign of their times; their class conflict was a manifestation of their particular situation and opportunities. They proposed democratic reforms to implement class rule. And their legacy has been lost amid the "liberal

paradoxes" proposed by contemporary historians and the heed-
less reassertion of older shibboleths that reduce their struggles to
"west" versus "east."

Notes

1. Calman Winegarden, professor of economics, University of Toledo,
developed the econometrics in Tables 3 through 5. His contribution enhanced
this article and is much appreciated. We wish to thank the Northern Illinois
University Press for allowing us to incorporate in this article portions of Marvin
L. Michael Kay's, "The North Carolina Regulation, 1766–1776; A Class Conflict,"
in Alfred F. Young, ed., *The American Revolution: Explorations in the History of
American Radicalism* (DeKalb, Ill., 1976). A special acknowledgment must be made
to Alfred F. Young of Northern Illinois University whose excellent editing of this
companion piece was of enormous help in writing the present article. We also
wish to acknowledge the help of the following individuals: Terri Hoffmann,
former analyst in Computer Services, University of Toledo, helped program
some of the data; Frank Schubert and David Rich, graduate assistants at the
University of Toledo, and Melisande Kay aided in the collection of data; and
Elizabeth Ruth Kay and Francine Cary helped edit the essay. The administrators
and personnel at the North Carolina Department of Cultural Resources, Division
of Archives and History, especially George Stevenson and William S. Price, Jr.,
have invaluably aided our research in their excellent archives. We wish to thank
the editors for their gracious help and commend them for navigating the articles
of this book through the rocky shoals of every joint effort. Last, grants from the
American Philosophical Society and the University of Toledo helped finance the
research.

2. A recent essay that illustrates these deficiencies is Edmund S. Morgan,
"Conflict and Consensus in the American Revolution," in Stephen G. Kurtz and
James H. Hutson, eds., *Essays on the American Revolution* (Chapel Hill, N.C.,
1973), pp. 289–309.

3. Historians who have stressed sectional interpretations to understand
the late colonial period in North Carolina include: Hugh Talmage Lefler and
Albert Ray Newsome, *North Carolina: The History of a Southern State* (Chapel Hill,
N.C., 1973), esp. pp. 173–90; Lefler and William S. Powell, *Colonial North
Carolina, A History* (New York, 1973), esp. pp. 217–39; Elmer D. Johnson, "The
War of the Regulation: Its Place in History" (M.A. thesis, University of North
Carolina, 1942), pp. 1–13 and passim; James Loy Walker, "The Regulator
Movement: Sectional Controversy in North Carolina" (M.A. thesis, Louisiana
State University, 1962), pp. 1–11, 111–15, and passim; Lawrence F. London,
"Sectionalism in the Colony of North Carolina" (M.A. thesis, University of North
Carolina, 1933); Lefler and Paul Wager, eds., *Orange County: 1752–1952* (Chapel
Hill, N.C., 1953), pp. 24–40. Walker tried to weave together the "consensus" and
"sectional" interpretations.

4. Multipliers of 4.1017 and 1.8868, respectively, may be used to convert white and black taxables to population totals. For data and aids used to develop these multipliers and the demographic analysis in the text see: North Carolina Department of Cultural Resources, Division of Archives and History, Raleigh (hereafter cited as State Archives): Secretary of State Tax Lists, 1720–1839; Legislative Papers, Tax Lists; Governor's Office, Lists of Taxables, Militia, and Magistrates, 1754–70 and Undated; Treasurer's and Comptroller's Papers, County Settlements with the State, Tax Lists; County Records, Bertie County Taxables; M. L. M. Kay, "The Institutional Background to The Regulation in Colonial North Carolina" (Ph.D. diss., University of Minnesota, 1962), pp. 23–43; Evarts B. Greene and Virginia D. Harrington, *American Population before the Federal Census of 1790* (Gloucester, Mass., 1966), pp. 157–72; Harry Roy Merrens, *Colonial North Carolina in the Eighteenth Century* (Chapel Hill, N.C., 1964), pp. 53–81, and passim. See Table 1 and notes.

5. See Merrens, *Colonial North Carolina in the Eighteenth Century*, pp. 37–49.

6. For population estimates see: Secretary of State Tax Lists, 1720–1839; Governor's Office, Lists of Taxables, Militia, and Magistrates, 1754–70, State Archives; William L. Saunders, ed., *The Colonial Records of North Carolina*, 10 vols. (Raleigh, N.C., 1886–90), 5:320, 575, 603; 7:145–46, 288–89, 539; Greene and Harrington, *American Population*, pp. 157–69; Kay, "Regulation in North Carolina," pp. 21–33. Anson, Orange, and Rowan were formed respectively in 1750, 1752, and 1753. Mecklenburg was formed in 1762 from Anson, and Tryon was formed in 1768 from Mecklenburg (David Leroy Corbitt, *The Formation of the North Carolina Counties 1663–1943* [Raleigh, N.C., 1950], pp. 8–11, 147–49, 167–69, 185–88, 205–6, 296).

7. See n. 10 below. Also see Merrens, *Colonial North Carolina in the Eighteenth Century*, pp. 162–72; Corbitt, *Formation of North Carolina Counties*, pp. 167, 185; Kay, "Regulation in North Carolina," pp. 442–81; Kay, "An Analysis of a British Colony in Late Eighteenth Century America in the Light of Current American Historiographical Controversy," *Australian Journal of Politics and History* 11 (1965): 174–75.

8. There was considerably greater variation in wealth distribution in North Carolina than is demonstrated in these counties, but time and labor requirements (along with the unavailability of adequate records for many counties) forced this limited but reliable sample.

9. State Archives: County Records—Rowan County, Record of Deeds, 1753–1800 (vols. 1, 2), 1755–62 (vols. 3, 4), 1762–90 (vols. 5, 6, 7); County Records—Orange County, Record of Deeds, 1755–85 (vols. 1, 2); County Records—Anson County, Record of Deeds (vols. 1, 3, 5, 6–7, B, C–1, H–1, K 1–294). The traditional sources we used to determine this information were primarily the Regulators' statements. These will not be listed here as they are cited in detail below.

10. Names of merchants and lawyers for Orange, Rowan, and Anson counties were obtained from the following sources: Johnston and Bennehan

Account and Invoice Book, 1769–75, Snow Hill, N.C., in Cameron Papers, 1700–1921, Southern Historical Collection, University of North Carolina, Chapel Hill; Lefler and Wager, eds., *Orange County*, pp. 24, 323–25, 328–29, 332, 337, 340; Kay, "Regulation in North Carolina," pp. 442–590 and passim; Charles C. Crittenden, *The Commerce of North Carolina, 1763–1789* (New Haven, 1936), pp. 97–98; Francis Nash, "Hillsboro, Colonial and Revolutionary," *North Carolina Booklet* 3 (1903): 6–8; Saunders, ed., *Colonial Records*, 7:506–7; 8:241–47, 273–75; Walter Clark, ed., *The State Records of North Carolina*, 16 vols. [numbered 11–26] (Winston and Goldsboro, N.C., 1895–1907), 22:425, 442, 454–55, 458–59, 475, 478, 870–76, 878–89; David L. Corbitt, ed., "Historical Notes," *North Carolina Historical Review* 4 (1927): 111–12; *Virginia Gazette* (Purdie and Dixon), 25 Oct. 1770; *Annual Register* (London), 1770; William S. Powell, James K. Huhta, and Thomas J. Farnham, eds., *The Regulators in North Carolina, A Documentary History* (Raleigh, N.C., 1971), pp. 253–55; State Archives: Orange County Court Minutes, 1752–66; Hillsboro District Minute Docket, 1768–88, Part I; Rowan, Court of Pleas and Quarter Sessions Minutes, 1753–72; Salisbury District, Minute Docket Superior Court, 1756–70; Anson County, Minute Docket County Court, July 1771–July 1777; Minutes, Anson County Court of Pleas and Quarter Sessions, 1771–77.

11. James Hasell wrote to Lord Hillsborough on 4 July 1771 that "above six thousand of them [Rebels] have submitted to Government and taken the oaths prescribed." Governor Josiah Martin, on 26 December 1771, stated that 6,409 men had taken the oath. Probably some Regulators and sympathizers did not sign the oaths, while a few who did had not been active in the movement. Thus, the above estimate of the total number of Regulators is reasonable (Saunders, ed., *Colonial Records*, 9:9, 78).

12. For evidence of the movement's expansion to other counties see, for example, William K. Boyd, ed., *Some Eighteenth Century Tracts Concerning North Carolina* (Raleigh, N.C., 1927), pp. 256, 257, 348; Saunders, ed., *Colonial Records*, 7:715; 8:537.

13. For a detailed narrative of the Regulation with complete documentation see Kay, "The North Carolina Regulation; A Class Conflict." For accounts of the Battle of Alamance and its immediate aftermath see John Spencer Bassett, "The Regulators of North Carolina," *Annual Report of the American Historical Association for the Year 1894* (Washington, D.C., 1895), pp. 201–6; Johnson, "The War of the Regulation," pp. 117–23; Saunders, ed., *Colonial Records*, 8:574–611, 634, 638–39, 641–43, 646–47, 664–77, 712–27; Clark, ed., *State Records*, 19:840–41, 843–45, 849, 853; David L. Corbitt, ed., "Historical Notes," *North Carolina Historical Review* 3 (1926): 482–83, 487–89, 492–501; *Virginia Gazette* (Purdie and Dixon), 30 May, 6, 13, 10, 27 June, 4, 25 July, 15 Aug., 7 Nov. 1771; *Virginia Gazette* (Rind), 15 Aug. 1771; *Gentlemen's Magazine*, June 1771, p. 290; State Archives: English Records, Colonial Office, Extract of Letter from Mr. Samuel Cornell to Mr. Elias Debrosses Merchant in New York, New Bern, 6 June 1771; War of the Regulation; Powell, Huhta, and Farnham, eds., *The Regulators in North Carolina*, pp. 469, 490–91, 492, 493–97, 506.

14. An intelligent, concise discussion of the role of deference in eighteenth-century America may be found in J. R. Pole, "Historians and the Problem of Early American Democracy," *American Historical Review* 67 (1962): 622–46. For an analysis of the theory of deference in seventeenth- and eighteenth-century Britain and America, see J. G. A. Pocock, "The Classical Theory of Deference," *American Historical Review* 81 (1976): 516–23. For a recent analysis that questions a liberal interpretation of the colonies prior to the Revolution and thereby lends support to the above class analysis see Rowland Berthoff and John M. Murrin, "Feudalism, Communalism, and the Yeoman Freeholder: The American Revolution Considered as a Social Accident," in Kurtz and Hutson, eds., *Essays on the American Revolution*, pp. 256–88. Kay developed the themes of class deference, class consciousness, and class conflict in an earlier essay, "Analysis of a British Colony," pp. 170–84.

15. The following is a listing of the major sources for Regulator statements. Two pamphlets were issued by the Regulators prior to the Battle of Alamance: Herman Husband's *An Impartial Relation* (1770), and his *A Continuation of the Impartial Relation* (1770). A third pamphlet, *A Fan for Fanning and a Touchstone to Tryon* (1771), by an unknown author, was printed after the Battle of Alamance. *An Impartial Relation* and *A Fan for Fanning* have been reprinted in Boyd, ed., *Eighteenth Century Tracts*, pp. 251–333, 339–92, while *A Continuation of the Impartial Relation*, ed. Archibald Henderson, is reprinted in *North Carolina Historical Review* 18 (1941): 48–81. A fourth pamphlet, a statement of grievances by the Granville County farmer spokesman, George Sims, was issued one year prior to the formation of the Sandy Creek Association, the immediate precursor of the Regulators in Orange County. Sims's pamphlet was partially reprinted in Husband's *Impartial Relation* and had an important effect upon the Regulators. It has been reprinted in its entirety in Boyd, ed., *Eighteenth Century Tracts*, pp. 182–92.

Most extant Regulator letters, petitions, minutes, agreements, and appeals made prior to the Battle of Alamance (eleven are recorded as "Advertisements") are reprinted in Saunders, ed., *Colonial Records*, 7:249–52, 671–72, 699–700, 702–3, 716, 726, 731–37, 758–67, 801–3, 806–9, 810–13, 847–48; 8:68–70, 75–80, 81–84, 231–34, 260, 536–37, 543–44, 640–41. The October 1768 joint petition of the Regulators from Orange and Rowan counties may be found in David L. Corbitt, ed., "Historical Notes," *North Carolina Historical Review* 8 (1931): 342–44. James Hunter's open letter to Maurice Moore (23 Nov. 1770) may be found in *Virginia Gazette* (Rind), 10 Jan. 1771.

16. Boyd, ed., *Eighteenth Century Tracts*, p. 303.

17. Kay, "The Payment of Provincial and Local Taxes in North Carolina, 1748–1771," *William and Mary Quarterly*, 3d ser. 26 (1969): 227–30. Kay developed this theme in "Some Economic Developments in the North Carolina Piedmont during the Late Colonial Period," a paper delivered before the Organization of American Historians in Los Angeles, 1970. See also Marvin L. Michael Kay and Lorin Lee Cary, " 'The Planters Suffer Little or Nothing': North Carolina Compensations for Executed Slaves, 1748–1772," *Science and Society* 11 (Fall 1976): 288–306.

18. See Kay, "Payment of Provincial and Local Taxes," pp. 218–39; Kay, "Provincial Taxes in North Carolina during the Administrations of Dobbs and Tryon," *North Carolina Historical Review* 42 (1965): 440–53; Kay, "Regulation in North Carolina," pp. 200–441 and passim; Kay, "The North Carolina Regulation; A Class Conflict."

19. A review of the Orange County Court Minutes (in the State Archives) from 1752 to 1766 (omitting the first and last year because of sparse records) reveals that during the years 1753–56, 1757–61, 1762–63, and 1764–65 there were respectively 180, 358, 223, and 576 civil cases. Taking population into account, this means that there were 36.53 cases per year for each 1,000 taxables during the period 1753–56. Cases per year for each 1,000 taxables for the three succeeding periods were: 36.29, 42.88, 94.55. Thus, in Orange County there was a discernible increase in court cases during the years 1762–63, but probably not enough to alarm the county's inhabitants. The precipitous increase during the years 1764–65 (and undoubtedly continuing in 1766) was certainly known among the inhabitants of Orange County and helped to precipitate the organization of the Sandy Creek Association during the summer of 1766. Inadequate court records prevent an analysis of Anson County, but Rowan County's records reveal a similar but considerably more moderate and later developing trend. Thus, analyzing the periods 1755–58 and 1761, 1762–63, 1764–65, and 1766–69, we find respectively 133, 54, 55, and 143 cases. This respectively equals for each period 26.6, 27, 27.5, and 35.75 cases per year for each 1,000 taxables. Perhaps the increase during the years 1766–69 agitated Rowan's inhabitants. See State Archives: Orange County Court Minutes, 1752–66; Rowan Court of Pleas and Quarter Sessions Minutes, 1753–72.

20. See n. 18 above.

21. See Clark, ed., *State Records*, 23:565–68, for inferior court procedures for small claims during the Regulator period. Also see an inadequate reform law passed during the height of the Regulation, January 1771, in ibid., pp. 846–49. With respect to the imprecision and inadequacy of fee laws see Bassett, "The Regulators of North Carolina," pp. 181–82; Kay, "Payment of Provincial and Local Taxes," pp. 231–35; and Clark, ed., *State Records*, 23:275–84. The last is a copy of the basic law concerning fees for the period under review. See Clark, ed., *State Records*, 23:814–18, 859–62, for acts passed toward the end of and after the Regulation.

22. Saunders, ed., *Colonial Records*, 8:83.

23. For accounts of the Sandy Creek Association see Boyd, ed., *Eighteenth Century Tracts*, pp. 257–61, 348–59; Saunders, ed., *Colonial Records*, 7:249–52.

24. Boyd, ed., *Eighteenth Century Tracts*, pp. 302–3.

25. Ibid., pp. 301–4.

26. Ibid., p. 323.

27. State Archives, War of the Regulation, 1768–73, printed in Saunders, ed., *Colonial Records*, 8:230–31.

28. The State Archives has compiled a list of assemblymen for each county and session. These lists were used to identify assemblymen. The

backgrounds of these assemblymen were checked in the records cited in notes 4, 6, 8–10, 19. Also see documentation to all the tables.

29. Ibid.

30. The petition of the Anson County Regulators is printed in Saunders, ed., *Colonial Records*, 8:75–80. The joint petition of the Orange and Rowan County Regulators is in ibid., pp. 81–84.

31. Ibid., p. 83.

32. Kay analyzed the inequitable nature of North Carolina's tax system in "Payment of Provincial and Local Taxes," pp. 218–39 and passim. He underestimated the injustice of the system in two ways. First, he was not aware of the important financial role of the practice of compensating owners for their executed slaves to which 25 percent of the yearly provincial budget was allocated. Since a disproportionate amount of these compensations went to large eastern slaveholders, they, on the average, were repaid all their tax payments. Second, although he recognized the importance of work levies, he could not quantify them. See n. 34 for a further discussion of this last point. See Kay and Cary, "North Carolina Compensations for Executed Slaves, 1748–1772," pp. 288–306 for an analysis of compensations made by the province to masters for their executed slaves.

33. Saunders, ed., *Colonial Records*, 8:77–78. See the following concerning the Granville District and the closing of the office in 1763: Saunders, ed., *Colonial Records*, 7:157; Beverley W. Bond, *The Quit Rent System in the American Colonies* (New Haven, 1919), p. 81; E. Merton Coulter, "The Granville District," *James Sprunt Studies in History and Political Science* 13 (1913): 33–56, esp. p. 52; C. B. Alexander, "Richard Caswell's Military and Later Public Services," *North Carolina Historical Review* 23 (1946): 18–21; David L. Corbitt, ed., "Historical Notes," *North Carolina Historical Review* 5 (1928): 339–41.

34. Saunders, ed., *Colonial Records*, 8:81.

35. Ibid., pp. 77, 84.

36. Boyd, ed., *Eighteenth Century Tracts*, p. 319. William S. Price, Jr., of the North Carolina Division of Archives and History and Kay are completing an article on roads and the militia in North Carolina during the years, 1740–75. On the basis of uncompleted but extensive research they believe that Husband's estimate was high. Nevertheless, work levies probably equaled £ 1 to £ 2 (North Carolina currency) yearly tax per taxable or up to nearly two times the yearly money taxes and fees per taxable.

37. Saunders, ed., *Colonial Records*, 8:68, 82–83.

38. Boyd, ed., *Eighteenth Century Tracts*, pp. 319–21.

39. See Kay, "The North Carolina Regulation; A Class Conflict."

40. Saunders, ed., *Colonial Records*, 8:257–58, 270–71; 9:12–13; Edenton Papers, 1717–1937 (1770), Southern Historical Collection, Chapel Hill; State Archives: Samuel Johnston Papers, 1763–1803; War of the Regulation; Hayes Collection, 1748– 1806.

Part Two

The War for American Independence: The "Southern Strategy" and Social Upheaval

5

British Strategy for Pacifying the Southern Colonies, 1778–1781

by John Shy

When news of the surrender of General John Burgoyne and his army at Saratoga in October 1777 had spread through North America and across the Atlantic, it became clear to all informed persons that the war raging in the mainland British colonies had entered a new, perhaps decisive, phase. After several years of little success on the battlefield, the American rebels not only had won a remarkable military victory, but their success surely would alter the international context within which the revolutionary war was being fought. France, previously no more than a covert supporter of the rebellion, probably would enter the war directly, encouraged by the success of her American clients, to seize this moment to reverse the defeat Britain had inflicted on France in the last war. So unfavorable did the situation seem to many Englishmen and their allies that they frankly advocated ending the American war in order to meet the far more dangerous threat from France. Major General Friedrich Wilhelm von Lossberg, for example, commanding German troops in Rhode Island, exuded pessimism over the prospects for ever pacifying the rebellious colonies: "We are far from an anticipated peace," Lossberg wrote, "because the bitterness of the rebels is too widespread, and in regions where we are masters the rebellious spirit is still in them. The land is too large, and there are too many people. The more land we win, the weaker our army gets in the field. It would be best," Lossberg concluded, "to come to an agreement

155

with them."[1] Informed sources believed that Lord North himself, head of the government, was for peace "at any rate," and Lord Howe, commanding the navy in American waters, was said to be "decided in his opinion that America must be abandoned."[2]

But Britain did not make peace in 1778, nor was the American war abandoned; instead, King George III and his more determined ministers decided to continue it on "a different plan" from that hitherto followed. The key element in the "different plan" of 1778 was the scheme to pacify the American South. This scheme, its implementation and its results, is the subject of this essay.[3] Ira Gruber of Rice University has carefully described British strategy and the motives behind it in the southern colonies, from the earliest effort of 1775–76 to support the armed rising of Scottish Highlanders in North Carolina, down to the ultimate failure of that strategy at Yorktown in late 1781.[4] His argument may be summarized here as the baseline from which the present inquiry begins.

In the beginning, Gruber says, munitions and some troops had been diverted to the South in order to exploit strong loyalist support reported to exist in Virginia and the Carolinas. British strategy in 1775–76 centered on New England and the North, but the king and his ministers hoped to gain major successes in the South in return for a fairly modest military investment. This secondary effort, plagued by haziness of conception and shortness of time, failed badly in the defeat of the loyalist Highlanders at Moore's Creek Bridge in February and the repulse of a British amphibious attack on Charleston in June 1776. Not until two years later would the British government and high command again think seriously about the strategic role of the South.

After the disaster at Saratoga in late 1777 and open French intervention early in 1778, the British gave the South a central role in strategy. Since previous campaigns had failed to break the back of rebellion in New England and the New York-Pennsylvania area, the South seemed to offer a last chance to win the war. Reports of extensive and militant southern loyalism were attractive to a government nearly frantic for new sources of military manpower and equally desperate to justify an increasingly unpopular war. Because French intervention brought new demands on British forces in North America, the first move south was weak—only three thousand men—and late—not until the end of 1778. But it was a spectacular success, seeming to justify all optimistic predictions: rebel resistance in Georgia collapsed quickly, and soon Charleston was being threatened.

The year 1779, as Gruber makes clear but does not especially emphasize, is a curious one for those seeking some coherence in British strategy; rather than quickly exploiting the initial success in Georgia, Sir Henry Clinton, the British commander in chief, spent months trying once more to bring Washington's main army to a decisive battle in New Jersey or New York. A small British raid in May on tidewater Virginia had seemed to give added proof of the strength of loyalism in the South, but not until more than a year after the first invasion of Georgia did the additional forces needed to capitalize on the victories of the previous winter actually arrive. Why the government and high command wavered in its original, clearly expressed plan to push the war in the South is a question better left for later discussion. In any event, delay did not appear to have done serious harm to British chances, for within weeks after the arrival of reinforcements in Georgia, Charleston was laid under seige, and rebel resistance had begun to crumble in South Carolina. Even before learning of its army's most recent successes, the London government reiterated to Clinton its desire to make the main war-winning effort in the South. Charleston fell in May 1780, with the biggest bag of rebel prisoners taken during the entire war, and in August, at Camden, the main rebel army in the South was literally destroyed. But in this summer of success basic weaknesses in British southern strategy became apparent, and inability to deal effectively with those weaknesses would pave the road to defeat at Yorktown in the following year.

Gruber points out that, as late as October 1780, twice as many troops remained in and around New York as were deployed in the South. Only after a second expedition went to the Chesapeake, followed by a third and a fourth during the winter and spring of 1781, each intended to support its predecessor against a strong rebel reaction, were a majority of British forces operating in what ostensibly had been for some time the main theater. By midsummer 1781, British troops in the Carolinas, under Cornwallis, had joined the combined Chesapeake forces, making Virginia, for the first time, the seat of war. The rest of the story is well known: the sudden arrival of a superior French navy off the Chesapeake and a rapid movement of a French and rebel army from the North closed a trap on the British forces in Virginia. The political earthquake in Britain set off by the surrender at Yorktown, more than any purely strategic effect, ended the war.

Gruber, in his meticulous account and judicious summing up, suggests that incoherence within the British high command, an incoherence compounded of Cornwallis's impulsiveness, of Clinton's apparent hesitation—in 1779, 1780, and 1781—about fully committing himself to the southern strategy, and of the reciprocal failure of their minds to meet on what they were trying to do, lay behind British failure. Though recognizing that British efforts to pacify the South had "foundered at last on determined opposition in a difficult country," Gruber also concludes that the "British had never really given their strategy a full trial."

What, exactly, was that strategy? Basic to it were a number of ideas. First was the belief, repeated frequently by those British officials and supporters with most direct knowledge of the South, that Georgia, the Carolinas, and even the Chesapeake were hotbeds of loyalism, ready to support royal authority whenever it appeared with sufficient force.[5] Second was a desire to cut off the principal channels of overseas trade through which foreign aid for the rebellion was being purchased; tobacco shipments from the Chesapeake and export of rice and indigo from the Carolinas were believed to be those channels. Third was the view that strategic and social geography—the proximity of the South to the West Indies where the major French threat soon would manifest itself, the strong pro-British Indian tribes along the southern frontier, the even more explosive potential of black slaves concentrated in the southern tidewater, and the extent of territory (which had made Lossberg despair) more thinly settled and loosely organized than in the North—favored a new aggressive campaign to conquer and control the South. Deprived of southern resources, the reasoning went, the rebellion would become weak and demoralized in the middle provinces and eventually could be isolated and dealt with in New England, where it had begun. Crucial to the whole concept of winning the war in the South, however, was what strategic theorists call "economy of force." No longer would British troops try to occupy and hold directly every square foot of territory; instead, the war was to be "Americanized"—territory once liberated would be turned over as quickly as possible to loyal Americans for police and defense, freeing redcoats to move on to the liberation of other areas. With care and patience, Americanization meant that a relatively small British force could conquer the whole South and thus win the war.

Understanding the concept of Americanization—a term, of course, not used at the time—enables us to grasp why adoption of a southern strategy did not necessarily entail an immediate, wholesale redeployment of British troops. Recognizing the military unorthodoxy of the concept provides a clue to why neither Clinton nor Cornwallis pursued it as consistently as they might have—never giving it "a full trial" in Gruber's words, setbacks and other distractions seeming to create doubts in their minds from early on as to whether the new plan actually could be made to work.[6]

Before 1778, British leaders had not thought very carefully about exactly how military operations were to be translated into political stability. Various feeble overtures had been made to the

Continental Congress, but clearly these were less important than
an unspoken assumption that military victories would produce,
more or less automatically, either serious political negotiations
with rebel leaders or a complete collapse of rebellion. By 1778,
however, experience had all but discredited this assumption, for
an impressive list of military victories had left a political settlement further away than ever. Although a new peace commission
was sent out in 1778, Britain's war leader, Secretary of State Lord
George Germain, put his hopes in "Americanization" as the
best—perhaps only—way to win the war.

The idea was attractively simple. A small British army
would liberate those thousands of southern Americans who,
openly or secretly, sincerely or from fear, longed for a return of
royal authority. These loyal Americans were to be armed, organized, and trained; hard-core rebels would be punished and
removed and suspicious persons kept under watch. When the
armed loyalists were strong enough both to defend and to police
their communities and districts, the British army would move
on. Step by step, from Georgia to the Chesapeake, the South
would be pacified. Previously, loyalists, if not neglected al-
together, had been recruited to join the king's forces, abandoning their homes and sometimes their families, or turning themselves into refugees living under the protection of British guns.
All that, in Germain's plan, was going to be changed, and he
spelled it out in a long letter to Clinton in March 1778: royal
authority in America ultimately would grow from the barrels of
guns held, not by redcoats and Hessians, but by Americans
themselves.[7] And the process would begin in the South.

The new plan contained a few problems immediately
apparent. One was the chronic uncertainty created by movements of the French navy in the North Atlantic; no military plan
could be implemented without reckoning the chance that a
French fleet, perhaps carrying an expeditionary force, suddenly
might disrupt it. Second, any opportunity to lure Washington's
army out of the hills and into a decisive battle must not be

missed, for destroying the Continental army might do in a day what would take a year or more to do in a methodical southern campaign of Americanization and pacification. Third, a small dilemma lurked in the letter in which Germain laid out the new plan. Assuming that operations in the South were best conducted in the cool weather between October and May, he urged Clinton to use available land and naval forces to raid the coast of New England, destroying rebel supplies and shipping, hitting the bases from which privateers preyed on British commerce, and bringing the war home to wavering Americans. The dilemma lurked not only in the optimistic idea of a seasonal shuttling of forces between North and South, but still more in the decision to strike terror into American hearts by amphibious raiding at the same time British soldiers were being asked to win American hearts and minds back to the royal cause. There was a certain fuzziness about how British armed forces were supposed to operate on American popular attitudes, whether they were to spread fear and demoralization or to induce a sense of security and self-reliance.

Despite these problems, whose significance is obvious in retrospect, there is little doubt that both Germain and Clinton, and later Cornwallis who would be directly responsible for implementing the plan, accepted its basic premises: that loyalism was an unexploited source of British strength, that British forces alone were inadequate to end the war and restore political stability, that the South was vulnerable to British operations, and that the exploitation of southern loyalism as a war-winning strategy would require careful management. One man who did not accept much of this thinking was the outgoing commander in America, the luckless Sir William Howe. In one of his last official dispatches, he dismissed the idea of southern loyalists being able to hold territory won by British troops. At best, Howe thought, the so-called loyalists would behave with "an equivocal neutrality. Experience," he concluded, "has proved this to be the case, in every province."[8] But Howe had been demonstrably a less thoughtful strategist than Germain, Clinton, or Cornwallis, and his status as an unsuccessful commander gave his views on the war little weight.

As Gruber reminds us, the new plan at first seemed brilliantly successful in Georgia and Virginia in 1779 and in South Carolina in 1780. What happened, then, to make the visceral Sir Billy Howe a better strategic prophet than his more cerebral, and apparently more optimistic, colleagues? Most obviously, the French intervened. In the same ship that brought the "new plan" to Clinton arrived a second letter, written two weeks later, in which Germain warned Clinton that the French were coming, ordered him to send large reinforcements to the West Indies, and effectively suspended the plan for southern pacification.[9] Not until early August 1778 did Germain return to his original idea. "The recovery of South Carolina . . . is an object of much Importance in the present State of things," he wrote, and told Clinton to put as much of the March plan into effect as he thought could be done successfully.[10] But just as Germain was regaining his confidence, Clinton was close to losing his nerve: frightened by French naval movements, he was seriously thinking of evacuating both Rhode Island and New York and withdrawing his army to Halifax.[11]

By September the French fleet itself had withdrawn, discouraging and angering the rebels by its failure to carry through a combined attack on Rhode Island, and Clinton was free to send troops to the West Indies and again turn his attention southward.[12] But at this moment he raised a point that would trouble British strategic coordination for the next three years. Once troops were sent southward, he insisted, barely enough would remain to hold New York and Rhode Island, and he would have to remain "on a most strict defensive next year," freeing Washington from the pressure that had kept the Continental army pinned to the protective highlands of New York and New Jersey.[13] Clinton continued to accept the importance of the South and of the need to exploit loyalism there, but he never ceased to assign at least equal priority to the confrontation with Washington in the lower Hudson Valley.

Germain, on the other hand, tended to shift priorities, almost from one month's letter to the next, even from paragraph to paragraph. Nothing was more important than the West Indies, he wrote, but he also thought the war might be ended if attacks on the American coastline cut off rebel trade. The evacuation of New York was unthinkable, of course, and no chance should be missed to destroy Washington; holding major seaports was a key to British strategy, Germain thought, yet the loyalists were another key, and Clinton should send expeditions out to encourage them. And, finally, there was the South, which more than once, when he felt that Clinton was too concerned with luring Washington into battle or reinforcing Canada, Germain would describe as an object of "vast" importance, "vast" being one of his favorite words.[14] Clinton, for his part, saw strategy as hard choices between competing objectives, and in reaction to Germain's chronic optimism emphasized, perhaps more than his situation actually warranted, the need to do one thing or the other. The new plan of March 1778, so forcefully stated, in time became blurred by this exchange of orders, complaints, charges, and clarifications that passed between the two men.

The early success of the expedition to Georgia, so weak and late in getting under way, would prove illusory, Clinton feared, if British forces could not hold firmly what they had occupied. As concerned with exploiting loyalism as was his chief, Clinton saw the main danger to lie in abandoning to rebel vengeance people who had taken risks to support the crown, and thus losing their goodwill and the credibility of British promises, perhaps forever.[15] Not only did Germain seem to overlook this danger in his reiterated desire to move as rapidly as possible to and through the South, but Clinton found it difficult to keep his more energetic but less experienced subordinates alert to the problem. Lamely explaining his advance to Augusta, Georgia, and subsequent withdrawal, Colonel Augustine Prevost told Clinton in March 1779 that he had been "bringing to the test the professions of loyalty of the back settlers, and by this appearance of support in their neighbourhood to countenance their rising, and give them an opportunity to do it successfully." When "no considerable numbers [of armed loyalists] appeared," Prevost pulled out. Clinton was not pleased.[16]

When, two months later, Commodore George Collier and Major General Edward Mathew, in charge of the small expedition to the Chesapeake intended to tie down Virginia troops and to destroy shipping, waxed enthusiastic about the rampant loyalism they had seen in Virginia, Clinton was dubious. It was no surprise, he informed Mathew, to find the people around Norfolk loyalist in sentiment. But, he continued, "if they have declared openly for you, it is an urgent reason for remaining to protect them; But I wish, that until we had determined to establish ourselves amongst them, the inhabitants had not been invited to join least our circumstances should oblige us to abandon them to the insult and oppression of the rebel faction. In a political light I fear the attachment of these . . . counties would not be very important, either as an example, influence, or internal strength."[17] A few days later, exasperated by his subordinate's eagerness to be reinforced and to continue operations in Virginia, Clinton was blunter. He sent Mathew a copy of a letter of his own, written to Howe in 1776, outlining the loyalist situation in the Chesapeake which Mathew was just now discovering with wide-eyed enthusiasm, and he explained to Mathew what staying in Virginia would entail: arming all the inhabitants around Norfolk, because any fewer than two thousand loyalists well organized and armed would be defeated and pillaged as soon as the British withdrew; building galleys to scout and raid the Chesapeake shore, keeping the rebels off balance and at arm's length; and immediately stopping the recruitment of blacks as soldiers for fear of antagonizing the loyal whites.[18] Mathew, in the end, got back on Collier's ships and came home to New York, as ordered.

Clinton's performance in 1779 needs both rational and psychological explanation. Waiting for reinforcements from Europe and for the return of at least part of the force he had sent to the West Indies in 1778, sure that a French fleet would reappear on the American coast in 1779, and above all afraid that his small victorious army in Georgia would be overwhelmed or forced to withdraw from liberated territory by rebel reinforcements, Clinton decided to use all his resources to pressure Washington in the Hudson Valley and prevent any detachment from the Continental army from moving southward. His estimate of the situation may have been too cautious, but it certainly was not unreasonable. There is, however, evidence that Clinton's powers of perception and decision were being sapped by something like nervous exhaustion. In a remarkable private letter to Germain, he complained bitterly of the weakness of his army and of being tied down by Germain's endless stream of orders, and insisted—in obvious reference to plans for the exploitation of loyalism—that the secretary of state stop listening to "the ill digested, or interested suggestions of people who cannot be competent judges. . . . For God's sake my Lord," he concluded in an incredible demand, "if you wish that I should do anything leave me to myself."[19] Reading Germain's letters, one can sympathize with Clinton's exasperation, while also recognizing that his outburst was irresponsible and disturbing.

Entry of Spain into the war in mid-1779 set off a new wave of panic in London and New York. Not until late October did the three thousand reinforcements, regarded by Clinton as the vital increment needed for any active operations, arrive, and by then a French fleet and American troops were attacking Savannah. Once again, panic set Germain and Clinton on two almost diametrically opposed tracks. While Germain conveyed bad news from the West Indies (the loss of St. Vincent and Grenada in the Leeward Islands) by calling for redoubled efforts everywhere else, Clinton prepared to evacuate Rhode Island in order to find the troops needed to expand operations from

Georgia into South Carolina.[20] Yet the two men could agree on the importance of the South: when Germain learned that Rhode Island had been evacuated, he accepted it as necessary to the conquest and pacification of the southern provinces, "upon the success of which all our hopes of a happy termination of the American war in a great measure depend."[21] With the repulse of the Franco-American attack on Savannah in late 1779, the last act of the war may be said to have begun.

Clinton, together with Cornwallis who recently had returned from England, took the large reinforcement to South Carolina, landing just above Charleston in early 1780. Clinton understood better than anyone else what Germain's war-winning plan required. From his arrival, he laid great stress on encouraging, protecting, and organizing loyalists, while being careful to do nothing that would discourage Americans who might be inclined to support royal authority.[22] Germain had harped constantly on reported American eagerness "to take up arms" at the first sign of a British military presence and also was pressing for the earliest possible restoration of civil authority in Georgia, which would demonstrate British good intentions. Clinton knew these matters were not so simple. Not only were loyalist attitudes highly susceptible to even momentary setbacks and extremely difficult to measure accurately, but the connection between loyalist *attitudes* and loyalist *behavior* was equally tenuous and obscure. Caution was Clinton's watchword. During his successful advance through South Carolina and the siege of Charleston, he declined to call for loyalist support in the province because he feared that the appearance of a French fleet and a consequent concentration of British troops, temporarily withdrawing from outlying areas, might expose some loyalists to the enemy and thus undermine British credibility everywhere.[23]

Immediately after the fall of Charleston in May 1780, Clinton sent James Simpson, former attorney general of South Carolina and perhaps the most influential of the southern "experts" who had been advising Germain, to sound opinion in the province. Simpson's first report, made at a crucial moment and promptly forwarded to Germain, deserves careful attention. Simpson had talked only to the leading men because he thought that the more numerous lower classes of people would follow their leaders. The leaders, he said, fell into four groups: those loyal by principle; those who were demoralized by revolutionary and military upheaval and ready to embrace royal authority as the best available form of government; those who still would defend the revolutionary experiment but saw no option except reluctant accommodation to royal authority; and those defiant ones who meant to continue the struggle. Although he found fewer loyalists by principle than he had expected, Simpson reported that the first two groups—the sincere and the demoralized—far outnumbered the last group—the defiant. But in closing he pointed to yet another category, those loyalists who had fled Charleston *before* the arrival of British forces and had taken refuge from their persecutors in the backcountry. These men were numerous and, having been driven from their homes, they had no intention of letting peace return to the province until the guilty had been punished. Under the circumstances, Simpson concluded that it was going to take "time and address" to restore royal government in South Carolina.[24]

Yet another issue British strategists never quite resolved is raised by the last part of Simpson's report. Clinton felt constantly pressured by what he considered the ill-informed optimism of Germain, old Admiral Marriot Arbuthnot, and a few others who saw virtually all Americans as being loyalists in their hearts, misled and coerced by a group of wicked leaders, but ready to support their king if given the chance to do so.[25] But he also felt increasingly pressured by another larger, better-informed group that advocated the use of fire and sword to defeat American rebellion. Hotheaded young officers like Banastre Tarleton and Patrick Ferguson were part of this group, and so were men like the Earl of Carlisle (head of the 1778 peace commission), Thomas Hutchinson (exiled former governor of Massachusetts), Admiral

George Rodney (commanding naval forces in the West Indies), and William Tryon (former governor of North Carolina and New York and serving actively as a major general with the army).[26] Clinton, Germain, and Cornwallis, for all their differences, never accepted the principle of a war of all-out terror, though each of them toyed with it at certain times for certain places; a strategy of terror flatly contradicted the belief that most Americans were basically loyal, but the use of terror did fit more easily with what Simpson had reported about diehard loyalist refugees in the Carolina backcountry—men who never would rest until they had taken vengeance for their sufferings.

Clinton knew about the propensity of loyalist refugees for terrorism long before he sailed to Georgia, and in a carefully worded letter to Germain he had tried to explain the problem they posed for any strategy based on loyalism. They were, he wrote,

a class of . . . men of a more ardent and enterprizing disposition, whose zeal and courage I have not yet been able to bend to the useful purposes they are by many thought equal to. Their former stations in life were above the level of the private soldier, and their spirits are not such as will permit them to submit totally to military control. Stung with resentment at the ignominious treatment they have received, and urged by indigence to venture their lives for the supply of their wants, their wish was to gratify their double impulse, and to ravish from their oppressors the property which had often in fact been their own. Such dispositions, as far as they induced the capture of obnoxious persons, of militia, and other soldiers, of forage wood, cattle and property of persons in rebellion, I was willing to encourage. . . . But fearing indiscriminate depredations, and having some cause to suspect that a spirit of licentiosness was the chief motive with many adventurers of this class, I endeavoured to restrain their irregularities. . . . These efforts have not as yet had the wished for effect.[27]

In plain words, Clinton knew that the most militant loyalists were essentially uncontrollable and if left free to fight their own war were little better than bandits who would sabotage every effort to restore peace, law, and order in South Carolina or any other rebellious province.

Caught between the enthusiasts for loyalism like Germain and Arbuthnot and the advocates of terrorism like Tarleton and Rodney, Clinton tried to combine his habitual caution with a bold stroke that would preempt the possibility of terrorism. By proclamation he released prisoners of war from parole and restored them to full citizenship, but also required them to take the oath of allegiance and to support efforts to restore peace to South Carolina. The proclamation was a mistake. Too lenient for the diehard loyalists to accept, it pushed former rebels, most of whom sought only to withdraw quietly from the struggle, to choose between a pretense of loyalism or a return to rebellion. Cornwallis, moving up the country, trying to organize a reliable loyal militia, complained that the proclamation was forcing dangerous men into the heart of his new organization, and soon he was modifying or ignoring the proclamation.[28]

Clinton did not wait to see the effects of his bold stroke. He reported to Germain that his rosiest predictions seemed to have come true ("there are few men in South Carolina who are not either our prisoners or in arms with us"), turned the war in the South over to Cornwallis, and sailed back to New York.[29] Less than three months later Clinton was singing a very different song. In a letter whose curious phraseology thinly masks his exasperation and fury, Clinton told Germain what he had always known in his more pessimistic moods and no doubt should have told him two years sooner: "The revolutions fondly to be looked for by means of friends to the British government, I must represent as visionary. These [friends] I well know are numerous, but they are fettered. An inroad is no countenance, and to possess territory demands garrisons. The accession of friends, without we occupy the country they inhabit, is but the addition of unhappy exiles to the list of pensioned refugees."[30] He must have known then, more than a year before Yorktown, that the southern strategy was not going to work.

Events of the summer of 1780 explain Clinton's renewed pessimism, now expressed in such blunt terms. A French expeditionary force had landed at Rhode Island, and the threat to New York was greater than it had ever been. Early reports from the Carolinas confirmed his worst fears about what could go wrong with a strategy that was heavily dependent on loyalists. Cornwallis had won smashing victories at Camden and elsewhere. But the loyalists of Tryon County, North Carolina, had risen prematurely and been defeated. Beyond the zone of British control, to the east, west, and north, rebel guerrillas began to disrupt the neat process of Americanizing the war. And while Cornwallis at first expressed satisfaction with the numbers and attitude of the loyal militia, he doubted that they ever would acquire the discipline and confidence needed to dispense with regular troops, "until," he concluded, "North Carolina is reduced."[31]

Cornwallis seemed ready enough to carry out the plan of pacification through Americanization, but from July 1780 he believed that its success depended on driving rebel forces far away from those areas where armed loyalists were trying to breathe life back into royal authority. He would invade North Carolina to protect South Carolina, arguing that no more regular troops were needed to hold both provinces than one because a North Carolina garrisoned by regulars would protect those Americans who were protecting South Carolina. And when North Carolina proved a geographical and political mare's nest, Cornwallis would argue that only the conquest of Virginia by British regulars would give loyalism a chance to flourish in North Carolina. Cornwallis clung pathetically to Germain's strategy for Americanization while undergoing a more bitterly disillusioning experience with loyalism than Clinton had ever had. Whole loyalist units defected to the rebels. Calls for loyalist support, even for information, went unanswered. As he advanced northward, supposedly pacified areas in his rear crumbled back into rebellion. Rebel terrorism was met with loyalist retaliation, and on, and on. Even Governor James Wright in Savannah and Governor William Bull in Charleston were appalled by the brutal spectacle of civil war, the very opposite of what Americanization was supposed to bring.[32] By the spring of 1781 the gap between strategic concept and operational realities was so wide that none of the three British leaders any longer knew what he was doing. Clinton sent successive diversionary expeditions to the Chesapeake, but otherwise seemed to withdraw into his familiar and soothing obsession with New York. Cornwallis may have believed his own rationalizations for what he was doing as he roamed through the Carolinas and, eventually, into Virginia, but there is a marked deterioration in the lucidity and logic of his letters.[33] Germain's optimism reached the pitch of hysteria as he seized on every scrap of favorable information and lectured Clinton on the same points that Clinton himself had been stressing a year and more before.[34]

In the end, American guerrillas did not defeat Cornwallis, nor would they ever have been able to defeat him decisively. Only a brilliant and lucky concentration of regular land and sea forces around the Yorktown peninsula defeated Cornwallis and ended the war. But to understand the bizarre chain of ideas and circumstances that brought Cornwallis to such an unlikely spot, so helpless to help himself, and cut off from the massive forces in New York, the West Indies, and Britain that might have supported him, we must understand how the British had planned to win the war by pacifying the American South.

Notes

1. 6 Jan. 1778, from the Jungkenn papers in the William L. Clements Library, University of Michigan, Ann Arbor, Mich., and translated in Ernst Kipping, *The Hessian View of America* (Monmouth Beach, N.J., 1971), p. 34.

2. "Journal from London (Most Secret)," 26 July 1778, in British Museum Additional Manuscripts (hereafter cited as BM Add. MSS.) 46491, p. 42, British Museum, London, and William Eden to Alexander Wedderburn, New York, 6 Sept. 1778, ibid., pp. 48–49.

3. Lord George Germain to General Sir Henry Clinton, 8 March 1778, "Most Secret," Historical Manuscripts Commission (hereafter cited as HMC) *Stopford-Sackville*, 2:96.

4. Ira Gruber, "Britain's Southern Strategy," in W. Robert Higgins, ed., *The Revolutionary War in the South: Power, Conflict, and Leadership* (Durham, N.C., 1979), 205–38.

5. Excellent on the role of loyalism in British strategy is Paul H. Smith, *Loyalists and Redcoats: A Study in British Revolutionary Policy* (Chapel Hill, N.C., 1964).

6. One well-informed observer's view of what was being attempted is in "Advices from [Andrew] Elliot," New York, 12 Dec. 1778, HMC *Carlisle*, pp. 392–93.

7. Germain to Clinton, 8 March 1778, HMC *Stopford-Sackville*, 2:94–99. Clinton received this letter on 9 May, at the same time he received the letter of 21 March, which modified the earlier directive and is discussed below.

8. Howe to Germain, Philadelphia, 16 Jan. 1778, Colonial Offiic (hereafter cited as CO) 5/95, pp. 127–28, Public Record Office, London.

9. Germain to Clinton, 21 March 1778, "Most Secret," CO 5/95, pp. 179–83, 194–97.

10. Germain to Clinton, 5 Aug. 1778, CO 5/96, pp. 49–52.

11. Clinton to Germain, New York, 27 July 1778, CO 5/96, pp. 123–26, extracted and summarized in HMC *Stopford-Sackville*, 2:116–17.

12. For example, Colonel Israel Angell of the Second Rhode Island Continentals entered in his diary on 23 Aug. 1778 that the French fleet "left us in a most Rascally manner and what will be the Event God only knows" (Edward Field, ed., *Diary of Col. Israel Angell* [Providence, R.I., 1899], p. 4).

13. Clinton to Germain, 15 Sept. 1778, CO 5/96, pp. 217–19.

14. Germain to Eden, 15 Oct. 1778, BM Add. MSS. 46491, pp. 54–55, is an example of his tendency to make everything "vital." Germain to Clinton, 23 Jan. 1779, "Secret and Confidential," CO 5/97, pp. 25–33, illustrates the effect of this tendency on his orders to Clinton.

15. Clinton to Germain, New York, 5 Oct. 1778, CO 5/96, pp. 347–49, and 4 April 1779, CO 5/97, pp. 467–70. The latter is also in HMC *Stopford-Sackville*, 2:124–25.

16. Prevost's letters to Clinton of 14 Feb., 1 March, and 11 June 1779, were enclosed in Clinton to Germain, 26 July 1779, CO 5/98, pp. 316, 323–24, and 355–56.

17. 20 May 1779, enclosed in Clinton to Germain, 18 June 1779, CO 5/98, p. 12.

18. 23 May 1779, in ibid., pp. 23–24.

19. 22 May 1779, "Private," CO 5/97, pp. 679–83.

20. Germain to Clinton, 27 Sept. 1779, "Secret," CO 5/98, pp. 169–87 (also in HMC *Stopford-Sackville*, 2:143–45), as well as a separate, "Most Secret" letter of the same date, suggesting that a chance to plunder the Spanish colonies would attract deserters from the Continental army; and Clinton to Germain, 26 Sept. and 9 Oct. 1779, CO 5/98.

21. 4 Dec. 1779, CO 5/98, pp. 709–18.

22. See, for example, Clinton's instructions to Major Patrick Ferguson, as

inspector of militia, 22 May 1780, extracted in William B. Willcox, ed., *The American Rebellion: Sir Henry Clinton's Narrative* . . . (New Haven, 1954), p. 441.

23. Clinton to Germain, 14 May 1780, CO 5/99, pp. 517–19.

24. Simpson to Clinton, 15 May 1780, enclosed in Clinton to Germain, 16 May 1780, CO 5/99, pp. 533ff.

25. Arbuthnot to Germain, 16 Dec. 1779, and 2 May [actually after 11] 1780, HMC *Stopford-Sackville*, 2:149, 161–62.

26. Tarleton to Clinton, Camp on Bronx, 2 July 1779 (enclosed in Clinton to Germain, 25 July 1779, CO 5/98); Ferguson to Clinton, 1 Aug. 1778, Clinton Papers, Clements Library; Carlisle to Lady Carlisle, New York, 2 July 1779, HMC *Carlisle*, 356; Hutchinson to the Earl of Hardwicke, London, 31 May 1779, BM Add. MSS. 35247 f. 186; Rodney to Germain, St. Lucia, 22 Dec. 1780, HMC *Stopford-Sackville*, 2:192; and Tryon to Clinton, New York, 20 July 1779 (enclosed in Clinton to Germain, 25 July 1779, CO 5/98).

27. 15 Dec. 1779, CO 5/99, pp. 55–56.

28. Franklin Wickwire and Mary Wickwire, *Cornwallis: The American Adventure* (Boston, 1970), pp. 182–83, discuss the effect of the proclamation. I do not share their opinion that a campaign of terror surely would have won the war in the South.

29. Clinton to Germain, 4 June 1780, CO 5/99, p. 589, also in HMC *Stopford-Sackville*, 2:167.

30. 25 Aug. 1780, CO 5/100, pp. 173–80.

31. Cornwallis to Clinton, 14 July 1780, enclosed in Clinton to Germain, 25 Aug. 1780, CO 5/100, pp. 221–26, also in B. F. Stevens, ed., *The Campaign in Virginia 1781*, 2 vols. (London, 1888), 1:235–41.

32. Cornwallis to Clinton, 6 , 29 Aug. 1780, CO 5/100, pp. 233–34, 515–19; Lord Rawdon to Major General Alexander Leslie, 24 Oct. 1780, ibid., p. 685; Rawdon to Clinton, 29 Oct. 1780, CO 5/101, pp. 85–90 (also in HMC Stopford-Sackville, 2:185–86, but misdated 28 Oct. 1778); Captain James Stuart to his brother Charles, Camden, S.C., 7 Jan. 1781, *Journal of the Society for Army Historical Research* 20 (1955): 135; and Bull to Germain, Charleston, 16 Feb. 1781, HMC *Stopford-Sackville*, 2:202.

33. William B. Willcox describes the Cornwallis revealed in his letter to Clinton of 23 April 1781 as "a man beyond the point of clear thinking. None of his reasons make sense." See "The British Road to Yorktown," *American Historical Review* 52 (1946): 12–13.

34. See, for example, Germain to Clinton, 3 Jan., 7 March, 4 April, and 2 May 1781, CO 5/101, pp. 1–8, 311–15, 337–44, 623–31.

6

Carolina and Georgia Patriot and Loyalist Militia in Action, 1778–1783

by Clyde R. Ferguson

Flora MacDonald, savior of Bonnie Prince Charlie at Culloden in 1746, underwent a peculiar historical metamorphosis. Once a defender of the exiled House of Stuart, in 1776 she gave allegiance to Hanover and was a North Carolina loyalist. The MacDonalds and many other Highlanders responded to royal Governor Josiah Martin's orders in January for the recruitment and assembly of a royal militia. "Allan leaves tomorrow to join Donald's standard at Cross Creek, and I shall be alone wi' my three bairns," wrote Flora. "There are troublous times ahead I ween. God will keep the right. I hope all our ain are in the right," she added.[1] Twenty-six days later at Moore's Creek Bridge, the loyalists, mostly Highlanders, suffered a disastrous defeat at the hands of North Carolina patriot militia led by Colonels Richard Caswell and Alexander Lillington. This calamity, following by only two months the dispersal of the South Carolina Tories under Colonel Thomas Fletchall, dealt the loyalist cause in the South a blow from which it never recovered. As in the North State, the perpetrators of the damage in South Carolina were patriot militia.[2]

Paul Smith's brilliant work, *Loyalists and Redcoats*, tells us that the royal governors, the British ministry, and some of the military leaders drew the wrong conclusions from these early setbacks. Undismayed by the defeat at Moore's Creek, which produced very "troublous" times for the North Carolina loyalists, Governor Martin was encouraged that they had risen at all. Royal Governor William Campbell of South Carolina saw the Fletchall uprising in a similar light despite the evidence that thousands of rebel militiamen had overwhelmed the Tory forces. Even the skeptical General Henry Clinton believed that Savannah might be captured and converted into a rallying point for the innumerable interior loyalists of the Carolinas and Georgia.[3] The seeds of the British "southern strategy" of 1778–81 were thus sown in 1775–76 at the same time the patriot militia were dismantling the components of the strategy. In the fall of 1776 the Cherokee Indians, another potential ally of the British in the South, were dealt a crushing blow by a triple-pronged pincers movement brilliantly and ruthlessly executed by rebel militiamen from Georgia, the Carolinas, Virginia, and Watauga.

This study deals with the British southern strategy of 1778–81 and the relationship of patriot and loyalist militia to its failure. Overconfidence of the Tories from 1775 onward played a role in the strategy's inception and was partially responsible for the resulting debacle. I contend that both loyalist and patriot militia played a more significant role in the southern war than is usually recognized and that they both tried to perform similar functions: suppression of political dissent and maintenance of an orderly society. In the civil war that was waged in the South, the two functions often were indistinguishable. Further, I argue that patriot militiamen performed both missions with greater success than their rivals and, indeed, did so from late 1775 onward. Conditions that existed prior to the implementation of the southern strategy thus were highly relevant to its outcome.

That rebel governments and militia made concerted and often successful efforts to stamp out every vestige of loyalist organization between 1775 and 1779 is clear. In a report to Colonial Secretary George Germain in 1779, James Simpson noted that the Tories who rose in 1775 and 1776 "and many more who were suspected of adhering to them had been the objects of almost unremitting persecution ever since." Simpson admitted that many Carolina and Georgia loyalists had changed sides and many had gone into exile, but he maintained that "there were still great numbers who continued firm in their opposition and were become most violent in their enmity to those by whom they had been oppressed."[4] Even Moses Kirkland, deputy Indian superintendent to the Seminoles in Florida, a committed loyalist and a wealthy South Carolinian in exile, hinted that the pressure on the Tories might become unbearable. "Do such Men merit the assistance and protection of their Sovereign?" queried the usually sanguine Kirkland.[5]

Although persecution sometimes does make martyrs, its effect over a prolonged period is to discourage the lightly committed. The combination of patriot persecution of Tories for three years and the virtual British abandonment of them during the same period proved disastrous. The claims of men like Kirkland, Simpson, and Colonel Thomas Brown of the Florida Rangers that the majority of southerners were loyal, that six thousand would spring to arms at the first appearance of a British army, were unwarranted. "While the regular armies marched and fought more or less ineffectually," wrote Walter Millis, "it was the militia which presented the greatest impediment to Britain's only practicable weapon, that of counter-revolution."[6]

Essentially the southern strategy depended on counter-revolution. The British plan for 1778–79 was to use a small body of regular troops to retake Georgia and South Carolina. Hoping to secure these conquests by the creation of a loyalist militia, the strategists expected to free the regular forces for further campaigning to the northward. The British also counted on elements of various southern Indian nations to cooperate with the army on call of John Stuart, Indian superintendent in the South.[7]

At least one American loyalist, and probably several others, helped formulate the various elements in this program.

On 13 and 21 October 1778, Moses Kirkland wrote letters to Henry Clinton and to the members of the Carlisle Peace Commission urging a strategy aimed at recovery of the South. By 3 November Clinton had decided to send out a southern expedition. He named Lieutenant Colonel Archibald Campbell to lead 3,041 "Rank and File" British and provincial regulars against Savannah, there to be joined by Major General Augustine Prevost and 2,000 troops from East Florida. Hopeful that civil government could be established in Georgia and South Carolina, the Carlisle Commission entrusted Campbell with blank civil commissions "to be produced and carried into Execution in Case the Course of Events" should give him "a reasonable Expectation of being able thereby to encourage and maintain any considerable Proportion of Inhabitants in a Return of Loyalty to their Sovereign; and of Affection to their Fellow Subjects." On 8 November Clinton informed Campbell that if successful against Savannah, he should "pursue such other Measures" as he should "think prudent and expedient for the Purpose of reducing the neighboring Provinces."[8]

Clinton and the Carlisle Commission thus allowed Campbell considerable political and military discretion in carrying out the southern expedition. The Archibald Campbell journal and the Kirkland letters, both significant sources that recently have come to light, reveal that Kirkland wielded great influence on the lieutenant colonel's conduct of the campaign against Georgia. A small but telling point was the matter of Prevost's assembly location. Clinton authorized the Florida troops to gather on the St. Mary's River, but Kirkland wanted assembly on the Altamaha, which would allow for a more rapid penetration of patriot-held Georgia. Writing from sea on 5 December 1778, *Lieutenant Colonel* Campbell urged *Major General* Prevost to consider "whether . . . a Movement from your Army towards the Altamaha River may not be eligible, even as soon as my Letter may be received."[9] By hurrying Prevost, Campbell was going against his personal desire to retain total control of the expedition. When the general finally arrived in Savannah on 15 January 1779, with but "900 rag tag & Bobtails" and assumed the overall command, Campbell "felt the Supercession severely," but admitted that "he was my Superior in Rank, and it was my Duty to obey."[10]

Kirkland's second recommendation with its various subpoints was followed almost to the letter by Campbell. Exaggerated Tory expectations thus became the basis for major elements in Britain's war strategy. Kirkland urged that one or two regiments with sufficient artillery and accompanied by the "Refugee Volunteers" from New York should seize Savannah and meet Prevost's army. Once a supply base was established at Savannah, Kirkland wanted the army to march rapidly to Augusta. This movement supposedly would secure Georgia and cut off "communication entirely between the Creek Indians and the Rebels." As deputy Indian superintendent, Kirkland knew that patriot George Galphin of South Carolina wielded much influence among the Lower Creeks and had thus far prevented their being utilized to support British objectives. From Augusta, according to Kirkland, "a Communication with all the Back-Settlements of the Two Carolina's will be open, and the Friends of Government will flock from all parts to that Post to join his Majesty's troops." Kirkland's third recommendation was that the British Indian superintendent should combine the Choctaw and Chickasaw with the Cherokee and move into support of the British troops on the South Carolina frontier. Kirkland also pointed out that John Stuart could provide these Indian auxiliaries, that the Regulators and Highlanders in North Carolina could be raised and organized into loyalist militia units, and that the entire program was feasible because the "great majority of the Inhabitants of North and South Carolina are loyal Subjects, groaning under the usurped authority of Congress."[11]

Campbell's actions and attitudes during the entire campaign reflected Kirkland's assumptions. The lieutenant colonel fretted like an old maid over the inadequacy of his artillery train.

He was convinced that a Mr. Bryson, "one of the most notorious Rebels in North America," was master of his artillery transport and intended to dock the ship in a patriot-held port. Before leaving New York, Campbell thought that he could conquer both Georgia and South Carolina because he expected aid from six thousand backcountry loyalists and the pro-British Indians.[12] Campbell did take an unknown number of "Refugee Volunteers" from New York to Savannah, among them the mysterious Colonel John or James Boyd. Believing that Boyd had great "Influence among the Back Woods Men of North and South Carolina," Campbell sent him into the interior to raise the loyalists shortly after the surrender of Savannah on 29 December 1778.[13] Before the attack on Savannah, Campbell informed Governor Patrick Tonyn of East Florida that "there is Reason to believe a considerable Body of Loyalists are happily disposed to join the Royal Standard: To encourage that laudable Spirit, and favour that Junction, I mean as soon as a proper Post shall be established at the Town of Savannah, to move with the Army as far up the Country as the Strength and Disposition of the Enemy will admit." Campbell hoped Tonyn could influence John Stuart to "make a Diversion in our favor by the Back Woods of Georgia, even as far as the Frontiers of South Carolina." Campbell also asked that Tonyn duplicate and distribute "among His Majesty's Loyal Subjects in the back Countries of North and South Carolina and Georgia" a proclamation intended for publication after the fall of Savannah. In general orders issued on 22 December 1778, Campbell revealed his assumption that the army's purpose was to rescue the majority of the people from the persecution of the minority. Officers were "not to suffer the Troops . . . to commit a single Act of Depredation or Plunder." The soldiers were "not to enter a Dwelling" without orders, and they would "shew every Mark of Lenity and Protection to the Inhabitants."[14]

On 3 January 1779, after the capture of Savannah, Campbell and Hyde Parker, commander of the naval squadron, proclaimed the "Royal Standard" raised and called on loyalists to rally and "rescue Their Friends from Oppression, themselves from Slavery." To other "well disposed Inhabitants," the British officers promised protection of person, family, and goods "on Condition that they shall immediately return to the Class of peaceable Citizens, acknowledge their first Allegiance to the Crown, and with their Arms support it." Meaning simply that neutrals would be protected only if they assumed the obligation to fight for the crown, this clause foreshadowed the infamous proclamation of 3 June 1780, through which Clinton changed the obligations for South Carolina militia after they surrendered on parole. To those actively opposing the "Re-establishment of Legal Government," Parker and Campbell promised the "Rigours of War."[15]

The reconquest proceeded as planned in January 1779. Boyd recruited in the Carolina backcountry; Campbell established several posts along the lower Savannah River and organized loyalist militia companies to patrol the countryside. On 21 January, Campbell learned that 1,000 loyalists were in arms in the backcountry, 5,000 less than expected but a force that demanded his immediate advance to Augusta. Three days later he departed from Ebenezer with 1,044 men, including the infamous unit of Florida Rangers under Thomas Brown. Campbell despised these men whom he described as "a mere Rabble of undisciplined Freebooters."[16]

Thrown into disarray by the British success at Savannah, the patriot militia soon began to take countermeasures, and the war in the South deteriorated into a fratricidal conflict characterized by ruthlessness and undisguised brutality. Several Georgia militia officers led by Lieutenant Colonel James Ingram met at Burke Court House to consider a response to the Campbell-Parker proclamation. Issuing a counterproclamation on 15 January, they gave the "disaffected" three days to resume allegiance to the American cause or be "deemed as Enemies & dealt with accordingly." Nine days before the departure of

Campbell for Augusta, Ingram and his men knew the enemy plans, and they passed this information to other patriot militia units in the backcountry.[17]

When General Prevost heard about the rebels at Burke Court House, he instructed Campbell to send Brown against them. Although fearing that this maneuver would either result in a loyalist defeat or alert the patriot militia to his own movements, Campbell issued the order. The Burke patriots bested Brown on 26 January, killing three men and capturing eleven. According to Campbell, the rebels then condemned three captured brothers and took them to South Carolina for execution. Campbell erected a gibbet on the Georgia side of the Savannah in view of the patriot camp and threatened to hang two for one. Though a prisoner exchange resulted, Campbell was deceived in his view that his actions would produce a more humane war in the future.[18]

The British lieutenant colonel's practices proved him hypocritical when he spoke of the civility of war. Hoping to use Indians in behalf of British objectives, he nevertheless opened a correspondence with George Galphin in an effort to maintain the neutrality of the pro-American Indians. Campbell was still pursuing the Kirkland logic that the movement toward Augusta could be used to isolate the rebels from the Lower Creeks. Eventually Campbell captured ninety of Galphin's slaves and sent them to lower Georgia to be held hostage for Galphin's good behavior.[19]

Campbell captured Augusta on 31 January 1779 and reported ten days later that he had organized 1,100 Georgians into twenty militia companies. Nevertheless, the British house of cards was about to collapse. Discussing the new companies, an engineer with Campbell wrote that "they could not be brought to any regularity; therefore no real, substancial services from them could be depended upon or, for some time looked for[,] but by people of too sanguine Expectations who would not consider that they were mostly *Crackers*, whose promises are often like their Boasts."[20] That the engineer considered Campbell "too sanguine" was clear. The lieutenant colonel, however, had some reasons to be confident. About 3 February he learned that Boyd was approaching with 600 loyalists—the number expected had dropped steadily—and Campbell ordered provincial units to advance above Augusta to secure the Tory's approach.[21]

Actually, Boyd had performed a remarkable feat. Recruiting largely from the area between the Saluda and Catawba rivers in the two Carolinas, he had assembled seven hundred to eight hundred men by 12 February, when he arrived at an upper ford on the Savannah.[22] There was no reason to expect, however, that either the small loyalist militia companies along the Savannah or the large force under Boyd could successfully compete with organized patriot militia units. Many of the latter had been actively engaged in suppressing political dissent since the fall of 1775.

The Ninety-Six Brigade, one of three created in a major reorganization of the South Carolina militia in 1778, apparently had territorial responsibility for approximately the upper quarter of that state. Commanded by newly promoted Brigadier General Andrew Williamson, many of the brigade's units were veteran by militia standards. The Upper Ninety-Six Regiment was commanded by Colonel Andrew Pickens. This regiment that long had borne the brunt of frontier patrol against the pro-British Indians began stabbing at the detachments above Augusta. On 14 February elements of Pickens's regiment and militiamen from the scattered Georgia units virtually annihilated Boyd's force at Kettle Creek. [23]

Ironically, the sanguine Campbell abandoned Augusta the same day. Aware that the increasing numbers of patriot militiamen might cut off his retreat to Savannah, the lieutenant colonel called a council of war that determined "there was scarcely a hope of our being now joined at Augusta with the Loyalists from the back Country." Rum also being short, no reinforcements expected, and the loyalist militia proving unreliable, it was "thought good policy to fall back."[24] Although 270 of Boyd's survivors finally caught up with Campbell, who tried to put a good face on his accomplishments in Georgia, his interior march proved a disaster for the loyalists. Many of the Kettle Creek prisoners were tried and condemned by South Carolina, and five were executed. The newly created loyalist militia companies disintegrated even before Campbell's retreat. The British engineer noted that when the militiamen were "ordered to Strengthen the posts that were allotted them, at the different crossing places along the River, it was plainly seen that they could not be depended upon; if their Asistance was seriously wanted; they could not be got to turn out or asemble."[25] Prevost considered the interior jaunt a fiasco. "I always thought that our being able to keep our post at Augusta, depended on the single Circumstance of the Back Country People's joining heartily in the Cause, as without that we must be certain of finding great Difficulty, if not Impossibility in preserving a Communication to such a Distance," wrote the general. "I do not think it would be prudent to persevere in a Measure that might bring the whole in Danger," he added.[26] Campbell virtually admitted the mistake in a letter to Prevost of 2 March: "When I consider the Strength of His Majesty's Forces in Georgia, and that of the Rebels on the opposite Banks of the Savannah, I am inclined to think it would be imprudent at this Juncture, to follow other Views than those of securing the Conquest already made."[27]

Campbell could set sail for England as he did on 11 March and leave his troubles behind him. The British government could decide that Georgia had been reconquered and order Sir James Wright to return as governor. Citizens of the state would have to live in the chaos that followed the invasion, however, and Wright would soon realize that the British forces had only recovered the lower part of Georgia. In April, Williamson ordered war on all the state's neutrals in an effort to coerce them into the patriot camp. Writing perhaps in the summer of 1779, the British engineer noted the intensity of the civil war that followed. The settlements "from Ebenezer to Augusta" were "in a ruinous, neglected State; two-thirds of them deserted, some of their Owners following the King's troops others with the Rebels, and both revengefully destroying the property of each other."[28]

The same backcountry militia units that prevented the junction of Boyd with Campbell also broke up the march of David Taitt with the Indian auxiliaries Kirkland and Campbell had requested. Only 120 of the 500 warriors that started for Augusta were able to break through the militia patrols and join the British army near Savannah. The patriot militia performed essentially the same functions in 1779 that they had been carrying out since the beginning of the Revolution: suppression of political dissent and protection of the frontier. Had Campbell succeeded in establishing a loyalist militia organization, it doubtless would have assumed exactly the same functions. When some of the Georgia patriot militiamen on frontier guard offered to surrender in February, Campbell ordered them to maintain their protective role. "Keep your usual Look-out against Indians," wrote Campbell. "Be faithful Subjects of the King; Cultivate your Lands, and enjoy the inestimable Blessings of Peace, Freedom and Happiness."[29]

Such tranquillity was impossible given the political divisions that resulted from the mini-invasion of 1779. The British had secured a base for future operations, but it was endangered by the Franco-American siege of Savannah in September and October. A premise of the southern strategy was that Britain should control the seas. She lost that control temporarily in the fall of 1779, and the possibility always existed thereafter that she could lose it again.[30] General Clinton nevertheless moved 8,500 men southward in early 1780, and Charleston, symbol of rebel resistance in the South, fell to British arms on 12 May. Occupation forces moved rapidly into the Georgia and South Carolina interior, and patriot resistance temporarily ceased.

Prior to the complete occupation of the two states, Governor Wright made slow headway in the reestablishment of royal authority in Georgia. Incursions into the low country by patriot militia bands plagued him as late as April 1780. He struggled with the problem of creating a viable militia and repeatedly postponed calling an assembly election because the interior remained under the control of a rebel government. In August 1780, he was still trying to establish the loyalist militia regiments that would free the British regulars to campaign northward. Typical of the problems Wright faced was the complaint of Captain Isaac Baillou of the First Regiment Foot Militia "that several of his Company pleaded Exemption from Militia Duty, on pretence that they had given their Parole to the Rebels." To counter a budding patriot resistance movement in the Georgia backcountry, Wright's council ordered that "a Stop should be put to such Practices, particularly as at this Time, there was not the Shadow of any Authority even on the Principles of Usurpation and Rebellion, to render such Parols binding."[31]

The interval between hostilities in the South was actually quite brief. Most South Carolina militiamen gave paroles in May or June, and many were back in action by July. By October 1780, patriot John Rutledge of South Carolina, the governor without a government, was giving authority to the resistance by commissioning its leaders as militia officers and investing them with powers to enforce the militia laws. As I interpret the resistance movement, Rutledge essentially recreated the three brigades that had existed prior to the occupation. To command these brigades, he named men who had gained reputations for success against the enemy. First commissioned and theoretically the superior was Thomas Sumter, who received command of Richard Richardson's brigade. This unit was responsible for defense of the piedmont. When Francis Marion performed distinguished service in the aftermath of the Battle of Camden, Rutledge named him to command the lowcountry brigade of Stephen Bull. Andrew Pickens received command of Andrew Williamson's Ninety-Six Brigade after leading seventy men from his old regiment to join General Daniel Morgan's Continental forces. By the time Morgan decided to make his stand at the Cowpens on 17 January 1781, Pickens had assembled six hundred militiamen from the Carolinas and Georgia. Most of the men who joined him apparently belonged to the old brigade regiments north of the Saluda and west of the Broad rivers.[32]

Although living under British occupation during much of 1780, South Carolinians compiled a remarkable military record. Patriot forces engaged in thirty-seven battles on the state's soil. In twenty-six the militia fought without the assistance of Continental troops. Later federal estimates placed the number of patriot militia at six thousand during 1780. Although the figure may have been exaggerated, it was the highest estimate for any single year of the long war. "I will not say much in praise of the militia of the Southern Colonies," wrote Lord Cornwallis, British commander in the South, "but the list of British officers and soldiers killed and wounded by them since last June, proves but too fatally that they are not wholly contemptible."[33] The state's loyalist militia organization, particularly in the backcountry, was also quite successful, at least in the period immediately following the state's subjugation. Major Patrick Ferguson, British inspector of militia, enrolled four thousand loyalists in the Ninety-Six area alone, but his overwhelming defeat at Kings Mountain in October sounded the death knell for the Tory militia system. After Kings Mountain, Tory commandant John Cruger at Fort Ninety-Six informed Cornwallis that "the loyal subjects were so wearied by the long continuance of the campaign . . . that the whole district had determined to submit as soon as the Rebels should enter it."[34]

North Carolina remained firmly within the patriots' grip. The British army in South Carolina received no intelligence from North State loyalists of the approach march of the Continental army under General Horatio Gates in August 1780. When the British regulars advanced to Charlotte in October, Lord Rawdon reported that the loyalists failed to furnish "the least information respecting the forces collecting against us."[35] The invasion of

North Carolina by the British in early 1781 has been criticized as an abandonment of the southern strategy, as a failure "to digest their acquisitions before gulping down more territory."[36] In partial justification of Cornwallis's decision, we should consider that the resistance in South Carolina fed on the North Carolina sanctuary and drew both supplies and men from that state. Cornwallis could neither pacify South Carolina while remaining in that state, nor do so by invading the sanctuary. The dilemma was not unlike that of General Creighton Abrams, who attempted to control South Vietnam while the rebels used Cambodia as a staging base. That the British general did not intend to abandon the southern strategy was made clear in a letter to Germain. Cornwallis explained that his purpose was to get between the Continental army and Virginia and defeat it and so "encourage our friends to make good their promises of a general rising to assist me in establishing His Majesty's Government."[37] Obviously, Cornwallis was receiving in 1781 the same exaggerated estimates of loyalist strength and determination that led Campbell into difficulties two years before.

Cornwallis gambled everything on overtaking General Nathanael Greene and the Continental army, and he lost. Once the American army eluded him, he moved to Hillsboro on 20 February, proclaimed North Carolina reconquered, and called for the loyalists to come in and establish their allegiance. "And I do hereby assure them," added his Lordship, "that I am ready to concur with them in effectual measures for suppressing the remains of rebellion in this province, and for the reestablishment of good order and constitutional government."[38]

The ability of the southern militia to frustrate British objectives was never more clearly illustrated than in the North Carolina phase of the war. The key to the militia's role was Andrew Pickens, the newly created South Carolina brigadier. In the aftermath of Morgan's retreat following the Battle of Cowpens, Pickens and 158 of his South Carolina and Georgia militiamen were drawn into the North Carolina campaign.

General William Davidson, commander pro tempore of the
Salisbury brigade, died opposing the British army's crossing of
the Catawba. His death allowed Pickens to take command of the
North Carolina militia; on General Greene's recommendation
the field officers of the Salisbury brigade elected Pickens as their
commanding officer.[39] Considering the provincial jealousies that
often frustrated interstate cooperation, this was a singular honor.
Pickens acted directly under the orders of General Greene to
gather a large force behind the advancing British army, to harass
it on its march, and to prevent enemy foraging parties from
supplying it. As Cornwallis raced northward, Pickens recruited
to the east of the Blue Ridge Mountains. As Cornwallis proclaimed the state recaptured, Pickens was approaching Hillsboro
from the west with approximately seven hundred recently
mobilized militia, and he had written to most of the over-
mountain patriot militia leaders requesting that they also advance against Cornwallis.[40]

In cooperation with detached Continental units, Pickens
disrupted the loyalist recruitment program. On 23 February,
Henry Lee informed Greene that Tories were swarming into
Hillsboro to take the oath of allegiance, "& I verily beleive, would
have mustered yesterday, had not our troops visited their
country." Pickens's militia had captured a British picket on the
outskirts of Hillsboro on the twenty-second.[41] Two days later
Pickens and Lee decimated a body of loyalists under the command of Colonel John Pyle. One of the strangest encounters of
the war, this battle resulted from Pickens's and Lee's desire to
destroy the green-coated legion of Banastre Tarleton. Pyle's
Tories unfortunately mustered between the two hostile forces.
When Lee's legion, also green-coated, attempted to bypass the
loyalists, shooting began, and the patriot dragoons and militia
destroyed the loyalist line. Lee was pleased by the victory, but
Pickens was chagrined. According to the South Carolinian, his
troops had almost caught up with the butcher Tarleton when
"our sanguine expectations were blasted by our falling in with a

body of from two to three hundred tories under the command of Colonel Piles." Lee and Tarleton both reported that bleeding loyalists came into their camps complaining of the brutality of the British dragoons.[42] The final irony occurred on 4 March when Tarleton chopped to pieces another body of loyalists who feared to identify themselves because of the Pyle incident. After these two encounters Cornwallis and the British army were not inundated with Tory recruits.[43]

One result of the assemblage near Hillsboro of mounted militia from South Carolina and the mountains was the achievement by the American army of cavalry superiority. The militia helped screen Greene's build-up for the decisive contest at Guilford Court House on 15 March. The most significant feature of Pickens's tactics was the constant movement by which his detached militia avoided surprise and also acted as a constant threat to any loyalist force's efforts to organize and assist Cornwallis.[44]

Using militiamen for an extended period also created problems, particularly when efforts were made to reduce them to components of a regular force. After Greene moved the Continental army back into North Carolina, he ordered many of the militiamen dismounted. Efforts to unhorse the militia had caused dissatisfaction throughout the war. The reluctance of militiamen to walk was one reason why Continental officers did not like to depend on them. Believing themselves needlessly exposed in the 2 March skirmish at Clapp's Mill and feeling misused after covering the regulars' retreat on 6 March at Wetzell's Mill, the militia began to desert in droves.[45] The North Carolina militiamen serving under Pickens were heading home, and the South Carolinians and Georgians were demanding to do the same. Pickens requested Greene's permission to lead them back. "I would serve my Country in any part," wrote the South Carolinian, "but I look on it I am capable of doing more good there than here. I am better known," he added, "perhaps another officer might suit these parts better." Then came a note

of reluctance: "I must confess I want to see what becomes of
Cornwallis; but should it be thought more advisable by you I
again repeat I had rather return."[46] Greene agreed with
Pickens—the Continental officer had learned to be tactful with
the militia leaders—and promised to follow him to South Carolina with the regulars as soon as they broke Cornwallis's leg.[47]

Although the British regulars held the field at Guilford
Court House, Greene did break that leg. "They have met with a
defeat in a victory," wrote the American commander, and the
evaluation was sound. As Don Higginbotham has written, his
Lordship "had put a European military machine through stresses
and strains collectively too much for it to bear."[48] Cornwallis's
retreat to Wilmington and subsequent advance into Virginia put
the quietus on the southern strategy. When Greene moved the
Continentals back into South Carolina in April 1781, the final
outcome of the war in the South was in sight. With the patriot
militia active and giving the Continentals even limited support,
the British and loyalists could not control the interior. Greene
understood this perfectly. Writing to Washington on 14 May, he
pointed out that if the British "divide their force, they will fall by
detachments, and if they operate collectively, they cannot command the country."[49] Upon his return to the South Carolina
backcountry in March, Pickens wrote that the patriots believed
the war was lost and were prepared to evacuate. By mobilizing
the militia, however, he gained a loose control of the area west of
Broad River by early April.[50] Following the onslaught of Continentals and militia in May and June 1781, the loyalists evacuated
the interior, and the British army pulled into a perimeter defense
near Charleston.

The story of the recapture of South Carolina has been
often told, and I will not repeat it here. The major contribution of
the patriot militia to the reconquest was the suppression of the
loyalists, a continuation of a function they had performed since
1775. At times the militia, particularly the veteran units, fought
brilliantly as integral parts of a regular force; the Battle of Eutaw

Springs in September was a good example. Formal battles, however, were never the militia's major forte, although it is often as auxiliaries to regulars that the institution has been judged, and found wanting. As the reconquest proceeded, the militia did assume another role that was closely related to the suppression of dissent—the restoration of social order. The new function was not dissimilar to one the loyalist militia had attempted to fulfill when the British held political sway over the backcountry.

The southern interior had a legacy of crime waves that resulted from the area's disruptive wars. Richard Brown has described the criminality of the 1760s in South Carolina after the Cherokee uprising of 1759–61. The plundering and banditry that marked the period was the major cause of the Regulator movement.[51] When loyalist Thomas Brown was attempting to pacify the territory around Augusta in June 1780, he informed Cornwallis that "the interior parts of this Province have been considered for some years past as a secure retreat for all the Villains and Murderers who have fled from Justice from the Southern Provinces, the principal difficulty . . . has been the suppression of plunderers and horsethieves who . . . ravaged the plantations of peaceable inoffensive inhabitants who have received protection as prisoners on parole." Although Brown promised to "hang without favor or distinction any person who presumed to plunder or otherwise disturb the peaceable inoffensive planters," he was soon appealing unsuccessfully for funds to establish a constabulary to create order. Daniel McGirth, once a leader of loyalist forces, was a chief villain, and Governor Wright offered a £50 reward to bring him to justice.[52]

As the patriots reconquered the interior, they faced the same problems and responded similarly. Elijah Clarke's militia captured James Dunlap, an infamous Tory leader, only to have him murdered by a "set of men chiefly unknown except one Cobb[,] an over Mountain Man." Pickens offered a $10,000 reward for the murderers' apprehension, but it was never claimed.[53] When the southern militia captured Augusta, unidentified men murdered Colonel James Grierson, the hated commander of the Second Georgia Regiment of Foot Militia. Pickens buried Grierson "with military honors," Greene offered a reward of a hundred guineas for information, but the murderers remained unpunished.[54] In June 1781, Greene received complaints against some of LeRoy Hammond's patriot militiamen. "The party plunders without mercy and murders the defenseless people just as private peak prejudice or personal resentments shall dictate," wrote the commander. Fearing that all the neutrals would be driven into the loyalist camp, Greene ordered Pickens to use capital punishment if necessary to halt the carnage. The commander issued similar instructions to Elijah Clarke with regard to the Georgia militia.[55]

When the loyalists evacuated the South Carolina interior in July, virtually denuding the country of supplies in the process, Greene ordered Pickens to use the militia to confiscate food from the well-to-do and distribute it to the impoverished.[56] Although the reconquest was still in progress, the Ninety-Six Brigade was tied up with such problems as protecting the surrendering loyalists, resuming patrol against Indian incursions, and preventing the endemic plundering. "I almost Dispair of totally suppressing it notwithstanding my best endeavours," wrote Pickens. "People who have Removed their Families to the remote parts of N: Carolina and Virginia, at least many of them seem to make a Trade of Carrying off Every thing valluable out of the country., Either the property of friend or enemy."[57] Wade Hampton reported similar conditions in the central part of the state. On 5 August, Governor Rutledge issued a proclamation against plundering and ordered all state militia to assist the civil magistrates in the recovery of stolen property.[58]

Before the war ended, Pickens, in an effort to create order, established a constabulary, the same kind of force Brown had desired for Georgia. Though defense against Tory militia units was one reason for creating the new force, Pickens made the basic purpose clear in his instructions to Captain William Butler:

"You will be particularly careful not to distress any of the good citizens of this State under any pretence, as the interest of this company is to protect, not injure; you will, therefore, effectually stop all plundering, of every kind, as no property is to be meddled with on any pretence whatever, unless such as may be taken in the field from men in arms against the State, which is to be the property of the captors, except what may be proved to belong to good citizens . . . who are to have their property delivered to them when proved, without any reward or deduction."[59]

This new force was continued by authority of the South Carolina assembly in March 1783. One of the last actions of the Revolution in the South was Butler's dispersion of the bandit band led by the Tory, "Bloody Bill" Cunningham. And as late as 1784, Colonel Thomas Brown was still in the field in East Florida, trying to run to ground his old comrade in arms, Daniel McGirth.[60]

This account of the role of patriot and loyalist militia in the South admittedly is incomplete. It hints at, but does not deal with, the war against the Indians, an activity the patriot militia assumed with a vengeance in late 1781 and throughout 1782. The destructive attacks against the Cherokees in 1776 were, of course, vital blows against the British southern strategy before it was adopted. Tory miscalculations, particularly Kirkland's, crippled the southern campaign in its early stages. The importance of a loyalist militia to that campaign and the essential failure of the Tories to raise a force that could control "conquered areas" have been emphasized. One cannot avoid the conclusion that there were not enough loyal citizens in the South to make the southern strategy feasible. Had the British decided to give massive support to the area at the beginning of hostilities, perhaps the outcome would have been different. Certainly the long delay made the task of raising a successful loyalist militia virtually impossible. Patriot governments and militia organizations were given three years to entrench their power before the British made a major effort to mobilize the Tories. The rebels used the time well.

One should not fail to note the striking similarity between the functions of patriot and loyalist militia. Whether revolutionary or counterrevolutionary, the militia was the chief arm to suppress political dissent. No matter which side of the ideological fence the militiamen occupied, they were the major prop of law and order in the revolutionary era. If either loyalist or patriot militia units were near the frontier, defense of that frontier became their key responsibility. The British could actually use the Indians more successfully against the South Carolina backcountry after the evacuation of the loyalists. The distinction of patriot and Tory made little sense to red men on the warpath. The Indians knew and respected the loyalists who lived among them and fought alongside them; other whites were the enemy.

As a final point I would reiterate my initial premise. Events of the period before the implementation of the southern strategy largely decided its outcome. Two major elements of the strategy were the rise of the loyalists and the assistance of the Indians. Largely against these two foes and long before Campbell descended on Savannah, the patriot militiamen made their greatest contribution to the establishment of American independence. Once the British had overrun and occupied South Carolina and Georgia, the loyalists were expected to be able to control the patriot militia. When the Tories failed to accomplish this mission, counterrevolution and thus British reconquest in the South were thwarted. Probably the patriot militia units could not have ejected the forces of occupation without the assistance of Greene's Continentals. Certainly the weak Continental army of the South could not have triumphed without the assistance of the partisan militia.

Notes

1. Catherine S. Crary, ed., *The Price of Loyalty* (New York, 1973), pp. 50–51.

2. Hugh F. Rankin, *The North Carolina Continentals* (Chapel Hill, N.C., 1971), pp. 31–32, 45–54; Robert W. Gibbes, ed., *Documentary History of the American Revolution* . . . *1764–1776* (New York, 1855), pp. 239–44, 246–48.

3. Paul H. Smith, *Loyalists and Redcoats: A Study in British Revolutionary Policy* (Chapel Hill, N.C., 1964), pp. 23, 25–26, 29–31.

4. Alan S. Brown, ed., "James Simpson's Reports on the Carolina Loyalists, 1779–1780," *Journal of Southern History* 21 (1955): 516.

5. Randall M. Miller, ed., "A Backcountry Loyalist Plan to Retake Georgia and the Carolinas, 1778," *South Carolina Historical Magazine* 75 (1974): 207, 213.

6. Walter Millis, *Arms and Men* (New York, 1956), p. 30; Gary D. Olson, "Thomas Brown, Loyalist Partisan, and the Revolutionary War in Georgia, 1777–1782," *Georgia Historical Quarterly* 54 (1970): 8–9.

7. Smith, *Loyalists and Redcoats*, pp. 79, 84, 86–87, 92–93.

8. Miller, "Backcountry Loyalist Plan," pp. 209, 212; Archibald Campbell, "Journal of an Expedition against the Rebels of Georgia in North America . . . , 1778," pp. 1–3, 5, original in Campbell family possession, Scotland, typescript in Georgia State Library, Atlanta, Ga. (hereafter cited as Campbell Journal).

9. Miller, "Backcountry Loyalist Plan," pp. 209–10; Campbell Journal, pp. 2, 17.

10. Campbell Journal, p. 67; Campbell to [William Eden], 19 Jan. 1779, Benjamin F. Stevens, ed., *Facsimiles of Manuscripts in European Archives Relating to America 1773–1783* . . . , 25 vols. (London, 1889–95), vol. 12, no. 1252. In his letter to Eden, Campbell revealed a lack of respect for the general: "Prevost seems a worthy man, but too old & unactive for this service. He will do in garrison, and I shall gallop with the light troops."

11. Miller, "Backcountry Loyalist Plan," pp. 210–11, 213; James H. O'Donnell, *Southern Indians in the American Revolution* (Knoxville, Tenn., 1973), pp. 15, 20–24, 52; Helen L. Shaw, *British Administration of the Southern Indians, 1756–1783* (Lancaster, Pa., 1931), pp. 88–89, 116–17.

12. Campbell Journal, pp. 1, 6, 8–9, 12.

13. Ibid., p. 99. For bibliography on the venture of Colonel Boyd, see Robert S. Davis, Jr., "The Recruitment of Col. James Boyd's Loyalist Regiment and the Events Leading to Their Defeat at the Battle of Kettle Creek, Ga. 14 Feb. 1779," File II, "Kettle Creek," Georgia Department of Archives and History, Atlanta, Ga.; Robert S. Davis, Jr., and Kenneth H. Thomas, Jr., "Kettle Creek: The Battle of the Cane Brakes, Wilkes County, Georgia," Georgia Department of Natural Resources, Historic Preservation Section, Atlanta, Ga.

14. Campbell Journal, pp. 15, 20, 22–23. "Marauders are the Bane and Disgrace of an Army, the stubborn Weeds of Riot and Licentiousness," wrote Campbell, "and will be exterminated without Mercy" (ibid., p. 21).

15. Stevens, ed., *Facsimiles*, vol. 12, no. 1238. Campbell admitted, in a letter to Germain of 16 Jan. 1779, that he had exceeded his instructions in calling

on Georgians to support their allegiance with their arms. "And this I resolved upon, from the Experience I have had, of its being the only true Impression, I could have of their Friendship." Campbell noted that only "One Jew Merchant, and an Anabaptist Preacher" objected to the requirement, and he sent them "off to the Rebels" (Campbell Journal, pp. 73–74).

16. Campbell Journal, pp. 65–66, 69–71, 76, 78, 81–83.

17. Paul L. Ford, ed., *Proceedings of a Council of War Held at Burke Jail* . . . (Brooklyn, N.Y., 1890), pp. 13–15, 17, 19–20.

18. Extract of letter from Camp at Fuzzel's place, 27 Jan. 1779, *South Carolina and American General Gazette*, 18 Feb. 1779; Campbell Journal, pp. 82–86.

19. Campbell Journal, pp. 89–90, 96.

20. Ibid., pp. 92, 103; Doyce B. Nunis, Jr., ed., "Colonel Archibald Campbell's March from Savannah to Augusta, 1779," *Georgia Historical Quarterly* 45 (1961), from which the quotation is taken, p. 286.

21. Campbell Journal, pp. 99–100.

22. Andrew Pickens to Henry Lee, 28 Aug. 1811, Lyman C .Draper Collections, Sumter Papers, State Historical Society, Madison, Wisc., 1:107[3] (hereafter cited as Dr., VV); Hugh McCall, *The History of Georgia* . . . , 2 vols. (Savannah, Ga., 1811–16), 2:202; Davis, "Boyd's Loyalist Regiment," pp. 2–4.

23. Pickens to Lee, 28 Aug. 1811, Dr., VV,1:107[2]–107[5]; *Gazette of the State of South Carolina*, 20 Jan. 1779; Thomas J. Cooper and David J. McCord, eds., *Statutes at Large of South Carolina*, 10 vols. (Columbia, S.C., 1836–41), 9:666; Campbell Journal, pp. 102–3.

24. Campbell Journal, pp. 108, 110. An unknown patriot source discussed this retreat and speculated that Campbell's advance to Augusta was instigated by "Kirkland and others" who promised all sorts of backcountry loyalist assistance (*South Carolina and American General Gazette*, 25 Feb. 1779).

25. Campbell Journal, pp. 114, 127–28; Davis, "Boyd's Loyalist Regiment," pp. 12–13; Nunis, ed., "Campbell's March," quotation on p. 286.

26. Prevost to Campbell, 17 Feb. 1779, Campbell Journal, p. 116.

27. Ibid., p. 121.

28. Williamson to Rutledge, 9 April 1779, Revolutionary Collection, Duke University Library, Durham, N.C.; Moultrie to Rutledge, 16 April 1779, William Moultrie, *Memoirs of the American Revolution* . . . , 2 vols. (New York, 1802), 1:368; Edward McCrady, *The History of South Carolina in the Revolution, 1775–1780* (New York, 1901), pp. 347–48; Nunis, ed., "Campbell's March," quotation on p. 286.

29. Charles C. Jones, ed., "Autobiography of Col. William Few of Georgia," *Magazine of American History with Notes and Queries* 7 (1881):348–49; Pickens to Lee, 28 Aug. 1811, Dr., VV, 1:107[5]; Campbell Journal, pp. 100–101.

30. Don Higginbotham, *The War of American Independence* (New York, 1971), pp. 353–54.

31. Lilla M. Hawes, ed., "The Proceedings and Minutes of the Governor and Council of Georgia, . . . September 6, 1779 through September 20, 1780," *Georgia Historical Quarterly* 35 (1951): 39–40, 46–49, 137, 139, 144–46, 148, 150–51, 209–13, 218–20.

32. McCrady, *History of South Carolina, 1775–1780*, pp. 525–27; David D. Wallace, *South Carolina: A Short History* (Chapel Hill, N.C., 1951), pp. 292–93, 299, 309; Robert W. Barnwell, Jr., "Rutledge, 'The Dictator,' " *Journal of Southern History* 7 (1941): 216, 219–20, 224; James Graham, *The Life of General Daniel Morgan* . . . (New York, 1856), pp. 268, 323. I have been unable to discover the exact territorial extent of the brigades. First commanding all of the militia, Sumter obviously led the regiments in the Saluda forks until Pickens's return to South Carolina in March 1781. In a letter of 13 April, Sumter said that Pickens had borrowed the four regiments. In July, Pickens still commanded these regiments while admitting they were Sumter's. During the siege of Augusta, Pickens commanded several regiments from the lower Savannah River area. In September, Rutledge said that he wanted to reallot the regiments and create a fourth brigade. By 18 September, Rutledge had removed the lower regiments from Pickens's control and made other adjustments. Apparently Pickens thereafter commanded all the backcountry regiments, and he apparently had commanded all of them since his return from North Carolina (Sumter to Greene, 13 April 1781, Rutledge to Sumter, 3 Sept. 1781, Dr., VV, 7:240–41, 461–64; Pickens to Greene, 25 July 1781, Greene Papers, Clements Library, University of Michigan, Ann Arbor, Mich.; Rutledge to S.C. delegates, 18 Sept. 1781, Joseph W. Barnwell, ed., "Letters of John Rutledge," *South Carolina Historical and Genealogical Magazine* 17 [1916]: 157).

33. Wallace, *South Carolina*, pp. 283, 310; Charles Ross, ed., *Correspondence of Charles, First Marquis Cornwallis*, 3 vols. (London, 1859), 1:81 (hereafter cited as *Cornwallis Correspondence*).

34. McCrady, *History of South Carolina, 1775–1780*, pp. 607–8; Smith, *Loyalists and Redcoats*, pp. 136–40; Robert D. Bass, "The Last Campaign of Major Patrick Ferguson," *Proceedings of the South Carolina Historical Association 1968* (Columbia, S.C., 1968), pp. 16–28; quotation from *Cornwallis Correspondence*, 1:63.

35. *Cornwallis Correspondence*, 1:63–64.

36. Smith, *Loyalists and Redcoats*, pp. 171–73; Higginbotham, *War of Independence*, quotation on p. 355.

37. Cornwallis to Germain, 17 March 1781, Henry Clinton Papers, Clements Library, University of Michigan, Ann Arbor, Mich.

38. Cornwallis Proclamation, 20 Feb. 1781, Banastre Tarleton, *History of the Campaigns of 1780 and 1781, in the Southern Provinces of North America* (London, 1787), pp. 256–57.

39. Greene to Locke, 9 Feb. 1781, Field Return, Pickens's brigade, 4 March 1781, Greene Papers, Clements Library; Walter Clark, ed., *State Records of North Carolina*, 16 vols. [numbered 11–26] (Winston and Goldsboro, 1895–1907), 16:vii; 19:969; William A. Graham, ed., *General Joseph Graham and His Papers on North Carolina Revolutionary History* (Raleigh, N.C., 1904), p. 203.

40. Greene to Pickens, 3 Feb. 1781, Greene Papers, Clements Library; Pickens to Greene, 19 Feb. 1781, Revolutionary Collection, Duke University Library, Durham, N.C.

41. Lee to Greene, 23 Feb. 1781, Greene Papers, Clements Library.

42. Tarleton, *Campaigns*, pp. 231–32; Graham, ed., *Joseph Graham*, pp.

319–22; Henry Lee, *Memoirs of the War in the Southern Department of the United States* (new ed., New York, 1870), pp. 253–59; Excerpt, Pickens to Greene, 26 Feb. 1781, William Johnson, *Sketches of the Life and Correspondence of Nathanael Greene* . . . , 2 vols. (Charleston, S.C., 1822), 1:453; Greene to Washington, 28 Feb. 1781, Item 150, 1:585, Papers of the Continental Congress, National Archives, Washington, D.C.

43. O. Williams to Greene, 4 March 1781, Greene Papers, Clements Library; Graham, ed., *Joseph Graham*, pp. 334–40; Clark, ed., *State Records*, 19:961–62; Charles Magill to Thomas Jefferson, 2 March 1781, Julian P. Boyd, ed., *The Papers of Thomas Jefferson*, 19 vols. to date (Princeton, N.J., 1950–), 5:44.

44. Graham, ed., *Joseph Graham*, pp. 326–28; Boyd, ed., *Papers of Jefferson*, 5:44.

45. Graham, ed., *Joseph Graham*, pp. 334, 340–41; Clark, ed., *State Records*, 19:960–61; Tarleton, *Campaigns*, pp. 335–38; Pickens to Greene, 5 March 1781, Greene Papers, Clements Library; Pickens to Lee, 28 Aug. 1811, Dr., VV, 1:107[6].

46. Pickens to Greene, 5 March 1781, Greene Papers, Clements Library.

47. Greene to Pickens, 8 March 1781, ibid.; Pickens to Lee, 28 Aug. 1811, Dr., VV, 1:107[6]. Governor John Rutledge and General Greene conferred with Pickens before he left the army. General plans for the reconquest of South Carolina were doubtless the chief subject of the meeting (Dr., VV, 1:107[6]).

48. Greene to Washington, 30 March 1781, Item 172, Papers of the Continental Congress, National Archives; Higginbotham, *War of Independence*, p. 370.

49. Jared Sparks, ed., *Correspondence of the American Revolution* . . . , 4 vols. (Boston, 1853), 3:312.

50. Pickens to Greene, 8 April 1781, Greene Collection, Duke University Library.

51. Richard M. Brown, *The South Carolina Regulators* (Cambridge, Mass., 1963), pp. 5–14, 29–40.

52. Heard Robertson, "The Second British Occupation of Augusta, 1780–1781," *Georgia Historical Quarterly* 58 (1974), quotation on pp. 428–29; Hawes, ed., "Proceedings and Minutes of the Governor and Council of Georgia," p. 201.

53. Pickens to Greene, 8 April 1781, Greene Collection, Duke University Library.

54. Pickens to Greene, 7 June 1781, Robert W. Gibbes, ed., *Documentary History of the American Revolution* . . . *1781 and 1782* (Columbia, S.C., 1853), p. 91; Greene Proclamation, 9 June 1781, Greene Collection, Duke University Library.

55. Greene to Pickens, 5 June 1781, Greene to Clarke, 7 June 1781, Greene Collection, Duke University Library.

56. Greene to Pickens, 15 July 1781, Greene Papers, Clements Library.

57. Pickens to Greene, 25 July 1781, ibid.

58. Hampton to Greene, 29 July 1781, Greene Collection, Duke University Library; David Ramsay, *The History of the Revolution of South Carolina* . . . , 2 vols. (Trenton, N.J., 1785), 2:506–8.

59. Pickens to Butler, 21 Aug. 1782, Robert W. Gibbes, ed., *Documentary History of the American Revolution . . . 1776–1782* (New York, 1857), pp. 210–11.

60. "South Carolina House of Representatives' Journal," 4 March 1781, pp. 248–49, South Carolina Department of Archives and History, Columbia, S.C.; Edward McCrady, *The History of South Carolina in the Revolution, 1780–1783* (New York, 1902), pp. 471–75, 628–31; *Gazette of the State of Georgia*, 6 March 1783; LeRoy Hammond to Greene, 2 Dec. 1781, Revolutionary Collection, Duke University Library; Olson, "Thomas Brown," pp. 200–201.

Part Three

The Revolutionary Impact
of War in the South:
Ideals and Realities

7
"What an Alarming Crisis Is This": Southern Women and the American Revolution

by Mary Beth Norton

In 1848, when Mrs. Elizabeth F. Ellet began to write the first history of women in the revolutionary era, she did not find her task an easy one. There is an "inherent difficulty in delineating female character," she told her readers; "a woman's sphere . . . is secluded" and usually does not "afford sufficient incident to throw a strong light upon her character." But Mrs. Ellet uncovered enough material to publish three volumes, then a fourth, on her chosen subject, for as she learned the Revolution so disrupted American society that it highlighted even the normally "secluded" role of women. She and many other authors limited the study of women in the Revolution nevertheless to a recounting of what she termed "individual instances of magnanimity, fortitude, self-sacrifice and heroism" in order to show the "vast influence of woman's patriotism upon the destinies of the infant republic."[1]

Mrs. Ellet omitted any consideration of loyalist women, and her approach to the Revolution, which has been adopted by her successors, concentrated on describing women's public contributions to the war efforts.[2] That focus is too narrow for a number of reasons. First, it is highly likely that a majority of female Americans did not participate actively on one side or the other; but because those women did not directly affect the war, does that mean that the war had no effect on them? Second, a narrative of women's activities during the war, while interesting in itself, tells us little about the meaning of those activities for the women involved. How did they perceive themselves and assess their experiences during the war years? Did their lives change in any way as a result of those experiences? Third, female blacks as well as whites lived through the wrenching years of warfare, yet few discussions of women in the Revolution mention them. Finally, the lives of women in the revolutionary era must be considered within the context of the times. The American Revolution was far more than just a war: it was also a search for a national identity, a social and economic upheaval of major proportions, a time of government building. These aspects of the Revolution no doubt affected women at least as directly as did the actual fighting.

This essay is an attempt to confront such questions as they relate to the lives of women in the South from roughly the 1760s through the 1780s. It does not pretend to be definitive, but rather suggests an approach to women's history in the late eighteenth century that stresses the effects of the Revolution; that explicitly connects social and economic circumstances to the shaping of women's roles; and that encompasses the experiences of women from various racial, political, social, and economic backgrounds.

I

Before one can assess the impact of the Revolution on southern women, one must begin by outlining the patterns of women's lives in the South in the years prior to the war. Those lives centered largely upon the household. Without today's—or even the nineteenth century's—labor-saving devices, female colonists had to spend the vast majority of their time caring for the needs of their families. But just as the economic conditions, geographic locations, and sizes of colonial households varied, so, too, did the duties and roles of the women within those households. For the purposes of this analysis, it is best to distinguish three separate types of households in which southern women led quite different lives: first, the rural homes of the poorer and "middling" parts of the white population; second, the urban households inhabited by members of the same group; and third, the large, multiracial households (whether rural or urban) that contained both the wealthiest whites and the black Americans who served them, the latter usually constituting a numerical majority of the family.[3]

Because poorer and middling southern women frequently were illiterate, or, if able to write, rarely were called upon to do so, historians seeking to study their lives must turn to the accounts of observers and to the records of their dealings with governments to gain insight into the conditions of their existence. In rural areas, such an investigation shows, white women worked in the fields or tended livestock in addition to caring for their houses and children. When Oliver Hart, a lonely South Carolinian separated from his wife by the war, daydreamed about her, he told her he saw her "on my Farm, busying yourself with your Poultry, traveling the Fields, admiring the Flocks and Herds, or within, managing the Dairy." That his characterization of his wife's role was accurate is revealed not only by the statements of such persons as the tutor Philip Vickers Fithian, who noticed white women planting corn in Virginia fields, but also by the contents of claims submitted by female refugees after the war to the loyalist claims commission in London. Rural women demonstrated a wide-ranging knowledge of farm tools and livestock, while admitting their ignorance of many aspects of their husbands' financial affairs. Their knowledge, in effect, revealed the dimensions of their lives. The Georgian Janet Russell, for example, mentioned that she regularly milked thirty-two cows and noted that she had counted the sheep on her farm "a few days before she came away." She and other rural southern loyalist women submitted claims documents that included long lists of the dishes and utensils they handled daily, of the spinning wheels and looms they occasionally operated, of the foodstuffs they prepared and stored, of the livestock they helped to feed, and of the clothing, linens, and furniture that were their prize possessions.[4]

The lives they led were hard and exhausting, with little respite or relief. The Reverend Charles Woodmason, an itinerant Anglican clergyman who traveled extensively in the Carolina backcountry, commented that the people there ate "fat rusty Bacon" and corn bread; lived in "open Logg Cabbins with hardly a Blanket to cover them"; and wore but scanty clothing and no shoes or stockings. He noted that the women were "so burthen'd with Young Children" that they could not "attend both House and Field," thus confirming the work demands made on rural women and recognizing that in many cases they were unable to meet them. One wonders how many rural white women were like the mother of a boy (the fourth of eight children) born on a Shenandoah Valley farm in 1769, whom he described thus: she "from my earliest recollection was weak & sickly . . . confined principally to her bed for the last two or three years of her life."[5]

In the towns, there were no crops to plant, no herds of livestock to attend (though there might be a cow or a few chickens), and as a result the lives of women of the "middling sort" who resided in urban areas were somewhat different. They prepared the food, but instead of cultivating crops in the fields they raised produce in small kitchen gardens or purchased it at city markets. They cared for numerous children, but the children might attend small schools run by women much like themselves for part of the day. They spun some wool and linen thread, but were more likely to buy their cloth at local stores. They also were more likely to engage in business activities on their own. In rural areas, the only way women could make money was by taking in travelers or by doing some spinning or weaving for wealthier neighbors, but in towns women could work alongside their husbands in taverns or shops or run independent businesses. In Charleston, for example, William Brockie sold "Fruit & Garden stuff" and his wife Mary was a mantua maker; Katherine

Williamson ran a grocery store while her husband Robert "worked at his Trade as a Bricklayer"; the widowed Janet Cumming made £400 annually as the most respected midwife in town; Eleanor Lestor took over her husband's liquor store after his death; and Mary and Robert Miller together kept a tavern. Most of these women were "in low life" (to use the phrase with which the claims commission described Mrs. Lestor), and they represented only a small proportion of the overall female population, but they led quite independent lives. When all the women just described became loyalist refugees, their experience in coping with manifold business problems stood them in good stead, as shall be seen.[6]

The lives of the wealthiest group of southern white women differed markedly from those of the poorer and middling sort. Foreigners and northerners almost invariably described well-to-do southern women as "indolent" because of the combined effect of "their living in so warm a climate and being surrounded by such a multitude of slaves." But appearances were deceiving to a certain extent. Such women were freed from the more monotonous and onerous household duties by the labor of female slaves, but in exchange they had to superintend large and complex families. One Virginia wife, complaining of how she and her husband could not leave home, told a friend that she and her female neighbors were "almost in a State of vegitation" because they constantly had to "attend to the innumerable wants" of their multiracial households. Appropriately, these women commonly were described as "good managers" or "remarkable Economists."[7] The skills they developed were those of command and of personnel management rather than of handwork and of "making do" with less than ample supplies of food or clothes.

They learned the habit of command early. In her diary, one little Virginia girl complained about the laziness of her black washerwoman and raged about a male slave who killed a cat: "a vile wretch of new negrows, if he was mine I would cut him to pieces, a son of a gun, a nice negrow, he should be kild himself by rites." A four-year-old North Carolina girl was described by a doting cousin as "strutting about in the yard after Susanna (whom she had ordered to do something) with her work in her hand & an Air of as much importance as if she had been Mistress of the family."[8] As adults, such women were entirely capable of directing the many-faceted activities of a plantation household. Eliza Lucas's 1742 description of how she spent her days is instructive here. Arising at five o'clock, she read till seven, saw "that the Servants are at their respective business," then ate breakfast. Afterward she practiced music, studied, and taught her younger sister until dinner time. She again turned to her music, then to needlework, and finally in the evening once again read or wrote. Although Eliza Lucas may have been more insistent on early rising than her female contemporaries (she recorded that at least one woman neighbor warned that the practice would age her unnecessarily), the diaries and letters of other wealthy southern women show a similar daily pattern: giving orders to servants in the morning, doing needlework in the afternoons, and reading, writing, or playing music at various times during the day.[9]

The labor of blacks allowed Eliza Lucas Pinckney and her counterparts to spend a good deal of time with their children. Unlike the poorer southern females, whose time had to be divided among a number of physically demanding tasks, well-to-do mothers (and fathers, too) could devote large amounts of their days to the care and education of their offspring. Mrs. Pinckney described the care of her daughter Harriott as "one of the greatest Businesses of my life," and she remarked upon the "pleasure it certainly is to cultivate the tender mind, to teach the young Idea how to shoot." Her attention to her eldest son Charles Cotesworth is well documented: by the time he was four months old she had decided "to teach him according to Mr. Locks method (which I have carefully studied) to play him self into learning." Her husband Charles made his son "a set of toys

to teach him his letters," and by the age of twenty-two months
Charles Cotesworth was so precocious that he "can tell all his
letters in any book without hesitation and begins to spell." Of a
similar nature was John Jaquelin Ambler's attention to his
daughter Betsy's education. She recalled in later years that "the
moment he left his chamber in the morning which was at an
early hour, we [she and her sister Mary] were called, and
throughout the day every hour from business was devoted to
us." Her father wrote passages for them to copy; he encircled
their arithmetic lessons "with flowers which had a happy effect
in drawing our attention;" he "carelessly" left "amusing books"
open on the table, where they would see and be attracted to
them; he encouraged them to write letters to the children of his
friends; and, most important, in Betsy's opinion, he used "the
Rod . . . most conscientiously."[10]

And what of the black women whose labor made all of this
possible? Their lives differed in obvious ways from those of the
whites, most notably, of course, in the inescapable fact of their
servitude. But married women of all descriptions in the colonial
South were, in a legal sense, "slaves" to their husbands, and
white female servants sometimes worked alongside black
women in both house and field. The tasks female slaves performed were equivalent to, if not exactly the same as, those done
by the poorer and middling whites: they worked in the fields,
prepared food, cared for children, and spun thread. But, significantly, specific individuals did not do all of these tasks, for
the sheer size of plantation households meant that the work of
slave women could be specialized in a way that that of poor
white women could not. During her lifetime, a slave woman
probably would serve her master and mistress in several
capacities: as a youngster, she might spin or mind smaller
children; as an able-bodied woman, she might work in the fields;
as an older woman she might again spin, work as a house
servant, or be a nurse or a midwife to both blacks and whites. But
she would not engage in these tasks simultaneously. And on

occasion a young girl would be singled out "to bring up in the
House," or would show such aptitude for a particular job that
she would be assigned to that task alone (as was Mulatto Milly,
the "principal spinner" on John Hatley Norton's quarter in
Fauquier County, Virginia). As a result, slave women living on
large plantations had opportunities to acquire a level of skill that
their white mistresses did not, and this may have contributed to
the development of such self-confidence as that exhibited by
"Miss Charlotte," an East Florida slave who in 1769 reacted to a
dispute between two whites over who owned her, one of them
reported, by "living with neither of us," but instead going
"about from house to house," saying "now she's a free
woman."[11]

Slave women in the mid-eighteenth-century South, unlike the vast majority of female whites, lived in truly extended
families, in which they, their siblings, parents, children, cousins,
and more distant relatives daily worked alongside each other,
and, moreover, often shared tasks and divided responsibilities.[12]
White women rarely had large kinship networks so readily
available to them. That family ties played a major role in the lives
of slave women is demonstrated by the records of planters and
overseers, in which a constantly recurring theme is that of black
females' unwillingness to be parted permanently from their
relatives. Historians have demonstrated that runaway slaves
often were seeking to reunite themselves with their families, and
kinship ties also motivated many other movements of slaves.
One Virginia planter, for example, told another that "Darby
wants to Cum to liv with me and as his wife is not sattisfyed with
out him" he would hire him. Similarly, there are numerous
documented cases of slave mothers refusing to move unless they
could be accompanied by their children and of husbands and
wives being moved together, though the presence of only one of
them was required at the new location.[13]

Whether black or white, rich or poor, however, the lives of
most colonial southern women can be summed up in one word:

"circumscribed." All were tied down by the care of their families. The nature of that care varied, as did the size and racial composition of the households, but the women bore responsibility for the day-to-day familial routine. They rarely traveled, and the demands of their regular duties seldom allowed them to venture outside their domestic sphere, though the shape of that sphere varied according to their race, place of residence, and economic status. Foreign travelers noted this quality in southern white women: Maryland females, observed an Englishman in 1745, had "an Air of Reserve and somewhat that looks at first to a Stranger like Unsociableness," but was rather the "effect of living at a great Distance from frequent Society and their Thorough Attention to the Duties of their Stations." A Venezuelan commented nearly forty years later on North Carolinians that the "married women maintain a monastic seclusion and a submission to their husbands such as I have never seen; . . . their entire lives are domestic. Once married, they . . . devote themselves completely to the care of home and family."[14]

It does not take much imagination to realize that women with little experience outside the confines of their households would find being in the midst of a disruptive civil war an unnerving experience. In the years after 1775, and especially in 1778 and thereafter, southern women had to cope with a myriad of unprecedented problems: armies on the march, guerrilla bands, runaway inflation, shortages of food and other supplies, epidemics spread by the military movements—all in the absence of the husbands, fathers, brothers, and sons they long had been told to look to for guidance. It was not an easy time.

II

Paradoxically, in light of the reputed paucity of sources for black history, it is easier to assess the impact of the Revolution on southern black women than on their white counterparts. This is essentially because to slaves the war brought a chance—a slim one, admittedly, but still a chance—for freedom. The Revolution, furthermore, by depriving planters of the British manufactured goods on which they previously had depended, also caused a significant rise in the production of cloth within plantation households. Thus some slave women were afforded the opportunity to develop new skills of spinning and weaving, and, by implication, perhaps gained somewhat greater independence and self-confidence.[15]

Before the nonimportation movements of the 1760s and 1770s, most planters of the tidewater regions seem to have purchased "negro cloth" as well as fancier goods from British sources, using the labor of their female slaves in the fields instead of in textile production. But when cloth no longer could be obtained from England, many planters established "wool and linen manufactories." In October 1775, John Harrower, an indentured servant in Virginia, commented that for the first time "coarse linnen for Shirts to the Nigers" was being made on the plantation where he lived. Several months previously, Robert Carter had begun planning for what was to become a large "Linnen and Woolen Factory" at his Aries plantation, ordering an overseer to "sett a part, Ten black Females the most Expert spinners belonging to me—they to be Employed in Spinning, solely." By spring 1776, Carter had discovered that this work force was not sufficient to supply his needs, and he told another overseer to hire a woman to teach six more slave girls to spin, if his wife could not take on that task herself. In April 1782, Carter was employing twelve spinners at Aries under the direction of a female overseer, and in August 1791, even though English goods had long since again become available, he still had seven female spinners working at Aries, along with three male weavers.[16]

Far more dramatic than the opening of this skilled occupation to slave women were the direct consequences of the war itself and, in particular, the results of British military policy regarding blacks. In November 1775, in an attempt to bolster his sagging cause, Lord Dunmore, the last royal governor of Virginia, issued a proclamation offering freedom to all blacks and indentured servants who would join him to fight the rebellion. Although only an estimated eight hundred slaves responded to Dunmore's call immediately, southern whites were terrified by the implications of the offer. One commented, "Hell itself could not have vomitted any thing more black than his design of emancipating our slaves." In July 1776, Robert Carter called together the black residents of his Coles Point plantation (which was dangerously situated on the Potomac) and suggested that Dunmore intended to sell those who joined him to West Indian planters. Carter's argument apparently dissuaded potential runaways at that time, but when the British army returned to Virginia in 1781 thirty-two of the Coles Point Negroes absconded during one nine-day period. Throughout the South, the story was the same: everywhere, the redcoats attracted slaves "in great numbers," according to the contemporary historian David Ramsay.[17]

Although a majority of runaways were male, women apparently sought freedom in greater numbers during the war than in peacetime. Jefferson noted twenty-three who "joined British" in his farm book, twelve of whom were women, and one of whom took her three children with her. The South Carolinian John Ball listed the names of fifty-three runaways to the redcoats in his plantation accounts; of these, only fifteen were adult women (many of whom left with their children), but none returned voluntarily, whereas at least ten of the men did. A woman named Charlotte may have instigated a mass escape. She originally fled on 10 May 1780, but "was brought home." A week later, however, she left again in company with fourteen other slaves, none of whom appears to have returned. That the sex ratios among runaways from the Jefferson and Ball plantations were not unusual is suggested by the lists of black evacuees prepared by British authorities at the end of the war. One Savannah list of 1,956 slaves is 41 percent male, 36 percent female, the remainder being children; and of the 3,000 blacks recorded as leaving New York City in 1783, 914 (or approximately 30 percent) were women.[18]

Even when the blacks did not run off, all was not well from the owner's point of view. Thomas Pinckney reported to his mother Eliza that the only slaves left on his Ashepoo plantation after a British raid in May 1779 were pregnant women and small children, who "pay no Attention" to the overseer's orders and "who are now perfectly free & live upon the best produce of the Plantation." Mrs. Pinckney had similar problems with her slaves at Belmont: she wanted them to come to her daughter Harriott's Santee plantation, she told Tom, but they were "attached to their homes and the little they have there [and so] have refused to remove." She concluded that if the blacks wished to join the British, neither she nor anyone else could stop them, "for they all do now as they please everywhere." More than a year later she complained of how she had been "Rob'd and deserted" by her slaves, remarking that it was impossible even to raise money by selling them because the "slaves in this country in genl, have behaved so infamously and even those that remain'd at home so Insolent and quite their own masters that there are very few purchasers" who would take them.[19]

Not all of the slaves who joined the British found freedom. Smallpox and camp fever were endemic in the British encampments, and many thousands of southern blacks died from those and other diseases. Of the runaways from Jefferson's plantations, only three (two men and a woman) seem to have joined the enemy and survived in freedom. Five more initially fled to the British, "returned & lived." The other fifteen died with the British or after they returned home, and Jefferson recorded the deaths of eleven more slaves as a result of disease caught from the returnees. Blacks who were the property of loyalists also ran the risk of being returned to their masters, and after the war it appears that some of the Negroes who were evacuated with the British army to the West Indies were sold as slaves.[20] But although the British formally agreed at the evacuation of Charleston and in the provisional peace treaty of November 1782 that they would not carry away slaves belonging to Americans, the army proved extremely reluctant to return to servitude blacks who had sought its protection. One South Carolina planter, all of whose slaves were in Charleston with the redcoats, was reduced in autumn 1782 to the futile hope that "they will not have transports enough to carry the negroes off." In all, the British carried with them approximately four thousand from Savannah, six thousand from Charleston, and four thousand from New York City. After the war, white southerners estimated their total losses in slaves at more than fifty-five thousand.[21]

If the British army attracted black Americans like a magnet, it repelled white Americans with similar force and efficiency. Everywhere the army went, fighting followed, and wherever there was fighting civilians, rebel and loyalist alike, left their homes to find places of greater safety. In January 1779, a South Carolinian told his brother, "the poor Georgians are flying over into this State, by Hundreds; many of them leaving their All behind." A few months later, as the British advanced northward, the people of his own state were experiencing "ravaging" and "Havoc." That year the revolutionaries successfully resisted the British invasion, but Charleston and much of South Carolina fell to royal forces in 1780. The victory did not bring peace to the province; quite the contrary. David Ramsay later recalled that after the surrender of Charleston, "political hatred raged with uncommon fury, and the calamities of civil war desolated the State." Then it was North Carolina's turn, and Virginia's. In 1781, Cornwallis's incursion into the latter state sent "every body scampering," to use the words of the young Yorktown girl Betsy Ambler. "What an alarming crisis is this," she wrote to a friend as she and her family fled before the advancing redcoats. "War in itself, however distant, is indeed terrible, but when brought to our very doors . . . the reflection is indeed overwhelming."[22]

In later years Betsy described her mother as having been especially "afflicted" by the family's repeated moves during the war; throughout the South white women had to endure similar hardships. Not only were many widowed by the war (reputedly there were 1,200 to 1,400 widows in the sparsely populated Ninety-Six district of South Carolina alone), but also they frequently had to face marauding troops and irregulars by themselves, since their husbands, fathers, and brothers were absent serving with one army or the other. Isolated in the countryside, groups of women and children gathered together for protection: at least twice during the war, for example, female friends of the Pinckney family sought refuge at Daniel and Harriott Horry's Santee plantation, and the wealthy widow Eliza Wilkinson, who lived in the sea islands south of Charleston, wrote of seeing "crowds of helpless, distressed women, weeping for husbands, brothers, or other near relations and friends, who were they knew not where, whether dead or alive." According to Mrs. Wilkinson, when the British moved through her neighborhood en route to Charleston in 1779, there were "nothing but women, a few aged gentlemen, and (shame to tell) a few skulking varlets" to oppose them.[23]

Mrs. Wilkinson had a frightening encounter with some British raiders, and her reflections on her experience are enlightening. For months she had assured herself that "our weak sex, '*incapable* of wrong, from either side claims privilege of safety,' " but a visit from "abusive" plunderers accompanied by armed Negroes disabused her of that notion. After the raiders had left with their booty, Mrs. Wilkinson found that she "trembled so with terror, that I could not support myself," and in the privacy of her room, she "gave way to a violent burst of grief." In the aftermath of the attack, she recorded that "we could neither eat, drink nor sleep in peace; for as we lay in our clothes every night, we could not enjoy the little sleep we got. The least noise alarmed us; up we would jump, expecting every moment to hear them demand admittance. In short, our nights were wearisome and painful; our days spent in anxiety and melancholy."[24]

For most well-to-do slaveholding whites like Mrs. Wilkinson, such troubles were unprecedented. Raised in luxury, accustomed to the constant attention and service of slaves, many were unprepared to cope with the situation in which they found themselves, and they recognized their own lack of resiliency. After the war, once-wealthy southern loyalist women frequently referred to the fact that they had been "accustomed to the Indulgence of Fashion & Fortune," had been "nurtured in the Lap of Affluence," or had been "born and breed to Affluence and indulgences of the tenderst Nature," when each explained her lack of success in handling "difficultys of which she had no experience in her former life."[25]

Contrast to this the behavior of southern women who had had previous experience in handling "difficultys," many of whom were of the poorer or middling sorts. They, too, encountered problems of unprecedented magnitude, but they— especially the urban businesswomen—seemed to land on their feet more often than their wealthier neighbors, and they were more willing to take the initiative and to act positively instead of sitting back passively waiting for the worst to happen.

Thus in 1780 a rural North Carolina woman impulsively followed her husband's militia unit to a battlefield, where she cared for the wounded of both sides until she learned he was unhurt. A Maryland carpenter's wife, whose drunken husband had enlisted on a privateer, physically resisted the marines who came for him and caused such an uproar by calling the recruiting officer "every vile name she could think of" that her husband was allowed to remain at home. Eleanor Lestor, the widowed Charleston shopkeeper, hid British sailors in her house and spoke "freely" against the rebel cause, and another "she-merchant" from Charleston, Elizabeth Thompson, assisted British prisoners of war, carried letters through the lines, and drove a disguised British spy through the American camp in her own chaise.[26] Other women like these followed their husbands to the armies of both sides and, though they lost many of their meager possessions, managed to surmount innumerable difficulties. The amazing saga of Susannah Marshall is a case in point. She and her loyalist husband William ran a tavern and boarding house in Baltimore before the war, until the rebels forced him to flee to the West Indies. She continued to operate their business, though the rebels looted the house, quartered troops in it, and prevented her from collecting from her debtors. In 1776 she chartered a ship to sail to Norfolk to join Lord Dunmore, but he had left the area by the time she arrived. Sailing back up Chesapeake Bay to Head of Elk, she there acquired another tavern and the local ferry concession. Allowed to leave the state in 1777, Mrs. Marshall invested her money in a cargo of foodstuffs, chartered another ship, and once again set sail. En route to the West Indies her ship was captured by the Americans, then recaptured by a royal cruiser. Since the cargo had been in the possession of rebels, it was forfeited under British law, and Mrs. Marshall salvaged nothing. Finally, she made her way to England, only to learn that her husband had died and to have her petition for a loyalist pension rejected by the authorities. Undaunted, she went to work as a nurse to support her family and in 1789 at last was awarded a permanent annual allowance by the British government.[27]

Susannah Marshall's tale doubtless was unique. But southern loyalist and patriot women alike saw their husbands murdered before their eyes, traveled hundreds of miles to escape one set of partisans or the other, endured repeated plunderings of their homes and farms, and survived physical ordeals far more damaging than the verbal abuse that so upset Eliza Wilkinson.[28] At the end of the war many were left with little more than the knowledge that they had managed to live through it all. Mrs. Wilkinson wrote, "It is some degree of satisfaction to look back on our sufferings, and congratulate ourselves on their being past, and that they were no *worse* when present." Eliza Lucas Pinckney wondered at the fate that had "so intirely deprived" her of a "Fortune sufficient to live Genteely in any part of the world," and a Georgia woman found her memories of wartime experiences so bitter that she absolutely refused to return to her former home.[29]

It is hardly surprising that in later years Betsy Ambler Brent, whose words supplied this essay with its title, entertained mixed feelings about the Revolution. The same event that had brought "independence and prosperity to my country," she mused in 1809, had involved "my immediate family in poverty and perplexity of every kind." Striving to discover the beneficial effects of the war, she found them not in public occurrences but rather in her own personal development: speaking of herself and her younger sister, she commented, "The only possible good from the entire change in our circumstances was that we were made acquainted with the manners and situation of our own Country, which we otherwise should never have known; added to this, necessity taught us to use exertions which our girls of the present day know nothing of, We Were forced to industry to appear genteely, to study Manners to supply the place of Education, and to endeavor by amiable and agreeable conduct to make amends for the loss of fortune."[30]

Surely Mrs. Brent's characterization of the war as requiring "exertions which our girls of the present day know nothing of" could have come from the pen of any other southern woman who had lived through the Revolution. Less wealthy families did not find their circumstances as greatly altered by the war as did the Amblers, but other southern women had had similar experiences. Accordingly, during and after the war the more highly educated and reflective among the white women began to raise questions about the social role to which they and their northern counterparts long had been confined. The fact that they did so constitutes an important consequence of the Revolution for American women; when coupled with the opportunity for freedom that the war offered to black females, it shows that, contrary to what historians usually have maintained, women did not simply "quietly sink back in their places and take up the old endless routine of their existence" after the war.[31]

III

Some colonial women always had railed against male conde-
scension. One thinks, for example, of the poet Anne Bradstreet's
defense of her literary capacities against carping male critics, or
of Esther Edwards Burr's almost equally well-known "smart
combat" with a Princeton tutor who had "mean thoughts of
Women." Such female outbursts of frustration were of a piece
with the raging of a North Carolina girl in 1784 against men who
"treat women as Ideiots" instead of recognizing them as
"reasonable beings."[32] Such anger was not new, even if it was
perhaps more commonly expressed in the aftermath of the
Revolution. But a great deal was new in other issues raised by
women during the 1770s and 1780s. Abigail Adams's correspondence with her husband John and her friend Mercy Otis Warren
contains often-quoted examples of such ideas; what is less well
known is that southern women expressed similar thoughts. The
Virginian Hannah Corbin, for example, asked her brother
Richard Henry Lee whether she, as a widow holding only a life
interest in an estate, rightfully could be taxed by the state on its
value, since she could neither vote nor alter the property in any
way.[33]

Somewhat more subtly, other southern white women
began to express dissatisfaction with certain of the proscriptions
that defined their lives. Two aspects of this trend stemmed
directly from wartime experiences. Under the common law, man
and wife were one person; a woman lost her independent legal
identity when she married. This meant, in terms of the Revolution, that a wife could suffer as a result of her husband's actions
and political beliefs, whether or not she shared them. Thus Anne
Hart, a resident of Charleston during the British occupation,
feared she would be banished from her home because her
husband Oliver had been a revolutionary activist early in the
war. David Ramsay later declared that such women had borne
their banishment with uniform "cheerfulness" and "resolution,"
but Anne Hart's letters indicate otherwise. Explaining her forth-

rightness by commenting, "I can speak free to my dearest," she wrote her husband of her "Anxiety" at the prospect of having to leave Charleston. She did not "condemn" him for what he had done, she said, but she was distressed because she was "liable to Banishment to transportation for Actions not her own." Of the other women in similar circumstances, she inquired, "What must those Wives expect from their Husbands, for whom they will suffer so much, what can they render to recompense for the Trouble they give?" The Revolution clearly had taught Mrs. Hart a lesson about women's inferior status before the law. One indication of her subsequent independence of mind was the fact that she was extremely reluctant to leave South Carolina to rejoin her husband in New Jersey after the war. [34]

The second example relates not to legal disabilities but to social limitations on the female role. With woman's sphere sharply defined to encompass only the household, the subject of politics was universally regarded as outside a woman's competence during the prewar years. And so in the 1760s and early 1770s when women discussed political matters in their letters, they invariably added a disclaimer: for instance, after making an acute loyalist analysis of America's current troubles, the wife of a Virginia Anglican cleric wrote in 1776, "Dont think I am engaging in politics. no; I assure you its a subject for which I have not either Talents or Inclination to enter upon." As the war continued, however, and women realized how important military and political events were in their lives, the formal disclaimers disappeared. A North Carolina woman, importuning her brother-in-law for more news in 1780, exuberantly declared, "you know I am a great politi-cian." And Eliza Wilkinson, referring to the critical days of 1779 during the first British invasion of South Carolina, recalled that "none were greater politicians than the several knots of ladies, who met together. All trifling discourse of fashions, and such low chat was thrown by, and we commenced perfect statesmen." Later she commented that the "men say we have no business with them [politics], it is not in our sphere." But, she wrote angrily, "I won't have it thought, that because we are the weaker sex as to *bodily* strength, my dear, we are capable of nothing more than minding the dairy, visiting the poultry-house, and all such domestic concerns, . . . Surely we may have sense enough to give our opinions to commend or discommend such actions as we may approve or disapprove; without being reminded of our spinning and household affairs as the only matters we are capable of thinking or speaking of with justness and propriety."[35]

Such sentiments were not unusual, if not exactly commonplace, in the writings of American women in the 1780s. But, strikingly, only north of the Mason-Dixon line did they have a significant impact. There men began to respond to the women's concerns and to expand their notions of what constituted women's sphere, to provide increased educational opportunities for women, and to publish (if not always to agree with) women's statements on their own behalf.[36] In the South no comparable developments occurred. There women expressed their sentiments privately, to each other and to their husbands, but they did not find men responsive to the issues they raised. The key question is why, and to find the answer it is necessary to return to a discussion of the impact of the war in the South.

By all accounts, the South suffered more from the Revolution than did the northern and middle states. The phases of the war fought on southern soil were both more destructive and more prolonged than those experienced by any northern region other than the immediate vicinity of New York City. The war in the North (with the same exception) largely concluded with the evacuation of Philadelphia in summer 1778, and so by the time the peace treaty was signed in autumn 1782 even the hardest-hit northern area had had time to recover. Not so the South. Long after Yorktown, guerrilla warfare continued throughout the Carolinas in particular, and not until after peace was officially proclaimed could recovery begin. And then it proved to be a long, slow process. Plantations had been laid waste, farms neglected, houses and fences left in disrepair, for far too long a time. Naval stores and indigo, two of the South's most important prewar exports, were now denied the bounties they had received when America was part of the British empire. Britain began to tax American rice and tobacco, thus necessitating a search for new markets and subjecting those products to increased competition in Britain itself.[37]

But most of all the South lacked labor. Those fifty-five thousand or more slaves lost during the war had been vital to the functioning of the southern agricultural economy. And so those planters who could afford it—and many who could not—began pouring their resources into the purchase of Negroes in order to bring their labor supply to prewar levels. Between 1783 and 1785, some seven thousand slaves were imported into South Carolina alone, and, because too many planters had gone deeply into debt to British traders, the South Carolina legislature in 1787 banned the further importation of slaves. In Georgia, the 1790 census recorded the presence of nearly thirty thousand blacks, where just seven years earlier slavery had "well-nigh disappeared," according to the leading historian of that state. And in both Virginia and South Carolina the 1790 census figures, when compared with 1782 estimates of the size of the black population, suggest a far higher rate of growth than would be expected from natural increase alone.[38]

Southerners frequently commented on the distressed economic conditions in the region during the postwar period. A Virginian in 1782 noted the "extreme poverty of our Country"; Eliza Lucas Pinckney described South Carolina as "greatly impoverished" by the loss of slaves; and a North Carolina woman recognized that her remaining blacks were now "va[lua]bel, . . . Chef of my Intrast." A Savannah resident observed in 1786 that "this place is far from having repaired the ruins of the late warr," and as late as 1799 an English visitor to Charleston remarked that the "people of this State tho' wealthy & very luxurious, have not yet got over the baleful effects of the revolutionary war. Their independance cost the Carolinians, much blood & treasure."[39]

The impact of this devastation upon society and social attitudes was incalculable. In the less-affected North, the postwar period could be one of experimentation with new ideas and social forms. Slaves could be emancipated, women could be educated, egalitarianism could be instituted in theory, if not in practice. But not in the South. There efforts were directed simply at rebuilding what had been lost, at conservatively reconstituting colonial society rather than at creating a new republican way of life. And so a Virginia planter in 1780 refused even to pay lip service to egalitarian rhetoric when he criticized the "little people": "Do they not know that a Gentleman is as necessary in a State, as a poor Man, and the poor as necessary as the Gentleman"? he asked. "So it must be! through all generations—for if we were all equall, one hour, nay one minute, wou'd make a difference according to mens Genious & Capacity." A Carolina boy born in 1785 recalled his youth as a time "when every nerve was strained to repair the broken fortunes of the Planters by the severest thrift and patient industry." It was not, his son concluded, "a good time to be born, for all the social relations of life had been badly disrupted." David Ramsay appropriately summed up the postwar years: "In such a condition of public affairs, to re-produce a state of things favorable to social happiness, required all the energies of the well disposed inhabitants."[40]

And what was the southern white woman's contribution to this rebuilding effort? According to Ramsay, "they aided by their economy and retirement from the world to repair the losses."[41] In other words, they retreated to the households that had shaped their lives before the war and to their standard prerevolutionary roles. Whether Ramsay's statement was factually accurate as far as the white women were concerned is questionable—indeed, the examples of Anne Hart and Eliza Wilkinson would seem to suggest otherwise—but it undoubtedly represented the wishes of their husbands, of whom Ramsay, of course, was one. For in rebuilding colonial society, in putting their resources into reconstructing an agricultural economy based on slavery, white southern males were ensuring, consciously or not, that the lives of their wives and daughters would continue to be determined by the nature of their households. Southern men were reinforcing a patriarchal society centered on an expanded household economy. In the North, the household became progressively less important in the economy as the years passed, as factories began to produce items formerly manufactured within the household, and as men increasingly worked outside the home. But in the South the household retained, perhaps even in certain areas expanded, its significance, as slavery gained an ever-tighter grip on the southern economy. Where the optimal family continued to be large and multiracial, and where the husband continued as the head of the increasingly important household, the wife's role necessarily contracted or remained the same. In the North, the family was left for the wife to supervise and eventually to control, at least theoretically.[42]

In short, the specific dimensions of the southern woman's role that Anne Firor Scott has termed "unusually confining" and the peculiarly rigid nature of the social hierarchy established by aristocratic white southern males that William R. Taylor has outlined both seem to have stemmed directly from the Revolution and its devastating aftermath.[43] The seeds were there before—there can be no doubt of that—but the difficult postrevolutionary years confirmed and solidified prewar patterns, whereas in the North the 1780s and 1790s saw significant alterations in colonial practices.

This observation can be illustrated by an examination of the changes, or the lack of such, in the image of women during the revolutionary era. Before the war, few or no regional differences can be discerned in the delineation of the ideal to which white women were expected to conform. Genteel colonial women in both the North and South read the same books and were told the same things: they were to be modest, pious, and submissive to their husbands; they must cultivate the feminine qualities of dependence, delicacy, and sensibility; and their chief accomplishments must be ornamental rather than useful.[44] In the 1780s, although some northern writers continued to compose their didactic literature in this vein, a new theme appeared, and indeed soon became dominant. As Linda Kerber has pointed out, the northern republican woman, though domestic, was characterized as "competent and confident," as one who ignored the "vagaries of fashion," as one who was "rational, benevolent, independent, self-reliant." And she was a woman who, moreover, had an important contribution to make to society at large. Yet in the South the image of women remained enmired in the colonial pattern. In 1789, when Charles Cotesworth Pinckney delivered a Fourth of July oration in Charleston, he described southern white women as having demonstrated "a sensibility so exquisitely delicate, a constancy so heroically firm" during the war that "admiration & delight are cold & inadequate terms to express the effect it had upon their enraptured Countrymen." Seeking a proper metaphor to express his admiration, Pinckney hit upon the following, a passive, stylized depiction if there ever was one: among the "massy ruins" of warfare were "a number of slender Columns, the most beauteous models of elegance & taste, erect & unimpaired notwithstanding the violence that occasioned the desolation which surrounds them." In sharp contrast, a northern orator in a similar speech just a year later emphasized the active and important role that republican women played in American society. Noting that the "female parent is considered of greatest importance" in raising children, that women's "thoughts and opinions are of the utmost conse-quence to the public," and that the influence of "female benevo-lence, candor and justice" would contribute to the "heightning of every improvement in political society," he reached the conclusion, startling for the eighteenth century, that women's control over manners was "of equal importance" in the republic to men's control of laws.[45] Despite the fact that in the years after 1800 progressively fewer northern authors seem to have approved an active role for women in politics and society, nevertheless the change in the years of the early republic was real. And there are few if any signs of a similar change in the South —a result, as has been argued, of the differential impact of the war.

Yet, ironically, in one case at least the more confining nature of the southern woman's role may also have generated the more successful revolt. In the early years of the nineteenth century, perhaps by coincidence, two brilliant young women, one northern, one southern, dreamed of becoming lawyers. The northerner, born in 1783 in Maine, wrote in 1802 that "the *law* would be my choice" of a profession. She expressed her desire to "arrive at an eminence which would be gratifying to my feelings," "to be a public character, respected and admired." She recognized, though, that as a woman she could not realistically aspire to such heights; she married, and died in 1809 of complications following the birth of her first child. Her name was Eliza Southgate Bowne, and today only a few persons are acquainted with her through her extraordinary published letters. The southerner, born in 1792 in South Carolina, first expressed her aspirations in 1808; like Eliza Southgate, her wishes were thwarted, and she wrote in later years, "Oh, had I received the education I desired, had I been bred to the profession of the law, I might have been a useful member of society." Unlike Eliza, she never married, and few beside herself would deny that she was a "useful member of society." In later life she went on to challenge both the system of slavery and the subordination of women. Her name was Sarah Moore Grimké.[46]

Notes

1. Elizabeth F. Ellet, *The Women of the American Revolution*, 3 vols. (New York, 1848, 1850), 1:xi; Elizabeth F. Ellet, *Domestic History of the American Revolution* (New York, 1850), p. 42.

2. For example, Elizabeth Cometti, "Women in the American Revolution," *New England Quarterly* 20 (1947): 329–46; Harry C. Green and Mary W. Green, *The Pioneer Mothers of America* (New York and London, 1913), vols. 2, 3; and Sally Smith Booth, *The Women of '76* (New York, 1973).

3. A good general survey is Robert V. Wells, "Household Size and Composition in the British Colonies in America, 1675–1775," *Journal of Interdisciplinary History* 4 (1974): 543–70. The impact of different sorts of households on women's lives is examined in greater depth in Mary Beth Norton, "Eighteenth Century American Women in Peace and War: The Case of the Loyalists," *William and Mary Quarterly*, 3d ser. 33 (July 1976): 386–409. Throughout this article the words "household" and "family" will be used interchangeably, as they were in the eighteenth century.

4. Oliver Hart to Anne Hart, 12 June 1781, Hart Papers, South Caroliniana Library, Columbia, S.C. (hereafter cited as SCL); Philip Vickers Fithian, *Journal and Letters of Philip Vickers Fithian 1773–1774: A Plantation Tutor of the Old Dominion*, ed. Hunter Dickinson Farish (Williamsburg, Va., 1957), p. 88; Janet Russell, claims testimony, Audit Office Papers, ser. 12, vol. 4, f. 73, Public Record Office, London (hereafter cited as AO). And see the testimony and loss schedules of other women in, for example, AO 12/46/166–68, 245–49; AO 13/25/395; AO 13/132/207–9; AO 13/138/432, 475.

5. Richard J. Hooker, ed., *The Carolina Backcountry on the Eve of the Revolution. The Journal and Other Writings of Charles Woodmason, Anglican Itinerant* (Chapel Hill, N.C., 1953), pp. 13, 16–17, 33, 39; John Coalter, autobiographical sketch to 1787, Brown-Coalter-Tucker Papers, box 1, Earl Gregg Swem Library, College of William and Mary (hereafter cited as W&M).

6. AO 13/125/639; AO 12/48/116; AO 12/50/347–48; AO 12/48/360; AO 12/48/179–82; AO 12/99/43. For examples of other Charleston businesswomen, see AO 12/46/77–80; AO 12/99/249, 290; AO 12/3/195. The accounts of a female Charleston tavernkeeper, Ann Little Norcliffe Cross, are preserved in the Paul Cross Papers, SCL. The work of rural southern women as spinners and weavers is revealed in such sources as Fithian, *Journal and Letters*, p. 131; Edward M. Riley, ed., *The Journal of John Harrower, An Indentured Servant in the Colony of Virginia, 1773–1776* (Williamsburg, Va., 1963), pp. 121, 134–35; and Robert Carter, Daybooks, 13:83–84, 195, 197, 209–11, 218; 14:5, 7, 105, 142, Robert Carter Papers, Duke University Library (hereafter cited as DL). A rural Virginia woman's descriptions of the Baltimore market may be found in "Diary of M. Ambler, 1770," *Virginia Magazine of History and Biography* 45 (1937): 156.

7. Harry Toulmin, *The Western Country in 1793: Reports on Kentucky and Virginia*, ed. Marion Tinling and Godfrey Davies (San Marino, Calif., 1948), p. 20; Ethel Armes, ed., *Nancy Shippen Her Journal Book* (Philadelphia, 1935), p. 236; Lucy C. Smith, Memoir of her Mother Lucy Grymes Nelson, Smith-Digges Papers, Colonial Williamsburg, Williamsburg, Va.; Fithian, *Journal and Letters*, p. 48. The last two descriptions have been pluralized. For similar comments, see Marquis de Chastellux, *Travels in North America in the Years 1780, 1781 and 1782*, ed. and trans. Howard C. Rice, Jr. (Chapel Hill, N.C., 1963), 2:422, 441–42.

8. "Diary of a Little Virginia Girl (Sally Cary Fairfax)," *Virginia Magazine of History and Biography* 11 (1903–4): 213; Helen Blair to James Iredell, 20 April 1789, Iredell Papers, DL.

9. Eliza Lucas Pinckney, *The Letterbook of Eliza Lucas Pinckney 1739–1762*, ed. Elise Pinckney (Chapel Hill, N.C., 1972), pp. 34–35, 33. See also Ann Kinloch, diary, April 1799, Langdon Cheves Collection, South Carolina Historical Society, Charleston (hereafter cited as SCHS); Lucy Armistead to Maria Armistead, 16 Feb. 1788, Armistead-Cocke Papers, W&M; Anne Clark to Dorothy Murray, 21 Nov. 1764, J. M. Robbins Papers, Massachusetts Historical Society, Boston (hereafter cited as MHS); "A Visit to Mt. Vernon—A Letter of Mrs. Edward Carrington to her Sister, Mrs. George Fisher," *William and Mary Quarterly*, 2d ser. 18 (1938): 198–202.

10. Pinckney, ed., *Letterbook*, p. 181; Eliza Lucas Pinckney to [Mrs. Boddicot], 20 May 1745, to Mary Lucas, [c. Dec. 1746], both in Eliza Lucas Pinckney Papers, DL; Elizabeth Ambler Carrington to Nancy Fisher, [c. 1807?], Elizabeth Ambler Papers (photostats), Library of Congress, Manuscript Division, Washington, D.C. (hereafter cited as LCMD). But in later life Charles Cotesworth Pinckney "used to dissuade all those over whom he had any influence from the premature instruction of their children, saying that from an over anxiety to make him a clever fellow he had run the risk of being a very stupid one," according to William Gilmore Simms's "Memoir of the Pinckney Family of South Carolina," Pinckney Family Papers, 2d ser., vol. 2, LCMD.

11. John Mercer to Battaile Muse, [n.d.], and John Hatley Norton to same, 23 Dec. 1781, both in Battaile Muse Papers, DL; Dorothy Forbes to Elizabeth Smith, 8 Sept. 1769, Murray Family Papers, box 4, New-York Historical Society, New York, N.Y. In November 1776, for example, Robert Carter decided against assigning a "very stout & strong" fifteen-year-old-girl to spinning duties, substituting for her a less healthy fourteen-year-old (see Carter, Daybook, 13: 218, 221, Carter Papers, DL). In November 1784, female slaves on Thomas Middleton's Goose Creek, South Carolina, plantation held the following jobs (in addition to field work): house servant, dairy maid, nurse, washer, and seamstress. His plantation book containing this list is in the Middleton Papers, Southern Historical Collection, University of North Carolina, Chapel Hill (hereafter cited as SHC-UNC). Women who worked on outlying quarters normally were field hands; see various inventories in the Muse Papers (for example, that of W. C. Seldon's Mountain Quarter, 10 July 1786, or that of Hugh Nelson's Frederick County estate, [1778]).

12. Allan Kulikoff has proved this point in his unpublished paper, "The Beginnings of the Afro-American Family in Maryland," which I thank him for sharing with me. That the pattern he describes was not peculiar to the Chesapeake may be shown by a reference to plantation books like that kept by Charles Cotesworth Pinckney the younger in South Carolina. Of the seventy-four slaves with which Pinckney and his wife began their married life in 1812, apparently only eleven were unrelated to the others. The book is vol. 1 of the second series of Pinckney Family Papers.

13. Francis Triplett to Battaile Muse, [n.d.], Muse Papers, DL; Anne Hart to [Oliver Hart], 23 July 1781, Hart Papers, SCL; Robert Carter to Clement Brooke, 27 July 1778, Letterbook 3, (book 3), pp. 45–46, Carter Papers, DL; James Mercer to Battaile Muse, 10 July 1777, Muse Papers, DL. See also Gerald Mullin, *Flight and Rebellion: Slave Resistance in Eighteenth-Century Virginia* (New York, 1972), pp. 109–10; and Peter H. Wood, *Black Majority: Negroes in Colonial South Carolina from 1670 through the Stono Rebellion* (New York, 1974), pp. 248–49.

14. Alice Morse Earle, *Colonial Dames and Good Wives* (Boston and New York, 1895), p. 15; John S. Ezell, ed., and Judson P. Wood, trans., *The New Democracy in America: Travels of Francisco de Miranda in the United States, 1783–1784* (Norman, Okla., 1963), pp. 5–6. This observation applies to black women as well. From documents in such papers as those of Battaile Muse, it is clear that female slaves traveled far less than their male counterparts.

15. Gerald Mullin argues persuasively in *Flight and Rebellion*, pp. 34–38, that the acquisition of artisan skills had this effect on male slaves. Although he does not explicitly apply his theory to women, there is no reason why it should not also be relevant to their experience.

16. Riley, ed., *Harrower Journal*, p. 121; Robert Carter, Letterbooks, 2:189; 3 (book 2), pp. 27–28; 5:11; and Deed of Emancipation, 1 Aug. 1791, all in Carter Papers, DL. On southern cloth production in general, see Julia Cherry Spruill, *Women's Life and Work in the Southern Colonies* (Chapel Hill, N.C., 1938), pp. 74–76; and James Curtis Ballagh, ed., *The South in the Building of the Nation*, vol. 5, *The Economic History 1607–1865* (Richmond, Va., 1909), pp. 231–33, 309–10.

17. Margaret Wheeler Willard, ed., *Letters on the American Revolution, 1774–1776* (Boston and New York, 1925), p. 233; Robert Carter, Daybook 13:175–78, Carter Papers, DL; Robert Carter to American Officers, 30 Oct. 1781, Letterbook 4:137, ibid.; David Ramsay, *Ramsay's History of South Carolina, from its First Settlement in 1670 to the year 1808*, 2 vols. (Newberry, S.C., 1858), 1:178. See also Oliver Hart to Joseph Hart, 16 Feb. 1779, Hart Papers, SCL; and Thomas Cabeen, petition to General Assembly, 19 June 1781, Legislative Papers, 39, North Carolina Division of Archives and History (hereafter cited as NCDAH), for accounts of slave losses in Georgia and North Carolina, respectively. On the impact of Dunmore's proclamation, see Benjamin Quarles, *The Negro in the American Revolution* (Chapel Hill, N.C., 1961), pp. 19–32; Mullin, *Flight and Rebellion*, pp. 130–36; and Ira Berlin, *Slaves without Masters: The Free Negro in the Antebellum South* (New York, 1974), pp. 16–18. A good general discussion of both British and American policy toward blacks during the war can be found in Donald Robinson, *Slavery in the Structure of American Politics, 1765–1820* (New York, 1971), pp. 98–130.

18. Edwin Morris Betts, ed., *Thomas Jefferson's Farm Book* (Princeton, N.J., 1953), p. 29; John Ball, plantation account book, 1780–84, John Ball Papers, DL; Quarles, *Negro in Revolution*, pp. 163, 172. Some of the runaways from Carter's Coles Point plantation were women; see Carter, Letterbook 4:137, 139, Carter Papers, DL. For examples of other female runaways to the British, see Eliza Lucas Pinckney to Thomas Pinckney, 13 Sept. 1780, Eliza Lucas Pinckney Papers,

SCHS; Samuel Stiles to William Telfair, 2 Feb. 1779, Edward Telfair Papers, DL; and John Hatley Norton to Battaile Muse, 23 Dec. 1781, Muse Papers, DL.

19. Thomas Pinckney to Eliza Lucas Pinckney, 17 May [1779], and Eliza Lucas Pinckney to Thomas Pinckney, 17 May 1779, both in Pinckney Papers, SCHS; Eliza Pinckney to [Mrs. R. E.——], 25 Sept. 1780 (draft), Pinckney Family Papers, ser. 1, box 5, LCMD.

20. Betts, ed., *Jefferson's Farm Book*, p. 29. Ramsay, *History of S.C.*, 1:178–79, 190, discusses the deaths of runaways from disease. For examples of loyalists' runaway slaves, see AO 12/46/78; AO 12/48/233; AO 12/50/391; AO 13/94/324; and AO 13/95/3. On resales in the West Indies, see Quarles, *Negro in Revolution*, p. 177.

21. John Lewis Gervais to Battaile Muse, 2 Dec. 1782, Muse Papers, DL. Estimates of losses and discussions of British actions may be found in Ramsay, *History of S.C.*, 1:270–72, E. Merton Coulter, *Georgia: A Short History* (rev. ed., Chapel Hill, N.C., 1960), p. 147, and Robert McColley, *Slavery and Jeffersonian Virginia* (2d ed., Urbana, Ill., 1973), pp. 82–87. Ira Berlin notes that after the war some former slaves who remained in America were able to pass as free and that many others were emancipated; see *Slaves without Masters*, pp. 15–50. The later lives of some of the blacks evacuated with the British are traced in Mary Beth Norton, "The Fate of Some Black Loyalists of the American Revolution," *Journal of Negro History* 58 (1973): 402–26, and Robin W. Winks, *The Blacks in Canada* (New Haven, 1971), pp. 24–60. The figures in the text are taken from Quarles, *Negro in Revolution*, pp. 163, 167, 172.

22. Oliver Hart to Joseph Hart, 14 Jan. and 18 July 1779, both in Hart Papers, SCL; David Ramsay, *History of S.C.*, 1:255–56; Elizabeth Ambler to [Mildred Smith], 1781, Ambler Papers, LCMD.

23. Elizabeth Ambler Brent to Nancy Fisher, 1809, Ambler Papers, LCMD, discusses their mother. David Ramsay (*History of S.C.*, 1:258) said there were 1,400 widows in Ninety-Six; Francisco de Miranda (*New Democracy in America*, p. 24) heard that there were 1,200. The gatherings at the Horrys' are mentioned in Thomas Pinckney to Harriott Horry, 11 June 1776, Pinckney Family Papers, ser. 1, box 6, LCMD, and C.C. Pinckney to Sally Pinckney, 26 May 1779, ibid., ser. 1, box 2. Mrs. Wilkinson's comments may be found in Caroline Gilman, ed., *Letters of Eliza Wilkinson, during the Invasion and Possession of Charlestown, S.C. by the British in the Revolutionary War* (reprinted, New York, 1969), pp. 12–13, 16. And see John Laurens to Benjamin Lincoln, 21 April 1780, Miscellaneous Manuscripts, SCL.

24. Gilman, ed., *Wilkinson Letters*, pp. 22–23, 31, 46.

25. AO 13/40/93 (Damaris Kennedy); AO 13/134/504 (Ariana Randolph); AO 13/132/257 (Henrietta Walker); and AO 13/32/126 (Isabella Logan).

26. Booth, *Women of '76*, pp. 248–49; *Autobiography of Charles Biddle, Vice-President of the Supreme Executive Council of Pennsylvania 1745–1821* (Philadelphia, 1883), p. 170; testimony re: Eleanor Lestor, 22 May 1786, AO 12/48/360–61; documents re: the case of Elizabeth Thompson, AO 12/46/77–79, AO 13/134/5, and AO 13/136/7.

27. Susannah Marshall's tale may be traced in AO 12/6/257–63, AO 12/99/244, AO 13/62/4, 7, and AO 13/40/173. The equally incredible experiences of another southern woman, Ann Finlayson of Georgia, are revealed in AO 13/34/482–97, AO 13/35/26, AO 13/137/215, and AO 12/101/250. Two loyalist women who had followed their husbands to the army mention that fact in AO 13/24/359, 386, and Thomas Pinckney commented on some revolutionary camp followers in a letter to Harriott Horry, 19 April 1779, Pinckney Family Papers, ser. 1, box 8, LCMD. And see Walter Hart Blumenthal, *Women Camp Followers of the American Revolution* (Philadelphia, 1952).

28. For examples: AO 13/36 pt 3/1270–71, AO 13/121/217, and AO 13/119/97; Elizabeth Steele to Ephraim Steele [19 April 1781], John Steele Papers, NCDAH; and document describing the death of Alexander Gaston, August 1781, William Gaston Papers, SHC-UNC.

29. Gilman, ed., *Wilkinson Letters*, p. 22; Eliza Lucas Pinckney to Alexander Garden, 14 May 1782, Pinckney Papers, SCHS; George Baillie, Jr., to John McIntosh, Jr., 7 Sept. 1783, John McIntosh, Jr., Papers, Georgia Historical Society, Savannah. See also Lucy Smith, Memoir of Lucy Grymes Nelson, Smith-Digges Papers, Colonial Williamsburg.

30. Elizabeth Ambler Brent to Nancy Fisher, March 1809, and [c. 1810?], Ambler Papers, LCMD.

31. Arthur M. Schlesinger, Sr., *New Viewpoints in American History* (New York, 1923), p. 132. I have changed the verb tense in the quotation.

32. Josephine Fisher, "The Journal of Esther Burr," *New England Quarterly* 3 (1930): 301–2; Helen Blair to William Blair, 20 Aug. 1784, Iredell Papers, DL. Bradstreet's retort is contained in a poem conveniently reprinted in Aileen Kraditor, ed., *Up from the Pedestal* (Chicago, 1968), pp. 29–30.

33. James Curtis Ballagh, ed., *The Letters of Richard Henry Lee*, 2 vols. (reprint ed., New York, 1970), 1:392–93. Relevant excerpts from Mrs. Adams's letters have been reprinted in Miriam Schneir, ed., *Feminism: The Essential Historical Writings* (New York, 1972), pp. 2–4.

34. Anne Hart to Oliver Hart, 19, 23 July 1781, Hart Papers, SCL; Ramsay, *History of S.C.*, 1:198. For a loyalist woman's ingenious but apparently unsuccessful attempt to make her dependent legal status work for her, see Elizabeth Dulany, petition to Maryland assembly, 27 Nov. 1787, AO 13/39/497, and related documents ff. 496, 509.

35. Elizabeth Feilde to Maria Armistead, 3 June 1776, Armistead-Cocke Papers, W&M; Elizabeth Steele to Ephraim Steele, 25 Oct. 1780, Steele Papers, NCDAH; Gilman, ed., *Wilkinson Letters*, pp. 17, 61.

36. These developments are discussed in Linda K. Kerber, "Daughters of Columbia: Educating Women for the Republic, 1787–1805," in Stanley Elkins and Eric McKitrick, eds., *The Hofstadter Aegis* (New York, 1974), pp. 36–59.

37. On the economic impact of the war in the South, see Curtis Nettels, *The Emergence of a National Economy 1775–1815* (New York, 1962), pp. 45, 49–51; and Gordon C. Bjork, "The Weaning of the American Economy: Independence, Market Changes, and Economic Development," *Journal of Economic History* 24

(1964): 543–44, 555–56. A useful study of a specific commodity is G. Terry Sharrer, "Indigo in South Carolina 1671–1796," *South Carolina Historical Magazine* 72 (1971): 94–103.

38. On slave importations and planter indebtedness, see Nettels, *Emergence of National Economy*, pp. 58, 82, 136–37; Merrill Jensen, *The New Nation* (reprint ed., New York, 1965), pp. 318–19; and Robert W. Fogel and Stanley Engerman, *Time on the Cross*, 2 vols. (Boston, 1974), 1:86–89. Population figures are given in Ballagh, ed., *South in Building of Nation*, 5:17–18; Stella Sutherland, *Population Distribution in Colonial America* (New York, 1936), pp. 238–39, 259; Evarts B. Greene and Virginia D. Harrington, *American Population before the Federal Census of 1790* (New York, 1932), pp. 141–43, 154–55, 179. The quotation on Georgia is from Coulter, *Georgia*, p. 166. On the closing of the slave trade in South Carolina: Patrick S. Brady, "Slave Trade and Sectionalism in South Carolina 1787–1808," *Journal of Southern History* 38 (1972): 601–20. A comparison of the best estimate of the slave population for South Carolina in 1782 (approximately 75,000; that is, 100,000 minus 25,000 slaves lost to their owners through death or emigration) with the 1790 census for the state, which shows a slave populace of 108,895, gives an annual growth rate of 4.7 percent when 2 to 3 percent would be a normal rate of natural increase. A similar comparison of 1782 and 1790 census figures for those Virginia counties on Cornwallis's line of march or bordering the York, Rappahanock, lower Potomac, and James rivers gives a nearly identical result: 4.6 percent rate of annual growth. The clear implication is that in both states planters were importing large numbers of slaves to make up their wartime losses. I wish to thank Robert Wells of Union College for his assistance in making these calculations.

39. John Hatley Norton to Battaile Muse, 7 Aug. 1782, Muse Papers, DL; Eliza Lucas Pinckney to [Mrs. R. E. ——], 25 Sept. 1780 (draft), Pinckney Family Papers, ser. 1, box 5, LCMD; Margaret Murray to Elizabeth Murray, 7 June 1782, Robbins Papers, MHS; Penuel Bowen to Nathaniel Barrett, 20 Dec. 1786, Bowen-Cooke Papers, SCHS; Caleb Cotton to his parents, 6 Aug. 1799, Cotton Papers, SCHS.

40. James Mercer to Battaile Muse, 17 Oct. 1780, Muse Papers, DL; Francis deBose Richardson, "Memoirs of Our Family," p. 21, SHC-UNC; Ramsay, *History of S.C.*, 2:247.

41. Ramsay, *History of S.C.*, 2:229.

42. On the South: William R. Taylor, *Cavalier and Yankee: The Old South and the American National Character* (New York, 1961), pp. 162–76. On changes in the North see Nancy F. Cott, *The Bonds of Womanhood: "Woman's Sphere" in New England, 1780–1835* (New Haven, 1977).

43. Anne Firor Scott, *The Southern Lady: From Pedestal to Politics 1830–1930* (Chicago, 1970), pp. 4–17, describes the ideal held out to white women in the antebellum South.

44. Cf. Spruill, *Women's Life and Work*, pp. 208–31, and Mary Sumner Benson, *Women in 18th Century America: A Study in Opinion and Social Usage* (reprint ed., Port Washington, N.Y., 1966).

45. Kerber, "Daughters of Columbia," in Elkins and McKitrick, eds., *Hofstadter Aegis*, p. 42; [Charles Cotesworth Pinckney], July 4th oration, Charleston, 1789, ser. 1, box 6, Pinckney Family Papers, LCMD; James Tilton, "An Oration Pronounced on the 5th July, 1790," *Universal Asylum and Columbian Magazine* 5 (Dec. 1790): 372–73.

46. Eliza Southgate Bowne, *A Girl's Life Eighty Years Ago*, ed. Clarence Cook (London, 1888), p. 102; Gerda Lerner, *The Grimké Sisters from South Carolina* (reprint ed., New York, 1971), p. 59.

8
British Caribbean and North American Slaves in an Era of War and Revolution, 1775–1807

by Michael Mullin

In *Common Sense* (1776) Thomas Paine accused Great Britain of inciting American slaves "to destroy us." In Virginia, where rebellion existed for more than a year before the publication of Paine's pamphlet, the last royal governor raised the king's standard at Norfolk and proclaimed liberty for slaves who would join the war against their masters. Lord Dunmore was his sovereign's personal representative, and his strategy, which unleashed the dread specter of a general servile war, was unprecedented and terrifying. But Virginia Negroes during the Revolution never rebelled, although several thousand did resist as solitary, unorganized fugitives who joined whichever army— British, American, or French—seemed to offer them the most favorable prospects of freedom.[1]

Elsewhere in the Chesapeake the planter's authority was more fragile, and slaves reacted more dangerously than in Virginia. In Dorchester County, Maryland, authorities in 1776 broke up a meeting of blacks and confiscated eighty guns, bayonets, and swords; and later on the Eastern Shore Negroes fought alongside Tory partisans.[2]

Blacks in South Carolina should have been even more dangerously rebellious than were Chesapeake slaves. Low-country Negroes, the most African of all North American slaves, had a fearsome tradition of organized resistance going back to the great Stono River rebellion of 1739. Although the evidence is inferential and sketchy (Charleston Police Board Minutes during the British occupation, loyalist claims, and correspondence of such military commanders as Sir Guy Carleton, Thomas Pinckney, and Nathanael Greene), South Carolina blacks apparently did not take advantage of their owners' predicament during the Revolution, nor did lowcountry planters exhibit the anxiety about their slaves' loyalty manifested by Maryland and Virginia slaveholders.[3]

At the close of the Revolution, North American planters realized that somehow a great disaster had been averted and praised slaves for their loyalty in the face of innumerable opportunities to act otherwise. The scion of the powerful Carroll family of Maryland wrote: "I think our negroes on the island have given proof of their attachment. . . . They might have gone off if they had been so disposed." When General William Moultrie returned to his South Carolina plantation in 1782, he was deeply affected by his slaves' reception. Each came forward, took his hand, and said, "God Bless you, massa! we glad for see you, massa! . . . The tears stole from my eyes and ran down my cheeks. . . . I then possessed about 200 slaves, and not one of them left me during the war, although they had great offers."[4]

Further south in the British Caribbean, planters, who encountered potentially even more destructive forces and events than the Americans did, also were fortunate to escape unscathed during years of war and revolution. In the sugar islands slaves outnumbered whites ten to fifteen to one; and maroonage (armed mountain villages of runaway Negroes) was a continual source of danger to whites and an inspiration to some lowland blacks. During this era of fundamental change in West Indian slavery, planters also faced increasing bankruptcies, declining profits, the revolution of former slaves in Santo Domingo (Haiti), British abolitionism, and their slaves' insistence that the end of the trade would be followed quickly by the abolition of slavery itself. Dissenting preachers, empire loyalists from America, and royalist emigrés from nearby French colonies—torn by civil wars and racial strife—came into the English islands and contributed to the atmosphere of crisis.

Behind this unnerving, kaleidoscopic scene loomed an even greater revolution in France, "by Men," the Jamaican assembly memorialized to the king, "who after overturning the Constitution of their own Country, and murdering their Sovereign, wished to carry their principles of Anarchy and Confusion, throughout the World." For planters the European dimension of the great French Revolution was sufficiently de-moralizing, but when the "Levelling *Influenza*" threatened to "spread thro' the ruder Multitudes on This Side of the Western Ocean," their reactions were feverish—and not unreasonable. For the French Revolution was a shattering reality in the Carib-bean, where the urbane governor of Guadaloupe, Victor Hugues, was busy deploying bilingual mulatto brigands, moun-tain fighters, in the British islands to incite maroons and planta-tion Negroes. Throughout the 1790s and Napoleonic era, then, a familiar image that sprang to mind whenever planters faced even the most inconsequential slave conspiracy was the ghastly possi-bility that it might become a "second St. Domingo War."[5]

These profoundly troubled reactions to the threat of a general servile uprising, however, came only from Jamaica—England's "jewel" of empire, staging area for counterrevolution against black and white jacobinism in the Caribbean, and an island with the largest and apparently the most dangerous slave and maroon communities in plantation America. But slaves elsewhere in the islands reacted differently to the crises of the era, as they had done in the American Revolution. Barbadians throughout the late eighteenth century, for example, praised their slaves' "quiet & well disposed" behavior, their "patriotism" and "tranquility."[6]

In retrospect the views of relatively peaceful slaves in wartime Barbados and South Carolina are more accurate and informative about those of all Anglo-American slaves during the era than are the words of Paine, the Virginians, and Jamaicans who thought blacks would "destroy" them. There never was a "second St. Domingo War" in any British or American plantation society at this time. To understand why this was so the following examination of the two major kinds of resistance that did take place—African uprisings and Creole conspiracies—also probes the question of why Africans and native American slaves seldom were able to overcome their ethnic and acculturative differences to cooperate as slaves had done in Haiti. While viewing slave rebels in their settings—mountains, plantations, and towns—on the one hand, and their varying rates of cultural change, on the other, I try as best I can to view the era from the slaves' vantage point by concentrating on what concerned them most: in the society at large, urbanization, accelerated by the endemic wars of the era; the French and Haitian revolutions, which meant much more to blacks than the American Revolution; and, on the plantations, the slaves' households and property, which they sometimes had to defend against other Negroes (maroons and French brigands, principally) as well as against whites. Essentially this essay is a proposal that Anglo-American slavery be examined in a comparative, hemispheric perspective on the basis of the slaves' varying rates of acculturation; this process depended upon the degree to which their owners and white supervisors participated in plantation management and the extent to which slaves controlled such vital resources as provision land and markets. In the islands plantation sanctions and values—partially of the slaves' own making—were based on the considerable control slaves exercised over food, markets, polygynous households, and heritable property. Upon this base Caribbean slaves created a Creole culture that was strongly African and achieved a degree of cultural autonomy unequaled on the mainland, particularly in Virginia, where the persistent, dominating presence of the master figure undercut the sources of slave authority (so prevalent in the islands) and encouraged slaves to assimilate to a culture that was largely not of their own making.

British and American slaves during this era participated in essentially two types of rebellion, actual insurrections and conspiracies. Different kinds of slaves with different strategies and objectives characterized each type. Insurrectionists and maroons were usually native Africans, many of whom were "new Negroes," men and a few women who only recently had been enslaved and imported to the new world. They followed the cultural sanctions of their African tribal ways and used the wild and formidable island interiors and the frontier areas of mainland America to establish either remote and relatively self-sufficient villages or camps for mounting raids on lowland plantations. Conspirators, on the other hand, were usually the sons and daughters of native Africans (called Creoles in the islands and country-born or American-born on the mainland), whose nonfield jobs as artisans and domestics, and situation as town Negroes accelerated their assimilation and made them unaccustomed and temperamentally unsuited to the maroons' techniques of wilderness survival and hit-and-run warfare. Creoles directed their elaborate schemes and ambitions at the whites' forts and port towns.

Maroons, who were ubiquitous throughout the mountainous islands, may be characterized in several ways: they were armed and organized; they lived either in camps or in more permanent villages with fairly stable economic and political arrangements around their root crops and small stock, headmen, conjurors, and obeahmen; they were not isolated from the plantations below, where they had wives and traded (wild hog meat for gunpowder and shot on one occasion); and they lived in relatively inaccessible mountain fastnesses. Comparatively flat, treeless, and dry islands like Barbados and Antigua had no reported instances of maroonage in the eighteenth century.[7]

By the 1760s, for example, maroons in Dominica—a wild, heavily forested, precipitous island—had built sturdy houses, planted gardens, raised poultry and hogs, fished in bountiful streams and the sea, and traded with plantation Negroes. They lived "very comfortably," wrote Thomas Atwood, a contemporary planter and historian, and they were "seldom disturbed." They also kept to themselves and never killed a white until 1778, when during the French occupation of the island their occasional nighttime forays became daytime raids of arson and pillage to the outskirts of Roseau, the capital city, with "conk shells blowing and French colours flying."[8]

In 1785 and 1786 the English used black soldiers, trackers, and spies to dismantle the major runaway settlements. In one camp of twenty or thirty they captured both English and French Negroes, including two women (one the governor's slave, Mary), and Monsieur Garshett, who had been in the woods for twenty years. They also killed Balla, a headman, probably by torture. Calling out to his tormentors to cut off his head because he could not be killed, Balla, the governor reported, "only . . . expressed much anxiety" about his obeah or charm, which he wanted buried, and his little five-year-old son whom "he bid to remember, the Beckys or White Men had killed his father."[9]

Armed and organized uprisings and maroonage in North America were virtually unknown at this time. The few instances of significant rebellion are described only in South Carolina sources (after the Revolution) and with none of the richness or depth of comparable Caribbean evidence. In December 1782, for instance, a Goose Creek planter wrote about fifty to one hundred "Black Dragoons who have been out four times within the last ten days plundering & robbing . . . last night they came as high as Mrs. Godins where they continued from 11 oclock till 4 this morning, & carried off everything they could . . . all her Cattle, Sheep, Hogs [and] Horses."[10]

When the British evacuated Charleston and Savannah some black irregulars chose to remain behind. Calling themselves "the King of England's soldiers," they raided at night and disappeared during the day into Savannah River swamps, and into a fortified encampment that was half a mile long, four hundred feet deep, with twenty-one houses and fields of crops surrounded by a four-foot breastwork of log and cane pilings. In May 1786 a combined force of militia and Catawba Indians defeated them, but a year later a very sparse governor's message to the legislature mentioned serious depredations of armed Negroes, "too numerous to be quelled by patrols," in the southern part of the new state.[11]

Even earlier, when most slaves were native Africans and the frontier was nearer at hand, maroonage in North America never matched its extent and intensity in the islands. On the American frontier armed and dangerous frontiersmen and land speculators and Indians, particularly the Over-the-hill Cherokees in the Carolinas—who had no equivalent in the Caribbean—fought runaway slaves for access to the wilderness.

As North American slaves lost tribal ways they seldom resisted slavery cooperatively. During the eighteenth century, few ran off in groups to establish remote settlements. While in the islands fugitives could join large and self-sufficient maroon villages on the ridges above their plantations, new Negroes in North America usually sat before smoldering fires in lonely camps in the woods alongside tobacco and rice pieces; and sometimes in the evening hours they came in to be fed at the doors of slave cabins and kitchens.[12]

These pictures of maroon and plantation blacks are somewhat misleading as they represent slavery in this era incompletely. The most significant changes in Anglo-American plantation societies took place in cities—not the countryside— and among free people of color (called freedmen or free Negroes in North America) and varieties of town slaves—domestics, artisans, dock roustabouts, watermen, and sailors. Whites throughout the mainland and islands overreacted to city slaves as they never had either to the plantation folk or the maroons, whose ways of resisting slavery were soon outmoded by the economic and cultural dvelopments that were pushing urban conspirators to the fore.

Endemic warfare after 1763 accelerated the growth of Anglo-American cities and the nonplantation (usually wartime) industries they incorporated. Slaves and free people of color were indispensable workers in mines and forges, munition and textile manufactories, and salt and rope works. These urban industries increased slave literacy and knowledge of colonial culture generally, while breaking down old and familiar patterns of plantation authority that traditionally had controlled slaves fairly well.

Varieties of documents from Baltimore to Bridgetown, Barbados—borough regulations, grand jury presentments, newspaper notices, and letters to the editor—make similar points regarding the expanding urban process and scene at this time: towns were rapidly getting out of control, and new police and regulations were needed to help identify and restrict city slaves and keep watch on their activities. In 1780 citizens in Augusta, Georgia, demanded more effective policing of slaves "rambling from place to place without written permits." In 1784 the captain of the James Street Fire Company in Bridgetown, Barbados, requested parish representatives to "suppress & abate such sheds & low houses erected & now erecting by negro & mulatto slaves & free negroes, which are not only public nuisances but afford fuel to spreading flames." Georgetown, South Carolina, citizens in 1790 asked for a stricter regulation of bread, liquor, and billiard licenses and an end to liquor sales to slaves aboard ships in the harbor. In Chatham County, Savannah, Georgia, in 1793 and 1796 whites demanded that Negro cartmen wear identification badges and insisted on better regulation of house rentals to Negroes and of dram shops, as their use of the latter encouraged them to steal. In Kingston, Jamaica, in 1797, a newspaper notice warned, "House-keepers cannot be too careful in seeing their doors & gates locked at this season of the year; & it is the duty of the Constables to take up all Negroes" in the streets after nine o'clock in the evening.[13]

Officials soon recognized that cities generated new kinds of organized resistance by slaves whose ways had become like the whites', but who were culturally even more threatening than the Africans. The solution of the Jamaica assembly was to keep slaves "constantly at home," while striking at the essentials of their potentially insurrectionary rites and associations—"disarm them, prevent caballing, drumming, sounding Conches & Horns, securing Rum & strong liquors, and also ammunition."[14] A contemporary historian, John Poyer of Speightstown, Barbados, warned in 1806 that "the coloured tribe not content with having their Balls, Routs & assemblies have established places of public rendezvous for Cockfighting & other Species of Gaming & in their general conduct have assumed an insolent & provoking deportment towards the legitimate inhabitants of the Island."[15] Poyer saw the rapid urbanization of large numbers of blacks in postwar Anglo-America as a contest between two cultures (his being the "legitimate" one) for control of Bridgetown. In Charleston, Henry Laurens, struggling in 1776 to rent and hire out his brother's town houses and black servants, finally threw up his hands and described urban slavery: "Your Negroes in some measure," he said, "govern themselves"—a contemporary view of urban blacks whom Ira Berlin appropriately has called "slaves without masters."[16]

In this context the rebellions designed by Anglo-American Creoles were similar regardless of their respective society's stage of development. St. George Tucker's account of Gabriel Prosser's conspiracy in Richmond, Virginia, in 1800—the largest and most ambitious up to that time in North America—is a most useful introduction to the origins and character of Creole conspiracies at the end of the century. "Nothing can stop the prodigious advancement of knowledge" among "this class of Negroes" (native Americans) whose new values and attitudes he attributed to the "unexampled rapidity" in the growth of wealth, population, and towns. Learning, "the vast march of mind," he added, "is the principle agent in evolving the spirit [the love of freedom] we have to fear" and had brought a change in Creole consciousness. The difference between Dunmore's black soldiers and Prosser's men was essentially ideological—in 1775, Negroes "sought freedom merely as a good, now they also claim it as a right."[17]

But urban conspirators, caught up in their "Balls, Routs & assemblies," their "caballing [and] drumming," never became insurrectionists—if that was ever their real intention. They no longer possessed the economic base, military leadership, athletic prowess, and ritual life of the runaway camps and maroon villages. "How should we think of such a thing," cried a conspirator under torture on Montserrat in 1768. "We have no arms! No powder! No camp, no any thing!" As incipient forms of black associationism, Creole conspiracies were based on towns, dancing, and music, elaborate oaths of initiation and allegiance, and overly ambitious plans of attack that included either seeking refuge outside or receiving help from outsiders. These common features warrant description in the slaves' own words to underline the conspiracies' remarkably consistent patterns from one colony or new state to another.[18]

Conspirators were typically among the least oppressed of nonfield slaves: our "most valuable Negroes on the Estate. . . . [The] most sensible of the Slaves" (Hanover Parish, Jamaica, 1776); coopers and boilers (St. Kitts, 1778); "Drivers and Head People" (St. Thomas in the East Parish, Jamaica, 1807); and blacksmiths, waitingmen, and town Negroes (Richmond, Virginia, 1800).[19]

Compared to the maroons' spartan existence in the mountains, urban conspirators, according to whites, aspired to or already lived the good life: once the capital of Richmond was taken, "on the day it should be agreed to [Gabriel] would dine and drink with the merchants of the City" (Virginia, 1800); "Their tables were covered with hogs, Guinea fowls, ducks and other poultry"; "they were not only in possession of the Comforts, but even the Luxuries of Life" (Tobago, 1801); and, "they arrived about Midnight & found a supper of fowls, bread, wine & rum. . . . One day when there was a dinner at Baptistes, he [the deponent] saw a great Cake at the table of Kings and Generals. But he was not admitted of the Party" (Trinidad, 1805).[20]

At their parties and rituals Creoles often talked about the French who were heroes to a great number of Negroes throughout the Americas. "They would drive the white people into the Sea [and] give the Country to the French" (St. George Parish, Jamaica, 1806); "Frenchmen were very good Masters for Negroes"; "As soon as the French came they [would] fight for them against the English"; and "they wanted to follow the example of Guadaloupe and St. Domingo . . . in the Chief's house was a print representing the Execution of the King of France" (Tobago, 1801); and "that the Negroes in the French Country (such is their Expression) were Men" (Clarendon Parish, Jamaica, 1791). The French were discussed more often in Gabriel Prosser's conspiracy than in any other. The Prosser organizers said Frenchmen were not to be killed because they were friends of liberty; the French would land at South Key and fight with them; a Frenchman at Corbin's in Middlesex County had first instigated the rebellion; and Jack Bowler, a leader, had received two kegs of gunpowder from a Frenchman.[21]

At the end of the century, as revolution swept through Europe and the islands, and whites for the first time employed regular Negro soldiers (the West Indian regiments), conspiracies became military in character, and Creole associations moved from gardens and barbeques to makeshift parade grounds. Simon Taylor, a leading Jamaican planter and politician, wrote a nervous letter about Negroes in St. Thomas in the East Parish who "had formed themselves into Society—that they mustered with wooden Swords, and wooden Guns and had appointed their Officers from Generals, to Sergeants and Corporals."[22]

When in 1805 dancing societies in Trinidad became military organizations, calling themselves "regiments" instead of "convoys," the authorities stepped in and uncovered the most significant conspiracy to date. The association, on plantations as well as in town, and with African as well as Creole members, had synthesized the major elements of this multinational island—Spanish, French, English official titles, and the ritual of the Catholic mass with wine and wafers as the flesh and blood of whites—into their rituals of rebellion. But this conspiracy bogged down in endless discussions and more planning than action, so it too was finally uncovered; and scores of men and women were executed or beaten severely, mutilated, or transported.[23]

Around their camp fires, the maroons spoke bluntly about giving whites a belly full or fighting them in broad daylight on the king's high road. At their entertainments Creoles talked in much greater detail about what they would do to whites—once the revolution began. But the Trinidad conspiracy of 1805 was as close as Anglo-American slaves came to organizing slaves of different nationalities and at different levels of cultural change. Unlike the Haitian revolutionaries, Boukman, the witch doctor, and the assimilated military leaders, Toussaint L'Ouverture and Henri Christophe, Anglo-American slaves in this era of revolution never were able to combine African traditions and Creole aspirations—tribal and assimilated styles of resistance—to free themselves. The following sections examine the slaves' material conditions that sharpened rather than synthesized their cultural differences.

Where a planter lived and his presence or absence from the estate helped define the nature of plantation organization, the degree to which master and slave participated in and controlled plantation authority and management, and the extent to which slaves achieved an economic base—provision grounds, markets, and heritable property—sufficiently strong to allow them to remain African in outlook and ways. But absenteeism was not as much a question of whether the planter lived on his estate as of the degree to which he came and went and the extent to which the plantation was his base of operations. This variable was intimately tied to the question of how slaves lived, where, with whom, and how they were fed or fed themselves.[24]

In the islands wealthy planters usually lived elsewhere (most often at "home" in England). Their slaves, who lived in villages of one hundred or more around the large, costly, and immobile sugar works, were the most permanent features on the estates. In North America, however, a vast continent with apparently endless vistas and resources, tobacco and rice required little capital equipment; slaves, particularly in tobacco regions, were spread out across the land in comparatively small and isolated settlements, and masters usually lived on their plantations.

Tobacco planters settled slaves on tracts of land called quarters where blacks lived in makeshift huts suitable for the area's migratory and often wasteful agricultural practices (George Washington, a "scientific planter," even used prefabs). Each quarter was worked by about ten or fifteen full hands under white overseers. Each slave lived in an environment that encouraged him to change his tribal ways quickly; that is, plantation authority in North America was personal and informal. In Virginia, owners were exceptionally and intensely patriarchal and close to each slave, who was known individually by the master and his family.[25]

An extensive network of navigable rivers in Virginia, a chronic absence of town life, and the gentry's desire to be "independent on every one but Providence," scattered settlers far into the interior of a vast country, where they built large and relatively self-sufficient plantations. Determined to be autonomous, tobacco planters encouraged slaves to change their traditions because their tanneries, blacksmith, and carpentry shops required educated (that is, Christianized) and skilled artisans. Virginia plantations were organized around the master's highly personal, indivisible, and unchallenged leadership. Planters as fathers, patriarchs who referred to slaves as "my people," the "black members of my family," carried their culture into the slaves' cabins, as they rode about their estates directly and persistently supervising the plantations' diverse routines and operations, while doctoring , advising, putting slaves into their varied tasks, intervening in their domestic spats and love affairs, and enforcing their own morality and values. Patriarchs as a matter of course provided slaves with their houses, fed them, and jealously regarded all plantation property and markets as their own.

The dynamic personalism that infuses the rich plantation records of such tobacco patriarchs as Landon and Robert Councillor Carter and George Washington is nowhere evident in comparable records for rice plantations. In the Carolina lowcountry, settled more than fifty years later than Virginia by Barbadians and Englishmen of the Restoration Era, a different kind of river system, a much higher percentage of unassimilated and untrained Africans among all slaves, and one of the largest cities in plantation America produced both different relationships between the land and its organization into plantations and different views about the desirability of changing African ways. Carolinians, like West Indians, believed that African ethnicity prevented serious security problems, that slaves who could read and write were dangerous.

Rice also made so much more money than tobacco (the weed's market declined sharply after about 1750), that by midcentury the lowcountry had the highest per capita income in America and what has been estimated as the fastest growth rate in the world. In structure South Carolina was a West Indian colony characterized by a well-defined export area, great fortunes, and capital, expertise and labor concentrated on the production of the cash crop with little attention paid to the kind of diversification (and hence self-sufficiency by means of slave acculturation and training) practiced by the rural Virginia aristocracy.[26]

Wealthy lowcountry planters were suburban aristocrats—like Sir Lewis Namier's English gentry, they were
equally at home in town or country. Concentrated on a plain of
sea islands and marsh that was extremely desirable agriculturally
but most unhealthy, they raised rice (and some indigo, corn,
potatoes, and livestock) and often traveled the year round from
their plantations to sea island and northern resorts, to Europe, or
more often to Charleston (especially during the mosquito-
malaria season from May to November), the source of the urban
goods and services that tobacco planters had to create on their
own plantations. Lowcountry slaves lived in denser, larger
settlements than did slaves in the Chesapeake, worked in gangs
of thirty or more supervised by black drivers, and participated in
work routines that were freer than those of either sugar or
tobacco Negroes. The lowcountry task system allowed slaves to
set their own pace and leave the fields—sometimes in the early
afternoon—when they were done. After a slave completed his
task "his master feels no right to call on him," wrote a St. Mary's,
Georgia, physician to his New England parents in 1806. Slave
"rights"—a familiar concept in rice and sugar areas—were
unheard-of in the Chesapeake. Through time Carolina and West
Indian slaves built up "rights" because their owners were
elsewhere and could not do much about them.[27]

In Caribbean societies where large slaveholders were
often absentees, plantation authority was managerial, impersonal, and more highly rationalized than on the mainland.
Absentees directed their representatives in the islands to make as
much money for them as possible and left the details of everyday
decisions to a variety of specialists in a comparatively well-
defined hierarchy of command—from town agents and attorneys, off the plantation, to resident managers, overseers, white
tradesmen, bookkeepers, and black drivers, on the plantation.
These men, who were far more transient than the more permanently situated slaves, in turn, found it most expedient and
profitable to allow plantation Negroes to do as much for them-

selves as possible with regard to building their own homes, raising small stock and provisions, and even marketing their considerable surpluses. Absenteeism became a vital part of the plantation existences of West Indian slaves (and not necessarily a negative feature of their lives as it is often presented). Island slaves used the income from the sale of surplus food to sustain such African traditions as polygynous and extended households and a family property estate, as well as elaborate cosmological beliefs and practices—witchcraft, ancestor worship, and elaborate funeral rites—vital expressions of authority within slave plantation communities that I have discussed elsewhere.[28]

Many West Indian slaves grew their own food and accumulated considerable property over time. Slaves throughout the islands owned flocks of fowl and small stock, such as pigs and goats. With other salable products—firewood, fruit, vegetables, and fish—they created large slave markets that became the internal marketing systems for most islands.[29]

Slaves supplied the king's ships with wood and water. A planter from Nevis testified in 1788 before the parliamentary slave trade hearings that slaves also sold grass and other kinds of fodder and cut wood. At his own table, he continued, "at least" half and "perhaps" three-fourths of the fresh provisions consumed were supplied by Negroes. Another witness said that half of the specie in his island was controlled by slaves. And another mentioned that three-quarters of all the poultry and pork eaten by planters (and all of that consumed by slaves) was produced by slaves and purchased from the master's own or someone else's Negroes. John Luffman, who has left an excellent traveler's account of Antigua in the 1780s, noted that the slaves' "attention" to their pigs, goats, and fowl "prevented" whites from starving when ships could not come in safely to St. Johns.[30]

Negro markets were extremely lucrative, and many slaves used their earnings to purchase salt provisions, furniture, utensils, and clothing. Some Negroes were known to "possess from £50 to £200 at their death; and few among them, that are at all industrious and frugal," wrote the Jamaican historian and planter Edward Long, "lay up less than £20 or £30 . . . which they gain by sale of their hogs, poultry, fish, corn, fruits, and other commodities, at the markets in town and country."[31]

In North American plantation societies land was comparatively cheaper and much more abundant and the weather was more consistently seasonable than in the islands; consequently, planters usually incorporated the growing of provisions into the slaves' daily tasks and carefully controlled the distribution of food. On the mainland, where slaves were usually fed allowances, they had very little property and quasi-official Negro markets did not develop. Only occasionally is there a glimpse of some solitary, unorganized market activity. A Maryland fugitive in 1777 was described as "a great trader with other Negroes." A Virginia slave told his master before he ran away a second time that while previously free he had "dealt freely in Williamsburg in the oyster and fish way, in their seasons." Evidence from plantation account books indicates that some slaves traded for money with whites. Henry Ravenel's daybook, one of the very few surviving accounts from an eighteenth-century lowcountry plantation, includes such entries as: "paid Amy £4 for a hog" (October 1764); "p[ai]d Chelsea's Negroes £2.15 for fowls" (15 December 1764); "p[ai]d Hector for a hog and rice £3.3.0" (9 January 1765). Other slaves were paid for baskets, trees, rails, corn, myrtlewax, beef, rice, and hogs. There were about as many entries for women as for men.[32]

North American slave property and markets were so meager that they are scarcely comparable to West Indian equivalents. Consequently, a Polish poet's description of the slave quarters of one of the wealthiest planters in North America may be representative. At George Washington's Mount Vernon, the visitor was startled by the general poverty of slave homes and food.

> We entered some Negroes' huts—for their habitations cannot be called houses. They are far more miserable than the poorest of the

cottages of our peasants. The husband and his wife sleep on a miserable bed, the children on the floor. A very poor chimney, a little kitchen furniture amid this misery—a teakettle and cups. . . . A small orchard with vegetables was situated close to the hut. Five or six hens, each with ten or fifteen chickens, walked there. That is the only pleasure allowed to the negroes: they are not permitted to keep either ducks or geese or pigs.[33]

By the end of the century slave property and how it was disposed of had become a conspicuous feature of West Indian family life, and it is described in a variety of sources with essentially two messages—black women were prominent as market Negroes and traders generally, but men seemed to control profits and used property as a kind of heritable family estate. Slaves, moreover, openly resisted interference with this custom, which was an indispensable part of the cultural and "political" autonomy they had achieved by the end of the century.

Planters from Jamaica and the Ceded Islands—mountainous with abundant provision grounds, plaintain walks, and largely undeveloped interiors by as late as 1800—left the richest evidence concerning the relationship between slave food, family, and inheritances. A Tobagan planter told Parliament in 1788 that while Negroes "certainly have no particular right to any property they may acquire because they cannot defend it by law against their Masters . . . opinion which is stronger than Law gives them that right in their acquirements that I do not know that it is ever violated." In fact, the Negroes' "peculium [private property] is so sacred," he continued, "that though it may amount to a considerable sum they always take it away and carry it to the plantation which they are purchased to the very doors, the window shutters of their Houses they have perhaps framed themselves even though the master's property has been taken in execution." A large Grenadian planter, who once was a St. Kitts attorney, said that he owned slaves worth "40, 50, 100" and "even a few" worth £200 sterling, and that the slaves' "property is regularly conveyed from one generation to another without any interference whatever." Edward Long, a contemporary Jamaican historian, was even more explicit about the slaves' property estate:

the black grandfather, or father (as they are called) directs in what manner his money, his hogs, poultry, furniture, cloaths, and other effects and acquisitions, shall descend, or be disposed of, after his decease. He nominates a sort of trustees, or executors, from the nearest of kin, who distribute them among the legatees, according to the will of the testator, without any molestation or interruption, most often without the enquire of their mother.[34]

Caribbean slaves were as determined to maintain customary courtship and marriage practices as they were to protect the property in land and markets that allowed them to maintain African patterns of domesticity. The sum of the evidence of various kinds is that the slaves' practice of having plural wives was African in origin and extremely difficult to modify according to both the whites' Christian morality and their gradual awareness at the end of the century that the slaves' courtship practices ("connexions," "Licentious behaviour") depressed birth rates, ruined their health by spreading venereal disease, and left them exhausted in the fields after a night of "rambling." "A West Indian," author of the best demographic study of that time, said that slaves may have no objection to being baptized, but "marriage is quite another thing." The master may advise a slave which of two women to take as his wife, but if he interferes directly this "leads to acts of poisoning & obeah." During the parliamentary hearings on the slave trade, the former manager of the Society for the Propagation of the Gospel's Barbados plantation mentioned that naturally planters wished to curtail slaves' "rambles" because they were debilitating, "but he is afraid to interfere too much in it."[35]

In North America planters were not "afraid to interfere" in their slaves' domestic lives. In Virginia, as we have seen, owners personally involved themselves in the most intimate details of their slaves' lives, including mate selection, placing black youngsters in nonfield jobs, and attending slaves who were ill. In South Carolina, however, the relationships among owners, overseers, and blacks concerning slave households are not as clearly delineated as they are in comparable island and Virginia documents. An invaluable picture, provided in 1740 by an Anglican commissary, describes a unique mainland slave community—a separate "Nation within a Nation."

Among us Religious Instruction usually descends from Parents to Children, so among them it must first ascend from Children to Parents, or from young to Old.
   There are as 'twere a Nation within a Nation. In all Country Settlements, they live in contiguous Houses and often 2, 3 or 4 Famillys of them in One House. . . . They labour together and converse almost wholly among themselves.[36]

The commissary's picture of the Carolina slaves' dense, unassimilated "Country Settlements" provides tantalizing clues to the sources of the Gullahs' isolated existences, which Alexander Garden associated with compact households and a patois or dialect that left them talking only among themselves. The image of a "Nation within a Nation" is powerful and was evoked in much the same way in Jamaica—but at the other end of the century. In a searching analysis of birth and death rates on his two plantations in a speech to the House of Commons on Chinese contract labor immigration to the West Indies, John Foster Barham, a prominent Jamaican absentee, concluded that moving his slaves from a lowland to a healthier mountain plantation would be impossible: "to interfere in their domestic lives" would be "dangerous and ineffectual" and could be accomplished only by altering their "political state."[37]

By the end of the eighteenth century the West Indian slaves' "political state," based on an elaborate system of food resources, kinship, and markets, had generated an irreversible body of traditional rights that gave slaves considerably more leverage and bargaining power than blacks had on the continent. On larger Caribbean estates authority was consensual and dispersed among supervisors and slaves; the latter made plantation organization work for them in ways we will never understand very well. In some cases, moreover, the British system of shared authority extended to entire societies—particularly if they were geographically peripheral and essentially nonstaple-producing. In the society of adventurers, turtlers, and logmen of the Bay of Honduras, nearly all of the five hundred whites lived on offshore islands, and most of their five thousand slaves lived on widely dispersed mainland plantations, some of which were more than 250 miles upriver. This type of settlement, however, did not produce runaway villages of bush Negroes as occurred in a very similar setting in Dutch Guinea; nor did Indians (as they did somewhat in South Carolina) keep slaves close to home; one report said Indians on the bay were "negligible."[38]

While at first view the weight of the evidence on slave households and property could lead to arguments that Caribbean slavery merely coopted Negroes, a closer examination indicates that in practice the system was complex. The contradictions inherent in the island provisioning system and the divided authority it entailed are exposed in the same documents. Alexander Campbell, a large property owner in the Ceded Islands, told Parliament in 1788 that the more money a slave received from his grounds, the more "firmly attached" he was to the estate. But it also "becomes the greatest consequence to the inhabitants," he added, "that all Negroes are properly supported." What he meant (on a Ceded Island beset by maroons, black Caribs, and French settlers from within and French squadrons from without) was that it was a "universal custom" for the nine hundred slaves on his fourteen plantations to have one afternoon off a week in which to grow crops on their own land and that Grenadan Negroes were usually given passes to visit relatives and to attend churches and markets. If these practices were not followed, whites feared slaves would rebel.[39]

Three years later, Negroes rose up on the neighboring island of Dominica because of problems involving many of the issues referred to in Campbell's testimony. Accounts of the rebellion demonstrate the extent to which estates—and even the tactics used to contain the insurrection—revolved around slave participation in organization and routines. The plantation run-away dimension of the 1791 Dominican insurrection (principally a war between English militia and French brigands from Mar-tinique and Guadaloupe) began among slaves in the French quarter of St. Patrick Parish and concerned a disagreement between managers and slaves regarding a trade-off—additional slave holidays for shorter slave provisions. When the lieutenant governor looked back at the rebellion's inception, he said the French planters "ha[d] in a great degree brought this on them-selves." Before they could actively pursue the brigands, the English realized that they first had to pacify the plantation people. Commanders and militia therefore were ordered to assemble the slaves and to discuss the issue of holidays (an irresponsible rumor); they were to show "no manner of resent-ment," nor to speak at all to the slave women, so as "to give them cause to complain, or raise jealousy" in the Negro men. They were not to mention punishments, and they were to pardon all slaves who returned from the hills, even those who were armed (suspected murderers excepted)![40]

The subtle nuances and shadings of authority *within* the slave community—sources and expressions of authority that were diverse and often conflicting—are even more difficult to explain, but illustrations are useful. The island provisioning system created paradoxes for both slave and free. Owners left slaves to themselves to grow and market their own food, only to realize sooner or later that their Negroes were far more au-tonomous than they wanted them to be. But slaves found that the rights that gave them more control over their plantations often made other Negroes their most immediate enemies, and these were Negroes who came onto the plantations to free them. While they marched unchecked, the Dominican maroons of 1791 sometimes announced to plantation slaves (whom we may imagine were suitably impressed) upon which plantation they would dine the ensuing evening. They dined that year in some of the largest, most elegant plantations on the island. Once they descended, drove the whites out, ordered the Negroes to kill a beef, which they ate with mutton and brandy, before inviting the slaves to join the feast. The next morning, the maroons distributed the food they did not want to carry away. But their inferred message—"look who is feeding you now!" "we are dining in your master's kitchen, where is your protection, join us!"— usually was ignored by plantation slaves who fled with the whites, "sulked" in the cane, or actually joined parties of militia as "confidential negroes"—the baggage men, trackers, and (later in the century) soldiers who pursued maroons.[41]

In the 1790s, during uprisings on Dominica, Grenada, and Jamaica, large numbers of slaves refused to leave plantations vacated by whites. Earlier, more than 250 slaves were left on Barham's plantation during an uprising in which most (if not all) of the white men, "and a great many of the ablest Negroes," were out two or three times a week in parties against the rebels. Meanwhile, on the estate a new, untried man, sent out under indentures, had replaced the overseer. But there was no sign of unrest, although the slaves were apparently without supervision—except their own—for more than a month.[42]

Antagonistic ethnic and tribal rivalries—another source of values and sanctions within the slave community—probably were all that kept Jamaica from becoming another Haiti. Uprisings often set blacks against blacks who were scouts, baggage men, or trackers—a situation dramatized during a 1798 uprising in Jamaica, when a rebel screamed at an African who was defending his master's property and identified him by his ritual face scars: "You d——d Chamba cut-fac'd Son-of-a B——h."[43]

Violence between plantation Negroes and organized runaways was sometimes awesome and probably stemmed either from tribal and ethnic rivalries or from competition between plantation Negroes and maroons for food and women—

the details will never be very clear. The runaways, as essentially unacculturated tribesmen, were experts in the psychology of terror generated by their hit-and-run raids. In Tobago, another Ceded Island, a Coramantee band in 1770 wounded a Negro watchman, twice failed to kill a head driver, and then successfully ambushed him on the public road. This party later entered the yaws house on the driver's plantation and killed three sick Negroes, including a mother and nursing infant. Balla, the Dominican maroon leader, descended onto a plantation in mid-July 1785, shot four whites, threw them into a fire while they were still alive, and shot their head Negro, before wounding—but not killing—the black man's wife and several children.[44]

The role of mainland Negroes in plantation sanctions and organization is described with little of the richness of comparable West Indian sources. But both sugar and rice regions used slave drivers extensively (who in North America before the antebellum era are described only in lowcountry documents), and the authority of South Carolina drivers was formidable. In practice their authority provides views of a slave community, a "Nation within a Nation," more like those in the islands than in the Chesapeake. In the antebellum era, Frederick Law Olmsted, whose traveler's accounts are unequaled, visited an old and established lowcountry rice estate and used words describing its policy—"consulted," "managed," "governed"—unheard-of in the land of the Carters and Byrds. Drivers, Olmsted observed, are often *"de facto* the managers." Usually the proprietor gave orders directly to them, "without the overseer's being consulted or informed"; and both owner and overseer "deferr[ed]" to the drivers about when to flood the fields. Overseers, moreover, who were "frequently" employed only "as a matter of form . . . consult the drivers on all important points, and are governed by their advice."[45]

The most revealing account of a rice driver's participation in a West Indian style of plantation community concerned the new state of Georgia's attempts to confiscate and use as a college

George Whitefield's (and heirs') Bethesda Orphanage and the plantation and slaves that supported it. When in the 1790s state officials moved in and arrested the caretaker parson, the struggle quickly spilled over into the community at large and uncovered local passions about overseas' philanthropy versus local control of slaves, loyalist property and local public acquisitiveness, high and low church. These issues, however, all stemmed from a confrontation on the plantation between the reverend and the slaves on one side, the sheriff's posse on the other, and the driver in the middle as makeweight and ultimate symbol of control at the orphanage. When the sheriff first rode in, he called out to the driver to hold the reins of his horse. "I countermanded it," the reverend noted, "& order'd another of the Negroes to do it." The sheriff's people remained; and in the evening, "about half past 8 . . . [they] went out in order to give the Driver orders for the next day." After his arrest the minister, in jail, heard that the slaves were "collected," but they had refused to obey the sheriff's command. A week later they were at work; either the driver, he suspected, had been bribed, or he was "overawed by Fear."[46]

  These pictures of the field hands' and drivers' relative autonomy in rice and sugar areas ought to be compared to the patriarchal style of plantation organization in Virginia, where masters, who possessed nearly all of what West Indian slaves considered their own, still often failed to be all things to their plantation families.

  The reactions of Anglo-American slaves to the opportunities and perils of the revolutionary era stemmed from the ways tobacco, rice, and sugar plantations were organized around resident or absentee owners and from the degree to which slaves participated in plantation management. The slaves' managerial role depended upon their control over food resources, markets, households, and heritable property.
  On tobacco plantations authority was monopolized by an

apparently powerful master figure whose personal supervision created considerable conflict among all members of the estate. Letters among planters, stewards, and overseers were often bitter, angry, and confused about who really was in charge. Such confusion originated in the master's inability to divide and delegate sufficient authority to those whom he expected to do their jobs most effectively as the slaves' immediate supervisors.

When challenged by even the lowest field hands, planters themselves were sometimes surprisingly ineffectual. Landon Carter's confrontations with his people fill up a copious diary and clearly indicate how shaky plantation organization on the patriarchal model could be in practice. Robert Councillor Carter's voluminous plantation records (which are at Duke University), however, reveal a man who superbly executed the patriarchal role, becoming the personal leader or chief of all of his four hundred slaves. Carter scarcely complained about even the most trivial day-to-day rebelliousness. But during the revolutionary war, even Carter lost slaves who deserted to the British (after he had made a personal appeal to them not to do so); for, like many other tidewater planters, he was vulnerable and defenseless before Lord Dunmore and the British fleet.[47]

Evidence of another kind, fugitive slave notices for new Negro runaways, also suggests that the Virginia owner had to be constantly and effectively present if all was to work smoothly. Some Africans reportedly ran off immediately after their master died; and a few, when recaptured and questioned, implied that they felt the personal bonds (whatever their precise nature may have been) vanished with an owner's death.

Once the patriarch's authority was challenged by someone who seemed as powerful as he was, or if he simply no longer could defend his plantation, slaves often sensed that they were on their own. But even then they had no place to go and relatively little to fall back on by way of family and property in plantation settings where the master owned and dominated virtually everything. The most extensively documented reaction of wartime rebellious slaves described disorganized fugitives who set out on the Chesapeake Bay in canoes or some other kind of open boat. Sometimes they were swamped, many drowned, and a few were reported picked up by the wrong ship—an American instead of a British one. This image conveys a sense of the relationship between plantation organization and authority in the Chesapeake and the wartime reactions of slaves, who as the least African and most thoroughly detribalized of all Anglo-American Negroes, had been cut adrift from the extended households, family estates, grounds, and markets that kept slaves together as a people further south in the lowcountry and Caribbean.[48]

South Carolina slaves during the Revolution are more difficult to characterize because surviving documents say little about them. But rebellious slaves there also seemed to have acted cooperatively as they had before the Revolution when in groups some joined friendly Indians, the Spanish in the Floridas, or the British evacuations of Charleston and Savannah. An unusually well-documented instance (which may be juxtaposed with the picture of wartime fugitives adrift on the Chesapeake Bay) told of thirty slaves—thirteen American-born and eleven African adults with six children—who followed British General Augustine Prevost's army toward Savannah before the "greatest part of them" split off and "followed" Creek Indians to a town "called Cawetta or Coweater."[49]

But most Carolina slaves remained behind on their plantations and within the relative security of their "Nation within a Nation," comprising compact settlements, crops, and an unusual tasking system of work. While I have argued that lowcountry slaves had much more to defend at home than did slaves in Virginia, many probably stayed where they were during the war simply for reasons of survival. While revolutionary Virginia was a remarkably tightly knit society, the civil war between Tories and patriots in South Carolina was ferocious and kept black and white backcountry folk close to home. Late in the war, for example, Savannah merchant John Habersham wrote General Nathanael Greene, hero of the long and bitter southern campaign, that Mulberry Grove plantation (given to Greene by a grateful southern people) could not be rented because "some object to its being too remote from Town, and consequently exposed to Murderers and Robbers."[50]

War and revolution swept through the islands more fiercely and for a much longer time than on the mainland, and slaves there were more conspicuously rebellious than were North American blacks. But African maroons and urban Creoles were unable to act in concert with the preponderant majority of plantation Negroes in an attempt to free themselves. In 1800 a leading Jamaican politician came as close as anyone to explaining the basis of shared authority on Caribbean plantations that often set black against black as well as against white. Henry Shirley wrote that after a season of fear about slave uprisings, good weather and abundant provision crops had brought Negroes substantial prices for their marketable produce, and slaves were now "happy and content."[51]

But to leave an impression of accommodated and acquiescent slaves in this era would be misleading. Even the Creoles, who were apparently so enmeshed in their owners' values, made their own decisions and tried to construct their own norms and ways in new urban settings. As conspirators they made their choices before the different revolutionary traditions of the late eighteenth century and showed a clear preference for the French and Haitian examples. Even the Prosser conspirators, the most assimilated of Creoles anywhere, chose to spare those whites—Quakers, Methodists, poor white women, and especially Frenchmen—who were outside the mainstream of our Revolution.[52]

Compared with the maroons, the Creoles come off badly. The runaways in the mountains were doing something about slavery, while Creoles down below only talked about it. Creoles thought about taking white wives after the slaughter; maroons had their wives with them in the hills; and so on. But the Creoles' task as revolutionaries was much more difficult than was the maroons'. Using their conspiratorial associations as meeting places for blacks of different nationalities, they were able to radicalize men such as Harold, a Trinidadian dancing convoy chief. He was a carter, not a field slave, a Christian born in Africa (of the Soso nation); he had bought his freedom and been a chief of the St. George convoy since Spanish times, and his association was called Grenada, after that island's mode of dancing. Behind the Creole's bluster, vacillating inaction, pomp, and pageantry there persisted in all of their conspiracies from Richmond, Virginia, to Port of Spain, Trinidad, a design to bridge formidable ethnic and acculturative barriers among men like Harold whose urban work had led them from the old values and sanctions of the historically isolated plantation Negroes and maroons into new, modern lives.

The outbreak of Creole associations of a distinctively military character in the early nineteenth century may be seen as an effort to use old ways of music and dance to secure a more natural and human culture within the inhumane economic system of white oppressors. Authorities know well this kind of countercultural warfare, they fear it, and respond accordingly. Even today in Jamaica some reggae songs are outlawed as subversive. In the stunning Jamaican film, *The Harder They Come*, the narcotics detective temporarily cuts off the country people's livelihood, the ganga (marijuana) trade to city markets, in order to suppress a song recorded by their folk hero whom the detective is trying to capture or kill. But Mister Hilton, a stereotypical capitalistic media mogul, reminds him, "no grass, no hit tunes mean no law and order—anarchy!" The political meaning and thrust of Afro-American culture in Third World cities like Kingston still has not crystallized; and whether it will tend to be assimilationist or revolutionary is unclear— reminiscent of Gavin Stevens's remark in William Faulkner's *Intruder in the Dust*, "The Past is never dead. It's not even past."[53]

Notes

1. Moncure D. Conway, ed., *The Writings of Thomas Paine*, 3 vols. (New York, 1894–96), 1:100. I wish to thank members of the Johns Hopkins University Departments of Anthropology and History Seminar in Atlantic History and Culture, and Rhys Isaac, in particular, for their helpful comments (17 October 1975) on this essay. The following proposal will be much more useful when monographs are completed about the issues I raise. I am currently preparing for Oxford University Press a book titled *Negro Slavery in the Old British Empire and North America during an Era of War and Revolution, 1750–1834.*

2. Ronald Hoffman, *A Spirit of Dissension: Economics, Politics, and the Revolution in Maryland* (Baltimore, 1973), pp. 147–48, 152–53, 184–85, 201, 204.

3. This section is based on conversations with Ron Hoffman, who is reading the extensive Nathanael Greene correspondence at Duke University and elsewhere while writing a book on the social and political dimensions of southern military campaigns during the Revolution. See also *Calendar of the Sir Guy Carleton Papers, Report on American Manuscripts in the Royal Institution of Great Britain*, 4 vols. (London, 1904–9); *Calendar of the General Otho Holland Williams Papers in the Maryland Historical Society* (Baltimore, 1940), esp. pp. 19–72; Thomas Pinckney's wartime letters to his sister Harriott, Blue Box No. 1, 1781–1782, Pinckney Papers, Library of Congress; Charleston (British) Police Board Proceedings, 1780–81; and South Carolina Loyalist Claims, South Carolina Department of Archives and History, microfilms of Public Record Office originals; see also, Bernard A. Uhlendorf, ed., *The Siege of Charleston . . . Diaries and Letters of Hessian Officers* (Ann Arbor, Mich., 1938).

4. Quoted in Benjamin Quarles, *The Negro in the American Revolution* (Chapel Hill, N.C., 1961), p. 121.

5. Jamaica Assembly Address to the King, 28 Nov. 1793; Council Address to Lieutenant Governor Williamson, both enclosed in Williamson to the Secretary of State, 30 Nov. 1791, Public Record Office, Colonial Office, London, 137/90 (hereafter cited as CO); extract of a letter from William Greene to Messrs. Aspinal and Hardy, Good Hope, Jamaica, 13 May 1798, CO 137/99 (some CO volumes have folio numbers, some do not).

6. Governor Cunningham to the Secretary of State, 22 Jan. 1781, CO 28/58; Seaforth to Lord Hobart, Pilgrim, Barbados, 6 June 1802, CO 28/68, f. 55; see also, Governor D. Parry to Lord Grenville, Barbados, 23 May 1791, CO 28/63.

7. The following is based on a paper I delivered at the Organization of American Historians Meeting (Boston, April 1975) entitled "Slave Resistance in an Age of Revolution: Major Insurrections and Conspiracies in the Old British Empire and North America, 1760–1807."

8. Thomas Atwood, *History of the Island of Dominica* (London, 1791), chapter 12.

9. Governor Orde to Sydney, Roseau, Dominica, 16 April 1786, CO 71/10, f. 21.

10. Thomas Bee to Governor John Mathews, Goose Creek, 9 Dec. 1782, Thomas Bee Papers, South Caroliniana Library, Columbia, S.C.

11. March 1787 letters from militia commanders and representatives for St. Peters Parish in a South Carolina Archives Miscellaneous file, Slavery before 1800, in which documents are now being reorganized according to their provenance (for example, Governor's Messages, Senate and Assembly Committee Reports). This material is in correspondence to the governor and a House Committee Report, 19 March 1787; see also Adele S. Edwards, ed., *Journals of the Privy Council, 1783–1788* (Columbia, S.C., 1971), pp. 186, 203–4; Quarles, *Negro in Revolution*, p. 174; and Reverend William B. Stevens, *A History of Georgia* . . . , 2 vols. (Philadelphia, 1859), 2:376–78.

12. Gerald W. Mullin, *Flight and Rebellion: Slave Resistance in Eighteenth-century Virginia* (New York, 1972), pp. 34, 40, 43–45, 55–57.

13. *Barbados Mercury* (Bridgetown), 14 Feb. 1784, Bridgetown Public Library microfilm; Augusta, Georgia, March 1780, Grand Jury presentment in Lilla M. Hawes, ed., *Papers of Lachlan McKintosh, 1774–79, Collections of the Georgia Historical Society* (Savannah, Ga., 1957), 12:88; Legislative petition from the Inhabitants of Georgetown, 19 Jan. 1790, South Carolina Archives; *Georgia Gazette*, 3 Jan. 1793, [n.d.] Oct. 1796; *Royal Gazette, Supplement*, 28 Oct. 1797, West Indian Reference Library, Kingston, Jamaica.

14. Stephen Fuller to Henry Dundas, 30 Oct. 1791, CO 137/89.

15. John Poyer to Governor Seaforth, 22 June 1806, "AN OPEN LETTER," reprinted in the *Journal of the Barbados Museum and Historical Society* 6 (May 1939): 163.

16. Henry Laurens to James Laurens, Charleston, Jan. 1776, Laurens Papers, Roll 13, South Carolina Archives microfilm. See Ira Berlin, *Slaves without Masters: The Free Negro in the Antebellum South* (New York, 1975).

17. [St. George Tucker], *Letter to a Member of the General Assembly of Virginia on the Subject of the Late Conspiracy of the Slaves, with a Proposal for their Colonization* (Richmond, Va., 1801), Virginia State Library microfilm.

18. "A Natural, Civil, and Religious History of MONTSERRET in the West-Indies, Including a Particular Account of the Struggles of the Free Coloured Inhabitants . . . by a Wesleyan Missionary who Resided Five Years in the Island," pp. 46–47, Ms., Biographical/West Indies, Box 1, Methodist Missionary Society, London.

19. "Extract of a letter from Sir Simon Clark to Benjamin Lyon Lucea, Jamaica, 23 July 1776; John Grizell to Lieutenant Governor Keith, Hanover, 27 July 1776, CO 137/71, f. 256v, ff. 262–63; CO 152/58, ff. 32–36v; Simon Taylor to Thomas Hughan, Kingston, 7 Jan. 1807, CO 137/120.

20. Mullin, *Flight and Rebellion*, p. 158; *Tobago Gazette, Extraordinary*, 1 Jan. 1802, enclosed in Governor Joseph Robley to Lord Hobart, Tobago, 2 Jan. 1802, CO 285/8; Council Minutes, Trinidad, 10 Dec. 1805, CO 298/2, f. 108.

21. Further Examination of Frank, Orange Vale, Jamaica, 8 Jan. 1807, CO 137/118; Brigidier General Hugh Lyle Carmichael's Report, 25 Dec. 1801, CO 285/8; Extract of a letter from Spanish Town, Jamaica, 6 Nov. 1791, CO 137/89; Mullin, *Flight and Rebellion*, pp. 143, 151–52.

22. Simon Taylor to Thomas Hughan, Kingston, Jamaica, 7 Jan. 1807, CO

137/120; Mullin, *Flight and Rebellion*, pp. 143, 148; Major General Adam Williamson to Secretary of State Dundas, Jamaica, 18 Sept. 1791, CO 137/89; Taylor to Hughan, Kingston, Jamaica, 7 Jan. 1807, CO 137/120.

23. I examined the Trinidad conspiracy more closely in a paper for the New York Academy of Sciences Conference on Slavery in the Americas (May 1976); the proceedings will be published. The conspiracy is in CO 298/2, ff. 97–148v.

24. This section is based on paper presented to the Southern Historical Association Meeting (Dallas, November 1974), "Slave Property, Families and Plantation Authority in the Old British Empire."

25. Descriptions of eighteenth-century Virginia plantation life are based on *Flight and Rebellion*, esp. chapters 1 and 2.

26. On the rice planters' wealth, see M. Eugene Sirmans, *Colonial South Carolina: A Political History, 1663–1763* (Chapel Hill, N.C., 1966), p. 226.

27. Daniel Turner to his parents, St. Mary's, Georgia, 13 Aug. 1806, Daniel Turner Papers, Georgia State Archives microfilm.

28. I have begun to explore the most important basis for authority among plantation slaves—the spiritual dimension—in a paper, "Obeah and Christianity in Four Eighteenth-century Anglo-American Plantation Societies" [Virginia, South Carolina, Jamaica, and Antigua], presented at the annual meeting of the American Historical Association (New Orleans, 1972).

29. Cf. Sidney W. Mintz and Douglas Hall, "The Origins of the Jamaican Internal Marketing System," *Yale University Publications in Anthropology*, No. 57 (New Haven, 1960), pp. 3–26; Richard Sheridan, *Sugar and Slavery: An Economic History of the British West Indies* (Baltimore, 1973), pp. 259–60; Richard Pares, *A West-Indian Fortune* (London, 1950), chapter 6–7.

30. James White to Bishop Gibson, Vere, 23 April 1724, Fulham Palace Papers, West Indies, vol. 17, f. 185; House of Commons Sessional Papers, Accounts and Papers (1790), pp. 84, 106, 262, 307 (hereafter cited as Sessional Papers). John Luffman, *A Brief Account of the Island of Antigua . . . in the Years 1786, 1787, 1788* (2d ed., London, 1788), p. 94; Atwood, *History of the Island of Dominica*, pp. 178–79.

31. Edward Long, *The History of Jamaica . . .* , 3 vols. (London, 1774, reprint ed., 1970), 2:410–11.

32. Dunlop's *Maryland Gazette or Baltimore Advertiser*, 4 Nov. 1777, William Bond advertiser; *Virginia Gazette* (Rind), 26 Sept. 1768; J[ame]s Mercer to Battaile Muse, 3 April 1779, Muse Papers, Duke University Library; G. Francklyn, *Observations . . . Shewing, the Manner in which Negroes are Treated in the West-Indies* (London, 1789), p. 32; Daybook of Henry Ravenel of Hanover, South Carolina Historical Society, Charleston.

33. Quoted in Paul Leland Haworth, *George Washington: Farmer* (Indianapolis, 1915), pp. 196f.

34. "Copy Evidence of Mr Franklyn 13th March 1794," p. 19, Minutes of Evidence on the Slave Trade, House of Lords Record Office, London; Long, *History of Jamaica*, 2:410.

35. [A West Indian], *Notes in Defense of the Colonies* (London, 1826), pp. 34, 37; "1826—Barbados—Codrington College, Remarks on Codrington Estate & Treatment of Slaves," Series C, West Indies, Box 8, Society for the Propagation of the Gospel, London.

36. Garden to the SPG Secretary, 6 May 1740, cited in Frank J. Klingberg, *An Appraisal of the Negro in Colonial South Carolina* (Washington, D.C., 1941), p. 106.

37. "Subjects Particular Respecting the Negroes in Reply to Mr. J. Sinclair," Miscellaneous Political Papers of John Foster Barham, Bundle 2, C. 381, Barham Papers, Clarendon Deposit, Bodleian Library, Oxford.

38. [?] to Lieutenant Governor Dalling, Kingston, 3 Sept. 1779, CO 137/75, f. 1.

39. Sessional Papers, 29, 141–42.

40. James Bruce to Lieutenant Governor Sir John Orde, Castle Bruce, 15 Jan. 1791; 3 Feb. 1791, Order to Lord Grenville; Thomas Beech to Orde, Widcombe, 16 Jan. 1791; Charles Bertrant to [the Governor ?], 18 Jan. 1791, CO 71/19.

41. Arthur Bertrand, Andre Botro, and Gruand to Lieutenant Governor Orde, Point Mulatre, 19 Jan. 1791, CO 71/19.

42. Daniel Barnjum to John Foster Barham, 23 Dec. 1760, Barham Papers, Clarendon Deposit.

43. The Deposition of Henry Paulett and Alexander Steel, planters of Trelawney Parish, Jamaica, 18 April 1798, CO 140/84.

44. "An Account of the Insurrection among the Cormantee Slaves at Tobago," 21 Nov. 1770, Papers of Captain Francis Reynolds, Gloucestershire Record Office; Minutes of the Tobago Council, 27 Nov. 1770, CO 288/2; Governor Orde to the Secretary of State, Government House, Dominica, 15 Dec. 1785, CO 71/9, f. 324.

45. Frederick Law Olmsted, *A Journey in the Sea Board Slave States in the Years 1853–1854*, 2 vols. (New York [1856], 1904), 2:66–67.

46. John Johnson, "Official Journal" (1791–92), Johnson Papers, Georgia Historical Society, Savannah.

47. Mullin, *Flight and Rebellion*, p. 133 and chapter 4.

48. Ibid.

49. "List of Negroes the Property of William Reynolds Sr., December 12, 1783," Miscellaneous file, Slavery before 1800, South Carolina Archives.

50. Ron Hoffman led me to this document, Habersham to Greene, "Private," Savannah, 1 Nov. 1782, Nathanael Greene Papers, Duke University Department of Manuscripts.

51. Shirley to Edward Shirley, Kingston, 21 May 1800, CO 137/104.

52. Mullin, *Flight and Rebellion*, pp. 143, 151–52, 200n.

53. Quoted in C. Vann Woodward, *The Burden of Southern History* (New York, 1961), p. 36.

9

"Taking Care of Business" in Revolutionary South Carolina: Republicanism and the Slave Society

by Peter H. Wood

History has to be rewritten in every generation, because, although the past does not change, the present does; each generation asks new questions of the past, and finds new areas of sympathy as it re-lives different aspects of the experiences of its predecessors. The experience of something approaching democracy makes us realize that most of our history is written about, and from the point of view of, a tiny fragment of the population, and makes us want to extend in depth as well as breadth.

Each generation, to put it another way, rescues a new area from what its predecessors arrogantly and snobbishly dismissed as "the lunatic fringe." . . . It is no longer necessary to apologize profusely for taking the common people of the past on their own terms and trying to understand them. [1]

You will recall that Rip Van Winkle slept through the entire American Revolution, and he was apparently none the worse for it. Maybe you have considered, as I have, the prospect of sleeping through the *entire Bicentennial*? Perhaps we shall all become drowsy and forgetful at once, like the characters in García Márquez's magnificent Latin American novel, *One Hundred Years of Solitude*.

Even as we doze off, the history of the Revolution will continue to be rewritten, or at least republished. Remarkably complete (and undeniably soporific) source materials concerning the founding fathers continue to flow unremittingly from the nation's academic presses, with no indications of early relief. *The Papers of Thomas Jefferson* are currently in their nineteenth volume;

each volume covers roughly three months of Jefferson's career, and there are thirty-five years to go. *The Adams Papers*, which are projected to go beyond one hundred volumes, so far have filled less than one-quarter of their shelf; even with a boost (such as it is) from *The Adams Chronicles*, I doubt if our grandchildren will see the end. *The Papers of James Madison* are in their ninth volume and have reached the important year 1787, which means they have only twenty-one years before Madison becomes president. The same pattern applies to *The Papers of Alexander Hamilton*, *The Papers of Benjamin Franklin*, *The Papers of Henry Laurens*, and others. This stack of sleep-inducing tomes concerns only primary sources and materials relating specifically to the founding fathers. The secondary literature surrounding the American Revolution is now equally dense, and at times more stimulating.[2]

In the past few years a good deal of the secondary writing touching the period has dealt with questions of race relations and slavery. Several impressive volumes, such as Jordan's *White Over Black* and Davis's *The Problem of Slavery in the Age of Revolution*, are so weighty as to constitute something of a "white man's burden" in their own right; others, such as Duncan MacLeod's suggestive essay, *Slavery, Race, and the American Revolution*, are slimmer and less well known. But almost all of these books (and I would include Edmund Morgan's important new study, *American Slavery, American Freedom: The Ordeal of Colonial Virginia*) continue to focus, however legitimately and effectively, more upon white people's relation to black America—their attitudes and institutions, their economic and psychological ordeals—than upon the lives and aspirations of black Americans.[3]

Nothing illustrates the dynamics behind this benign neglect of the black experience in revolutionary America more clearly than a passage from Donald Robinson's *Slavery in the Structure of American Politics, 1765–1820*, published in 1971. In his introduction, Robinson states candidly, "When this study began six or seven years ago, I sought to analyze the role of black people in the founding of the United States. . . . But most of the evidence

pointed in a different direction." Using words that reflect the
mark left by Stanley Elkins's study of slavery a decade earlier,
Robinson continues:

In national politics, black people were almost entirely mute, politically
passive. Being victims of almost total human repression, they were
restrained from all but indirect and non-political expressions of their
passions and resentments. . . . Gradually, the intention of my project
was modified. *Instead of studying the role of blacks in the founding, I began to
concentrate on the performance of whites, as it was affected by the presence of
blacks. . . . What has emerged is a book, not about black people, but about white
people.*[4]

As Kurt Vonnegut would say, "And so it goes." It is
hardly a worthy compliment to that respected senior scholar,
Benjamin Quarles of Morgan State University, to observe that his
excellent study on Negroes in the Revolution is the best book in
the field; it remains, for all intents and purposes, the *only* book
dealing at extended length with the experience of black people in
the period of the Revolution.[5] Confronted with the paradox of
race slavery and republicanism in the revolutionary era, white
authors traditionally have raised the matter to the lofty, impersonal level of an inconsistency in political theory. The human
impact of this deep-seated contradiction has been all but ignored. Dick Gregory, that most serious of American humorists,
recently put his finger on the problem. In his book about
American history, *No More Lies*, Gregory wrote: "The myth of the
founding fathers features only those white folks whose wealth
and privilege allowed them the benefit of education, and therefore they spoke and wrote the inspiring words of the American
Revolution. The reality of American independence requires some
paternal integration. While the now-famous white patriots were
articulating the spirit of independence, some little known black
folks were taking care of business."[6]
   In these pages I want to take my down-to-earth cue, as
well as my title, from Gregory, to engage in a little historical
"integration," not on a lofty conceptual level, but in a more

immediate and localized way. I shall focus down in time and space to deal particularly with black workers in South Carolina just prior to the American Revolution, weaving together some incidents I have encountered in my research that have not been pulled together before.[7] As the English historian Christopher Hill states in the passage quoted at the outset, "It is no longer necessary to apologize . . . for taking the common people of the past on their own terms." So I shall not apologize, as I might once have done, for focusing on those southerners whom Robinson and others have felt to be passive, unconsidering, and inert.

At the time of white independence, 90 percent of the blacks in America lived in the five southernmost states. They constituted about a third of the population of the entire region, and in some parishes they outnumbered European-Americans by ratios of five and ten to one. The Carolina lowlands was one area where Afro-Americans had been in the majority for more than half a century, and there, in the heart of the rice- and indigo-producing country, it is no mere rhetorical flourish to say that "black folks were taking care of business." Indeed, the eighty thousand Negroes who made up roughly six-tenths of South Carolina's colonial population in 1770 were taking care of business in three distinct, if related, ways. Each is worth examining briefly in turn.[8]

In the first place, blacks were, not surprisingly, handling the bulk of the colony's physical labor. They were forced to clear land and raise crops, to dig canals, and tend cattle. However involuntary and onerous such work may have been, it was not always simplistic drudgery, mere sweat and toil. Definite skills were involved, often partially or wholly African in origin, as with raising rice, building dugout canoes, and catching shrimp. Ironically, Negroes familiar with indigo as a dye in West Africa may have had a hand in the reintroduction of that crop as a new commercial staple in Carolina in the 1740s. From the perspective

of thousands of enslaved workers who gave their lives to the
laborious cultivation of this plant in succeeding generations, its
intensified production was less a triumph than a tragedy. By
coincidence, the energetic planter-diarist often credited with this
commercial "achievement" is also the author of a suggestive
letter regarding the pervasive quality of Negro labor.[9] Living
"alone" shortly before the Revolution, Eliza Lucas Pinckney
wrote to her daughter describing the activities of her household
as follows:

> Mary-Ann understands roasting poultry in the greatest perfection you
> ever saw, and old Ebba the fattening them to as great a nicety. Daphne
> makes me a loaf of very nice bread. You know I am no epicure, but I am
> pleased they can do things so well, when they are put to it. . . . I shall
> keep young Ebba to do the drudgery part, fetch wood, and water, and
> scour, and learn as much as she is capable of Cooking and Washing.
> Mary-Ann Cooks, makes my bed, and makes my punch, Daphne works
> and makes the bread, old Ebba boils the cow's victuals, raises and
> fattens the poultry, Moses is imployed from breakfast until 12 o'clock
> without doors, after that in the house. Pegg washes and milks. Thus I
> have formed my household, Nobody eats the bread of idleness when I
> am here, nor are any overworked. . . . Mary-Ann has pickled me some
> oysters very good, so I have sent you a little pott by the boat. Moses gets
> them at low water without a boat.[10]

The folks taking care of business for Mrs. Pinckney were more
numerous, and therefore perhaps less overworked, than those in
other Carolina households, but the pattern was generally the
same. "The gentlemen in the country have among their negroes,
as the Russian nobility among their serfs, the most necessary
handicraftsmen, cobblers, tailors, carpenters, smiths, and the
like, whose work they command at the smallest possible price, or
for nothing almost," wrote a European visitor at the time of the
Revolution. "There is hardly any trade or craft which has not
been learned and is not carried on by negroes."[11]

But if blacks were, in the simplest sense, taking care of
business by performing a variety of tasks, in a second sense they
were taking care of business in a more complex and assertive

way. All slavery systems, as far back as the Greeks, have aroused speculation about the degree to which slaves are able, morally, mentally, and physically, to gain control over their masters.[12] Early South Carolina was no exception, and evidence suggests that Charleston blacks, though supposedly forbidden from earning wages, seeking profits, or organizing collectively, were nevertheless literally and surprisingly controlling business in a number of avenues. They were not only doing the work; they were devising ways to regulate that work.[13]

Well before the mid-eighteenth century, there were numerous complaints about the ways blacks manipulated the local economy of Charleston, and these complaints continued through the revolutionary period and beyond. In 1763 the Grand Jury of Charleston protested that Negro apprentice chimney sweeps had combined to fix prices, one of the earliest such labor actions to be recorded in North America. The following year the Board of Commissioners published an order intended to fix rates for the work of licensed slave porters whose owners allowed them to rent out their labor by the day in exchange for a set return on the investment. The payment for "Labour in Ships at the Wharves" and "For cleaning of wells, or other employ requiring them to stand in water" was to be ten shillings per day, while "rolling of rice [barrels], or other common porterage" was to command seven shillings and six pence. The order prohibited workers from roaming through the city, looking for different work at higher rates, but it clearly was ineffective. In 1771 the local Grand Jury recommended an alteration of the Negro Law "to empower the Commissioners of the Streets to punish such Negroes as refuse to work unless it be such work as shall be agreeable to themselves and such pay as they may require."[14]

But while enslaved workers were accused of refusing to work and fixing wages, on the one hand, they were charged with taking over jobs and controlling market prices, on the other. In 1770 (and again in subsequent years) the Grand Jury recommended revising the Negro Law "so as to prevent idle slaves

interfering with poor honest White people supporting themselves and families amongst us." It is hard to see when these
particular slaves were "idle," for they were, in the words of the
Grand Jury, "being suffered to cook, Bake, Sell Fruits, dry
goods, and otherwise traffic, Barter &c in the Public markets &
streets of Charles Town." Two years later a letter to the *South
Carolina Gazette* charged that failure to enforce the laws regulat-
ing slaves affected "poor white people in a greater degree than is
generally imagined. They are not sufficiently encouraged here,
while the negroes receive too much countenance."[15]

According to this white observer, who signed himself as
"Stranger," Negro enterprise was countenanced too freely on
the waterways around Charleston. Most of the fishing, piloting,
and transporting was done by blacks, frequently without the
required white surveillance. The previous year Provost Marshall
William Pinckney had served notice that he would enforce the
law requiring owners of coastal vessels to have at least one white
person aboard their boats, noting that disregard for the law had
caused plantations along the Ashepoo River to be robbed frequently "to the great damage of the proprietors." Now the
observant and critical "Stranger" pointed out that slaves who
made illegal use of boats and canoes were able to fence stolen
goods on a regular basis, "and, at their pleasure, to supply the
town with fish or not." He argued that these fishing Negroes, as
they were called, were able "of course to exact whatever price
they think proper, for that easily-procured food, so necessary for
the subsistence of, and formerly as a great relief to, the poorest
sort of white people." He charged that as their control had
increased over the past ten years, the price of drumfish had risen
almost tenfold to sixty-five shillings.[16]

Intermittent control of seafood prices was part of a larger
covert effort to develop and retain a stake in Charleston commerce generally. By the late eighteenth century black women had
assumed an important role in the town's daily economic affairs,
not unlike the place traditionally held by female entrepreneurs in

the trading centers of West Africa. (The tradition of Negro market vendors and street callers has persisted distinctively in Charleston well into the twentieth century.) Leila Sellers, in her study of *Charleston Business on the Eve of the American Revolution*, refers to the "slaves who monopolized the market business" despite restrictive regulations,[17] and she quotes the valuable observations of the "Stranger." He commented at length on the Negro women around Charleston's Lower Market,

who are seated there from morn 'til night, and buy and sell on their accounts, what they please in order to pay their wages, and get as much more for themselves as they can; for their owners care little how their slaves get the money so they are paid. These women have such a connection with and influence on, the country negroes who come to that market, that they generally find means to obtain whatever they choose, in preference to any white person; thus they forestall and engross many articles, which some hours afterwards you must buy back from them at 100 or 150 per cent advance. I have known those black women to be so insolent as even to wrest things out of the hands of white people, pretending they had been bought before, for their masters or mistresses, yet expose the same for sale again within an hour afterwards, for their own benefit. I have seen country negroes take great pains, after having been spoken to by those women, to reserve what they choose to sell to them only, either by keeping the articles in their canoes, or by sending them away, and pretending they were not for sale, and when they could not be easily retained by themselves, then I have seen the wenches as briskly hustle them about from one to another that in two minutes they could no longer be traced.[18]

This was not Robert Fogel and Stanley Engerman's world of successful and satisfying entrepreneurial middle management. Instead it was, in several senses, a "black market," a serious and extensive effort—opportunistic but unceasing—by black Americans to participate in the rewards of an economic system for which they provided the foundation.

These assertions of economic independence are just as noteworthy—and just as illegal—as the numerous violations of British Navigation Laws for which white merchants have been romanticized by colonial historians. I make this comparison purposefully, for I wish to argue in the remainder of this essay that the connections between white activism and black activism prior to the Revolution were not accidental. Several incidents reveal curious and notable linkages that suggest that numerous blacks were ready to take care of business on yet another level. For if black Carolinians were doing much of the physical work, and if they were struggling for a minimal share in the profits being generated by that work, they also were aspiring to a more legitimate place in the society that exploited them. That is to say, taking care of business for many, if not all, involved trying to gain greater control of their own lives, trying to obtain what we would now crudely define as "liberty and independence."

The white minority accepted the fact that enslaved persons were quick to take advantage of anything that weakened, disturbed, or distracted the controlling culture. When fire destroyed much of Charleston in 1740, rumors of an imminent slave revolt reached as far as Boston.[19] And when hurricanes devastated the port town twelve years later, Governor James Glen issued a proclamation outlining punishments for the "divers wicked and ill-disposed persons," slave or free, who sought to "take advantage of the calamity with which it has pleased God to afflict the inhabitants." Negro slaves were allowed to sift the wreckage only under white supervision or with a permit from the property owner; violators would "be sent to the workhouse, there to be corrected for such offence."[20]

It was not always acts of God that provided black captives with a strategic opening. The Stono Rebellion of 1739, the largest and best-timed slave uprising in the history of the North American colonies, was initiated south of Charleston within twenty-four hours of the time word reached South Carolina that the English had gone to war with Spain.[21] But that conflict, the so-called War of Jenkins' Ear, brought little social dislocation to the lowland region compared to the turbulent events of the next quarter century associated with the onset of a full-scale colonial revolution. Both in 1765 following passage of the Stamp Act and in 1775 in the wake of the initial bloodshed at Lexington and Concord, anti-British crowds took to the streets of Charleston, and in each instance overt civil unrest among the white inhabitants, protesting their "colonial slavery" to England, was accompanied by signs of threatened unrest among the black half of the town's populace, challenging their condition as chattel slaves.

In late October 1765, Henry Laurens, thought to be in possession of the stamped paper Parliament had ordered for the implementation of the Stamp Act and which had reached Charleston five days earlier, found his residence surrounded by a crowd of radicals chanting, "*Liberty Liberty and stamp'd paper.*" Laurens, a wealthy merchant who was uncertain as yet of his political stance toward the English crown and whose wife was "far gone with child," handled the disruptive event as best he could. Several days later he looked on uneasily as the town celebrated the resignation of its stamp officers with the largest demonstration in local history. It was led by Christopher Gadsden's triumphant Sons of Liberty, who unfurled a British flag in the streets with the word LIBERTY emblazoned across it.[22]

Needless to say, this public display was watched closely by blacks in Charleston. The African-born slave, Olaudah Equiano, may have witnessed this celebration from aboard the sloop *Prudence* in Charleston Harbor, for he noted in his remarkable autobiography, "I saw the town illuminated, the guns were fired, and bonfires and other demonstrations of joy shown."[23] But the best evidence of black attentiveness comes from Laurens himself, for as the crisis over the Stamp Act continued, the former slave trader recorded that, "A peculiar incident, revealing in what dread the citizens lived among the black savages with whom they were surrounding themselves, was furnished in January by some negroes who, apparently in thoughtless imitation, began to cry 'Liberty.'" According to Laurens, "The city was thrown under arms for a week and for 10 or 14 days messengers were sent posting through the province in the most bitterly cold weather for 19 years. Nothing was proved; but one negro was banished because some of his judges said in the general course of his life he had been a sad dog—and perhaps that it was necessary to save appearances."²⁴ Not until a decade later would white violence and black unrest again coincide dramatically in Charleston. Then, on the eve of revolution, a Negro leader once more was singled out and punished as a scapegoat, on limited evidence, for a suspected plan that went far beyond the limits of "thoughtless imitation."

The year 1775 was one of heightening distrust and animosity in England's North American empire. Deep-seated suspicions of long standing were renewed and intensified at every level—between king and colonists, governors and assemblies, Whigs and Tories, masters and servants—and more than once a sense of vigilance merged into an acceptance of vigilantism. In London, crown officials claimed to uncover an elaborate scheme (said to include at least one young American) for kidnapping George III and sending him back "to His German Dominions";²⁵ while on the colonial frontiers, from Canada southward, spokesmen expressed the fear that British officers were plotting with loyal Indian tribes to overrun white Protestant settlements in the interior. A declaration by Congress dated 5 July 1775, "setting forth the causes and necessity of . . . taking up arms," claimed that, "We have received certain intelligence that General Carleton, the Governour of Canada, is instigating the people of that Province, and the Indians, to fall upon us."²⁶ This document, drafted by Thomas Jefferson and John Dickinson, signed by John Hancock, and issued by George Washington upon his arrival in Massachusetts to take command of the rebel army, went on to state: "And we have but too much reason to apprehend that schemes have been formed to excite domestick enemies against us."²⁷ Naturally, these fears of "domestick" insurrection were greatest in the southern colonies. In Virginia, Governor Dunmore made it known, shortly after confiscating the colony's gunpowder from its Williamsburg magazine in April 1775, that in case of disorder he expected "all the Slaves on the side of Government." When a group of blacks promptly presented themselves at Dunmore's door for duty, he turned them away, but he informed the Earl of Dartmouth that, given adequate arms, he expected "to collect from among the *Indians*, negroes and other persons" a force large enough to contain the colony's white dissidents.[28]

In Maryland, Governor Robert Eden apparently was thinking along similar lines, although in April a delegation had persuaded him to issue four hundred stands of arms to contain suspected slave uprisings in four counties.[29] During the summer, a Whig minister in Maryland complained, "The governor of Virginia, the captains of the men of war, and mariners have been tampering with our Negroes; and have nightly meetings with them; and all for the glorious purpose of enticing them to cut their masters' throats while they are asleep. Gracious God! that men noble by birth and fortune should descend to such ignoble base servility."[30] Later in the fall, the patriot Committee of Inspection for Dorchester County, Maryland, reported, "The insolence of the Negroes in this county is come to such a height, that we are under a necessity of disarming them which we affected on Saturday last. We took about eighty guns, some bayonets, swords, etc. The malicious and imprudent speeches of some among the lower classes of whites have induced them to believe that their freedom depends on the success of the King's troops. We cannot therefore be too vigilant nor too rigorous with those who promote and encourage this disposition in our slaves."[31] One local resident named James Simmons was tarred, feathered, and banished on the accusation of fomenting a slave insurrection.[32]

Similar signs of class unrest between masters and slaves were clearly evident in Georgia and in North Carolina, where Janet Schaw noted in July 1775 that white residents had heard that the king "was ordering the tories to murder the whigs, and promising every Negro that would murder his master and family that he should have his Master's plantation." She added dramatically, "This last artifice they may pay for, as the Negroes have got it amongst them and believe it to be true. Tis ten to one they may try the experiment, and in that case [white] friends and foes will all be one."[33] By this time, the possibility that rebellion by white dissidents in any southern colony might be offset by a revolt of enslaved blacks was a pressing matter for consideration among persons of every social, political, and racial group. This awareness could be found from the highest to the lowest rungs of the culture, with widely differing expressions and implications, throughout the South.

But the consciousness that a possible social revolution lay behind any political revolution that might be brewing (a prospect, incidentally, common to most such transforming moments in human affairs) was expressed most early, most often, and most logically with respect to South Carolina, because of its high concentration of enslaved people. At the beginning of 1775, General Thomas Gage had sent from Boston to Charleston a private letter for John Stuart, the British Indian superintendent of the Southern District, reflecting upon this matter. "It is to be hoped," he wrote, "for your own Sakes that the Delegates you send to Philadelphia will be moderate People, but you Carolinians are as hot as your Climate—however it is well known that if a Serious Opposition takes place, you can do but little—You have too much to take care and think of, but should you proceed [to] much greater lengths it may happen that your Rice and Indigo will be brought to market by negroes instead of white People—"[34]

The delegates to whom Gage referred sailed for Philadelphia on 3 May 1775. They had scarcely departed Charleston Harbor when a private letter arrived from Arthur Lee, the Whigs' attentive and industrious correspondent in London, suggesting that a plan had been laid before the British administration for instigating American slaves to revolt.[35] It is impossible to deter-

mine the origins of this report—whether from the statements of
Dunmore in Virginia, Gage in Massachusetts, Dartmouth in
London, or some other source—much less how much weight to
give it—but Lee's letter had extreme implications for everyone in
South Carolina, and rumors of his message must have spread
rapidly through Charleston among Whigs and Tories, slaves and
freemen. To reinforce the sense of unrest, the first word arrived
on 8 May of the open hostilities and bloodshed at Lexington and
Concord three weeks earlier. "Upon news of the affair at
Lexington," states one report, "the people of Carolina were
thrown into a great Ferment."[36] Now Gage's prediction of the
culture turned upside down would be tested.

Conditions were extremely tense in the ensuing weeks.
Rumors spread that Stuart, the Indian agent, was party to a
British plan for counterinsurgency, and on 26 May he withdrew
toward Florida, fearing for his safety. When the Provincial
Congress met in Charleston on 1 June, it immediately dispatched
two of its members to pursue Stuart, "showing printed Bills to
the militia now under arms thr'out the Province, containing the
Grossest aspersions of his Character, and setting forth that he
was employed to arm the negroes and Indians."[37] According to
an official British account drawn up a year later, "the Colonel of
the Malitia Mr Pinckney ordered the Inhabitants to do Patrole
Duty and to Mount Guard every night, which duty had till then
been done by a Town Guard," on the basis of "Certain information which they pretended to have received that an Insurrection
of the negroes was meditated." The memorandum continues:
"The news papers were full of Publications calculated to excite
the fears of the People—Massacres and Instigated Insurrections,
were Words in the mouth of every Child—The pretended
Discovery of an intention to Instigate Insurrections of the negroes and bring down the Indians was the pretence for tendering
an Instrument of Association to every Person in the Province."[38]

This oath of loyalty to the patriot cause, which referred
explicitly to the "Dread of instigated Insurrections in the Col-

onies," was widely circulated in early June.[39] The Provincial Congress with Henry Laurens presiding met on a Sunday, 4 June (no doubt as much for symbolic reasons as through a sense of urgency, since that date was the king's birthday and had been observed as a holiday in earlier years) and passed an order that all who refused to sign a pledge of association were enemies to their country.[40] In addition, the South Carolina Council of Safety warned against "instigated insurrections by our negroes," and a special committee was established "to secure the province against an insurrection of slaves or counter-Revolutionary moves."[41] On 6 June the *South Carolina Gazette and Country Journal* printed a news item from New Bern, North Carolina, regarding Lord Dunmore's seizure of the gunpowder at Williamsburg earlier in the spring. According to the report, "The monstrous absurdity that the Governor can deprive the people of the necessary means of defense at a time when the colony is actually threatened with an insurrection of their slaves," merely by claiming the powder to be under the king's jurisdiction, "has worked up the passions of the people there almost to a frenzy."[42]

By now passions were equally high in Charleston. When two loyal residents were reported spreading the "good news" that Negroes, Roman Catholics, and Indians were to receive British arms, the General Committee of Correspondence chose to make an example of them, and on 8 June "two poor wretches," James Dealy and Laughlin Martin, were "tarred, feathered carted about the streets and then put on board a Vessel bound for England."[43] In addition, a number of blacks were arrested upon suspicion of being involved in the plot. Several were punished for using impudent language, but most were released within a week for lack of evidence, while only one free black named Thomas Jeremiah was retained in prison under suspicion. By 13 June the next issue of the local paper reported that the militia companies were patrolling regularly, "the salutary Consequences of which are every Day more apparent; The nightly Meetings and Riots of the Negroes are entirely suppressed."[44]

In July, the planter Gabriel Manigault wrote a letter to kin in England stating, "We have been alarmed by idle reports that the Negroes intended to rise, which on examination proved to be of less consequence than was expected, however a Strick watch has been kept for fear of the worst." Young Gabriel Manigault, receiving this news in September, wrote to his grandmother in Charleston, "I am very glad to find by Grandpapa's Letter, that there was not so much reason to be afraid of the Negroes, as was at first suspected."[45] But he was unaware of events that had taken place during August repeating, in exaggerated form, the patterns that had occurred in June. And in August, as in June, discussions, threats, and acts involving whites and blacks in Carolina were inextricably entwined.

The newly appointed colonial governor, Lord William Campbell, who reached Charleston in the early summer, found the story still circulating that the "Ministry had in agitation not only to bring down the Indians on the Inhabitants of this province, but also to instigate, and encourage an insurrection amongst the Slaves. It was also reported, and universally believed," Campbell stated, "that to effect this plan 14,000 Stand of Arms were actually on board the Scorpion, the Sloop of War I came out in. Words, I am told, cannot express the flame that this occasion'd amongst all ranks and degrees, the cruelty and savage barbarity of the scheme was the conversation of all Companies." He went on to report that on Friday, 11 August, Thomas Jeremiah was again "brought to trial, if such a process deserves that name."[46] On Saturday afternoon, less than twenty-four hours later, a white soldier named Walker was seized by a mob of several hundred "for some insolent speech he had made."[47] In reporting this incident, His Majesty's surgeon to the force in Carolina, Dr. George Milligen, made special note of the fact that 12 August was the birthday of His Royal Highness, the Prince of Wales. He claimed that around two o'clock the local mob, "offended at something the Gunner of Fort Johnson had said, seized his person, stript, tarred and feathered him and then putting him in a Cart paraded through the Town with him till 7 o'clock using him very cruelly all the time."[48]

A week later, when Governor Campbell related this mob scene to Lord Dartmouth, he was obliged to report in the same paragraph "Another Act of Barbarity," more "tragical in nature," which he clearly felt to be part of the same picture. For having been tried summarily under the Negro Act of 1740, Thomas Jeremiah had been sentenced "to be hanged, and then burned to ashes, on Friday the 18th." He could not be saved even by the best efforts of Governor Campbell, who wrote after Jeremiah's death, "I have only the perfect comfort to think I left no means untried to preserve him. They have now dipt their hands in Blood, God Almighty knows where it will end."[49]

As one of a small group of skilled black navigators who served as licensed harbor pilots, Jeremiah "had often piloted in Men of War" through the shoals around Charleston Harbor, a type of work that could be extremely important and highly suspicious when British ships were close at hand.[50] A black named Sambo who also worked in the harbor had testified against "Jerry" in a deposition, "that about 2 or 3 months ago being at Simmons Wharf, Jeremiah says to him, Sambo, do you hear anything of the war that is coming, Sambo answered no, Jeremiah replies; yes there is a great war coming soon—Sambo replies, what shall we poor Negroes do in a schooner. Jeremiah says set the Schooner on fire, jump on shore, and join the soldiers—that the war was come to help the poor Negroes."[51] Even more damaging had been the testimony of Jemmy, a slave owned by Peter Croft, whom Jeremiah first denied recognizing but who was shown to be his wife's brother. On 16 June, Jemmy had sworn before a justice of the peace that ten weeks earlier, while in Charleston at Mr. Preolia's Wharf, he was approached by Jeremiah, "who declared he had something to give Dewar a runaway slave belonging to Mr. Tweed, and wished to see him, and asked Jemmy to take a few Guns to the said Dewar, to be placed in Negroes hands to fight against the Inhabitants of this Province." The pilot told him further, Jemmy testified, "that he Jeremiah was to have the Chief Command of the said Negroes; that he Jeremiah said he believed he had Powder enough already, but that he wanted more arms which he would try to get as many as he could."[52]

Sentenced to hang as a coconspirator, Jemmy had revised his testimony and obtained a reprieve on 17 August, the day before the scheduled execution, but his brother-in-law, Thomas Jeremiah, went to the gallows, unrepentant and unpardoned. Governor Campbell, anxious to intervene for Jeremiah for both strategic and humanitarian reasons, was advised against resisting the white patriots' determination to execute him by both the attorney general and the chief justice. "My blood ran cold when I read what ground they had doomed a fellow creature to death," wrote the frustrated official, saying his efforts at intervention "raised such a Clamour amongst the People, as is incredible, and they openly and loudly declared, if I granted the man a pardon they would hang him at my door."[53]

A local minister who visited the condemned man shortly before the hanging related to Governor Campbell that "his behavior was modest, his conversation sensible to a degree that astonish'd him, and at the same time he was perfectly resigned to his unhappy, his undeserved fate. He declared he wished not for life, he was in a happy frame of mind, and prepared for death." According to the governor, Jeremiah "asserted his innocence to the last, behaved with the greatest intrepidity as well as decency, and told his implacable and ungrateful Persecutors, God's Judgement would one day overtake them for shedding his innocent blood."[54]

Henry Laurens, who had been caught in the middle of white and black responses to the Stamp Act crisis ten years earlier, again found himself in a conspicuous and difficult position. The president of the Provincial Congress was convinced that "Jerry was guilty of a design and attempt to encourage our Negroes to Rebellion and joining the King's Troops if any had been sent here," but he was equally aware that the weak evidence of the prosecution, the brutal nature of the sentence, and the noble bearing of the victim cast a doubtful light on the emerging patriot leadership. Laurens hastily sent a long letter to his son, John, in London, intended "to contradict false reports which may be, among others, propagated to the prejudice of the poor Carolinians whose impolicy and, in many instances, mad conduct, will appear glaring enough without the aid of one Lie."[55]

Laurens was not alone. Others caught up in the white revolutionary movement took pains both to justify and to distance themselves from the turbulent actions of the previous week. On 18 August, the day Thomas Jeremiah's harsh sentence was to be carried out, the South Carolina House of Assembly forwarded a message to Governor Campbell. "In times like the present when the continent is engaged in one arduous struggle for their Civil Liberties," the statement began, "if Individuals will wantonly step forth and openly . . . condemn measures universally received and approved, they must abide the consequences." The legislators thus invoked the civil liberties of some citizens to justify the brutal treatment of others, as in the tarring of Walker or the hanging of Jeremiah. Then, using a device that would have a long and venerable future, the political leaders divorced themselves apologetically from the crude acts of their constituents. "It is not in our power in such cases," they stated bluntly, "to prescribe limits to Popular Fury."[56]

That afternoon Thomas Jeremiah was hanged and burned. Among the white residents of Charleston, neither his accusers nor his defenders could fully comprehend or acknowledge the meaning of his life and death.[57] But fellow blacks, both enslaved and free, even without knowing the details of his case, must have sensed his real and symbolic significance in a powerful way. Hoping to take advantage of white unrest, he had been caught in the crossfire of the incipient colonial revolt and had paid with his life. Whatever his innermost thoughts and motives, this free pilot represented an expanded definition of "taking care of business." Whatever his "guilt" or "innocence," his experience illustrated the thoroughly enmeshed and interdependent nature of African and European lives in the revolutionary South. Thomas Jeremiah was a curious and inspiring anachronism who seems to have been engaged in the right revolution at the wrong time. Whether his particular ambitions were decades away from possible realization, or only premature by a matter of weeks and months, is difficult to assess. As events transpired in the race-conscious republic, it would be generations before his particular liberty ship reached harbor safely.

Notes

1. Christopher Hill, *The World Turned Upside Down* (New York, 1972), pp. 13–14.

2. For a much fuller résumé of this "trackless wilderness" of publications, see Bernard Bailyn's address to the International Historical Congress, San Francisco (August 1975).

3. Winthrop D. Jordan, *White Over Black: American Attitudes toward the Negro, 1550–1812* (Chapel Hill, N.C., 1968); David Brion Davis, *The Problem of Slavery in the Age of Revolution, 1770–1823* (Ithaca, N.Y., 1975); Duncan J. MacLeod, *Slavery, Race and the American Revolution* (Cambridge, England, 1974); Edmund S. Morgan, *American Slavery, American Freedom: The Ordeal of Colonial Virginia* (New York, 1975).

4. Donald L. Robinson, *Slavery in the Structure of American Politics, 1765–1820* (New York, 1971), pp. 6 ff. Emphasis added.

5. Benjamin Quarles, *The Negro in the American Revolution* (Chapel Hill, N.C., 1961). See also Sidney Kaplan, *The Black Presence in the Era of the American Revolution* (Washington, D.C., 1973). Kurt Vonnegut has made his own succinct comments about slavery and American history; see particularly the opening pages of *Breakfast of Champions* (New York, 1974).

6. Richard Claxton Gregory, *No More Lies: The Myth and the Reality of American History* (New York, 1971), p. 100.

7. My friend and fellow scholar, David M. Zornow, has been studying blacks in revolutionary Charleston and generously has shared with me the text of his excellent 1976 Harvard College honors thesis, now in the Harvard Archives. He and I hope to combine our research into an article in the near future; meanwhile, I am grateful for his counsel.

8. The best single summary of colonial demography is the impressive

recent volume by Robert V. Wells, *The Population of the British Colonies in America before 1776: A Survey of Census Data* (Princeton, N.J., 1975).

9. On the general theme of labor in early Carolina, see Peter H. Wood, *Black Majority: Negroes in Colonial South Carolina from 1670 through the Stono Rebellion* (New York, 1974), chapters 2 through 5, or the condensed discussion in Peter H. Wood, " 'It Was a Negro Taught Them': A New Look at African Labor in Early South Carolina," *Journal of Asian and African Studies* 9 (July and Oct. 1974): 160–79. For a recent illustration of the ideological confusion still felt by historians describing altered production on the Pinckney estate, see G. D. Lillibridge, *Images of American Society: A History of the United States*, 2 vols. (Boston, 1976), 1:75, where black slaves are shown at backbreaking labor over the caption, "Indigo processing—Eliza Pinckney's success."

10. Harriott Horry Ravenel, *Eliza Pinckney* (New York, 1896), p. 245. Cf. David L. Coon, "Eliza Lucas Pinckney and the Reintroduction of Indigo Culture in South Carolina," *Journal of Southern History* 42 (Feb. 1976): 61–76.

11. Johann David Schoepf, *Travels in the Confederation, 1783–1784*, trans. and ed. Alfred J. Morrison (Philadelphia, 1911), pt. 2, p. 221.

12. In this tradition, consider the literary speculation of Ebenezer Kellogg, a Yale graduate teaching languages at Williams College, who went south for his health in the early nineteenth century. One of his half-whimsical letters from Charleston states: "The character and situation of the black population of this country is one of the most interesting subjects of observation to strangers who visit it. Their number is such as might entitle them to be regarded as the first portion of the population, and the whites only as a kind of agent for them, performing a very important part in the interior economy of this mixed society, but a part subservient rather than superior to the blacks: And I sometimes amused myself in walking about the streets, when I met five negroes as often as one white person, with sketching in my mind the plan of a description of the city, with all its business and organization, a description accommodating to this idea. The blacks are the most numerous, and of course, in the eye of the philanthropist, the most important part of the community. There would be something of verisimilitude in such a representation as should make the whites toil, and bustle, and oversee the blacks only for the benefit and by the authority and consent of the blacks themselves" (*South Carolina Historical and Genealogical Magazine* 49 [Jan. 1948]: 9).

13. For brief comments on slave history as labor history, see *Southern Exposure*, 3, no. 4 (1976): 97–98. For a vivid incident concerning a wildcat strike or "revolt" by black workers facing a speed-up in the production of barrel staves on a Louisiana plantation in 1775, see the excellent new sourcebook edited by Willie Lee Rose, *A Documentary History of Slavery in North America* (New York, 1976), pp. 105–7.

14. *South Carolina Gazette*, 3 Nov. 1763, 1 Oct. 1764; Journals of the Court of General Sessions, 1769–76, 21 Jan. 1771, South Carolina Department of Archives and History, Columbia, S.C.

15. *South Carolina Gazette*, 25 Jan. 1770, 24 Sept. 1772.

16. Ibid., 30 April 1771, 24 Sept. 1772.

17. Leila Sellers, *Charleston Business on the Eve of the American Revolution* (Chapel Hill, N.C., 1934), p. 106.

18. *South Carolina Gazette*, 24 Sept. 1772.

19. Shortly after the fire, the merchant Robert Pringle wrote to his brother in London, noting "the great Risque we Run from an Insurrection of our Negroes which we were very apprehensive off [sic] but all as yet Quiet by the strict Guards & watch we are oblig'd to keep Constantly night & Day" (Robert Pringle to Capt. Andrew Pringle, 22 Nov. 1740, Pringle Letterbook, South Carolina Historical Society, Charleston).

20. *South Carolina Gazette*, 18 Sept. 1752.

21. See Wood, *Black Majority*, p. 314. David Zornow has pointed out to me that Lieutenant Governor William Bull, who was instrumental in foiling the rebels' effort to escape to St. Augustine, recalled much later that the incident "took its rise from the wantonness, and not oppression of our Slaves, for too great a number had been very indiscreetly assembled and encamped together for several nights, to do a large work on the public road; with a slack inspection" (Letter of 30 Nov. 1770, British Public Record Office Transcripts [hereafter cited as BPRO Trans.] 32:381–83, South Carolina Archives).

22. David Duncan Wallace, *The Life of Henry Laurens* (New York, 1915), pp. 118–20. When Laurens's wife bore a daughter the following month, some of his patriot friends referred to the child as "Liberty" Laurens, apparently to goad the father about his politics.

23. "The Life of Olaudah Equiano, or Gustavus Vassa, the African. Written by Himself," in *Great Slave Narratives*, selected and introduced by Arna Bontemps (Boston, 1969), pp. 95–96. According to Equiano's recollection, this display was "on account of the repeal of the stamp act," news of which reached Charleston the following year, but the dates he provides for his travels, although slightly uncertain, suggest that he was actually in Charleston late in 1765 when colonists celebrated their success in blocking initial enforcement of the Stamp Act.

24. Wallace, *Laurens*, p. 120. It is intriguing to note that Laurens's maternal grandfather, Augustus Grasset, a noted merchant and government official in New York, had been killed in the Negro insurrection there on 7 April 1712 (ibid., p. 5). During the Revolution Laurens's son John, as an aide to General Washington, would become an advocate of arming South Carolina slaves and enlisting them to fight in the revolutionary cause, with the assurance of eventual freedom. On John Laurens, see Robert M. Weir, "Portrait of a Hero," *American Heritage* 27 (April 1976): 16–19, 86–88. On the threat of black violence in the wake of Stamp Act demonstrations, see BPRO Trans., Council Journal for 17, 25 Dec. 1765, 25 Jan. 1766; Journals of the South Carolina Commons House, 14, 17 Jan. 1766, South Carolina Archives.

25. Pauline Maier, *From Resistance to Revolution: Colonial Radicals and the Development of American Opposition to Britain, 1765–1776* (New York, 1972), p. 259.

26. *Sources and Documents Illustrating the American Revolution 1764–1788*, selected and ed. S. E. Morison, 2d ed. (New York, 1929), p. 144.

27. Ibid. When Jefferson drafted the Declaration of Independence a year later, he again linked these allegations, though in reverse order. The last in a long list of charges against King George were, "He has excited domestic insurrections amongst us, and has endeavoured to bring on the inhabitants of our frontiers the merciless Indian savages" (ibid., p. 159). Historians have paid far more attention to the latter charge than to the former. To cite one interesting example, William Gilmore Simms, the nineteenth-century novelist and historian who wrote extensively about revolutionary South Carolina, makes considerable reference in *Joscelyn* to the fear of Indian attacks in the lowcountry in 1775, while refraining from any mention of the related suspicions of black insurgency.

28. Quarles, *Negro in Revolution*, pp. 21–22. Quarles notes that on 15 May, from Boston, General Thomas Gage, "in a letter to Dartmouth touched on Dunmore's proposal: 'We hear,' wrote the British commander, 'that a Declaration his Lordship has made, of proclaiming all the Negroes free, who should join him, has Startled the Insurgents.' " In fact, as Quarles explains, Dunmore did not issue such a formal proclamation until November.

29. Ibid., p. 14; Ronald Hoffman, "The 'Disaffected' in the Revolutionary South," in Alfred F. Young, ed., *The American Revolution: Explorations in the History of American Radicalism* (DeKalb, Ill., 1976), p. 281.

30. "Extracts of a Letter from a Clergyman in Maryland to his Friend in England," 2 Aug. 1775, in Peter Force, ed., *American Archives* . . . , 4th ser., 6 vols. (Washington, D.C., 1837–46), 3:10. (This quotation and the next are drawn from Hoffman's excellent article cited in note 29.)

31. Report of the Dorchester County Committee of Inspection, Fall 1775, Gilmor Papers, Maryland Historical Society, Baltimore, Md.

32. Maier, *From Resistance to Revolution*, p. 284.

33. Janet Schaw, *The Journal of a Lady of Quality*, ed. Evangeline W. Andrews and Charles M. Andrews (New Haven, 1923), p. 199. For details, see Francois Xavier Martin, *History of North Carolina* (New Orleans, 1829), pp. 353–55, and William L. Saunders, ed., *Colonial Records of North Carolina*, 10 vols. (Raleigh, N.C., 1886–90), 10:41, 94–95, as well as Jeffrey J. Crow, *The Black Experience in Revolutionary North Carolina* (Raleigh, N.C., 1977), chap. 4. On Georgia, see *Georgia Gazette*, 12 July 1775.

34. John R. Alden, "John Stuart Accuses William Bull," *William and Mary Quarterly*, 3d ser. 2 (July 1945): 318.

35. *South Carolina Historical and Genealogical Magazine* 47 (July 1946): 191. In this communication, D. D. Wallace also comments on Gage's threat—or warning—to Stuart cited in note 34.

36. Alden, "John Stuart," p. 318.

37. Ibid., p. 320.

38. Ibid., pp. 318–19. According to this account, when Lieutenant Governor Bull inquired why the city was under arms, "the Colonel answered that they had information of some bad designs in the negroes and that the steps taken by him were Judged necessary for the security of the Town. His Honour seemed intirely satisfied with his Reason, and without any enquiry into the

nature of the Information or Evidence, that the negroes meditated an Insurrection, approved of the Colonels Conduct and gave him a writen order for his Justification."

39. For the text of the Association oath, see *South Carolina Historical and Genealogical Magazine* 8 (1907): 141. The loyalist Thomas Knox Gordon, who later filed a claim with the English government, stated in his memorial (n.d.): "In the beginning of the year 1775 the Malcontents being very anxious to have some plausible pretence for arming with great industry propagated a Report that the Negroes were meditating an Insurrection." Gordon goes on to explain how he tried to quash this rumor (Audit Office 12, vol. 51, ff. 289–91, Public Record Office, London). Another South Carolina official, Thomas Irving, makes a similar statement in his memorial (vol. 51, ff. 306–7). I am indebted to Mary Beth Norton for these references.

40. Wallace, *Laurens*, p. 207. On changing responses to the king's birthday, see Maier, *From Resistance to Revolution*, p. 210. The Association was first adopted by the provincial congress on 3 June. See B. D. Bargar, "Charles Town Loyalism in 1775: The Secret Reports of Alexander Innes," *South Carolina Historical Magazine* 63 (July 1962): 126–28.

41. "Journal of the Council of Safety for South-Carolina," *South Carolina Historical Society Collections* 2 (1858): 40; Richard Walsh, *Charleston's Sons of Liberty: A Study of the Artisans, 1763–1789* (Columbia, S.C., 1959), p. 69.

42. This dispatch from New Bern was datelined 19 May. Samuel A. Ashe, *History of North Carolina*, 2 vols. (Greensboro, N.C., 1908), 1:435–36, relates that several days later an emissary arrived in the North Carolina capital from New York, "and informed Governor Martin that General Gage was about to send him the arms and munitions desired, and there was reason to suppose that the shipment had been discovered. A report also had been propagated that the governor had formed a design of arming the negroes and proclaiming freedom to those who should resort to the king's standard, and the public mind was much inflamed against him."

43. Walsh, *Sons of Liberty*, p. 71; Bargar, "Charles Town Loyalism," pp. 132–33. In his report to the Earl of Dartmouth, dated 10 June, Innes wrote, "Your Lordship will easily see with what art the *Herd* has been led on from one step to another and now the language is that there is no drawing back as they have gone so far."

44. *South Carolina Gazette and Country Journal*, 13 June 1775. The case of Thomas Jeremiah (or Jeremiah Thomas as he may actually have been known) is mentioned briefly in Pauline Maier, "The Charleston Mob and the Evolution of Popular Politics in Revolutionary South Carolina, 1765–1784," *Perspectives in American History* 4 (1970): 177, in James W. St. G. Walker, "Blacks as American Loyalists: The Slaves' War for Independence," *Historical Reflections* 2 (Summer 1975): 51, and in Maier, *From Resistance to Revolution*, pp. 283–84. But the most thorough treatment to date is in the honors essay of David M. Zornow, "A Troublesome Community: Blacks in Revolutionary Charles Town, 1765–1775," Harvard Archives.

45. "The Papers of Gabriel Manigault," *South Carolina Historical Magazine* 64 (Jan. 1963): 2, and letter from Woodmanstone, England, 5 Sept. 1775, in Manigault Family Papers, South Caroliniana Library, Columbia, S.C.

46. BPRO Trans., 35:192–93, 197–98.

47. *South Carolina Historical and Genealogical Magazine* 27 (July 1926): 129. Peter Timothy, member of the Council of Safety and printer of the *South Carolina Gazette*, writing to William Henry Drayton on 13 August, continues his account: "There is hardly a street through which he was not paraded nor a Tory House where they did not halt. . . . At. Fen. Bull's they stopt, call'd for Grog; had it; made Walker drink D——n to Bull, threw a bag of feathers into his Balcony, & desired he would take care of it till his turn came; & that they would charge the Grog to the Acct. of Ld North, finally the wretch was discharged at Milligan's door. The people were in such a humour that I believe there was scarce a non-subscriber who did not tremble, & Wells had his Shop close shut" (ibid., p. 129). Fenwick Bull was an agent of the English government and no relation to the Carolina Bulls.

48. "Mr. Milligen's Report of the State of South Carolina," written at sea after leaving the province, 15 Sept. 1775, quoted in Chapman J. Milling, *Colonial South Carolina* (Columbia, S.C., 1951), pp. xix–xxi. Milligen continued, "About six o'clock they took it into their heads to pay me a visit with him . . . I was immediately surrounded by a vast crowd, three or four hundred snakes, hissing, threatening, and abusing me."

49. BPRO Trans., 35: 184–88, 207–8. Campbell wrote: "Your Lordship will I am sure excuse my warmth when I acquaint you, that yesterday under colour of Law, they hanged & burned, an unfortunate wretch, a Free Negroe of considerable property, one of the most valuable, & useful men in his way, in the Province, on suspicion of instigating an Insurrection, for which I am convinced there was not the least ground. I could not save him My Lord! the very reflection Harrows my Soul!"

50. BPRO Trans., 35:196. On the strategic importance of Negro pilots, see Wood, *Black Majority*, pp. 204–5, and Quarles, *Negro in Revolution*, p. 152. For evidence of discussions regarding the tactical significance of ships in Charleston Harbor, see Bargar, "Charles Town Loyalism," pp. 131, 133.

51. BPRO Trans., 35: 216.

52. BPRO Trans., 35: 215.

53. BPRO Trans., 35: 198–99. The governor added, "I received too a letter from a man of the first Property in the Province, who had always express'd great friendship, representing in the strongest terms the dreadful consequences that would attend my pardoning him, concluding with this remarkable expression, that it would raise a flame all the water in Cooper River would not extinguish."

54. BPRO Trans., 35:200–202. Campbell recorded that the Reverend Mr. Smith "candidly told me that he attended the Black as much from a desire to ascertain the reality of an instigated insurrection as from motives of humanity."

55. Henry Laurens to John Laurens, 21 Aug. 1775, Henry Laurens Papers, South Carolina Historical Society, Charleston. For an earlier encounter of

Jeremiah's with the white legal system, see Miscellaneous Records, Book RR, p. 239, and Book OO, p. 264, South Carolina Archives. I am indebted to David Zornow for these references.

56. Maier, *From Resistance to Revolution*, p. 279.

57. Governor Campbell based much of his argument for Jeremiah's innocence on the belief that a prosperous free Negro would have no grounds for fostering resistance and on the reassuring fact that no evidence of incitement or involvement by whites could be found. Significantly, he explained the unrest in the slave community and the testimony against Jeremiah in terms of white behavior: "The constant exercising of the Militia, and other martial appearances, joined to their imprudent conversations at their tables before their domestics, could not escape the notice of those unhappy wretches, and naturally led them to converse among themselves on the reasons for it. One of these conversations was, it is said, overheard, and several of those poor ignorant creatures taken up, who terrified at the recollection of former cruelties were easily induced to accuse themselves and others to escape punishment" (BPRO Trans., 35:195–96).

Contributors

Lorin Lee Cary, Associate Professor of History at the University of Toledo, wrote his doctoral dissertation on the labor union organizer, Adolph Germer, at the University of Wisconsin in 1968. His articles on labor history and colonial North Carolina slavery have appeared in the *Wisconsin Magazine of History*, the *Journal of the Illinois Historical Society*, and *Science and Society*. He received the Harry E. Pratt Memorial Award for the best article published in the *Journal of the Illinois Historical Society* in 1973. Currently he is completing a book on slavery and social structure in colonial North Carolina with Marvin L. Michael Kay, writing a study of labor organizers in the twentieth century, and with Francine Cary examining the black population of Nantucket, Mass.

Clyde R. Ferguson, Assistant Professor of History at Kansas State University, studied at Duke University with John R. Alden. Interested in irregular warfare during the revolutionary war in the South, Ferguson is currently engaged in a study of the revolt in the Carolina backcountry.

Jack P. Greene is Andrew W. Mellon Professor in the Humanities at the Johns Hopkins University. He has published widely in the field of southern colonial history and is currently completing work on the emergence of corporate identities in three plantation societies—Virginia, Jamaica, and South Carolina—during the seventeenth and eighteenth centuries.

Marvin L. Michael Kay, Associate Professor of History at the University of Toledo, wrote his doctoral dissertation on the North Carolina Regulation at the University of Minnesota in 1962. His articles on colonial North Carolina and the Regulation have appeared in the *Australian and New Zealand American Studies Association–First Biennial Conference Proceedings*; *Australian Journal of Politics and History*; *North Carolina Historical Review*; *William and Mary Quarterly*; *Science and Society*; and in a book edited by Alfred F. Young, *The American Revolution: Explorations in the History of American Radicalism* (DeKalb, Ill., 1976). He is currently preparing a book on the North Carolina Regulators; with Lorin Lee Cary a monograph on slavery in North Carolina, 1748–72; and with William S. Price, Jr., a social analysis of roads and the militia in North Carolina, 1740–75.

Pauline Maier was recently appointed Robinson-Edwards Professor of History at the University of Wisconsin, Madison, after having spent several years on the faculty of the University of Massachusetts, Boston. She has published numerous articles including "Popular Uprisings and Civil Authority in Eighteenth-Century America," which originally appeared in the *William and Mary Quarterly* and won the Douglass G. Adair award. Her first book, *From Resistance to Revolution; Colonial Radicals and the Development of American Resistance to Britain, 1765–1776*, was published by Alfred A. Knopf in 1972. More recently she edited, with Jack P. Greene, *Interdisciplinary Studies of the American Revolution* (Beverly Hills, 1976). During the fall of 1976 she served as the Anson G. Phelps lecturer at New York University.

Michael Mullin, Professor of History at California State University, Sacramento, is the author of *Flight and Rebellion: Slave Resistance in Eighteenth-Century Virginia* (New York, 1972) and editor of *American Negro Slavery: A Documentary History* (New York, 1976). He is presently preparing a book for Oxford University Press on slavery in the American South and British Caribbean in an age of war and revolutions, 1750–1834.

Mary Beth Norton is Associate Professor of History at Cornell University. A graduate of the University of Michigan and of Harvard University, where she received her Ph.D., she has written numerous articles on the American revolutionary era and on women and loyalists in particular. In 1972 Little, Brown and Company published her doctoral dissertation, *The British-Americans: The Loyalist Exiles in England, 1774–1789*.

John Shy, Professor of History at the University of Michigan, is the author of *A People Numerous and Armed: Reflections on the Military Struggle for American Independence* (Oxford, 1976) and *Toward Lexington: The Role of the British Army in the Coming of the American Revolution* (Princeton, 1965).

Robert M. Weir is Associate Professor of History at the University of South Carolina. His articles on colonial and revolutionary America have appeared in *American Heritage*, the *Journal of Interdisciplinary History*, the *South Atlantic Quarterly*, the *William and Mary Quarterly*, and he is the author of a forthcoming study of the Revolution in South Carolina.

Peter H. Wood is Associate Professor of History at Duke University. His book, *Black Majority: Negroes in Colonial South Carolina from 1670 through the Stono Rebellion* (New York, 1974), won the Albert J. Beveridge Award of the American Historical Association. He is currently preparing Volume 2 of Louisiana State University Press's series, *A History of the South*. It will concern the southern colonies from 1689 to 1763.

Index

A

Abrams, Creighton, 187
Adams, Abigail, 220
Adams, Henry, 42
Adams, John, 14, 220
Adams, Samuel, 7, 14, 17, 20
Adams Chronicles, The, 269
Adams Papers, The, 269
African ethnicity, 238–39, 248, 250,
    252–55, 257–58
African uprisings: characteristics of,
    238–39; in Caribbean in 1790s,
    255–58. *See also* Maroons
Alden, John R., x
Ambler, Betsy, 209, 215, 219
Ambler, John Jaquelin, 209
Americanization: as crucial part of
    southern strategy, 159, 160, 170
*American Slavery, American Freedom: The
    Ordeal of Colonial Virginia*, 269
Andover, Mass., 28, 29
Anglicans: and Puritan Ethic, 42
Annapolis, Md., 6
Anson, George Lord, 60
Anson County. *See* North Carolina;
    Regulators
Antigua, 239, 250
Arbuthnot, Marriot: as advocate of
    terrorism, 167, 169
Atwood, Thomas, 240
Augusta, Ga., 163, 178, 180–84, 191,
    242
Authoritarianism: trend away from,
    27, 29
Authoritarian Personality, The, 26
Autonomous personality: develops in

eighteenth century, 27, 29, 31. *See
    also* Rebellious personality

B

Bacon's Rebellion, 58
Baillou, Isaac, 185
Bailyn, Bernard, ix
Baldwin, Abraham, 50 (n. 22)
Ball, John, 213
Balla (headman), 240, 258
Baltimore, Md., 6, 218, 242
Barbados, 238, 239, 242
Barham, John Foster, 254, 257
Battle of Alamance, 134
Beaufort County. *See* North Carolina;
    Regulators
Berkeley, Norborne, 59
Berkeley, William, 58
Berlin, Ira, 243
Bertie County. *See* North Carolina;
    Regulators
Bethesda Orphanage, 259
Blacks. *See* Negroes; Slavery; Slaves
Bladen County. *See* North Carolina;
    Regulators
Blair, John, Sr., 60, 87, 89
Bland, Richard, 62, 70; as political
    writer, 71, 75–76, 84, 86; demands
    impersonal government for
    Virginia, 88; as candidate for
    speakership, 94; asserts gentry's
    values, 95
Bolling, Robert: spearheads discussion
    of Chiswell case, 88–91; condemns
    Robinson, 92; sued, 99
Boston, 57, 276, 280

299

Botetourt, Baron de. *See* Berkeley, Norborne

Boucher, Jonathan: characterizes revolutionaries, 26, 33

Boukman (witch doctor), 246

Bowler, Jack, 245

Bowne, Eliza Southgate, 227

Boyd, John (or James): as loyalist partisan, 179–80, 182–84

Bradford, William, 7

Bradstreet, Anne, 220

Bridgetown, Barbados, 242, 243

Brinton, Crane, 11

Britain: and seventeenth-century revolutions, 14–15; restrictions of, shatter American trust, 28–29; and family analogy with colonies, 34–35; expects colonies to act rationally, 37–38; as counter-example of decay, 57; and parliamentary taxation, 71–86; and southern strategy, 156–71, 175–94; and postwar economy, 223

British army: and evacuation of blacks, 213–15; and irregular warfare, 215–16. *See also* Revolutionary War

Brockie, Mary, 206

Brockie, William, 206

Brodie, Fawn, 38, 53 (n. 43)

Brown, Richard, 191

Brown, Thomas: as loyalist partisan, 176, 180, 181, 191–93

Brunswick County. *See* North Carolina; Regulators

Bryan, Jonathan, 50 (n. 22)

Bryson (rebel), 179

Bull, Stephen, 185

Bull, William, II, 4; as loyalist personality, 35–36; appalled by civil war, 170–71

Burgoyne, John, 155

Burke, Thomas, 40

Burke Court House, Ga., 180, 181

Burr, Esther Edwards, 220

Burrows, Edwin, 28, 29, 35

Burwell, Lewis, Sr., 99

Butler, William, 192, 193

Byrd, William, III, 87, 99

C

Caldwell County. *See* North Carolina; Regulators

Calhoon, Robert, 35

Calvinism: tradition of, as values of Revolution, 14, 21

Cambodia, 187

Camden, S.C., 157, 185

Campbell, Alexander, 255

Campbell, Archibald: and southern strategy, 177–84, 194, 195–96 (n. 15)

Campbell, William: as royal governor of South Carolina, 175, 283–85, 292 (n. 49), 293 (n. 57)

Canada, 163, 278

Carleton, Guy, 236, 278

Carlisle, Earl of (Frederick Howard), 167

Carlisle Peace Commission, 177

Carroll, Charles (elder), 9, 14, 15, 16

Carroll, Charles: background and politics of, in Maryland, 6–10; his Catholicism, 12; and values of Revolution, 15–17

Carter, Charles, 62

Carter, Landon, 33; as rival to Speaker Robinson, 62, 69–70; opposes Stamp Act, 71, 77, 80, 84, 87; supports Peyton Randolph for speaker, 95; as planter, 248, 260

Carter, Robert (of Nomini Hall), 43, 212, 213; as patriarch, 248, 260

Carter, Robert Wormley, 33

Cary, Archibald, 62, 77

Caswell, Richard, 174

Catawba Indians, 241

Catholicism: as bar to office and voting in Maryland, 6, 12; and fear of loyalism, 282

Ceded Islands, 252, 255

Charleston, S.C., 4, 25, 35, 47, 156, 157, 166, 167, 170, 184, 190, 206, 214–17, 220, 221, 223, 226, 240, 243, 249, 261;

and blacks in the Revolution,
273–87
*Charleston Business on the Eve of the
American Revolution*, 275
Charlotte, N.C., 186
Chase, Samuel: his background and
politics in Maryland, 6–9
Cherokee Indians, 175, 191, 193, 241
Chickasaw Indians, 178
Children. *See* Family life
Chiswell, John: accused of murder, 71;
scandal of, 87–102 passim
Choctaw Indians, 178
Christophe, Henri, 246
Clapp's Mill, N.C., 189
Clarke, Elijah, 191
Class conflict: in North Carolina,
109–46 passim; class differences
between Regulators and
opponents, 127–34
Clerks. *See* Regulators, class
differences with opponents
Clinton, Henry, 175, 177, 180, 184;
offers to pardon North Carolinians,
7; and southern strategy, 157–71
Collier, George, 164
Colonel Dismounted, The, 75
Commissioners. *See* Regulators, class
differences with opponents
Common Sense, 36, 235
Confederacy (southern), 21
Consensus historians, 109–10
Continental army: destroyed at
Camden, 157; cooperates with
militia, 188–90, 194
Continental Congress: warns of Indian
and slave insurrections, 278
Copperheads: compared with
revolutionaries, 20
Corbin, Hannah, 220
Corbin, Richard, 60
Cornwallis, Charles Lord: and the
southern strategy, 158, 161, 166–71,
173 (n. 33); comments on patriot
militia, 186; in southern war,
187–91, 215

Coroners. *See* Regulators, class
differences with opponents
Cowpens, S.C., 186, 187
Creek Indians, 178, 261
Creole conspiracies: characteristics of,
238–39, 243–46, 262–63
Croft, Peter, 284
Cromwell, Oliver, 14
Cross Creek, N.C., 174
Crosthwaite, William Ward, 46, 47
Cruger, John, 186
Culloden, 174
Cumberland County. *See* North
Carolina; Regulators
Cumming, Janet, 207
Cunningham, Bill, 193
Currency Act of 1764, 92

D
Dartmouth, Earl of (William Legge),
279, 281
Davidson, William, 188
Davis, David Brion, xiii, 269
Dealy, James, 282
Deane, Silas, 7
Declaration of Independence:
compared with childhood
rebellion, 37, 45; read in
Charleston, 47; and domestic
insurrections, 290 (n. 27)
Declaration of Rights (Virginia), 55
Deference: in decline in eighteenth
century, 27; as expression of class
and power arrangements, 109;
rejected by Regulators, 135
Demography: of North Carolina,
111–14
Dickinson, John, 278
Digges, Dudley, 62
Dinwiddie, Robert, 59, 65
Dixon, John, 88
Dominica, 240, 255–57
Drayton, Glen, 34
Drayton, John, 32–34
Drayton, William Henry, 33, 44
Drysdale, Hugh, 59
Dunmore, Earl of (John Murray): offers

freedom to slaves, 212–13, 218, 235, 244, 260, 278–79, 281–82
Dutch Guinea, 255

E
East India Company, 4, 18
Ebenezer, Ga., 180, 184
Eden, Robert, 279
Education: and role of women, 208–9. *See also* Locke, John
Elkins, Stanley, 270
Ellet, Elizabeth, 203
Elliott, Barnard, 46, 47
Engerman, Stanley, 275
Equiano, Olaudah, 277
Erikson, Erik, 38, 39
Eutaw Springs, S.C., 190–91
Eyre, Severn, 88

F
Family life: and relationship to Revolution, 25–47 passim; in transition in eighteenth century, 30–31; and analogy with Britain, 34–35; conflict in, 39–40; and qualities esteemed in sons, 41–45; importance of, to slaves, 210; responsibility of women, 211
Fanning, Edmund, 140
Farmers. *See* Regulators
Fathers: autonomy of, produces autonomous sons, 27–28; repressed hostilities toward, unleashed on George III, 36; and parricide, 40–41
Faulkner, William, 263
Fauquier, Francis: as royal governor of Virginia, 59–60, 67, 77, 80, 82, 86
Ferguson, Patrick, 167, 186
Ferguson, Thomas, 42
Feuer, Lewis, 40
First Regiment Foot Militia, 185
Fithian, Philip, 32, 43, 49 (n. 20), 205
Fleming, John, 77, 80
Fletchall, Thomas, 174

Florida, 176, 177, 179, 193, 210, 261, 281
Florida Rangers, 176, 180
Fogel, Robert, 275
Fort Johnston: burned by North Carolina revolutionaries, 5
Fort Ninety-Six, S.C., 186
France: and its influence on British strategy, 155–60, 162, 165, 166, 169
French: seen as allies by slave insurgents, 245
French Revolution, 237, 238

G
Gadsden, Christopher, 22 (n. 11), 277; his background and politics, 4–8; alienates royal governor, 12; defines Revolution's moral message, 13; compares colonists with slaves, 17–18; notes negative effects of slavery, 19; describes William Bull, 36
Gage, Thomas, 7, 280–81
Galphin, George, 178, 181
Gandhi, Mohandas K., 39
García Márquez, Gabriel, 268
Garden, Alexander, 254; as loyalist personality, 35–36
Garshett (maroon), 240
Gates, Horatio, 186
Gentry: in Virginia, reaffirms dominance, 99–102
Germain, George, 175, 187; and the southern strategy, 160–71
George III: as father figure, 36; as source of disorder, 45; decides on new strategy, 156; and kidnapping scheme, 278
Georgetown, S.C., 242
Georgia, 37, 218, 223, 258, 279; in southern war, 157–94 passim
Glen, James, 276
Glorious Revolution (1688), 14
Gooch, William, 59, 60
Granville County. *See* North Carolina; Regulators
Greene, Jack P., 27, 28, 31, 40

Greene, Nathanael, 236, 262; in
    southern war, 187–94
Gregory, Dick, 270
Grenada, 257
Greven, Philip, 28
Grierson, James, 192
Grimké, Sarah Moore, 227
Gruber, Ira: his analysis of the
    southern strategy, 156–59, 162
Grymes, Benjamin, 95
Guadaloupe, 237, 245, 256
Guilford Court House, N.C., 189, 190
Gullah, 254

H
Habersham, John, 50 (n. 22), 262
Habersham, Joseph, 50 (n. 22)
Haiti. See Santo Domingo
Halifax, Nova Scotia, 162
Hammond, LeRoy, 192
Hampton, Wade, 192
Hancock, John, 7, 278
Hansford, Charles, 69
Harder They Come, The, 263
Harnett, Cornelius, 8, 12; leads
    resistance in North Carolina, 5;
    characterized as Sam Adams of
    North Carolina, 7; wealth of, 9;
    defines patriotism, 13
Harold (Creole), 263
Harrison, Benjamin, 50 (n. 22), 62, 77
Harrower, John, 212
Hart, Anne, 220–21, 224
Hart, Oliver, 205, 220
Hartley, Sarah, 46, 47
Hartswell, Richard, 93
Henry, Patrick, 5, 18, 29, 52 (n. 40);
    attacks Stamp Act, 80–82
Higginbotham, Don, 190
Hill, Christopher, 271
Hillsboro, N.C., 114, 187–89
Hindus, Michael, 31, 34
Honduras, 255
Horrocks, James, 68
Horry, Daniel, 216

Horry, Harriott, 216
Households: profile of, in colonial
    South, 204–11
House of Burgesses (Va.): leadership
    of, characterized, 69–70; protests
    Stamp Act, 77–81; and strength of
    gentry, 83; reform impulse of,
    96–98
Howe, Richard Lord, 156
Howe, Robert, 7
Howe, William, 161, 164
Huger, Benjamin, 47
Hugues, Victor, 237
Huntington, Samuel P., 59
Husband, Herman, 133, 140, 141, 144
Hutchinson, Thomas, 167

I
Impartial Relation, 140
Indians: considered as part of British
    strategy, 37, 159, 261, 278, 281–83;
    in southern war, 176, 178, 179, 181,
    182, 184, 192–94. See also Cherokee
    Indians; Chickasaw Indians;
    Choctaw Indians; Creek Indians;
    Seminole Indians
Ingram, James, 180, 181
Intruder in the Dust, 263
Iredell, James, 53 (n. 43)
Izard, Ralph, 50 (n. 22)

J
James II, 14
Jefferson, Thomas, 5, 18, 278, 290 (n.
    27); and tensions in colonial family,
    33, 38, 42–45, 53 (n. 43); and flight
    of his slaves, 213–14
Jemmy (slave), 284–85
Jeremiah, Thomas: as black loyalist,
    282–87
Johnston, George, 80
Johnston, Samuel, 145
Jordan, Winthrop D., xiii, 41, 52 (n. 40),
    53 (n. 43), 269
Justices of peace. See Regulators, class
    differences with opponents

K

Kerber, Linda, 226
Kettle Creek, Ga., 182, 183
Kings Mountain, S.C., 186
Kingston, Jamaica, 242
Kirkland, Moses: as loyalist adviser to
    British, 176–78, 184, 193

L

Laurens, Henry, 243; and tensions in
    colonial family, 37, 43–44, 49 (n.
    20), 50 (n. 22); and the Stamp Act,
    277–78; presides over provincial
    congress, 282; comments on black
    insurgency, 285–86
Laurens, John, 50 (n. 22), 286, 289 (n.
    24)
Lawyers. See Regulators, class
    differences with opponents
Lee, Arthur, 12, 23 (n. 25), 70, 280–81
Lee, Henry, 188, 189
Lee, Ludwell, 43
Lee, Philip Ludwell, 10
Lee, Richard Henry, 36, 43, 62, 69, 70,
    220; opposes Stamp Act, 5, 72–73,
    77, 80, 84; background and politics
    of, 6–12; and values of Revolution,
    13–16; and danger of slavery,
    17–19; demands impersonal
    government for Virginia, 88;
    candidate for speakership, 94
Lee, Thomas (father of Richard Henry
    Lee), 72
Lee, Thomas (son of Richard Henry
    Lee), 43
Lee, William, 10, 37
Lestor, Eleanor, 207, 217
Liberty: as part of Anglo-American
    political thought, 56; loss of, feared,
    57–58
Lillington, Alexander, 174
Locke, John: as political theorist, 14; as
    theorist on rearing children, 30, 34,
    42, 48 (n. 14), 208
Long, Edward, 253

Lossberg, Friedrich Wilhelm von, 155,
    159
L'Ouverture, Toussaint, 246
Lowndes, Rawlins, 37, 50 (n. 22)
Loyalists: compared with supporters of
    North in Civil War, 20; distinctive
    personality of, rejected, 35–36;
    know vulnerability of colonies, 37;
    as basis of southern strategy,
    156–71; defeated in Carolinas, 174;
    and militia of, discussed, 175–94
    passim; and postwar claims by
    women, 205–6, 217–18; reprisals
    against, in Charleston, 282–87
Loyalists and Redcoats, 174
Luffman, John, 250
Luther, Martin, 39
Lux, William: background and politics
    of, in Maryland, 6–9
Lynch, Thomas, Jr., 50 (n. 22)

M

MacDonald, Flora, 174
McGirth, Daniel, 191, 193
McIntosh, Lachlan, 50 (n. 22)
MacLeod, Duncan, xiii, 269
Madison, James: chides northern
    revolutionaries, 7
Maier, Pauline, 35
Maine, 227
Manigault, Gabriel, 49 (n. 20), 283
Marion, Francis, 185
Maroons: and African uprisings in
    Caribbean and North America,
    239–41, 246, 255–57, 262–63
Martin, Laughlin, 282
Maryland, 211, 217, 235–36, 251, 279;
    its revolutionary leaders, 6, 9, 12,
    14, 16
Marriage: decline of parental control
    over, 31
Marshall, Susannah, 217–18
Marshall, William, 217
Martin, Josiah: as royal governor of
    North Carolina, 8, 174–75

Martinique, 256
Maryland Gazette, 6
Mason, George, 33, 44, 86; attacks
    slavery, 18; angered by Britain's
    parental style, 34
Massachusetts, 28, 29, 278
Mathew, Edward, 164
Mazlish, Bruce, 29, 39
Mecklenburg County. *See* North
    Carolina; Regulators
Mercer, George, 5, 82
Mercer, John, 65, 84, 87
Merchants. *See* Regulators, class
    differences with opponents
Militia: role of, in southern campaign,
    174–94
Militia officers. *See* Regulators, class
    differences with opponents
Miller, Mary, 207
Miller, Robert, 207
Milligen, George, 283
Millis, Walter, 176
Milner, James: spearheads discussion
    of Chiswell case, 88–90
Mobility: in North Carolina, 116–23
Montague, Edward, 74, 75
Montgomery County. *See* North
    Carolina; Regulators
Montserrat, 244
Morgan, Daniel: in southern war,
    185–87
Moore, Maurice, 32
Moore's Creek Bridge, N.C., 156, 174
Morgan, Edmund S., xiii, 19, 38, 42,
    269
Mortality: of parents, 33
Moultrie, William, 236

N
Namier, Lewis, 249
Nation, Christopher, 141
Negro Act of 1740, 284
Negroes: emancipation of, linked to
    colonization, 19; population of, in

North Carolina, 111–14; and the
    Regulation, 134; and irregular
    warfare, 216; and postwar
    population growth, 223, 233 (n.
    38); in urban areas, 241–43; as laborers
    in South Carolina, 271–75; activism
    of, in colonial South Carolina,
    276–87. *See also* Slavery; Slaves
Nelson, Thomas, 60
Nelson, William, 60, 91
New Bern, N.C., 282
New England: values of, admired by
    southern revolutionaries, 13–14;
    and colonial family, 29–30
New Hanover County. *See* North
    Carolina; Regulators
New Jersey, 157, 162, 221
New York, 7; as part of British strategy,
    156–58; 162–64, 169–71, 178–79
New York City, 213, 215, 222
Nicholas, Robert Carter, 62, 74, 75; and
    Robinson scandal, 86–102 passim
Ninety-Six Brigade, 182, 185, 192
No More Lies, 270
Norfolk, Va., 5, 85, 164, 218, 235
North: and revolutionary tradition, 20;
    and postwar social
    experimentation, 224–27
North Carolina, 5, 7, 12, 19, 32, 33, 40,
    53 (n. 43), 208, 211, 215, 217, 220,
    221, 223, 279; class conflict in,
    discussed, 109–46; economy and
    demography of, 111–14; wealth
    distribution in, 115–16; mobility
    patterns of, 116–23; political power
    arrangements of, 123–27; class
    differences between Regulators
    and opponents, 127–34; and the
    Regulation, 134–46; and southern
    war, 156, 158, 170, 174–75, 178–79,
    186–87, 189, 192. *See also* Regulators
North, Frederick Lord, 156
Norton, John Hatley, 210

O

Olmstead, Frederick Law, 258
One Hundred Years of Solitude, 268
Onslow County. *See* North Carolina;
    Regulators
Orange County. *See* North Carolina;
    Regulators
Oswald, Richard, 37

P

Paca, William: opposes Stamp Act, 6
Page, John, 99
Page, Mann, 99
Paine, Thomas, 28, 36, 235
Papers of Alexander Hamilton, The, 269
Papers of Benjamin Franklin, The, 269
Papers of Henry Laurens, The, 269
Papers of James Madison, The, 269
Papers of Thomas Jefferson, The, 268
Parker, Hyde, 179, 180
Parliament: and issue of taxation, in
    Virginia, 71–86
Parricide: and analogy with
    Revolution, 40–41
Pasquotank County. *See* North
    Carolina; Regulators
Patriarchalism: declines in colonial
    society, 28, 30; pronounced in
    South, 32; and Freudian fantasy,
    41; and postwar southern society,
    225; and plantation organization,
    247–48, 259–61
Patriots: and militia of, discussed,
    174–94 passim
Pendleton, Edmund, 33, 57, 62, 64, 77,
    97, 102
Penn, John, 50 (n. 22)
Pennsylvania, 156
Personality development. *See* Family
    life; Autonomous personality;
    Patriarchalism; Rebellious
    personality
Philadelphia, 222, 280
Pickens, Andrew, 50 (n. 22); and
    southern war, 182, 185–92, 197 (n.
    32)

Pinckney, Charles Cotesworth, 208–9,
    226, 229 (n. 10)
Pinckney, Eliza Lucas, 42, 208, 214,
    218, 223, 272
Pinckney, Harriott, 208, 214
Pinckney, Thomas, 214, 236
Pinckney, William, 274
Pistole fee controversy, 65
Pitt County. *See* North Carolina;
    Regulators
Plantation: organization of, in British
    Caribbean and North America,
    246–63. *See also* Slaves
*Problem of Slavery in the Age of
    Revolution, The*, 269
Premarital pregnancy: reaches all-time
    high in eighteenth century, 31
Prevost, Augustine: as officer in British
    army, 163–64, 177–78, 181, 183
Prosser, Gabriel: and his revolt in
    Richmond, Va., 243–45, 262
Purdie, Alexander, 88
Puritan Ethic, 42
Pyle, John: his loyalist force
    massacred, 188–89

Q

Quarles, Benjamin, xiii, 270
Quincy, Josiah, Jr.: characterizes
    Harnett, 6–7; and Gadsden, 8

R

Ramsay, David: describes Revolution
    in South, 213, 215, 220, 224
Randolph County, *See* North Carolina;
    Regulators
Randolph, Edmund, 61, 63–65, 67
Randolph, John, 59, 60, 63, 70, 95
Randolph, Peyton, 33, 61, 77, 88, 94, 97
Ravenel, Henry, 251
Rawdon, Francis Lord, 186
Rebellious personality: in Revolution,
    26, 44–45. *See also* Autonomous
    personality
Registers. *See* Regulators, class
    differences with opponents

Regulation. *See* Regulators
Regulators (of North Carolina), 110–46
    passim; class differences with
    opponents, 127–34; reject
    deference, 135; demand
    democracy, 136; grievances of,
    136–38; and 1769 assembly
    elections, 140–41; suggest reforms,
    141–44; as potential loyalists, 178
Regulators (of South Carolina), 191
Religion. *See* Anglicans; Calvinism;
    Catholicism
Republican woman: emerges in North,
    226
Restoration, 58
Revolution: southern historiography
    of, ix–xiv; southern leaders of, 3–21
    passim; values of, 13–21; and
    relationship to colonial family life,
    25–47 passim; calls forth childhood
    experiences, 35–37; and question of
    charismatic leaders, 39; as means of
    restoring order, 44–45; paradoxes
    of, 45; and its origins in Virginia,
    55–102 passim; and its impact on
    women, 203–27; and threat of
    servile insurrection, 235–37; and
    slave unrest in South, 277–87
Revolutionary War: and Britain's
    southern strategy, 155–71; as a
    civil war, 174–94, 261–62; and
    social disorder, 211–19;
    devastation of, in South, 222–24
Rhode Island, 155, 162, 165, 166,
    170
Rice. *See* Plantation; Slaves
Richardson, Richard, 185
Richmond, Va., 243, 244, 263
Rind, William, 87, 88
Riot Act, 145
Ritchie, Archibald, 5, 7, 82
Robinson, Charles, 133
Robinson, Donald, 269–70
Robinson, John, 12, 59, 71, 77; as
    popular and powerful

politician, 60–62; as speaker and
    treasurer, 69–70; and scandal
    following his death, 86–102
    passim
Rodney, George, 168, 169
Roseau (Dominica), 240
Routledge, Robert, 87
Rowan County. *See* North Carolina;
    Regulators
Royle, Joseph, 87
Rush, Benjamin: as pioneer
    psychiatrist, 34
Russell, Janet, 205
Rutledge, Edward, 33, 50 (n. 22)
Rutledge, Hugh, 50 (n. 22)
Rutledge, John: and tensions in
    colonial family, 33, 37, 43–44, 50
    (n. 22); as republican governor
    of South Carolina, 185, 192, 197
    (n. 32)

S
Saint Mary's, Ga., 249
Saint Thomas, 245
Salisbury, N.C., 114
Sambo (Charleston black), 284
Sandy Creek Association, 138, 139,
    150 (n. 19)
Santo Domingo: and African
    uprisings, 236–38, 245
Saratoga, N.Y.: and defeat of
    Burgoyne, 155–56
Savannah, Ga., 165, 166, 170, 175,
    177, 178, 179, 180, 182, 184, 194,
    213, 215, 223, 240, 242, 261
Saveth, Edward, 30
Schaw, Janet, 279–80
Schoepf, Johann David, 64
Scott, Anne Firor, 225
Scottish Highlanders: as loyalists,
    156, 174, 178
Sellers, Charles G., Jr., x
Sellers, Leila, 275
Seminole Indians, 176
Seven Years' War: and Maryland's

double tax on Catholics, 12; and colonial contribution, 67, 74

Sheriffs. *See* Regulators, class differences with opponents

Sidney, Algernon, 14

Simmons, James, 279

Simms, William Gilmore, 290 (n. 27)

Simpson, James: and Britain's southern strategy, 166–68, 175–76

Sims, George, 149 (n. 15)

Slavery: seen as evil by southern revolutionaries, 17–19; exacerbates conflicts in family, 32; and its effects on morals, 67; slaveholding patterns in North Carolina, 111–14; and political power in North Carolina, 123–27; and class differences between Regulators and opponents, 127–34; in British Caribbean and North America, compared, 238–63; and historiography of Revolution, 269–71. *See also* Negroes; Slaves

Slavery, Race and the American Revolution, 269

Slavery in the Structure of American Politics, 1765–1820, 269

Slaves: and comparison with white children, 32; as measure of mobility in North Carolina, 116–23; held as hostages, 181; and household chores, 207–8; and life of women, 209–10; and war's impact, 211–15; and postwar labor shortage, 223; and threat of servile insurrection, 235–37, 276; on tobacco and rice plantations, 247–49, 251–54, 258–61; on Caribbean plantations, 249–58; and unrest in revolutionary South, 277–87. *See also* Negroes; Slavery

Smith, Daniel Scott, 31, 34

Smith, Paul, 174

Some Thoughts Concerning Education, 30

Sons of Liberty, 41, 277; in Charleston, 4; in Cape Fear, 5; in Norfolk, 5; in Baltimore, 6; southern and northern groups, compared, 7; in Norfolk, respond to Stamp Act, 85; their arguments borrowed by Regulators, 139

South: role of, in Revolution, ix–xiv; revolutionary leadership of, 3–21 passim; and revolutionary tradition, 20–21; and British plans for pacification, 156–71; and civil warfare, 174–94; and the colonial household, 204–11; and devastation of Revolution, 222–24; and postwar patriarchal society, 225–26

South Carolina, 4, 12, 13, 32, 33, 35, 37, 42, 215–16, 221, 223, 227, 235–36, 238, 240, 248, 255, 258, 261; and southern war, 157–94 passim; and blacks in the Revolution, 271–87

South Carolina Gazette and Country Journal, 282

Southern strategy: elements of, 158–59; and relationship to patriot and loyalist militia, 175–94

South Vietnam, 187

Spain, 165, 276

Speightstown, Barbados, 243

Spotswood, Alexander, 58

Stamp Act, 4–6, 18; and its challenge to Virginia elite, 71–86; and unrest in South Carolina, 277–78

Stevens, Gavin, 263

Stith, William, 68

Stono River rebellion, 236, 276
Stuart, John: as British Indian
    agent, 176, 178–79, 280–81
Sumter, Thomas, 50 (n. 22), 185,
    197 (n. 32)

T
Taitt, David, 184
Tarleton, Banastre: as British advocate
    of terrorism, 167, 169, 188–89
Taylor, Simon, 245
Taylor, William R., 225
Terrorism: and the southern campaign,
    167–71, 191–93
Thompson, Elizabeth, 217
Thornton, Presly, 87
Tobacco. See Plantation; Slaves
Tobago, 245, 258
Tonyn, Patrick, 179
Tories. See Loyalists
Townshend duties, 4
Trinidad, 245, 246, 263
Tryon, William, 145, 168
Tryon County. See North Carolina;
    Regulators
Tucker, St. George, 63, 243–44
Turner, Frederick Jackson, 110
Turner thesis, 27
Two-penny Acts, 66

U
Upper Ninety-Six Regiment, 182
Urban household, 206–7
Urban markets: control of, by Negroes,
    250–51, 273–75

V
Virginia, 29, 32, 33, 37, 42, 205, 207,
    210, 212–13, 215, 220, 221, 223–24,
    235–36, 278; and revolutionary
    leaders, 5, 7, 10, 12–13, 16, 19; and
    origins of Revolution, 55–102
    passim; and stability of its politics,
    59; and sectional split in politics,
    rejected, 62–63; and its corporate

self-image, 63–65; and signs of
    internal moral decay, 67–68; and
    response to Stamp Act, 71–86; and
    response to Robinson and Chiswell
    scandals, 87–102; and southern
    campaign, 156–92 passim; and
    plantation organization, 238, 244,
    247–48, 251, 253, 259–61
Virginia Gazette, 72, 88, 96
Virtue: as part of Anglo-American
    political thought, 56; decline of,
    feared, 57–58, 98
Vonnegut, Kurt, 270

W
Walker (soldier), 283
Wallace, Michael, 28, 29, 35
Waller, Benjamin, 62
Walton, George, 50 (n. 22)
Walzer, Michael, 42
War of Jenkins' Ear, 276
Warden, G. B., 17
Washington, George, 190, 278; and
    tensions in colonial family, 33; and
    charismatic leadership, 39; and
    Stamp Act, 85; and British strategy,
    157, 160, 162, 163, 165; as planter,
    247–48, 251
Watauga, 175
Wayles, John, 99
Wealth distribution: in North Carolina,
    115–16
Wells, Robert, 30
West Africa, 271, 275
West Indies, 159, 162, 163, 165, 171,
    214, 250, 252, 254
Westmoreland Association, 82
Wetzell's Mill, N.C., 189
Whigs. See Patriots; Revolution
White, Alexander, 70
Whitefield, George, 259
White Over Black, 269
Wilkes fund controversy, 12
Wilkinson, Eliza, 216, 218, 221, 224
Williams, Robert, 25, 46

Williams, Mrs. Robert, 25, 46
Williamsburg, Va., 55, 99, 251, 279, 282
Williamson, Andrew, 182, 183
Williamson, Katherine, 206–7
Williamson, Robert, 207
Wilmington, N.C., 190
Women: patterns of lives, 204–11;
    confront social chaos of war,
    211–19; and Revolution's impact on
    roles, 220–27
Woodmason, Charles, 206
Wright, James: as royal governor of
    Georgia, 170, 183–85, 191
Wythe, George, 50 (n. 22), 62, 74, 75, 77

Y
Yorktown, Va., 156–58, 169, 222

A NOTE ABOUT THE EDITORS

Jeffrey J. Crow is head of the General Publications Branch, Historical Publications Section, North Carolina Division of Archives and History. He is the editor of the North Carolina Bicentennial Pamphlet Series, the author of *The Black Experience in Revolutionary North Carolina* (1977), and coauthor with Robert F. Durden of *Maverick Republican in the Old North State: A Political Biography of Daniel L. Russell* (1977).

Larry E. Tise is the director of the North Carolina Division of Archives and History. He is the author of *The Yadkin Melting Pot: Methodism and the Moravians in the Yadkin Valley, 1750–1850* (1968) and the general editor for and author of four volumes in the Winston-Salem in History Series.

A NOTE ABOUT THE BOOK

Composed by The University of North Carolina Press
in Mergenthaler VIP Palatino

Printing and binding by Kingsport Press, Kingsport, Tennessee

Published by The University of North Carolina Press